Ideology in
Social Science

Robin Blackburn
Lucio Colletti
Norman Geras
David Goddard
Maurice Go
E.
C.
Ra
Tom
Edwa
Martin   olaus
Nicos Poulantzas
Martin Shaw
Gareth Stedman Jones
J. H. Westergaard

D1290525

IDEOLOGY IN SOCIAL SCIENCE

Readings in
Critical Social Theory

Edited by
Robin Blackburn

Fontana/Collins

This selection first published in Fontana 1972
Second Impression June 1973
Third Impression February 1975
Fourth Impression September 1976

Copyright © in the editor's introduction and arrangement of
this selection, Robin Blackburn 1972
Copyright © in 'Economics: the Revival of Political Economy'
by Edward Nell and the postscript to 'Sociology: the Myth of
Classlessness' by J. H. Westergaard, *New Left Review* 1972

Made and printed in Great Britain by
William Collins Sons and Co Ltd, Glasgow

CONDITIONS OF SALE
This book is sold subject to the condition that
it shall not, by way of trade or otherwise, be lent,
re-sold, hired out or otherwise circulated without
the publisher's prior consent in any form of
binding or cover other than that in which it is
published and without a similar condition
including this condition being imposed on the
subsequent purchaser

Contents

Acknowledgments

For kind permission to reprint the essays contained in this
Reader the Editor wishes to thank the following journals and
publications. The chapter number under which the essays are
arranged in this collection is placed in brackets after the
author's name.

The *New Left Review* for the essays by Martin Shaw (2),
David Goddard (4), Gareth Stedman Jones (6 and 10), J. H.
Westergaard (7), Robin Blackburn (8), Tom Nairn (9), Nicos
Poulantzas (11), Ralph Miliband (11), Norman Geras (13), Martin
Nicolaus (14). The essays by J. H. Westergaard and Robin Blackburn appeared in *Towards Socialism*, edited by Perry Anderson
and Robin Blackburn (Fontana, 1965). Norman Geras' essay was
originally entitled 'Essence and Appearance : Aspects of "Fetishism" in Marx's *Capital*'. The essay by Edward Nell and the
postscript to J. H. Westergaard's essay appear here for the first
time. 'Post-Liberal-Democracy?' by C. B. Macpherson (1) first
appeared in the *Canadian Journal of Economics and Political
Science*, October 1964. 'The Professional Organization of Sociology : A View from Below' by Martin Nicolaus (3) is reprinted
from *The Antioch Review*, Vol. XXIX, No. 3, by permission of
the editors. 'Karl Marx's Contribution to Historiography' by
E. J. Hobsbawm (12) is reprinted from *Diogenes*, No. 64, Winter
1968, by permission of the editors. 'Structure and Contradiction in *Capital*' by Maurice Godelier (15) is reprinted from the
translation by Ben Brewster in the *Socialist Register*, 1967 by
permission of the editors and publisher. 'Marxism : Science or
Revolution?' by Lucio Colletti (16) is reprinted from his book
From Rousseau to Lenin (London, 1973) by permission of New
Left Books.

Introduction

The essays in this collection seek to challenge the prevailing ideologies in the social sciences and to indicate scientific alternatives to these ideologies. It may seem curious to claim that a reader in critical social thought is aiming to combat ideology. After all, are not the critics simply the champions of another ideology, or even, perhaps, the champions of ideology itself against the neutral and positive approach of the true social scientist? It is certainly a distinguishing feature of the contributions to this book that their argument develops some general theory about the nature of society. Is not such a theory, however plausible the assumptions on which it rests, and however sympathetic the value judgments which it reflects, more or less bound to stand in the way of detached social inquiry? Some may feel that the best way forward for social scientists is to leave politics to the politicians and values to those with a taste for metaphysics. Their proper task is to supply that body of information and evidence which can be ascertained independently of any political position or value judgment. In this view 'ideology' is constituted by all those generalised social theories and world views which hover above the *terra firma* of established fact and empirically tested hypothesis.

In this Reader a number of the essays counterpose science to ideology but they do so in an entirely different sense. For them ideology is by no means defined by the conscious choices made by the social theorist about how society works but rather precisely by those assumptions of which the theorist is least aware and about which he is least explicit. The very notion that social research can be conducted other than on the basis of the prior development of concepts and theories is held to be ideological. The choice of a particular field of investigation, the choice of a given range of concepts with which to investigate that field, all express assumptions about the nature of society and about what is theoretically significant and what is not. The essay by Gareth Stedman Jones entitled 'History: the Poverty of Empiricism' attacks the error of imagining that the study of society can be based on the simple accumulation of facts from which theories are then deduced. As he shows, the assumption that there exists a realm of facts independent of theories which establish their meaning is fundamentally unscientific. Science proceeds by challenging the deceptive obviousness of everyday observation and common sense.

When it comes to society the 'obvious', given appearance of social relations is particularly misleading and treacherous. The problem is not just confined to those specific ideologies which justify the material or political interests of the dominant social class. Indeed in the nature of things these ideologies are fairly easy to recognise and, where necessary, to discount. The critiques developed in the first part of this book really concern the less evident 'general' ideologies which conceal the real contradictions of capitalism and imperialism today. They do this not by openly justifying prevailing institutions but by arresting social thought at inadequate and superficial concepts. Right from the outset the division of labour between the various social sciences (economics, sociology, anthropology, history, political science) parcels up investigation in such a way as to prevent the underlying determinants of the social formation coming into view. In different ways this theme is developed by most of the contributions to the first part of this collection. Liberal political theory ignores the basic economic forces, while economics becomes a technical exercise which neglects and obscures class relations. History rarely ventures beyond a timid empiricism while sociology soars into empty abstraction. The real forces at work in the present epoch of wars and revolutions are lost either in the absorption with detail or in suprahistorical speculation.

Whereas the critiques in the first part of the book mainly concentrate on attacking the general orientation of the different academic 'subjects' and 'disciplines', the second part focuses on some of the vital questions which are ignored—or even denied—in consequence: class conflict, the nature of capitalism, the emergence of the working class, the determinants of political power and the history of imperialism. J. H. Westergaard confronts the myth that changes in capitalist social organisation have led to a withering away or amelioration of class division. Drawing on a wide range of evidence he demonstrates that this view was erroneous even during the height of the post-war imperialist boom. This essay was originally published in 1964; a valuable postscript examines developments since that date (pp. 152–63). In Chapter 8 the thesis that capitalism is no longer dominated by the making of profits and the accumulation of capital is scrutinised and rejected. It is argued that the over-riding goal of the enterprise in the context of the capitalist market must be the most profitable organisation of the resources it commands, above all of the labour power it purchases. Increasing rivalry between the capitalist states has led in nearly all of them to attempts to regulate wages and to introduce other forms of capitalist planning. Far from mitigating the classic contradictions of capitalism these developments unite them in a clearer and more explosive form.

Tom Nairn, basing himself on Edward Thompson's *The Making of the English Working Class*, discusses the ways in which the British ruling class was able to crush the early revolts of the working class and to instil into it the ideological legacy of the earliest, most primitive and partial bourgeois revolution. As well as being a powerful treatment of this theme, Tom Nairn's essay can be seen as a plea for a new emphasis in the writing of labour history. In a complementary essay Gareth Stedman Jones insists on a continuity in the history of the United States, namely a non-territorial variety of imperialism. Even really outstanding works of academic history such as Barrington Moore's *Social Origins of Dictatorship and Democracy* miss the crucial significance which the imperialist past—and present—has for the first capitalist states. Thus Barrington Moore argues in a most illuminating manner that a bourgeois revolution of the British, French or American type was needed to establish the social foundations for parliamentary democracy: what he fails to investigate is that these states were also the first and most successful exponents of colonialist plunder and imperialist domination and that this fact helps to explain the viability of bourgeois democracy within them. Of course once a bourgeois democracy has been established its institutions, with all their built-in class guarantees for capitalist power, acquire a certain relative autonomy. This and other questions are debated in the exchange between Nicos Poulantzas and Ralph Miliband which arose out of the publication of the latter's book *The State in*

Capitalist Society. Part of the value of this exchange comes from the fact that it raises important issues both of substance and method which do not begin to get discussed even in the best academic criticism of pluralist political theory.

The third part of the Reader is devoted to examining and developing the concepts and theoretical framework which are needed to equip a genuinely scientific study of social relations. These essays all take Marxism as the indispensable starting point for this work, but this does not mean that they pose some uniform and homogeneous alternative to bourgeois ideology. Within Marxism there is continual development and discovery based both on political struggles and on new interpretations of what was really important in the writings of Marx himself. E. J. Hobsbawm discusses the progressive discovery of the implications of Marx's method for the writing of history while Martin Nicolaus insists on the crucial significance of Marx's *Grundrisse*, the recently published first draft for what later became *Capital*. Differing interpretations of *Capital* itself are furnished by Norman Geras and Maurice Godelier. Compared with the partial and empiricist ideologies which dominate the academic disciplines, Marxism seeks to produce a conceptual framework within which social relations as a whole can be studied. The attempt which Marxist theory makes to be comprehensive is one sign of its scientificity since it discourages unexamined assumptions or the acceptance of ready-made notions either from existing disciplines or from the everyday discourse of capitalist social relations. The Marxist study of social formations is unified by its focus on the different mechanisms whereby surplus labour is extracted from the direct producers. But these mechanisms, in their different ways, require political institutions to defend them and ideologies to justify them. Thus Marxism does not deny the relative autonomy of the different levels of social practice, even though it refuses to study them in isolation from one another.

There is inescapably an arbitrary element in the selection of essays for a Reader such as this. In each section there are a host of further questions which could be explored. The purpose of this Reader is, however, simply that of providing a few sign-posts out of the maze of bourgeois ideology in academic social theory. But once this ideology has been identified and explained, however provisionally, it becomes clear that the important task is to abolish the conditions which generate it.

In a most important final essay Lucio Colletti insists that the scientific character of Marxism must be understood to demand revolutionary politics for which it provides the necessary basis.

Robin Blackburn, 1972

Part One
CRITIQUES

1

Politics: Post-Liberal-Democracy?

C. B. MACPHERSON

In its heyday liberal theory developed a generous vision of the nature of democracy which contrasts sharply with the ideologies of élitism which now dominate political science. C. B. Macpherson argues that the fatal flaw of the classical theories was that they failed to comprehend the central economic dynamic that underlay the liberal conception of society.

C. B. Macpherson is Professor of Political Science at Toronto University and author of The Political Theory of Possessive Individualism.

It is quite generally thought to be commendable, but only marginally worthwhile, for a political theorist to devote any great attention to economic assumptions, much less to economic theory. The general separatist trend of political science is quite understandable. As political science becomes a more confident, more developed, and more extensive discipline, the natural tendency is for it to seek a greater measure of independence. Along with the trend to separatism in political science has been a marked trend towards empirical, value-free analysis. The concern with values, which was central in the great theoretical writing on politics in the past, has been pushed out to the fringes of the subject as empirical work has proliferated.

I am going to suggest that both these trends are now rather dangerous, that they are a result of overconfidence in the strength of liberal-democracy. I shall argue that political science is now more than ever in need of rethinking its normative theory, and of doing so in full consciousness of the bearing of economic systems and economic assumptions on that theory. Political values have become more, not less, in need of central attention in political science, and economic assumptions more, not less, important in political theory.

Thus there is a good deal of loose writing these days about something called 'post-capitalism'. The same publicists and theorists who use this term are apt to talk also about post-Marxism. The idea in both cases is the same: to suggest that the thing now hyphenated has in fact disappeared and has been replaced by something really quite different. If one cannot deny, in either case, that something superficially similar to the old thing is still around, one can perhaps exorcize its spirit by calling it 'post-'. Thus, as capitalism, old-style, has become increasingly difficult to justify in terms of any acceptable social ethic, it becomes highly advantageous to find that it has given way to something else.

And as Marxism, old-style, continues to give trouble, it can perhaps more easily be dealt with by announcing its demise and replacement.

There is just a sufficient grain of truth in the alleged facts—the transformation of capitalism and of Marxism—to make the new concepts plausible. Capitalism has become a managed economy. It is managed partly by price-making firms and combinations of firms, themselves increasingly directed by the need to use administrative and other technological skills—to give full employment to accumulated administrative capital. And it is managed partly by the state, in pursuance of the goal of full employment of the labour force, a goal willingly shared and enforced by at least those capitalists who see that the stability of the whole system is a prerequisite of their profits and their power and that such stability does not permit a repetition of the great depression. A capitalism managed in those ways is not quite the same as the old model, which left everything to unmanaged competition between productive units none of which could by themselves make prices. I shall suggest, however, that this entitles us only to say that capitalism has developed, not that it has been replaced.

My primary concern in this paper is neither with the economics of capitalism nor with the philosophy or sociology of Marxism, but with the politics of individualism. The three are, however, not unrelated. Perhaps we can come at the whole thing best by asking, with tongue not entirely in cheek, whether it is now proper to promote a concept of post-liberal-democracy. There are really two questions here. First, has liberal-democratic theory already changed so much, since its first formulation, as to merit a new name? In other words, have we *got* a post-liberal-democratic theory? I shall suggest that the answer is no. Secondly, is the theory as it now stands adequate in justifying the liberal-democratic state and society as they now are or as they might be improved, or do we need a still further changed theory, so changed as to merit a new name? In other words, do we *need* a post-liberal-democratic theory? I shall suggest that the answer is yes.

In seeking to assess the changes in liberal-democratic theory, what should we take as our benchmark? We need not go very far back in time to find the first formulation of what we now regard as liberal-democratic theory—probably no further back than J. S. Mill, although the formal democratic case was made along with the liberal case by Bentham earlier in the nineteenth century. Liberal theory proper—the theory of individual rights and limited government—goes back, of course, to the seventeenth century. But until the nineteenth century, liberal theory, like the liberal state, was not at all democratic; much of it was specifically anti-democratic. Liberal-democratic theory thus came as an uneasy compound of the classical liberal theory and the democratic principle of the equal entitlement of every man to a voice in choosing government and to some other satisfactions. It was an uneasy compound because the classical liberal theory was committed to the individual right to unlimited acquisition of property, to the capitalist market economy, and hence to inequality, and it was feared that these might be endangered by giving votes to the poor.

The central problem of liberal-democratic theory was to reconcile the claims of the free market economy with the claims of the whole mass of individuals to some kind of equality. It cannot be too often recalled that liberal-democracy is strictly a capitalist phenomenon. Liberal-democratic institutions have appeared only in capitalist countries, and only after the free market and the liberal state have produced a working class conscious of its strength and insistent on a voice. The importance of the market, that is of the full capitalist market system in which labour itself is a marketable and normally marketed commodity, was well understood by the liberal theorists of the eighteenth and nineteenth centuries. So it is not surprising that economic assumptions, assumptions about the ultimate worth of different systems of relations between men in the process of producing material wealth, were never far below the surface of the classical liberal political theory, from, say, Locke to Bentham.

But there is a curious and interesting movement of these assumptions from the eighteenth century to the present. By the end of the eighteenth century, classical liberal theory had reached its mature form in Bentham's utilitarianism. Utility, defined as a quantity of pleasure minus pain, was taken as the sole criterion of individual and social good. The good of society was the maximization of the aggregate of individual utilities. And although Bentham was scornful of the natural rights postulates of earlier liberal theory, he put such a postulate into his system in another form; in aggregating individual utilities each individual was to count as one. The liberal state was then justified as the state most calculated to maximize utility. It could provide most efficiently what might be called the basic political utilities—security of life, freedom of individual movement, security of property. It would also maximize the material utilities of the whole society. Or rather, it would permit the market to maximize those utilities. With a liberal state guaranteeing a free market, everyone's natural desire to maximize his own utility, or at least not to starve, would bring everyone into productive relations which would maximize the aggregate utility of the society. Thus Benthamism, reinforcing and reinforced by the teachings of classical political economy, came close to justifying the liberal state on the main ground of its permitting the market to maximize material utilities. Bentham was clear that the market must be left to determine the allocation of the material product among the individuals who contributed to it by their labour or land or capital, although he saw that this would mean persistent inequality. He acknowledged, indeed, that there was a case for equality of wealth or income. This followed from the principle of diminishing utility—the principle that a second loaf of bread doesn't give a hungry man as much satisfaction as the first loaf, or more generally, that the more you have of anything the less the utility to you of any increment. Given this principle, and given that each individual's satisfaction was to count as one, it followed that the aggregate satisfaction or aggregate utility of the whole society would be greatest if everyone had equal amounts of wealth. But as soon as Bentham had thus demonstrated the case for equality he argued that it had to yield to the case for productivity. Without security for unequal property there would be no incentive to capital accumulation, and without capital accumulation there would be practically no productivity. Besides, without a large labour force whose incentive was fear of starvation, the market could not maximize productivity.

This was where classical liberal theory stood just before the demands of the common people for a political voice began to make themselves felt. Economic assumptions bulked very large in the liberal political theory; the liberal case was largely a material maximizing case.

With John Stuart Mill the emphasis became very different. He may be regarded as the first serious liberal-democratic theorist, in that he was the first liberal to take seriously, and to feel sensitively, the claims of the nascent democracy. He had some reservations, indeed, about a fully democratic franchise. He would not give the vote to those who were illiterate, nor to those who paid no direct taxes, but he was willing to have both literacy and direct taxes extended to the poor. And even those who were to have the vote were not all to have equal votes. The better educated, being more capable of political judgment, were to have more than one vote each. In these respects Mill's democracy was somewhat more qualified than Bentham's.

But in a more fundamental respect Mill must be counted more of a democrat. For he took people not as they were but as he thought them capable of becoming. He revolted against Bentham's material maximizing criterion of the social good. He could not agree that all pleasures were equal, nor that the market distributed them fairly. He held that men were capable of something better than the money-grubbing and starvation-avoiding existence to which Benthamism condemned them. He rejected the maximization of indifferent utilities as the criterion of social good, and put in its place the maximum *development* and use of human capacities—moral, intellectual, aesthetic, as well as material productive capacities.

This was, we may say, an act of democratic faith. It was a turn away from the market. It was a refusal to allow that the market should determine the value or worth of a man. It put other values higher than market values. Yet in the end, Mill found himself helpless, unable to reconcile his notion of values with the political economy which he still believed in. The world's work had to go on, and he could see no way in which it could be carried on except by competitive private enterprise. He saw clearly that the prevailing relation between wage-labour and capital was condemned by his own criterion of good, and he thought that it would before long become insupportable by the wage-labourers. His only way out was the hope that a network of co-partnerships in industry, or producers' co-operatives, might turn every worker into his own capitalist, and so enable the system of enterprise to operate without the degradation of wage-labour.

It is easy to see now that Mill, in spite of his ranking as an outstanding economist, did not grasp the essence of the capitalist market economy. It was his failure to do so that enabled him to reject the market morality. The founding father of liberal-democratic theory, we are compelled to say, was able to rise above the market morality only because he did not understand the market society.

The same must be said of the next outstanding figure in the English liberal-democratic tradition. T. H. Green, a philosopher with no pretensions as an economist, may be more readily forgiven for his economic naivety. Like Mill he despised and rejected the market morality. He did so even more strongly than Mill, perhaps because he did not have Mill's problem of trying to be faithful to the utilitarian philosophy. Yet he held that the free development of individual personality required the right to accumulate unlimited property through the mechanism of the market, and even required the full right of inheritance. (This was a step backward from Mill, who wanted high inheritance taxes in order to iron out the inequalities produced by the working of the market.) Green recognized that the existence of a proletariat—his own word—was inconsistent with the rationale of private property, which required that everybody should have enough property, over and above a bare subsistence, to enable him to develop and perfect himself. But he had so little insight into the nature of capitalism that he could attribute the existence of a proletariat not to the nature of capitalist enterprise but to the continuing effect of an original forcible seizure of land in feudal times, and subsequent 'unrestricted landlordism'. By putting the blame on feudalism, and on the continuing rights of unproductive landowners, he exempted capitalism from any responsibility for the condition of the bulk of the people. To say the least, this shows rather less grasp of the essentials of the capitalist market economy than Mill had.

Mill and Green, between them, set the pattern of English liberal-democratic political theory from their time on. It is probably fair to say that there have been since then no new insights sufficient to carry liberal-democratic theory over the hurdles which they have failed to surmount. They had rebelled against the morality of the market, but their rebellion, even at the level of theory, had failed.

What has happened since then? While the liberal-democratic theorists have been, so to speak, coasting on Mill and Green, a new step was taken in liberal economic theory. The new step was the development of marginal utility theory. More sophisticated than the classical theory, and much better able to explain the price system, it had the additional effect of diverting attention from the question of the distribution of the social product between social classes, a question to which Adam Smith and Ricardo had paid some attention. The marginal utility theory, or neo-classical theory as it came to be called, contained some implied value judgments. It implied that the capitalist market system did maximize utility, and that it gave everyone—labourer, entrepreneur, capitalist, and land-owner—exactly what his contribution was worth.

The system tended to an equilibrium at which every factor of production—each lot of labour, of capital, of land, and of enterprise—got a reward equal to the marginal productivity of its contribution. This theory, first worked out in the 1870s and brought to definitive form by Marshall, still in its essentials holds the field. It has had to be modified in some respects, of course. Allowance has had to be made for monopolistic developments. And after Keynes demonstrated that the system did not automatically tend to equilibrium at maximum utility, but could find an equilibrium at any measure of underemployment of resources and labour, the theory had to be modified to admit the necessity of continual government action in order to keep the system up to the mark. But with these adjustments, the neo-classical theory can still be taken as providing a justification for a slightly modified system of capitalist enterprise. The modified market system can be held to be justified on the grounds that it maximizes utilities and that it distributes rewards according to marginal productivity. It is true that few modern economists do explicitly use their theory to justify anything. Most of them decline to draw value judgments from technical theory. Indeed, it is clearer to the economists than to the non-economists who have absorbed the elements of orthodox theory that the maximization of utility by the market can only be demonstrated by assuming a certain income distribution, and that the marginal productivity theory of distribution is not a demonstration of an ethically just distribution of wealth or income. It has, however, been easy for political theorists to overlook these limitations of economic theory.

I think it fair to say that liberal-democratic theory, having failed to resolve the dilemma encountered by Mill and Green, has fallen back pretty heavily on this modified free enterprise theory for the main justification of the liberal-democratic state. It is true that current liberal-democratic theory still insists, very properly, on the central importance of certain individual freedoms—of speech and publication, of religion, of association. It still asserts the ultimate moral worth of the individual, and speaks of the self-development of the individual as the ultimate good. But it has persuaded itself that this good is to be achieved through the market, as modified of course by the welfare state. Its central value judgment is the value judgment it finds in the modified neo-classical economic theory, that the best society is the modified market society because it maximizes utilities and distributes them according to each man's deserts.

Seen in this light, current liberal-democratic theory appears to have taken two steps backward from the original liberal-democratic position formulated by Mill. The first step may be described as a reversion to the pre-democratic classical liberal emphasis on maximization of the material utility. Liberal-democratic theory has retreated back beyond John Stuart Mill to the value judgments of Bentham—to the indifferent weighing of the utilities of individuals, with their existing habits, tastes, and preferences taken as given, as the ultimate data.

The second step has carried the liberal-democratic theorists, along with the neo-classical economists, back even beyond the original classical economists. The classical economists were fighting against something as well as for something. They had refused to accept the values of the society they lived in, with its element of rentier morality and of what was in their view wasteful expenditure. For them, the uses to which labour was put by the existing social order were not automatically justified by the fact of their existence. They distinguished between productive and unproductive labour and had some harsh things to say about the latter, and about the social and political arrangements that called it forth. In short, they were sizing up the existing scale of values and passing a critical judgment on it. The same cannot be said about the neo-classical economists. They concern themselves only with the scale of values that is actually registered in the market. The individual utilities on which their system is based are given by the preferences and tastes of individuals as they are. In maximizing utility or welfare, all wants are equal. Whatever is, is right.

This position has not been reached and held without some difficulty. The main difficulty was that the marginal utility theory relied for its explanation of relative prices on the principle of diminishing utility. The more you have of anything, the less your desire for still more of it. This seemed to entail (as Bentham had allowed it did entail) that the richer you become the less satisfaction you could get from each additional lot of wealth. To admit this would be to recognize an order of urgency of wants in every man, ranging from the most basic necessities to pure frivolities. To recognize an order of urgency of wants would be to cast serious doubts on the ability of the market system, with all its inequalities of income, to maximize the aggregate utility of all members of the society, which ability is offered as the system's great justification.

The difficulty has been met by the simple device of refusing to admit that the satisfactions of an individual can be compared over time. A man who was poor yesterday and well-to-do today can indulge desires which he could not indulge before. He has new and different desires, and who is to say that the satisfaction he gets from indulging these is less than the satisfaction he got from meeting different wants when he was a different man? As soon as intertemporal comparisons of utility are ruled out, the socially dangerous implications of the principle of diminishing marginal utility are avoided. Utility can be said to be maximized no matter what the inequality of wealth or income.

Yet as Galbraith has pointed out, in discussing the marginal utility theorists from a somewhat different angle, they are here on very slippery ground. For they shut their eyes to the fact that the more affluent a society becomes the more the wants which are satisfied by the market have been created by the process of production itself. There is no reason, Galbraith argues, why we should attach the same urgency or the same moral value to wants created by the system as to wants original with the individual. Galbraith here seems to align himself with Rousseau, who insisted on the moral distinction between the original or natural desires and the artificial desires created by a competitive and unequal society.

The point I should like to emphasize is that one can only make a distinction between natural and artificial wants if one rejects the postulate that all men inherently desire to emulate others, or innately desire ever more. If you allow that postulate, and only if you allow it, there is no basis for the distinction. For if you allow it, then whatever new thing one man gets others will want, and the want will be just as genuine, will flow just as much from his inherent nature, as any apparently more natural or more basic wants.

The marginal utility theorists, then, are making the assumption of universal innate emulation, or innately insatiable wants. We may say that in doing so, they, and the liberal-democratic theorists in so far as they rely on the utility theorists, have gone not two steps but three steps backwards. They have gone back before even that arch-competitor of the seventeenth century, Thomas Hobbes. For even Hobbes started from the assumption that only some men naturally wanted ever more, while others would naturally be content with the level of satisfactions they had if the system did not force them to enter the competition for more in order to keep what they had. The system which compelled this was, as I have argued elsewhere, a system whose stipulated qualities can be found only in a capitalist market society. Hobbes saw that it was the society that made all men emulative, that thrust them all into the desire for 'precellence'. It was the social relations which created the desire. Our modern theorists, in having failed to see this, may be called pre-Hobbesian. We must not press this point too far. For Hobbes was to a considerable extent a prisoner of his own model of society; having constructed the model of a capitalist market society he treated it as a model of society as such. But at least when he did this it was an advance in thought. There is less excuse for doing it again three hundred years later.

The main lines of the changes I have pointed to in the development of liberal-democratic theory may now be summarized. The theory begins with a solid inheritance of classical liberal theory, which made it the great virtue of the liberal society and the liberal state that they maximized the aggregate utility of the whole membership of the society, or that they allowed the market to do so. Each individual was to count as one, and all utilities were as good as each other. With John Stuart Mill and Green this market morality is rejected. The goal is no longer the maximum material utility of men as they are, but the fullest development and enjoyment of men's faculties. This was a finer vision, and a democratic one. But they failed to deal with the inconsistency between this vision and the necessary requirements of the market economy, the essentials of which they did not fully see. Since then, I have suggested, liberal-democratic theory has followed the same lines and, having failed to master the central problem, has slipped back into increasing reliance on the old argument of maximum utility. It has done so a little shamefacedly, aware perhaps that this is scarcely up to the vision which Mill had offered of a free society whose aim was higher utilities, higher values. But it has done so. It has not noticeably rejected the marginal utility analysis which refuses to make intertemporal comparisons of utilities.

We began this enquiry into the changes in liberal-democratic theory with a question: has it changed enough to merit a new name? Is there now a post-liberal-democratic theory? The answer is evident. What we have now is not post-liberal-democratic theory, but recessive liberal theory. It would be nearer the mark to call it pre-democratic liberal theory.

We had also a second question: is the theory, as it now stands, at all adequate in justifying the liberal-democratic state and society as they now are or as they might be improved, or do we need a still further changed theory, so changed as to merit a new name. In other words, do we need a post-liberal-democratic theory? It will be apparent by now that I think we do need a post-liberal-democratic theory.

The extent of the need is to be measured not merely by the extent to which current theory is regarded as a step or two backward from the original liberal-democratic theory, but also by the extent to which the liberal-democratic society and state have themselves changed since the original theory was created to justify or demand them. If the society and state have changed significantly, in a direction different from the change in the theory, the distance to be made up is even greater. Or, happily, the society and state may have changed in ways which tend to resolve in fact the difficulties that Mill and Green could not resolve in theory. The central difficulty was that the market economy, with its concentration of capital ownership, and its distribution of reward in accordance with the marginal productivity of each of the contributions to the product, maintained a massive inequality between owners and workers, an inequality which stood in the way of any extensive development and fulfilment of individual capacities. There was the further difficulty that the market society encouraged or demanded a money-grubbing, maximizing behaviour, which distorted the quality of life: the market might maximize utilities, but only by denying qualitative differences in utilities. Have the market society and the liberal state changed in ways that diminish or remove these difficulties?

We cannot here attempt a systematic answer to these questions. The most we can do is to notice one or two relevant trends. I will risk the generalization that the changes in the liberal-democratic *state*, since the introduction of the democratic franchise, have been less fundamental than the changes in the society and economy. By changes in the state I am thinking in the first place of changes in the ways governments are chosen and authorized. It is true that very considerable changes in the ways governments were chosen and authorized did come with the introduction of democratic franchise. As electorates increased in size, party organization became more important and party discipline stronger. Hence, the responsiveness of elected representatives to their constituencies diminished, as did the responsiveness of governments to elected representatives. But these are not changes in the liberal-democratic state, they are changes as between the pre-democratic liberal state and the liberal-democratic state. Apart from these there have been no great changes in the mechanism of choosing and authorizing governments, unless the proliferation and institutionalization of pressure groups as part of the standard method of determining government policy be so considered. When we turn to what governments do with their power there is a more noticeable change. But here we move into the area of changes in the society and economy. For it is these changes which have called forth the regulatory and welfare state.

When we look at changes in the society and the economy, two changes stand out: the decline of pure competition and the rise of the welfare state. The two changes may be summed up as a move away from a relatively unregulated free enterprise economy to a system more heavily managed and guided both by large private economic organizations and by the state.

These changes have become most striking in the last few decades. They are not confined to the last few decades, of course. But the cumulative effect of welfare measures, of monetary and fiscal policies designed to prevent depressions and maintain full employment, of control and direction of foreign trade and home production, and all the rest, has given our market economies quite a different look even since the 1930s. Equally important has been the change in scale of the productive units. The move has been from markets in which no producer or supplier could make prices, to markets in which prices are increasingly made by firms or groups of firms who can do so, and who are sometimes able to enlist governments or groups of governments in their arrangements.

This is familiar enough. And it throws us back to the question mentioned at the beginning of this paper: how much has capitalism changed? Are we in an era of post-capitalism? I do not think we are. The change is not as great as some would suggest. It all depends, of course, on how you prefer to define capitalism. If you define it as a system of free enterprise with no government interference, then of course our present heavily regulated system is not capitalism. But I find it very unhistorical to equate capitalism with *laissez-faire*. I think it preferable to define capitalism as the system in which production is carried on without authoritative allocation of work or rewards, but by contractual relations between free individuals (each possessing some resource be it only his own labour-power) who calculate their most profitable courses of action and employ their resources as that calculation dictates.

Such a system permits a great deal of state interference without its essential nature being altered. The state may, as states commonly do, interfere by way of differential taxes and subsidies, control of competition and of monopoly, control of land use and labour use, and all kinds of regulation conferring advantages or disadvantages on some kinds of production or some categories of producers. What the state does thereby is to alter the terms of the equations which each man makes when he is calculating his most profitable course of action. Some of the data for the calculation are changed, but this need not affect the mainspring of the system, which is that men do act as their calculation of net gain dictates. As long as prices still move in response to these calculated decisions, and as long as prices still elicit the production of goods and determine their allocation, we may say that the essential nature of the system has not changed.

One may grant that the regulatory role of the modern state, and the transfer payments involved in the welfare state, are not a contradiction of capitalism, but may still argue that capitalism has been transformed into something else by its other most obvious novelty. This is the rise of the modern corporation to a point where a few firms, whose behaviour is less competitive than (to use Schumpeter's fine word) 'corespective', can make prices and dominate markets, and whose decisions are said to be determined less by desire to maximize profits than to build empires and to grow. The appearance of this phenomenon does indeed cast doubts on the justifying theory implicit in neo-classical economics, for in these conditions there is no reason to believe that the corporation's price-making decision will maximize production or utilities. But it does not alter the basic nature of the system. The driving force is after all still maximization of profit, for it is only by accumulating profit that the corporation can continue to grow and to build empires. The only thing that is different is the time-span over which maximum profit is reckoned.

Our present managed economy, managed both by the state and by the price-making corporation, is not, in my view, to be regarded as a transcendence of capitalism. It is still capitalism. But it has made nonsense of the justifying theory that capitalism maximizes social utility. And so, to the extent that modern liberal-democratic theory has reverted to the maximizing justification, that theory is further out of step than it was in the days of more nearly pure competition.

On the extent to which the welfare state has diminished the old inequality of opportunity and increased the chances for fuller development of individual personality, there will be differences of opinion. Improvements in the general level of health and literacy should, other things being equal, improve the quality of life for the great mass of individuals. But other things are not equal. For the very system of production which has afforded the welfare state has brought other changes. It has, necessarily, organized the work process in such a way that, for most people, their productive labour cannot be itself regarded as a fulfilment or development of their capacities. Fulfilment and development of individual capacities becomes, therefore, increasingly a matter of the development and satisfaction of wants for all kinds of material and, in the broadest sense, aesthetic or psychic goods.

But here again the system has changed things. For the market system, based on and demanding competition and emulation, creates the wants which it satisfies. The tastes and wants which people learn to satisfy as they rise above bare subsistence are, as we have seen, tastes and wants created by the productive system itself. And as the system increasingly moves away from a pattern of widespread competition between many producers (when it was still possible to think of it in terms of consumer sovereignty) to a pattern of competition for power between fewer and larger corporate units and groupings, which are increasingly able to control prices and products, the tendency of the system to create the wants which it satisfies will become stronger. There is no reason to expect that the wants and tastes which it satisfies will reflect or permit that full development of the individual personality which is the liberal-democratic criterion of the good society.

On balance, then, the changes in the liberal-democratic society seem to have made the justifying theory less, rather than more, adequate. When the changes in the society are taken in conjunction with the changes in the theory, the theory seems less fitted to the society than was the case at the beginning of the liberal-democratic period. One of the changes in the society has gone in the opposite direction from the change in theory. That is, while the theory since Mill has come to rely more heavily on the maximizing of utilities justification, the society has moved towards a more managed system whose claim to maximize utilities can no longer be granted. The other main change in the society has not made up for this, has not provided a way out of the central difficulty of the original liberal-democratic theory. That is to say, the change to the welfare state and the managed market cannot be counted on to provide an improvement in the quality of life as judged by the liberal-democratic criterion. We can only count on the manufacture and control of tastes.

2

The Coming Crisis of Radical Sociology

MARTIN SHAW

The publication in 1970 of Alvin Gouldner's The Coming Crisis in Western Sociology *represented a decisive advance over all previous critiques of sociology to have emerged from among the ranks of the sociologists themselves. In this work Gouldner mounts a devastating attack on the dominant schools of contemporary sociology so that it is quite appropriate that Martin Shaw's review of this work should provide an overview of the impasse that this tradition now faces.*

Martin Shaw is a lecturer in sociology at Durham University.

What is sociology? The textbook myth is that it is 'the scientific study of society'. But this is a notion that few sociologists would straightforwardly defend. If it is not this, however, what is it? There is no easy answer. In fact there is a large question-mark, presently getting larger (not least in the minds of the sociologists and their students), over the nature of the 'discipline'.

For anyone concerned with finding the answer to this problem A. W. Gouldner's book, *The Coming Crisis of Western Sociology* (Heinemann) is a text of major importance. Gouldner's focus is 'theoretical', and sociological 'theory' is a very special world. This focus is, however, the right one. Students may study sociology, and governments, local authorities, and college administrations may support it, because they believe it provides 'facts' and 'practical' policy guidelines. Up to a point it does; and this empirical underbelly of sociology is essential to its institutional growth. But even when, as in Britain which (as Perry Anderson has argued) has never produced its own 'classical' sociological theory, empirical research is to the fore, there is always an *ideological* component—the belief in 'the facts' is itself an important ideology. And in the modern expansion of sociology, this 'theoretical' or ideological component has been pushed to the centre of the discipline.

For *as sociology*, even the most minute, 'factual' study must be referred eventually to the body of thought which is called 'sociological theory'. This is what defines sociology as a profession : the carving out of a structure of ideas, a context of argument, of a particular kind. Within this framework, empirical study is validated. Only by endowing his work with 'theoretical' significance can the empirical researcher aspire to a place in the upper echelons of the profession. The big boys are all 'theoreticians'; they have a kind of magic, separating them from everyday discussion of society, which the pure empiricist does not possess.

For if the material basis of the recent expansion of sociology is capitalism's need, vaguely perceived by educational planners, for certain kinds of white-collar technicians, this is not the material basis of sociology. Sociology is primarily an intellectual, or more specifically ideological, response to the major social and political struggles of the last 200 years, which has been translated into an academic, professional, context. And it is important to note that the 'professionalization' of social thought, while effectively ensuring its co-existence and collaboration with the powers-that-be, is also a way of preserving its relative autonomy. Which explains why independent spirits (if not militant revolutionaries) can exist within it; which in turn helps to explain the irate response of academic sociologists to the charge that sociology as such is bourgeois ideology.

Sociology as ideology

But this it is. Sociologists operate, by and large, with a *reductionist* conception of ideology; they think that to be called bourgeois ideologists means that they are charged with being capitalism's yes-men. They point out, quite rightly, that only some of them are, while others are declared opponents of many social evils and established powers. They point out too, that while some sociology is conservative, other schools of sociology exist which provide the basis for radical social criticism. Surely this can't all be bourgeois ideology?

Ideology, however, is not apology, although it may and often does entail it. Ideologies are world-views which, despite their partial and possibly critical insights, prevent us from understanding the society in which we live and the possibility of changing it. They are world-views which correspond to the standpoints of classes and social groups whose interests in the existing social system and incapacity to change it makes it impossible for them to see it as a whole. A large number of different ideologies have been devolped by thinkers tied to bourgeois society, and there is constant development and change. But they are all part of *bourgeois ideology*, not because they express the immediate interests of the ruling class or are developed by it, but because they are limited, in theory, by the limits of bourgeois society in reality; because their development, including even their criticism of bourgeois society, is governed by the development of bourgeois society and is unable to go beyond it. As such, as bourgeois ideology, they face certain theoretical dilemmas, the solution to which lies in going beyond the standpoint of bourgeois society; just as in practice there are certain problems which cannot be solved within its framework. But because they assume it, they are condemned to reproduce the problems and to reproduce the same one-sided answers which will not solve them in reality.

It is the way in which it is structurally determined which eludes even a perceptive historian of the devolpment of sociology like Gouldner. He can trace many of the links very accurately, both within thought and between thought and society. He can portray trends. But he cannot understand sociology as a component part of bourgeois social thought as it has developed, from the days when it was a part of a process of revolutionary change, until today when the bourgeois social relations which it takes as given are a monstrous barrier to human progress.

Sociology and conservatism

'Sociology today,' Gouldner claims, 'is akin to early 19th-century Hegelianism, especially in the ambivalance of its political implications. Despite Hegelianism's predominantly conservative and authoritarian cast, it contained powerful radical implications that Marx was able to extricate and to incorporate into a transcending system of thought. The extrication of the liberative potential of modern Academic Sociology is a major task of contemporary cultural criticism.' A lot hinges on the *illegitimacy* of this comparison.

Hegel himself wrote that in his time 'revolution was lodged

and expressed as if in the very form of thought'. Reason 'swept Germany as thought, spirit and concept', while 'in France it was unleashed as effective reality'. He himself regarded his thought as the philosophical expression of the forces which in France produced the great Revolution of 1789. The conservative cast of his later political philosophy, while consonant with the 'mystical form' of the dialectic in Hegel, was, as Marx showed, in opposition to its 'rational kernel' whose implications were thoroughly revolutionary. As the nineteenth century wore on, and the bourgeoisie edged over to the side of counter-revolution, this opposition became more acute and Hegelianism as such had to be overcome by Marx to develop the implications of its main concepts.

The youthful Talcott Parsons, high priest of modern sociology, gave no such revolutionary hostages to fortune. Nor did any of his fore-runners, the thinkers who make up the pantheon of 'classical' sociology. And this was not accidental: it was not revolution, but counter-revolution, which was lodged in the form of their thought.

Gouldner himself designates the first period of Academic Sociology by the name of 'Sociological Positivism'. It was created not by the 'middle class' but by the 'dispossessed aristocracy', by a marginal group, a sect even, for whom even the bourgeois transformation of society was a mixed blessing. They developed a 'positive philosophy', as Marcuse has described in *Reason and Revolution*, in opposition to the 'negative', critical dialectic of Hegel. The 'founder of sociology', Auguste Comte, planned for a revival of medieval hierarchy and religion in a new 'scientific' guise. 'Academic Sociology, in its Positivistic heritage ... emerges from the failure of Comteanism as a practical social movement for cultural reconstruction' (Gouldner).

Positivism as an ideology of conservative social reconstruction was translated into positivism as an ideology of empirical social research. The continuity lay in respect for the given order and its progress. On the methodological level they were 'scientistic', stressing the objective, external character of social reality and the naturalism of social study. In social philosophy, a belief in social evolution survived. Neither of these was to be undisputed in later sociology. In the period of 'classical sociology', at the end of the last century and the beginning of this—the period of the crisis of classical imperialism—the belief in social progress collapsed, and the methodological certainties of positivism were enveloped in doubt. In the work of Max Weber, for example, a pessimistic perspective of global bureaucratization replaces evolutionary optimism. And in his methodology, the surviving elements of positive social science are surrounded by cultural relativism and subjectivism. And this, as commentators within academic sociology have noted, was a typical movement. It was an expression of the real crisis of traditional conservatism and liberalism in the face of the juggernaut of imperialism and the direct challenge of social revolution. For Weber, while supporting the counter-revolution in Germany at the end of the First World War, could see little hope of a constructive relationship between the values he upheld and the trend in capitalist development. Another 'classical' sociologist, Vilfredo Pareto, could only find a way out by supporting the first steps in Mussolini's development of the fascist state.

Conservatism and liberalism within bourgeois social thought start as radically opposed, while liberalism is still tinged with social revolution or radical reform, but survive in an epoch of capitalist maturity and decline only as relative emphases within an ideological sphere of basic agreement. What is significant is the extent to which, in the analytical sphere as well as in the cruder world of political argument, it is conservatism which has won the upper hand in the constitution of the ideological framework. The *concepts* of the liberals and even the radicals have their roots in the conservative tradition. Most of the 'classical' sociologists—like the majority of their successors—might have described themselves as in some sense liberals, but their conceptual heritage was from political conservatism. Emile Durkheim, probably the true 'father' of modern sociology, is the clearest proof of this. The ideological links are persuasively argued for in Robert Nisbet's recent *The Sociological Tradition*.

Sociology's place in bourgeois thought

The reasons for the success of conservatism and theoretical concepts derived from it in bourgeois thought are complex, but are all related to the path along which capitalism has developed. Just as the social character of production under capitalism becomes more apparent even to our rulers and receives a kind of bastard recognition from them (e.g. the nationalization of Rolls-Royce), so it becomes more apparent to our social theorists and receives an equivalent form of recognition from their pens.

Society cannot be seen simply as a natural organism, in which economic laws are given for individual actors, as it was seen in classical economics. Recognition of the social character of human relations begins to permeate all the varieties of bourgeois social thought, and cannot even be eliminated from its economics. But most of all it is to be seen in the rise and development of sociology as an independent form of thought, with a much more intense ideological character than the other bourgeois social sciences. The inadequacy of the individual nature contrast in social thought is expressed not so much in a thorough-going criticism of the social sciences (above all economics) in which this is chiefly embodied, as in the rise of new forms of thought.

Gouldner sums up the consequent characteristic of sociology: 'This means that Academic Sociology traditionally assumes that social order may be analysed and understood without making the concerns of economics focal and problematic ... sociology is a discipline which takes economics and economic assumptions as givens.... Academic sociology polemically denies that economic change is a sufficient or necessary condition for maintaining or increasing social order.' He later argues that it comes into existence: '1. Where industrialization has, at least, reached the "take-off point" and become self-sustaining. 2. Where, in consequence, social theorists and others can more readily define and conceptualize their society's problems as non-economic or purely "social", which is to say, as distinct from economic problems.' But this is a profoundly ideological explanation. It begs the question of whether society's problems really *are* non-economic. And of course this is not true. A non-ideological formulation of what Gouldner hints at would be to say that sociology arises and assumes the economic problems are *solved*, when economic problems have become transparently social problems which *cannot be solved* within the framework of bourgeois economics. That is to say, when the social character of capitalist production, veiled by bourgeois economics, has become apparent in the revolt of the chief force of production, the working class, sociology arises as a theory of how to respond to this revolt *without* abolishing the capitalist mode of production. Sociology recognizes the social character of production—but by denying that it is to do with production, which is a matter for 'economics'!

The structural character of the ideological function and

nature of sociology is thus clear. It is the direct heir to the impasse in bourgeois economic thought which Marx cut through in the middle of the nineteenth century, and from which bourgeois economics has only retreated since then. The political economists, with the labour theory of value, had come within a hair's breadth of grasping that economic relations between commodities were based on social relations between classes in the process of production. Marx developed their arguments, and turned them against them, showing the full revolutionary implications of the labour theory of value. Economists after Marx gradually turned away altogether from the theory, and from all recognition of the social character of economics, although they have more recently developed the 'social' aspect as a residual or additional category to 'pure' market economic relations. The other side of this decline and fragmentation of bourgeois social thought (also manifest in the decline and eventual trivialization of philosophy after Hegel), is precisely the rise of sociology to deal with what economics cannot deal with—social relations between classes, in their political, trade union, ideological and cultural aspects—without dealing with their real basis in the capitalist mode of production.

It is thus that conservative concern for the values and morality, which is itself a concern for the non-economic aspects of social relations so neglected by liberalism, becomes central to sociology. Sociology is the historically necessary expression, in social theory, of the way in which bourgeois society turns against its own origins—against the individual capitalist living for the market. Indeed Gouldner sees sociology as a reaction against 'utilitarian culture' and 'middle-class society'; what he does not specify is that it is a reaction within capitalism, a part of its development rather than in opposition to it. (Which really goes to show the confusion in such terms as 'middle-class society', which are euphemisms for capitalism at a particular stage.) The function of this ambiguity will be clear: it is to provide a basis for distinguishing mainstream and oppositional sociology, and a let-out for the latter from the facts of its own ideological heritage and determination.

The present crisis

To be fair: Gouldner develops a sharp critique of contemporary mainstream sociology and he does not build up the more radical strands in any very extravagant way—indeed he carefully knocks down a couple of the 'radical' heroes—so that sociological reviewers like T. B. Bottomore in the *New York Review of Books* have even complained that they have been badly treated. And yet he does provide a let-out for radical sociology, a basis for assuming that it can develop like left Hegelianism did, because he ignores the effect on sociology of its own place in the development of social thought. The Hegelian opportunity is not there for *sociology* to grasp, because sociology has been built on the basis of its rejection, and in opposition to Marx who did take it. Nor is there a roughly analogous opportunity, because this earlier development has naturally changed the nature of the problems of social theory. Radical sociology will have to go 'back' to the crisis of nineteenth-century bourgeois thought, before it can solve its own problems. And in doing so, it will have to repudiate sociology much more thoroughly than Marx repudiated Hegel. Let us show why this is, by following Gouldner in examining modern theoretical sociology.

'If the key polemical target of Positivistic Sociology has been the *philosophies* of the French Revolution,' he writes, 'the common polemical target of the thinkers of the classical period was Marxism.' Sociology was indeed increasingly shaped, both consciously and unconsciously, by the need to respond to the Marxist challenge. For this reason the criticism of sociology becomes more complicated as sociology has to cope not just with the problem of interpreting society within the framework of bourgeois social relations; but also with the problem of the alternative theory which does not adopt that limitation. Karl Korsch recognized this, when writing his *Karl Marx*; he regards classical political economy as a relatively pure form of bourgeois thought, because it is not involved in debate with Marxism, and therefore takes the critique of political economy as a *basis* for the criticism of later, more impure forms of bourgeois thought like modern sociology. Sociology tends to make a virtue out of what was only a necessity with the political economists; for example, while the political economists merely represented bourgeois conditions as eternal and natural, the 'schools of "general" or "formal" sociology have even raised the "unspecific" treatment of their subject matter to the very *principle* of their new and assumedly "disinterested" scientism'.

To a very large degree, however, the relations between sociology and Marxism were not overt; the polemic was not always

explicit, and in any case the influence was not merely at a polemical level. This was partly because Marxism was not seen as
'sociological'—because it was not academically represented within sociology, and because it was seen as an 'economic' doctrine.
Marxism, after all, was represented not merely by Marx, but
by German revisionism and, later, by Stalinism. What sociology
did, in opposition to these mechanistic and economic-determinist 'Marxisms' as well as to Marx, was to develop a theory of
society stressing the moral and 'ideational' elements. This theory,
in its most developed form, which Gouldner calls 'Parsonsian
structural-functionalism' after Talcott Parsons, certainly made
unspecificity a principle! Gouldner's merit is that he does pinpoint the fact that this very unspecific doctrine was a response
to very specific problems. Not only does he explain how it grew
out of a circle at Harvard which was based on a conservative
anti-Marxist position—although it avoided direct confrontation
with Marxism. He also argues cogently that the 'problem of
order' in Parsonsian sociology is not purely abstract and therefore irrelevant—it is concerned with the problem of order in
capitalist society which, in the 1930s, had just gone through
the profound crisis of the Great Depression. He argues that it
is the response of academic conservatives who stressed the importance of moral integration of society, in opposition to the
statism of the New Deal as well as Marxism. The highly abstract character of Parsonsian ideology he attributes to an
inability to connect with the New Deal, leading to a retreat
from practical involvement by Parsons. (This may be part of
the explanation, but there is a more basic reason : sociology
could not depict the contemporary problem of order as being
specific to capitalism, without raising the possibility of a different kind of social order.)

Having characterized the dominant school of modern sociology in this way, Gouldner is able to locate the source of its
instability. This lies in the strain which this ideology has under-
gone in being transformed from a fairly traditional conservative
theory of the need for value-consensus for social stability, into a
theory that the existing order *is* based on such consensus, and
that the state and its agencies can and do actively create that.
In the process of being made into the institutionally dominant
doctrine of a massively expanded academic sociology, an ideology of spontaneous social regulation has given way to a kind
of 'sociological Keynesianism'. It is a justification of a mon-

strous, all-powerful 'social system', now expressed in the agencies of the welfare (and warfare) state, in whose hands the underlying population is clay.

The crisis of modern sociology is, as far as Gouldner is concerned, primarily a crisis of this theory. As a number of critics have pointed out, it is not so much 'coming' as already in our midst. From the late fifties on, both in Europe (where it was never so thoroughly accepted) and in the USA, the assumptions of value-consensus and moral integration of the social structure began to crack. Sociology had accepted a greater ideological burden than the other sciences, as part of the division of labour between them. It had also, because of the nature of its subject matter rather than of its specific ideological superstructure, attracted many liberal, reforming and radical academics. In the gradually developing crisis of post-war Western society, the tension between the sociologists and the dominant ideology of 'Parsonsian structural-functionalism' has grown. We have seen the birth of new strands of sociological theory expressing, in many different ways, the unease of sections of the sociological profession at the ideological commitment of their discipline to various aspects of the existing order.

Despite some brief and perceptive strictures Gouldner does not choose to deal with these theories systematically; the omission makes it more difficult to uncover the real problems and the limitations of sociology. Of course, one of the reasons Gouldner does not attempt this is precisely the theoretical weakness and eclecticism, even by comparison with Parsons, of much radical sociology. There is no systematic counter-theory.

On the one hand there are those, such as the currently fashionable 'ethnomethodologists', who as Gouldner points out, adopt an approach which borrows from Parsons. They see the world as held together, not by a semi-sacred morality, but by a dense collective web of tacit understandings concerning the most mundane and 'trivial' matters. But the individuals between whom such trivial understandings exist are abstracted from systematic social relationships and the contradictory forces from which they arise. It is a trivialization of the social individual by placing him in a world of total subjectivity, in which the structuring of social relationships becomes invisible. This ideology offers itself as a kind of nihilistic protest, an *ersatz* radicalism within an academic context. As Gouldner points out; 'It is a substitute and symbolic rebellion against a larger structure

which the youth cannot, *and often does not want to*, change.'
(Emphasis added.) Alongside them have existed other writers
whose view of the men and society is even more akin to Parsons',
in stressing the objective and constraining character of social
relations as such, but who unlike Parsons do not see social
relations in terms of social systems, but in terms of the individuals who participate in them. The radicalism, such as it is,
of such writers consists in an existential *cri-de-cœur*, and a practical emphasis on the ability of the individual to manipulate the
roles and social relations imposed on him by society. How
radical this is is well expressed by Gouldner in his criticism
of Erving Goffman. The individual can make his own identity
—in the same way that an actor can create a new role, or an
ad-man create a new product. 'Dramaturgy' (the name of Goffman's doctrine, which likens society to drama) only 'reaches
into and expresses the nature of the self as pure commodity,
utterly devoid of any necessary use-value: it is the sociology
of soul-selling'.

One trend in sociological theory is, then, the emphasis on
the importance of 'the trivial', i.e. the finer details of social
relations and the marginal adjustments we can make in them, as
if even these could somehow escape the gravitational force of
capitalist relations of production, and the contradictions they
generate. But on the other hand there are sociological writers
who have challenged Parsonsianism on a more substantial level
—by pointing, for example, to divergent material interests in
society, to the persistence of ruling élites, and continuing conflict. Gouldner ignores this trend, no doubt because it has thrown
up little in the way of a general sociological theory. Certainly
this is a relevant consideration. For theoretically, such criticisms
have often been seen as modifications of, or as complementary
to, the dominant model in sociology; they have been largely *ad
hoc*. Indeed 'conflict theory', as an oppositional trend in sociology, seems to consist of assertions that there *is* conflict in
society, rather than of a serious explanation which is part of
a coherent alternative theory. Challenges to the dominant
theory on this level, which is potentially the most explosive,
have remained curiously limited. Where, for example, is the
'conflict theorist' who has claimed the May Events of 1968 in
triumphant vindication of his idea? To my knowledge such
a person does not exist. The oppositionists are as much an

ideological reflection of bourgeois society as the conservative sociological establishment.

The litmus test is still the attitude of sociologists to Marx. Whereas Talcott Parsons and his followers largely ignore Marx, or indulge in crude and ignorant polemic, radical sociologists add Marx to the tradition they share with the conservatives. The early Marx is adduced as a support for an ahistorical phenomenology; the late Marx as a founding father of conflict theory. Sociology invariably tears elements of Marx's thought out of its context, which embraces both a theoretical grasp of capitalism and the practice of the workers' revolution to overthrow it. Instead, Marx's ideas are converted into abstractions independent of capitalism and of Marxism which can be married to other equally 'independent' abstractions.

As yet Marx and Marxism are not assimilated, they remain a pole of social thought outside sociology as such, even if they are alleged to contribute to sociology. Gouldner has a peculiar way of recognizing this, when he designates Marxism a 'period' of sociology, along with three others (positivistic sociology, 'before' Marxism; classical sociology, and Parsonsian structural-functionalism, 'after' Marxism). This particular formula is contradicted within the book, as Gouldner talks about 'Marxist sociology' and 'academic sociology' as continuous and still-present poles. Marxism can hardly be a 'period' of sociology when it is present throughout all other 'periods': So what counts is whether Marxism is a sociology, or part of sociology, at all.

Marxism is a sociology in the sense that it seeks to express and develop the revolutionary logic of capitalist society. It entails a sociology in the sense that it requires us to grasp the dynamic of the class struggle. But Marxism does not see the logic of society as sociological, in the sense that social relations can be abstracted from economics, from the forces and relations of production. Nor does it believe they can be grasped sociologically, in the sense of study abstracted from action, from participation in the revolutionary transformation of society. Marxism is not therefore a part of a sociology, but seeks to abolish sociology in the specific sense. 'The real contradiction between Marx's scientific socialism and all bourgeois philosophies *and sciences*, consists entirely in the fact that scientific socialism is the theoretical expression of a revolutionary process, which will end with the total abolition of these bourgeois philosophies and sciences, together with the abolition of the material relations that find their ideological expression in them.' (Karl Korsch.)

Gouldner is not alone among radical sociologists in being conscious of this fact, and in seeking to neutralize its importance by too often identifying Marxism with its disintegrating Stalinist shell, rather than with the revolutionary tradition of thought and action. Nor is he alone in trying to justify his eclectic, neutral attitude to Marxism by pointing to the real problems of its development, and the reluctance of the New Left itself to adopt unreconstructed dogmas. But what is most important is that, also like other radical sociologists, he has to give backhanded recognition to the viability of Marxist social thought. And there can be no doubt why: the real crisis of capitalism, of which the crisis of Western sociology is a part, is giving birth to the spectre of a revolutionary theory and practice which will overcome the fragmentation of social being and social consciousness that is capitalism. In this crisis, the ideology of sociology is threatened. The answer is not Gouldner's tame assertion that the sociologist must become self-aware, but to overcome 'sociology' in the development of the revolutionary self-consciousness of the working class.

3

The Professional Organization of Sociology: A View from Below

MARTIN NICOLAUS

In recent decades there has been a phenomenal growth in all branches of sociology, especially in the United States, together with a great expansion of its involvement with industry and government. Martin Nicolaus links a scrutiny of the social role of organized sociology to an investigation of its intellectual roots. Nicolaus argues that most academic sociology is conducted from the vantage point of the dominant class in the society and devotes its energies to gathering information about the underlying population which is useful to the ruling institutions. He urges the radical sociologist to put this procedure into reverse—to investigate the activities of the powerful from the vantage point of the exploited and oppressed.

Martin Nicolaus is a former lecturer in sociology at Simon Fraser University (Canada) and is now a militant in the West coast revolutionary movement. He was awarded the Isaac Deutscher Memorial Prize for two studies of Marx's Grundrisse *(one of which will be found in the third section of this book); he is currently engaged on translating the* Grundrisse *into English.*

The trunk of political power has many branches. One of these is the professional organization of sociology, the American Sociological Association. The upper, fatter portion of this branch is grafted seamlessly, with contractual cement, to the civil, economic and military sovereignty which constitutes the trunk. From that source, the organization spreads outward and downward along the institutional scaffolding, carrying the authoritative views on matters of social reality into the universities, junior colleges, and high schools. In addition to the general dissemination of propaganda, professional sociology has the major specific functions of aiding industrial, civil, and military authorities in the solution of manpower control problems of a limited order, and of preparing university candidates for careers in the official bureaucracies. As a source of legitimation for the existing sovereignty, and as a laboratory of refinements in the processes by which a tribute of blood, labour, and taxation is extracted from the subject population, the professional organization of sociology today represents the concrete fulfilment of the charter vision of its founding fathers.

Sociology is not alone among the professions which are an extension of sovereignty by other means. That it shares this constituent function with the organizations of other disciplines is affirmed in the authoritative *International Encyclopedia of the Social Sciences* (1968), by a sociologist of world repute, who has long played the role of advocate general for all the postwar professions. Under the rubric 'Professions', Talcott Parsons moves the relationship between the professions and the power structure into extraordinarily sharp focus with the use of a homely metaphor; he writes: 'The fundamental origin of the modern professional system, then, has lain in the marriage between the academic professional and certain categories of practical men.'

The professions, in other words, play a female role. In the form of marriage which typically obtains within the professional stratum, and to a great extent elsewhere as well, the female partner is in an economically dependent status, and hence routinely subordinate to the male partner's will. This relationship may be described as an institutionalized appropriation by the superior of the subordinate's services, in return for money or commodities. Accurate also, though circumspectly phrased is sociologist Parsons' view of the prevailing *quid pro quò*. The author, most recently, of a work, *American Sociology*, which was commissioned by the Voice of America, Parsons writes that these 'practical men' '... have taken responsibility, on a basis more of specialized competence than of a diffuse religious or ideological legitimation, for a variety of operative functions in the society.' This testifies to the author's continuing sensitivity to the prevailing drift. In this year of war, inflation and recession, the men who 'have taken responsibility' for 'operative functions' such as expanding the empire, driving the labour force and collecting taxes, do indeed suffer from a lack of any intrinsic source of 'diffuse religious or ideological legitimation'. In thus describing what it is that the professions in general supply to their unofficial conjugal master, sociologist Parsons has also described his own profession, in particular, with pinpoint accuracy. The analogy which is thus established between the modern professional body on the one hand, and the enterprise commonly known as the oldest profession, on the other, can stand as crowning evidence of the synthetic powers on which Parsons' eminence as spokesman for sociology justly rests, and as proof of his unerring grasp of essentials.

The formal political organization of the contemporary academic professional bodies is the product of a long historical development. A brief examination of the pivotal figures and events in the growth of sociology will show that the current posture of this profession, in method, theory and practice, is fully congruent with its charter vision, and proceeds in an orthodox line from the contributions of its pioneers.

While social thought in general is as old as civilization, sociology as a special field is comparatively recent in origin, arising long after the medieval university's division of labour had become consolidated in early industrial society. It was perhaps in part this lack of a feudal patent which accounts for Auguste Comte's enthusiasm for things medieval. Among the conservatives of his day, this father of sociology (or, some hold, godfather) was counted a distinct reactionary. Unlike the majority of his contemporaries, who rejected the rational, humanist spirit of the French Enlightenment, Comte (1798–1857) rejected also the achievements of the seventeenth century, of the Renaissance, and of the Reformation. The only circle of his own time with which he felt a close affinity was a group known as the 'retrograde school'. 'Long live the retrograde school, the immortal group under the leadership of Maistre,' he wrote, referring to a gathering of papists, gothics, race-mystics, ultramonarchists, and theocrats who are the intellectual ancestors of twentieth-century monarchism, anti-Semitism and fascism.[1] The core of the Comtean vision of society, which it was the mission of sociology, using the 'positive' method, to realize, lies in the marriage of modern capitalist-industrial productive forces with the kind of social and political relationships which obtained

1. Quoted by Robert A. Nisbet, *The Sociological Tradition*, New York, 1966, p. 13.

at the peak of theocratic feudalism. To achieve this end, he proposed the establishment, at public expense, of a caste of scientist-priests (*les sociologues*), whose function it would be to endow the industrial and other secular authorities with the unquestionable, transcendental sanction they intrinsically lacked. The Parsonsian perspective cited above expresses the Comtean idea precisely.

But sociology remained a vague current within philosophy until, near the turn of the century, Comte's compatriot Emile Durkheim succeeded in having the first university chair created specifically in sociology. Abandoning the broadly deductive, philosophical vein, Durkheim wrote in his path-finding work, *The Rules of the Sociological Method*, that sociologists study 'facts', specifically, 'social facts'. These were to be recognized and distinguished from, for example, 'psychological facts', by the sign of the 'constraint' which they exercised. That is, a phenomenon is 'social' when its operation is beyond the control not only of any individual but also of the population as a whole; when it imposes itself on the inhabitants of a country with compelling force. Towards these basic data, sociologists are to adopt, following Comte, a 'positive' stance. Since Comte took great pains to have his methodology match his political ideology, the precipitate of the Durkheimean formulas is a reverent empiricism, which supplies scientific sanction for a patriotic posture towards the facts of social compulsion. Or, to paraphrase a passage by Karl Marx on academic political economy, sociology merely formulates the laws of oppressed social life. To this basis, Durkheim later added an additional dimension by postulating that the structure of oppression in any given society originates in, and expresses, the collective unconscious will of the population. With these certificates, sociology was admitted into the French universities.

In Germany, sociology achieved academic acceptance with a similar strategy, albeit couched in a different vocabulary. Apart from the thinly-veiled medievalism of Tönnies and the lacy intuitions of Simmel, the arena was dominated by the great Max Weber's epic campaign against the influence of Marx. This battle culminated in the sociologist's ultimate identification of the Prussian military bureaucracy, in its ideal-typical form, as the highest social embodiment of rationality. Weber also introduced into sociology the comparative method, which compares the laws of two or more oppressed societies in order to deduce the laws of oppressed societies in general. Weber summarized the method, theory and practice of the modern social sciences in two speeches to Munich university audiences during a period of student unrest a few years prior to the beer-hall putsch. In these addresses, the doctrine of 'value-free social science', under which ·banner the German universities were integrated into the Prussian bureaucracy during the Nazi period, received its seminal and constituent expression.

In the United States, sociology originally served primarily as a conduit through which European conservative social thought was introduced into the American academic milieu. To these currents, of which the later work of the 'functionalists' Parsons, Merton, Coser, and others is the naturalization and the creative synthesis, the early American practitioners added a Protestant social-meliorist bent (which proved of short duration) and the 'participant-observation' method. The latter originally meant taking conscience and notebook in hand while going slumming; today it finds application as a form of social espionage.[2] For two decades after its organizational incorporation as the American Sociological Society in 1905, sociology prospered, at least numerically, as the wholesome attitudes which it dispensed found increasing favour with college authorities. However, compared to its booming rival, psychology, sociology barely vegetated internally, remaining primarily a lecturing occupation, until an experiment in industrial management aroused widespread business interest in its practical applications.

Dissatisfied with the slow pace of output at its Hawthorne plant in Chicago, the Western Electric Company in 1927 hired a team of Harvard psychologists and cultural anthropologists to explore the problem. After selecting several small groups of workers for special attentions, and spying on and cross-examining the remainder, the researchers came to the conclusion that neither individual nor cultural factors could adequately account for the collective slow-down in production. Harvard business specialist Elton Mayo, in his widely-distributed assessment of the experiments, concluded that the explanation must be sought

2. See Alan P. Bates, *The Sociological Enterprise*, Boston, 1967, p. 147: 'On other occasions, the sociologist may simply arrange to be present at a social event (perhaps a riot, crowd or audience) in which he is professionally interested. He remains outside the situation, so to speak, but closely observes what goes on.'—And reports to his patrons.

in the realm of sociology, and advanced tentative hypotheses which drew on Durkheim and the Comtean synthesis.

As the depression intervened, however, and the rise of unionism at the Hawthorne plant called for more direct forms of labour force control, sociology was not able immediately to capitalize on the reputation which the prominence of Mayo's conversion had gained for it. Throughout the depression, the profession's ranks thinned and its influence waned. Not until the Second World War did the opportunity for a breakthrough again present itself. Faced with unprecedented demands on its officer corps' ability to manage and control millions of fresh recruits, the Pentagon contracted with a team of sociologists headed by Samuel Stouffer for the development of a set of questionnaires, tests, indices, and measurements. Published in four volumes after the war as *The American Soldier*, and containing no analysis of the demobilization riots which occurred in the Pacific towards the war's end, this military project was the cornerstone of a sociological research enterprise whose growth has continued without significant interruption since that time.

In 1958, the name of the scholarly organization was changed from American Sociological Society to Association (A S S to A S A), symbolizing the submergence of the traditional W A S P lecturing-sermonizing occupation under the new order of professionalism, which elaborates the theoretical principles of the older tradition via a sophisticated research technology so as to produce results with immediate commercial value to corporate and governmental purchasers. In 1960, the A S A moved its headquarters to Washington D.C., and engaged a full-time lobbyist at a salary reputed to be $20,000 annually. As the frictionless control of the subject population has continued to be problematic for the civil, military, and economic authorities, so the sociological profession has prospered. Amounting to 1600 persons in 1946, membership in the A S A today stands at more than 12,000.

In his aptly-titled book, *The Sociological Enterprise*, sociologist Alan P. Bates, an influential A S A functionary, draws attention to: '. . . a point that is obvious enough but nevertheless significant: like any other discipline, sociology is supported by society, which pays the salaries of people called "sociologists" and the expenses of their research'.[3]

3. *The Sociological Enterprise*, p. 71.

A less official sociologist, Irving L. Horowitz, provides a more detailed breakdown of this 'society' which pays these 'people called sociologists':

> Given the complex nature of social science activities and their increasing costs—both for human and for machine labor—the government becomes the most widespread buyer. Government policy-makers get the first yield also because they claim a maximum need. Private pressure groups representing corporate interests are the next highest buyer of social science services. ... The sources of funds for research tend to be exclusively concentrated in the upper class.[4]

Or: given the increasingly expensive nature of social research, those who engage in it, who make their living from it, are compelled to turn with outstretched hand towards the civil, military, and economic soyereignty, and prove themselves 'useful'. This social fact is basic to any understanding of the politics of the organized sociological profession.

In the post-war era the road to prominence, hence office, within the profession has been paved with research publication. Once he obtains financing for a research venture, the sociologist builds up, through publication, his professional reputation. This form of capital is then convertible into academic promotion, which yields better access to more research funds, permitting further publication, yielding further promotion, even closer proximity to the big money, and so on up, until, as supervisor of graduate students, the successful sociological entrepreneur is in a position to start and manage younger persons on the same spiral. The inevitable consequence of this career-pattern, if ability is held constant, is to reward servility. The structure is such that the achievement of prominence in the profession is a direct function of the decisions of outside financial powers. That the strings are contractual as well as salarial matters little. With a few exceptions, chiefly among the pre-war eminences, today's prominent sociologists are the direct financial creatures, functionally the house-servants, of the civil, military, and economic sovereignty.[5]

4. Horowitz, *Professing Sociology*, Chicago, 1968, pp. 270–1.
5. The financial dependence is already pointed out by Mills in *The Sociological Imagination*; is common knowledge in the profession; repeated and summarized at length by Horowitz, op. cit., pp. 159–73.

A post-war exception like the late C. Wright Mills only proves the rule. Though the most widely-read sociologist outside the academic world, Mills was barred by his university from training graduate students, for fear that he would raise up others in his image. Given the persistence of the structural constraints inherent in the exercise of the profession, which are partly rooted in the academic structure generally, the chance of another Mills arising in sociology is about equal to the chance of a Fidel Castro emerging in the State Department. Unless this structure changes profoundly, it is safely predictable that the next generation of prominent sociologists will be just as bought as the present one is.

These constraints influence the politics of the profession not only indirectly, by preselecting the group from which the professional notables, officers of the Association, etc., are drawn, but also directly, through the financial structure of the A S A.

A motion to compel the Association to issue a complete financial report was defeated at the 1969 convention, so that detailed disclosure of who owns whom will probably have to wait liberation of the files *à la* Harvard and Columbia. (1001 Connecticut Avenue, N.W.) The one and only general sociological law that has ever been discovered, namely that the oppressors research the oppressed, also applies within the A S A. While it encourages its members to engage in the full disclosure of the financial, political, sexual, mental, and other affairs of the subject population, it maintains a tight secrecy around its own affairs. Enough is known, however, to dispel the notion that the A S A is a club or society in the ordinary sense, i.e. that it is financed primarily by membership dues. According to a book entitled *A Sociology of Sociology* (1969), by sociologist Robert W. Friedrichs—a work that is as narcissistic as it sounds—the A S A as early as 1960–1 received 80 per cent of its budget from the government and corporation contracts it 'services'. It is unlikely that the proportion has declined since then.

Politically speaking, an organization which receives such a proportion of its resources from above cannot be properly said to 'represent' its membership. It succeeds, rather, for the opposite reason, because it 'represents' the imperial treasury to its membership: or, better, that it represents its members' desire to be connected to that source. The political model after which the A S A is fashioned does not, therefore, resemble the standard pyramid, in which power originates in the base and rises towards the apex. The opposite is the case; to understand this power structure, one has to visualize a cluster of grapes on a vine, or barnacles on a ship.

The matter of direct-imperialist research provides an ample illustration of this truth. The scandals of the Michigan State-sponsored Vietnam Project, of Project Camelot, Pax Americana, and others, have taught discretion but not abstinence. For example, while the panel on 'military sociology' was omitted from the 1969 convention of the A S A, perhaps as a result of Sociology Liberation Movement opposition in 1968, the ends for which the military is the means continue to be promoted, if anything, with greater pomp. At a 1969 convention panel entitled 'New Social Networks Among Interdependent Societies', the main attraction was 'Discussion and Remarks by the Guest of Honour, His Excellency Saedjatmoko, Ambassador of the Republic of Indonesia.' The panel should have been titled 'Social Change by Mass Murder', but in that unadorned diction would have been offensive to the sight, and would have failed its purpose of socializing sociologists in socio-cide.

It would be an error to believe that direct military and imperialist penetration into the sociological profession encounters general resistance from within. The whole postwar research boom was begun with Pentagon research, it should be remembered; and, as sociologist Irving L. Horowitz reports, the leading sociologists have long been lobbying and pressuring for more. The case of Horowitz himself provides an enlightening perspective. Among the liberals in the profession, the editor of *Trans-Action* magazine (nicknamed *Deal*) was instrumental, in 1965, in exposing Project Camelot for the espionage operation that it was. A year later, however, the same Horowitz—as he records in his new volume of collected papers, *Professing Sociology* (1968)—appears on what can only be called his political knees before a congressional subcommittee, pleading for the establishment of an 'independent' social science research funding agency. (The Voice of America is also 'independent'.) His testimony argues against 'secret research' only on grounds of its alleged inefficiency and wastefulness, and contains such pearls as 'Congress is uniquely qualified to be the keeper of science'.[6] The occasional verbal hostilities that do occur between government and social science must be understood as analogous to the

6. Horowitz, *Professing Sociology*, p. 256.

oaths and nips that pass between master Thornton and his dog
Buck in Jack London's *Call of the Wild*:

> Buck had a trick of love expression that was akin to hurt.
> He would often seize Thornton's hand in his mouth and close
> so fiercely that the flesh bore the impress of his teeth for
> some time afterwards. And as Buck understood the oaths to
> be love words, so the man understood this feigned bite for a
> caress.

What holds for self-defined marginal figures on the order of
Horowitz holds *a fortiori* for the professionally orthodox; the
caress from there is with gums alone.

Maintenance and lubrication of this liaison with the economic,
military, and civil sovereignty is the main but not the only
significant business of the Association. Its array of committees
undertakes, among other things, the business of disseminating
the results of this connection outward around the world and
downward into the colleges and high schools. The committee
on publications, for example, besides keeping rein over the
A S A's half-dozen official quarterlies and monthlies, produces
a series of monographs and readers in which the official view
of the social scene is retailed overseas and at home. The committee on 'International Cooperation' maintains liaison with
Soviet and East European sociologists, including 'rescue' services
à la Congress for Cultural Freedom; and pursues a programme
'to encourage the growth of sociology and support the isolated
sociologists in the developing countries of Africa, Asia, and the
Middle East.' (Latin America is apparently considered already
in the bag.) A committee on 'International Order' dispenses wish-
ful platitudes of the order of '... if the conditions may be
changed so there will be no more Vietnams.'[7] The committee
on 'Social Studies Curriculum in American Secondary Schools'
promotes under the social science label variations on the theme
of 'I Pledge Allegiance' into junior colleges and high schools;
a parallel body assists in the indoctrination of teachers for these
courses. Since the great majority of sociology BAs are hired by
the official bureaucracies, the cycle of sovereignty-sociology-
sovereignty is neatly closed at both ends.

Given these underlying structural realities, it will come as no
surprise to learn that the formal political mechanisms of the

7. Quotes are from the A S A Convention Program.

A S A resemble those of colonial India, i.e. guided democracy within the upper caste. A S A 'members' are divided into four major strata, entitled fellow, active, associate, and student. Only occupants of the first can hold office, and only occupants of the first two, who make up about forty per cent of the total, are eligible to vote in such Association affairs as the executive committee chooses to permit them to decide. The upper caste, which elects the president, vice-president, and a twelve-member Council, is composed of full-time responsible Ph.D.'d professional sociologists employed by universities, business, or government. The Council is—apart from such power as the permanent executive staff may retain to itself—the supreme governing body within the Association. It appoints all committees, including the nominating committee for next year's elections, and can accept or reject committee recommendations as it sees fit. Nor is it bound by resolutions passed or decisions made by the voting membership at 'business' meetings; once elected, its power is beyond appeal.

Quite apart from any effect the activities of the recently organized insurgent caucuses may have had, all has not been well within the organized sociological profession, even on its own terms. The glimpses into the inner core which the official record affords give a picture of spreading unrest within the upper ranks themselves.[8] The journals, for example, are plagued by editorial troubles. There is a repeated complaint about the lack of 'creative theoretical articles'. A new standing committee on 'professional ethics' has had to be minted; the Association, for the first time in its history, finds it necessary to take out libel insurance; and, worst of all, the influx of new members between 1968 and 1969 was the lowest in four years or more. What accounts for these phenomena of disquiet, and what is their significance?

Charles P. Loomis, who chairs an A S A committee, allowed himself, in the official record, to compare the flock of overfed, business-suited Rotarians who make up the A S A core to what he calls 'various minority groups', because of the fact that both 'are the first to suffer from depression or cutbacks and the last to gain from increases.' While the comparison is 'professional' at its worst, i.e. by implication racist—it does contain an inter-

8. Official Reports and Proceedings of the American Sociological Association, *passim*.

esting and significant grain of truth. Any body which is as parasitic upon the economic structure as is the A S A is necessarily highly sensitive to economic fluctuations. And it is a fact that when the economy is on the upswing, both sociology and the subject population, each in its sphere, prospers relatively, while when a recession hits, both suffer absolutely, each in its sphere. What accounts for this correlation?

At the turn of the century, a leader of the Social Democratic Party in Germany, who understood the society of her day so well that its authorities ordered her assassination, provided the key to an understanding of this question when she wrote: 'The German social scientists have always functioned as an extension of the police. While the latter act against Social Democracy with rubber truncheons, the former work with the weapons of the intellect.'[9] Had she been a sociologist, perhaps a Mertonian, Rosa Luxemburg would have expressed herself in slightly different words; she might have said: police and sociology are functional alternatives. Sociological research thrives on a low level of social unrest, widely diffused; but when, as in recessions and depressions, unrest changes from passive to active, when resistance breaks out in overt acts, in strikes, revolts, riots, and revolutions, then the 'weapons of the intellect' which sociological research supplies to the authorities become increasingly functionless. What counts as 'hardware' within sociology counts as 'software' for sovereignty. When the subject population has had enuogh of being studied, researched, analyzed, and tabulated, and actively demands instead to be fed, housed, clothed, schooled, served, alive, and sovereign, then the sponsors of research shift their assets towards the sponsorship of a different science, an alternate profession. As the evidence of the United States over the last four or five years shows, the positive correlation between the functionally contradictory prosperities of sociology and the subject population is explicable by reference to the inverse correlation between the functionally alternate prosperities of the sociological and the police professions.

When the ruling class switches its funds from sociological hardware to the hardware of sovereignty, the sociological profession has little alternative but to retreat behind the line of truncheons, hoping that the social organization of repression will be inefficient enough in the eyes of its masters to warrant sociological research, so that something, at least, can be salvaged.

9. Quoted in Peter Nettl, *Rosa Luxemburg*, abr. Oxford, 1969, p. 141.

The appearance of articles and books on the sociology of the police, and the presentation of a paper on 'The Professional Cop' in a panel on 'Sociology of the Professions' at the 1969 A S A convention are signs that this opportunity, however small, is not being wasted.

The changeover from one function to another can catch many a man of conscience in its gears, producing anguish. Sociologist Richard Flacks, a former officer of S D S, told a Sociology Liberation Movement panel audience in the San Francisco Hilton this past September [1969] that his questionnaire-and-interview studies of students who participated in campus insurrections prior to Chicago, August 1968—the crest of the changeover— had strictly preserved the anonymity of his respondents from official eyes. Nevertheless, he confessed, contrary to every intention, the published findings of his studies fed ammunition to the kind of politics that sees the root of the student movement in overly-permissive parents. It was with this notion of the students as spoiled children, it will be remembered, that Chicago's Mayor Daley urged his troopers not to spare the rod: the rising function appropriates the products of the waning function. Delivered of this *mea culpa*, this individual confession of a collective burden, Flacks proceeded to a meeting of the new professional ethics committee, there perhaps to argue with chairman Lewis Coser (who was one of the initial sponsors of Camelot) whether or not where the rockets come down is any business of Werner Von Braun.

As the functional changeover takes place from the sociological to the police professions, the level of anxiety in the councils of the former takes a perceptible upward turn. When the pool of funds shrinks, the frogs within it start hopping; none wants to be at the edges, and the premium on lily-pads near the centre is terrific. As the sciences operate with a system of individual payment for socially-produced work, a noticeable contraction in the aggregate of research funds produces a marked change in the tenor of scholarly discourse. 'Creative theoretical articles'—the kind that pay nothing and take much time—cease to appear; if a man has ideas that might make for interesting research, he is best advised, if he regards his career, to keep them to himself. The boundaries between what is my idea and what is your idea acquire an increasing commercial importance, with the result that the incidence of 'plagiarism' and 'unethicality' rises, scholarly disputes take on an increasingly economic, hence 'personal' and 'libellous' character, and the aggregate output of any ideas at all declines.

Given its dependence on the treasury just described, in times of tight money the professional organization of sociology follows its patron to the political right, along with the rest of the academic world. Radical and liberal sociologists have been or are being fired at the University of Chicago, Connecticut, Chico State (California), Mills College, George Williams, and Simon Fraser, without any spontaneous sign of interest or concern from the A S A. On the scholarly level, the drift to the right is observable in the pages of the A S A's official *American Sociological Review*, where the totalitarian implications of the functionalist method when coupled to technological means and modes of research can be studied in full theoretical bloom. Those familiar with both sociology and politics will recognize where the A S A stands from the official Theme of the 1969 convention: 'Group Conflict and Mutual Acceptance'—Simmel/Coser and Billy Graham, the left wing of functionalism and the right wing of Richard Nixon, the ancient bedmates brought to the altar.

By September of 1969 the rightward shift of the professional framework had produced a response in the opening tactic of the Sociology Liberation Movement's 'counter-convention', which convened irregularly in a church a block from the Hilton. The organizers chose to commemorate, in a lengthy panel discussion, the spirit of Pitirim Sorokin, the late refugee from the 1917 revolution, whom already Lenin had pegged as a weathervane. After achieving the A S A presidency, sixteen years behind his Harvard colleague and arch-rival Parsons, Sorokin came to see fault with the Vietnam war, as being immoral, expensive and probably unconstitutional. This deathbed gesture towards radicalism, the first of his American career, sufficiently established him in the view of his S L M sponsors to justify minting a box of 'Sorokin Lives' buttons, a tactic which the A S A neatly topped by announcing the establishment of a Sorokin Award, thus winning the first round.

The drift of the younger people, however, was in the opposite direction. A few years ago, one of the Supreme Sociologists, I believe it was Lipset, was reported to have made his exit from the convention hotel by unhooking his name badge and tossing it bridally towards a group of graduate students, who (reportedly) scrambled to pick it off the floor. This year there was none of that; the charisma was in the negative. Lipset was denounced in absentia on 'his' panel as an Air Force intellectual; the S L M truth squads, not the panelists, won the applause; and one young man said it all with an oversized name tag bearing the legend, 'Professor Bullshit, Honky U.' The S L M was a soporific in its isolated sanctuary, but inside the Hilton it crackled.

Theodor Adorno, the eminent Frankfurt philosopher of praxis, had died during the week preceding the convention. But, as his era had passed over a year ago, when he used police against an in-house application of his theory by his students, he went unmourned in San Francisco. As the panels droned and grated on, the news filtered in of the death of Ho Chi Minh and galvanized the S L M forces into action. The next evening at the plenary session, as A S A president Turner stood with his manuscript of 'The Public Perception of Protest' in hand, the words of his address leaped off the page and became flesh : members of the S L M seized the microphones and spoke movingly for twenty minutes in memory of Ho Chi Minh.

The S L M caucus, the Women's Caucus, and the Black Caucus, separately and together, beleaguered and attacked the upper caste from every angle, without quarter. Although their votes counted for nothing, the insurgent forces had the majority on nearly every resolution submitted to the business meeting. Whether the elders liked it or not, the movements of blacks, students, and women were no longer the subjects of research monographs, but forces to be dealt with in the immediate present.

The professional organization of sociology appears to be caught in the pincers of history. The market tides are turning against the product on which its prosperity chiefly depends. It has barely recruits and hardly legitimacy enough for its own consumption. As the uprisings of the subject population diminish its credit in the budgets of its patrons, so they demystify it in the eyes of its followers. What 'science' is this, that only holds true when its subjects hold still? Strange 'laws', that presuppose humanity in formaldehyde! What scientists are these, who peer into everything below, yet see nothing ahead? Now finally it dawns on these minipopes, Rotarians, dreamers and technocrats that they are trapped between the descending sky and the rising of the earth, abandoned by angels and disciples at once.

Yet the devil is old, as Weber warned. The 'liberation of sociology', which the most militant caucus in the social sciences inscribed on its banner, is a noble cause; but even the devil knows it is a contradiction in terms. Sociology is not an oppressed people or a subjugated class. It is a branch of the tree of political power, an extension of sovereignty by other means. It has survived many a borer-from-within, a pecker-from-without, and carver-of-initials-in-the-bark. To 'liberate' the branch means not to sit on it whistling the 'Marseillaise' or the 'Internationale', but to saw it off. If that is forgotten, this movement will lead not so much to the liberation of sociology as to the proliferation of A S A panels, sections, and committees on the 'sociology of liberation'. In the last analysis, the only moves toward liberation within sociology are those which contribute to the process of liberation *from* sociology. The point is not to reinterpret oppression but to end it.

4

Anthropology: the Limits of Functionalism

DAVID GODDARD

In this essay David Goddard develops a critique of the function-
alist school long dominant in Anglo-Saxon anthropology. Con-
ventionally the functionalist method has been criticized for its
inability to explain social conflict. Yet clearly any social theory
which gave a thoroughly convincing and adequate account of
social integration would have provided at least the basis for a
theory of conflict at the same time. Goddard argues that the
root failure of the functionalist approach was the absence of a
satisfactory concept of structure.

David Goddard is Assistant Professor of Anthropology at
Simon Frazer University. He will shortly publish a book about
Claude Lévi-Strauss.

Anthropological studies in Britain grew up in the context of
European, and especially British colonialism as a *part* of the
colonial situation. Anthropologists for the most part did not
question the colonial situation and the fact that they participated
in it by investigating subjugated peoples. As they took the
colonial situation for granted, often capitalizing on it and sometimes actively supporting it, they did not perceive that colonialism created a colonial people—'the native peoples'—under
the economic, political and spiritual domination of an alien
power which possessed and ruthlessly used the means of
violence against them. Instead, they chose to see colonial
peoples in terms of a 'primitive' concept, denying in effect their
colonized status.

This singular blindness to the reality of the situations of the
colonized cannot be dismissed as the helplessness of white
liberalism under conditions of imperialism so easily as it has

been by Katharine Gough.[1] On the contrary, imperialism was the normal world for anthropologists (whose existence it had made possible), just as it was for the English bourgeois intelligentsia as a whole. They avoided questioning the foundations and ideology of imperialism because it never occurred to them to do so. They were liberals, as Gough says, but liberalism then as now, however radical, was such a rationalization of the contradictions that it amounted to a denial of their existence.

However, the failure of anthropology to articulate a total conception of the colonial situation cannot be entirely understood in these terms. Characteristic of British culture since the nineteenth century has been its inability to put the whole of society in question. Even in the post-1945 context of an increasing geo-political and economic crisis, the intelligentsia have firmly avoided questioning the basis of the social order. There is, as Perry Anderson has said, a deep, instinctive aversion among the intelligentsia as a whole to engaging in any fundamental critique of the *totality* of social and cultural life.[2] Since the nineteenth century, Britain has differed from every other European country in that its intellectuals have never attempted to engage in an analysis of the underlying structures of culture and society. The very notion of 'underlying structure' has escaped them, a conceptual blindness epitomized by the superficial empiricism of all the social and historical sciences and by the interminable games of ordinary language analysis in philosophy. Instinctively they have confined themselves to the appearance of things, never attempting to analyse the relationships latent in the things themselves. Equally significant has been the constant evasion of the notion of totality, as both cause and consequence of their refusal to accept the notion of structure. For structure in its Hegelian, Marxist or structuralist usages is a *totalizing* concept in that it seeks to effect a dynamic but never complete synthesis or closure of a domain of experience. It attempts to grasp a total phenomenon in terms of the relationships which constitute it. But British thought has never looked into this rationalist abyss, either to situate itself or to

1. Katharine Gough, 'Anthropology: Child of Imperialism,' *Monthly Review*, Vol. 19, No. 11, 1968.

2. 'Components of the National Culture', *New Left Review*, No. 50, July–August, 1968.

situate its society as a total historical phenomenon requiring critical structural explanation.

Pseudo-structures

British social anthropology has, however, worked with a notion of structure, but without ever bringing it into an intelligible relation with these considerations. Structure has been identified with the totality of empirically given social relationships in tribal societies. It is, that is to say, the *social* structure of the society. To all intents and purposes it is therefore coterminous with the totality, a closed, stable system tending towards equilibrium. This structural approach has been the unifying theme of social anthropology since Radcliffe-Brown, and, in consequence, the first task of the anthropologist has always been seen as 'to give an account of the social structure of the people he has studied.'[3] Structure is therefore a simple and not a complex notion because it relates directly and virtually without mediation to the empirical reality of social life.

The principal concern of social anthropology has been with the problem of social order: how does it come about that, once the field-worker has accustomed himself to the bewildering flux of strange impressions, the social life of the people he is studying presents itself as a stable, orderly, repetitive reality, that there appear to be regular modes of action and/or orientation to others? For the anthropologist, the small-scale social systems of the primitive presented a unique opportunity to study the coherence of society in microcosm, and establish the bases of social integration. Yet this is not to say that the problem of order appeared simply as an *abstract* problem to the anthropologists, a question raised by the nature of anthropological theory itself and requiring critical examination. It was, in fact, imposed by the very presupposition of an isolable, primitive totality, which underlay every ethnographic investigation; but it appeared to the anthropologists as a problem imposed by the phenomena themselves.

Social anthropology discovered its solution to it in the institutional arrangements of social life which regulate the relationships between individuals. Social conduct is governed by habitual, customary, and juridical norms, to which overt or covert sanctions are attached to ensure conformity, and which struc-

3. M. Fortes, *Dynamics of Clanship Among the Tallensi.*

ture the social life of individuals in their orientation to others in a regular and predictable fashion. This focused the analysis of primitive life on rules of conduct as mechanisms of social control, on the types of rules that obtain in particular kinds of social groups (e.g. kinship or political groups), and on the consequences which complexes of norms have for the *organization* of social relationships in given sectors of the social existence. The fabric of society was thus discovered, not in culture (as a given totality of customary ways of behaving), but in institutions considered as regulative social relationships. Hence the 'structural approach' to primitive society consisted in describing minutely the organization of social institutions as systems of norms and their orderly articulation with each other—kinship systems, economic systems, juridical systems, and political systems. Broadly speaking, this was regarded as the social structure of the society, and corresponded to Durkheim's conception of morphological structure. The 'dynamic' element in this highly descriptive approach to social phenomena was added by the concept of function. Institutions were seen as functioning parts of the social system which maintained it in a more or less stable equilibrium condition. In so far as institutions continued to play this role in contributing to the maintenance of the total social order they were seen as 'functional' for it. Ultimately this conceptual approach focused on the control mechanisms that function to ensure conformity with the normative order. It led directly to a perception of social life as approximating to a seamless web of highly integrated institutionalized relationships enclosing and regulating the lives of primitives in all their manifest activities.

The concept of social structure which was thus developed consequently remained highly empirical in scope. In the last analysis it simply referred to the totality of real social relationships obtaining in a given social group which could be directly observed and which were organized in a 'network'. As it was put by Radcliffe-Brown in his 1940 essay 'On Social Structure' '... direct observation does reveal to us that ... human beings are connected by a complex network of social relations.'[4] The integration of this conception of structure into the functional approach had however already been fully formulated by Radcliffe-Brown: 'Individual human beings ... are connected by a

4. A. R. Radcliffe-Brown, 'On Social Structure' in *Structure and Function in Primitive Society*, London, Cohen and West, 1952, p. 190.

definite set of social relations into an integrated whole. The continuity of the social structure, like that of an organic structure, is not destroyed by changes in the units ... The continuity of structure is maintained by the process of social life, which consists of the activities and interactions of the individual human beings and of the organized groups into which they are united. The social life of the community is here defined as the *functioning* of the social structure. The *function* of any activity is the part it plays in the social life as a whole and therefore the contribution it makes to the maintenance of the structural continuity.'[5]

So within the pseudo-totalization of social anthropology there is really nothing more than the idea of an aggregate of social relations (the social structure) maintained in being by the on-going 'process of social life'. The primitive totality is merely an empirical whole having a certain manifest pattern or arrangement, institutional or normative in character. In effect, the normative series, as observed and also lived, remains unreduced in social anthropology; it is simply described and its order noted. Further analysis consists only in attempting to delineate the 'general or normal form' of the normative series or 'structure', arrived at by simple induction.

While the Polish born anthropologist Malinowski must be credited with revolutionizing British anthropology in the 1920s as a result of his immensely detailed studies of the Trobriand Islanders, and also of exciting wider intellectual interest in what had previously been a rather esoteric subject, it was Radcliffe-Brown rather than Malinowski who provided the scientific criteria for modern anthropological research and laid down the conceptual parameters for *social* anthropology. Malinowski, it is true, pioneered in-depth field methods[6] (as a result of his

5. *The Concept of Function*, p. 180.
6. Malinowski's ideas on intensive investigation were quite new at the time in England although Boas and his students, Kroeber and Radin in the United States, were already spending long periods in the field. Malinowski, however, did get anthropologists off the district officer's verandah by insisting that primitive culture must be observed at first hand in its day-to-day workings. His views on the collection of data were also much more sophisticated than those of later anthropologists who imagined they were observing directly phenomena which resulted from a series of prior acts of conceptualization. This led to the criticism, as structural studies were refined, that structure was too often regarded as 'more real than

involuntarily prolonged visit to the Trobriands) and established the functional approach to the analysis of culture. But his functionalism was 'reductionist' inasmuch as it was grounded in a psycho-biological theory of needs, and thus ran counter to the main drift of anthropology which, from Radcliffe-Brown's reading of Durkheim on, was sociological rather than psychological (or, for that matter, cultural).

Comparing the methods of ethnology and social anthropology in his 'charter of revolt'[7] Radcliffe-Brown claimed that social anthropology was an inductive, generalizing science, anti-historical and anti-psychological, whose aim was the establishment of universal sociological laws governing the relations between social phenomena by comparative analysis of social systems. The initial attack was mounted against 'conjectural history' as consisting of no more than hypothetical reconstructions of historical events or stages. Both evolutionism and diffusionism

---

other aspects of the social system'. Cf. P. Kaberry, *Malinowski's Contribution to Field-work Methods and the Writing of Ethnography*, in R. Firth (ed.), *Man and Culture*, New York, Harper, 1964. Malinowski, to the contrary, seemed much more aware of the relation between observation and description, which is perhaps why the social life of the Trobrianders never appeared in his work as 'over-specified'. Yet, paradoxically, Malinowski was not an empiricist in the traditional British sense (although his work was highly empirical as this statement in *Coral Gardens and Their Magic* indicates: 'The main achievement of field-work consists, not in a passive registering of facts, but in the construction and drafting of what might be called the charters of native institutions ... While making his observations the field-worker must constantly construct: he must place isolated data in relation to one another and study the manner in which they integrate ... "Facts" do not exist in sociological reality any more than they so in physical reality; that is, they do not dwell in the spatial and temporal continuum open to the untutored eye. The principles of social organization, of legal constitution, of economics and religion, have to be encountered by the observer out of a multitude of manifestations, of varying significance and relevance. It is these invisible realities only to be discovered by inductive compilation, by selection and construction, which are scientifically important in the study of culture.' Vol. 1, p. 317.) Malinowski owed more to Durkheim and *The Rules of Sociological Method* than is commonly thought, and certainly by E. R. Leach, by whom this passage is quoted.

7. 'Methods of Ethnology and Social Anthropology' in *Structure and Function in Primitive Society*.

were subjected to this criticism. Similarly psychological explanation of social phenomena was dismissed as irrelevant to a social anthropology considered as an independent science. Like Durkheim, Radcliffe-Brown regarded the object of study as 'the process as a whole' and not individuals with their particular thoughts, feelings, and motives ('of no interest or importance for our purpose').[8] Hence social anthropology was to be a science of social systems aiming to establish the bases of their present functioning, presumed to be regular and *hence* capable of being expressed in statements of law. The method of functionalism itself did not amount to a rigorous set of methodological or theoretical requirements that analysis of social systems should meet (it was never codified by either Radcliffe-Brown or later anthropologists), but referred to the general orientation or approach to social phenomena to be taken by anthropologists. In his well-known essay on the concept of function, for instance, Radcliffe-Brown has no more to say than the following on the question of functionalist 'theory' : '. . . if functionalism means anything at all it does mean the attempt to see the social life of a people as a whole, as a functional unity.'[9] 'The function of a particular social usage is the contribution it makes to the total activity of which it is a part. Such a view implies that a social system (the total social structure as a society, together with the totality of social usages in which that structure appears and on which it depends for its continued existence) has a certain kind of unity, which we may speak of as a functional unity.'[10] In fact, functionalism in British anthropology came to mean little more than this—an assumption that a social totality had a functional unity of some kind which was to be empirically established—especially since the more radical formulation of functionalism by Malinowski was rejected.

More interesting for present purposes is the relation between Radcliffe-Brown's view of scientific method and his conception of social reality. The one reveals the other especially clearly in this case : 'My view of natural science is that it is the systematic investigation of the structure of the universe *as it is revealed to us* through our senses.'[11] Thus the task of the scientist is

8. Ibid., p. 17.

9. 'The Concept of Function' in *Structure and Function in Primitive Society*, p. 185.

10. Ibid., 181.

11. Ibid., p. 190 (italics added).

merely one of recording the observable regularities of the universe and of collating them in the form of empirical generalizations or 'laws'. The status of reality is only accorded to observable phenomena therefore; there are no hidden relations, principles, or forms, nor is the scientist engaged in the construction of models or theories of such relations or principles in order thereby to *explain* what he observes. Such a view of science leads no further than to description of observable regularities, their classification through comparison with apparently similar phenomena, and the abstraction of general uniformities discerned as a result of classifying the forms of the phenomena in question. It is evidently the classical inductivist position of traditional British empiricism: 'All phenomena are subject to natural law, and consequently it is possible, by the application of certain logical methods, to discover and prove certain general laws, i.e. certain general statements or formulae, of greater or lesser degree of generality, each of which applies to a certain range of facts or events. The essence of induction is generalization; a particular fact is explained by being shown to be an example of a general rule.'[12]

Its consequence for the development of theory is that all concepts are necessarily empirical concepts referring to the observable processes of social life. There can be no analytic 'break' with the phenomena in order to penetrate their inner nature. Sociological analysis cannot progressively strip away the outer forms of the real (as in psychoanalysis) in order eventually to reveal the immanent structure of the real, but is limited to finding an observable social order at the phenomenal level. Hence the unremitting emphasis on the normative arrangements of social systems by means of which 'orderly and workable systems of social relationships defined by social usage' are made possible.[13]

The influence of Maine

Full discussion of the consequences of this conception of science and the crisis it has provoked in social anthropology must be reserved until later. However, it can be pointed out that by confining investigation to regularities observed in institutional organization, Radcliffe-Brown in effect destroyed

12. 'Methods of Ethnology and Social Anthropology', p. 7.
13. 'The Study of Kinship Systems' in *Structure and Function*, p. 62.

the distinction erected by Montesquieu in *L'Esprit des Lois*, between normative and natural laws. If sociological laws are no more than statements of 'regularities among (normative) phenomena', then they are no more than sociological restatements of the customary and legal rules by means of which people maintain stable social relationships among themselves (e.g. 'the principle of sibling unity').[14] They certainly cannot be held to express 'in their most general signification ... the necessary relations arising from the nature of things.'[15]

The principal influences on the formation of this social anthroplogy were a highly selective study of Durkheim's early work, and the tradition of historical and comparative jurisprudence in England. The debt to Durkheim was more or less consciously acknowledged, but the general ideas to be found in comparative law were assimilated in a much less conscious fashion. Still, Maine's *Ancient Law* was as mandatory theoretical fare for the post-Radcliffe-Brown generations of social anthropologists as Durkheim's *Division of Labour*. Maine's *Ancient Law* was of course much closer to the main stream of social theory in the late nineteenth century than the work of other legal historians at the time, Vinogradoff, Maitland, Pollock, whose work has been less clearly recognized as having exercised a profound influence on anthropological theory and the formulation of certain key concepts such as agnation, cognation, corporation, matriarchy, patriarchy. Maine was within the evolutionary tradition and saw the historical development of law as an evolution from status to contract, a shift from legal rights, duties and commands based on personal status to the objectivation and codification of law in impersonal statutes having universal application (a move, in other words, from archaic custom to law proper). Maine thus reflected and also anticipated other

14. By means of which a wide-ranging kinship organization is made possible with a limited classificatory terminology.

15. Montesquieu, *L'Esprit des Lois*, Book I, p. 1. Montesquieu formulated the distinction between natural and normative law as follows: 'Man, as a physical being, is like other bodies governed by invariable laws. As an intelligent being, he incessantly transgresses the laws established by God, and changes those of his own instituting.' A natural science of society, which Radcliffe-Brown wished to establish, would have to treat man as a social being governed, as in his physicality, by invariable laws: the position taken by Durkheim but not by his Anglo-Saxon epigones.

similar conceptual dichotomies which have remained central in twentieth-century social theory.[16]

But where Maine was important, and where he agreed with other contemporary students of the history of law who were not evolutionists, was in his recognition that the institutions of law are a complex of rules in society, among other sets, by which men order their lives. He investigated law not as an autonomous structure with its own internal principles of determination, but as related to other social institutions (kinship, political, economic) which it influenced and which also influenced it in its character and development. Secondly, he regarded law as having derived from custom in the 'life of the folk' of medieval and ancient communities, that is, as developing from a loose, uncodified system of rules to eventual crystallization in fixed and explicit rules. So law in comparative jurisprudence was considered from a broadly sociological point of view: law was a means to understanding society, and society was a means to understanding law. Radcliffe-Brown applied these ideas directly to societies ruled by custom, which he held in most instances lacked law, and regarded customary and legal rules (where they existed) as systems of organized sanctions functioning as mechanisms of social control. All rules are supported by sanctions, whether diffuse or codified. Similarly in *The Division of Labour*, the main Durkheimian influence on Radcliffe-Brown, Durkheim thought that law was the basic organizational aspect of social life. Whether fixed or not, norms of conduct (backed by sanctions in the form of custom, convention or usage) and law regulated social relations; and in *The Division of Labour* law was treated as the outward manifestation of forms of social solidarity which consisted of social relationships. Thus the type of law associated with mechanical solidarity (characteristic of undifferentiated or segmented societies where the division of labour is minimally institutionalized and in which individuals 'resemble' one another socially) is repressive in nature. Under conditions of organic solidarity (where, because of an advanced division of labour, individuals

16. Tönnies (*Gemeinschaft* and *Gesellschaft*), Weber (types of rational action), Durkheim (organic and mechanical solidarity), Redfield (folk-urban continuum), Becker (sacred-secular) have all conceived the development of modern institutions in a similar fashion. These dichotomous schemata have received their apotheosis in Parsons' pattern variables of action.

are highly differentiated from each other in social terms) the law is restitutive rather than repressive in character. Hence law is not simply a convenient index of social solidarity, as was thought by some of Durkheim's later interpreters—rather as the incidence of suicide was an index of the lack of social solidarity —but law, as the most explicit aspect of the total normative system of society, was seen by Durkheim to play a fundamental role in the regulation of social solidarity itself.

The jural focus

But *The Division of Labour* was the only book of Durkheim's in which he approached the analysis of society in its jural aspect, while in England this defined the scope of anthropology altogether. Under Radcliffe-Brown's influence social anthropology remained rooted in problems Durkheim had half-analysed but which he subsequently lost sight of in his studies of morality, religion, and the mind. The primary phenomenon distilled out of Durkheim and comparative law was the 'jural relationship', that is, relationships in primitive societies which had legal or quasi-legal character. In practice the concept was applied to all social relationships from customary to legal which were supported by sanctions of a more or less binding character. Hence it did not simply apply to the institutional regulation of disputes between groups and individuals or to the redress of wrongs through quasi-legal forms, but to a whole range of social relations which were obligatory in regard to the expectations of the conduct of the individuals who were parties to the relationships.

In particular, social anthropology concerned itself with the organization of kinship as the principle focus of social cohesion in primitive societies. Kinship systems were analysed as rules having obligatory status which regulated the conduct of particular categories of kin towards one another. Given the almost universal complexity of these rules and their practical application, and the complexity of the classificatory terminologies which were articulated with the rules (especially rules regulating marriage choices, but also descent and inheritance), it should not surprise us that a great deal of social anthropology has been taken up with the problem of describing kinship organization in a very detailed way, classifying the basic rules of kinship (called 'structural principles'), and comparing one system with another in the hope of finding certain key correspondences which could be summarized in 'general sociological laws'. In certain acephalous (non-hierarchical, chiefless) societies, the jural organization of kinship relationships, and especially of the relations between descent groups, was regarded as the basic integrative structure of the social system, providing its political as well as its social integration. This was the case of the Nuer, studied by Evans-Pritchard, an extremely large tribal society held together by a very complex differentiation of descent groups through the mechanisms of fission and fusion. As can be seen from this example the concern with kinship organization as a quasi-legal and stable structure entering into and usually structuring other areas of social activity (religious, economic, etc.) led directly to a consideration of forms of authority and domination in society, that is, to the organization or lack of organization of primitive political systems, again regarded as having a jural character. In the case of the Neur, political organization consisted of the relationships between descent groups incorporated in broader and broader social groupings (clans) having literally a corporate character. Non-acephalous societies having chiefs and a pyramidal structure were analysed in a similar way, that is, from the point of view of the articulation of kinship with forms of political authority.

As a result of such an orientation, the concept of social structure, regarded as consisting of these jural-type relationships, obviously became central. To understand the normative organization of the social structure came to be regarded as the key to understanding the society as a whole.[17] In most cases the concept of social structure was developed by the anthropologists in close relation to the actual empirical research undertaken. There are consequently differences in emphasis as between different individual definitions. Evans-Pritchard's view that social structure consists of relations between groups is thus clearly drawn from empirical observation of Nuer society and its complex organization of descent groups: 'Structural relations are relations between groups which form a system. By structure

17. *African Political Systems*, ed. by M. Fortes and E. E. Evans-Pritchard, Oxford, 1940, and *African Systems of Kinship and Marriage*, ed. by A. R. Radcliffe-Brown and D. Forde, Oxford, 1950, exemplify this approach to the study of tribal social organization. See particularly Radcliffe-Brown's introductory essay in the second volume.

we therefore mean an organized combination of groups ... The social structure of a people is a system of separate but interrelated structures.'[18] Here he differs from Radcliffe-Brown who emphasized, as we have mentioned, that social structure was simply 'the network of actually existing social relationships'. Firth, from his studies of the Tikopia, considered the social structure to be composed of certain key relationships: 'The essence of this concept is those social relations which seem to be of critical importance for the behaviour of members of the society, so that if such relations were not in operation, the society could not be said to exist in that form.'[19] Nadel, on the other hand, defines it more abstractly, using the concept of role which had not previously been introduced into social anthropology : 'We arrive at the structure of a society through abstracting from the concrete population and its behaviour the pattern or network (or "system") of relationships obtaining "between factors in their capacity of playing roles relative to one another".'[20]

But despite differences in conceptualization all contain a central reference to relations between actual, empirically given social phenomena, whether those phenomena are individuals, groups, or roles. These relationships are either given in the facts as observed directly, or arrived at by simple abstraction from the facts. Thus structure refers to no more than the actual organization of society.

However, the 'facts' in this instance are normative facts, phenomena of institutional regulation given to both observation and the consciousness of those whole lives are ordered by them. Certainly they are a legitimate body of phenomena, as Durkheim showed by arguing that the facts of the moral life could be analysed with the precision of natural science. But the question in social anthropology is the mode of their treatment, the manner in which they are conceptualized and whether, as Durkheim held, they are subject to principles of inner structuration. Neither of these questions have been considered in British anthropology, despite overt homage to Durkheim. The

18. E. E. Evans-Pritchard, 'The Nuer', in *African Political Systems*, pp. 262–3.

19. R. Firth, *Elements of Social Organization*, Boston, Beacon Press, 1964, p. 31.

20. S. Nadel, *The Theory of Social Structure*, London, Cohen and West, 1957, p. 12. The quoted part of the passage is from Parsons.

'facts' are merely seen as given in a certain organization.[21] Their methodological status is not put in question. It is precisely this which is problematic. Even though social facts are superficially treated as 'things' and explained by reference to other social facts (the sociological perspective absorbed from Durkheim), there is no tendency to recognize that normative facts may be shaped by 'facts' that are non-normative and which may be hidden from view, requiring a critical analysis to uncover them. So, for instance, the category of 'interests' as structuring the normative orientations of actors and as arising from structural relationships which are non-normative (and which only become normative in a manner which distorts their true nature) is not taken into consideration. Interests, and conflicts resulting from them, are, on the contrary, analysed as effects of tensions in normative requirements and, moreover, as contributing through their (normative) resolution to the social integration of the system.[22] The convergence between method and theory could not be more complete. Inductive empiricism prohibits analysis of anything which is not accessible to inspection and which requires an 'operation' on observable phenomena to bring what is hidden to the light of day. But the substantive orientation of theory to normative phenomena inhibits the anthropologist from attempting to go beyond the description of their empirical arrangement.

In consequence, the assimilation of Durkheim was, to say the least, highly selective and incomplete. Durkheim's rationalist, Cartesian mode of analysis of social phenomena by reducing them to their constituent elements, was interpreted uneasily as a 'sociological positivism' and thus made to correspond as nearly as possible to the methodological conditions of traditional empiricism. The 'metaphysical' elements in Durkheim—society as a phenomenon *sui generis*, the apparently outrageous analysis of religion—were quietly suppressed or conveniently forgotten. His 'disdain' for empirical facts was berated, his view that one crucial experiment or experimental situation could serve to establish the validity of a sociological or natural law was treated with incredulity. It would not be too much to say that social

21. A conception corresponding to the empiricist and holist view of gestaltism and organicism: a 'whole' is merely an arrangement of parts.

22. Cf. M. Gluckmann, *Custom and Conflict in Africa*, Oxford, Blackwell, 1961.

anthropology, while owing its scientific character and its sub-stantive focus very much to Durkheim, nevertheless entirely misundertood his thought. The real strength of the Durkheimian methods, its analysis of phenomena into the elements which constitute them, was never received into British anthropology.

5

Economics: the Revival of Political Economy

EDWARD NELL

The prevailing schools of economic theory are unable to explain the most acute problems of contemporary capitalist economies: inflation combined with unemployment, the distribution of income between social classes, the persistence of poverty, the expansionary drive of the major corporations. Edward Nell argues that to grapple with these questions will require a revival of political economy in the classical sense, with a renewed focus on the class system which structures and constitutes the economy.

Edward Nell is a Professor of Economics at the New School for Social Research.

Since the latter decades of the nineteenth century orthodox economic theory has made its main business the demonstration that a well-oiled market mechanism will produce the most efficient allocation of scarce resources among competing ends. This preoccupation has in turn dictated a characteristic mode of analysis, in which the economy is divided horizontally, so to speak, into 'agencies', or institutions, which whatever their other differences, always operate on the same side of the market and so respond in roughly similar ways to market incentives. Thus Rockefellers and share-croppers are both households, G M and the corner grocery are both firms. Households demand 'final goods' and supply labour and other 'factor services' (meaning the use of capital and land); firms demand labour and other 'factor services' and supply 'final goods'.

This way of subdividing the economy fits neatly into the framework of 'rational choice'. Firms supply goods and demand factors in the amounts and proportions that will maximise their profits, given their technical possibilities and opportunities.

Households supply factor services and demand goods in the amounts and proportions that will maximise their 'utility' (most perfectly satisfy their preferences), given their 'initial endowments', a polite and covert way of referring to property holdings. The amounts finally chosen, the equilibrium supplies and demands, will be simultaneously compatible solutions to all these different individual maximising problems.

The task of high theory, then, is twofold; first, since the models are complex, *to show that there are, indeed, such simultaneous, mutually compatible solutions*. This is not obvious, and in fact not always true. Secondly, of equal mathematical and of greater ideological importance, are what might be called the Invisible Hand Theorems, which *show that the system of market incentives will direct the economy towards the equilibrium prices, supplies and demands*. In other words, the theorems demonstrate that the system is automatically self-adjusting and self-regulating.

Orthodox economic theory has many strengths. Market incentives often *do* direct the system in various predictable ways. Maximising is, under some conditions, an indispensable part of rational behaviour, and so must be spelled out. That it is all done at an exceptionally high level of abstraction is not only no objection, it may be a positive merit. The analysis is not cluttered with irrelevancies.

But when all is said, apart from defending the freedoms appropriate to private enterprise from hare-brained schemes of social reform, the theory of the optimality of competitive markets has never provided much practical insight into the working of the economy. Since it presupposes effective market incentives and institutions devoted to maximising behaviour, it cannot easily be applied to the study either of pre-market economies, or of post-market ones—i.e., ideal communist (or anarchist) societies. Still, traditional theory could probably be forgiven these shortcomings if it provided a good model for studying the working and misworking of present-day capitalism. Unfortunately, it is not even a good model for this, and for a very simple reason.

Basically, orthodox theory is a theory of markets and market interdependence. It is a theory of general equilibrium in *exchange*, extended almost as an afterthought, to cover production and distribution. It is not a theory of a social system, still less of economic power and social class. Households and firms are considered only as market agents, never as parts of a social structure. Their 'initial endowments', wealth, skills and property, are taken as *given*. Moreover, the object of the theory is to demonstrate the tendency towards equilibrium; class and sectoral conflict is therefore ruled out almost by assumption.

As a result, the orthodox approach has comparatively little interesting to say about such important socio-economic questions as the distribution of wealth and income. It cannot say how these came about; it cannot say how different they might be under another kind of economic system, and it cannot describe the evolution and development of the institution of private property.

It does, however, have one major claim to social and historical relevance. It offers a definite though limited theory of the division of the value of net output between land, labour and capital. This is known as 'marginal productivity' theory. Briefly, it states that each agent in the system will tend to be rewarded in proportion to and—as a limiting case—in direct equivalence to the contribution it makes to output. Thus a man earns what he (literally) makes; a landlord reaps what he (metaphorically) sows.

But with the revival of interest in the great problems of Political Economy in recent years, this central claim has come under increasingly heavy attack. Moreover, in the last few years, this attack, which began in particular objections to specific orthodox doctrines, has developed into an alternative conception of the economic system. It is no longer simply a rival theory of growth and distribution—a 'non-neo-classical' theory—nor can it be regarded merely as a return to the approach of the Classical Greats, Smith, Ricardo and Marx. It is both of these, but it is considerably more. In currently fashionable terminology, it is the emergence of a new paradigm.

To see this, let us contrast the emerging view of income distribution with orthodox marginal productivity theory. At first glance, marginal productivity theory appears eminently sensible. As we have seen, it states that 'factors'—land, labour and capital—will be hired as long as they produce more than they cost to hire. Since expanding the employment of any one factor, the others held constant, will (the theory assumes) cause the returns on the extra units of that factor to decline (it having proportionately less of the others to work with), extra employment will cease when the declining returns just equal the cost of hiring the factor. The total earnings of any factor will then be equal to its amount times its marginal product, summed up over all the industries in which it is used. Clearly the relative shares of 'factors', land, labour and capital, depend on the technology (which determines how rapidly returns diminish) and on the supplies of the factors available.

So far so good. To be sure, this story depends on the existence of markets, specifically on markets for labour, land and capital, so that the theory will not be much use in examining the emergence or abolition of the market system. But also, in a sleight of hand so deft as to have passed virtually unnoticed for an intellectual generation, it attributes responsibility for the distribution of income (under market competition) wholly and solely to the impersonal agency of *technology*. No man, nor god, least of all politics, in this most political of economic affairs, has decreed what the shares of labour and capital are to be in the total product. They are the accidental, but inescapable, and unalterable, consequence of the technology we happen to have. Only through technical changes, inventions which alter the engineering possibilities, can relative shares be changed. For if income shares are to change, the ratio of the proportional changes in the marginal products must differ from the ratio of the proportional changes in the amounts of factors employed. Which is to say that everything depends on how rapidly marginal returns to the different factors diminish, relatively to one another, and this is a matter which depends only on technology.

So the class struggle is an illusion; unions are valuable only as mother-substitutes—providers of security and a sense of identification. Minium wage legislation, by restricting the level of employment offered, and in no other way, may or may not raise wages—if the marginal product rises proportionately more than the employment falls such legislation *could* raise labour's share. But in both cases the effect will depend wholly on what the technology permits. Only moves which change the relative marginal products of labour and capital can affect income distribution (though even they might not if, for example, the movement in the relative amounts of labour and capital employed just offsets the changes in marginal products). For whereas profits and wages depend to some extent on the available amounts of labour and capital, they hinge chiefly on the technical opportunities, which determine what the marginal productivity of each factor will be. Indeed, the influence of factor supplies is felt through, and only through, marginal productivity. Hence *technology* is what finally determines income distribution. Aggregate demand, monetary policy, inflation, unions, politics, even revolution, are, in the end, all alike, irrelevant.

That the technical possibilities available influence income distribution is surely undeniable. Clearly if it is known that a machine can do a certain job, the labourer now doing it would be unwise to ask, and unlikely to get, more in pay than it would cost to install and run the machine. But this in no way depends on diminishing marginal returns; substitution of machines for men and *vice versa*, although what marginal productivity theory is talking about, can be examined without its straitjacket.

In any case, the technical possibilities of substitution are only one set of influences among many which bear upon the division of national income. For example, the orthodox story in singling out the influence of technology neglects that of, say, differential rates of inflation. This is not a merely accidental oversight. Ideologically significant choices are never simple and, while they may occur, in the first instance, by chance, it is not by chance that they get incorporated into the text-books, even if the motivation is seldom explicit or conscious. Here the ideological content could hardly be clearer. No one is responsible for technology (so the story goes); it is 'given'—the result of cultural and historical influences quite separate from the economic system. But if technology is the chief determinant of income distribution, then apart from its influence, only minor changes are possible. Even monopoly power and the influence of the state make only a marginal difference. The theory, in short, relieves politics and property of any responsibility for the existing division of earnings and patterns of consumption, no small coup in the ideological fray.

Socialist and New Left economists, indeed social critics generally, have always gagged on this. Property and power, they maintain, are the essential elements in class struggles and sectional conflicts; it is ridiculous to say they do not matter, that the outcome, given the competitive market, is predetermined by the accidents of technological inventiveness. From their vantage point, income distribution, the division of society's annual product among the members of society, is *the* central question. By way of contrast, for the orthodox economists the problem of *allocation* stood at the centre; their questions were how the members of society choose to spend their incomes, and how suppliers adjust to this. But if we put income distribution at the centre of the stage, these questions seem relatively minor. The framework of rational choice looks flimsier and more makeshift; essentially a consumer theory, it has come to resemble so many consumer products, ingenious, brilliant, but unsuited to human needs. Like the automobile, its surface dazzles, but its functioning can be destructive.

This is not to say that the Political Economist rejects the theory of rational choice outright; he rejects it merely as an appropriate framework for the analysis of production and distribution in the aggregate. The appropriate framework is one which reveals the *links* between sectors and classes, how the products of one industry or set of industries are used as inputs by other industries, whose products, in turn, are used by still others; how the earnings of one class are spent supporting production in some sector or industry. Inter-industry and inter-sectoral relations are crucial to understanding how changes in demands or in technology transmute themselves into prosperity for some, disaster for others. Links between revenue from sales, social classes, and spending are crucial for understanding how the distribution of income is established and maintained in the face of considerable changes in the composition of output and in government policy.

The difference may seem more one of emphasis than of substance, but putting income distribution at the centre and relating it to different patterns of linkages, of payment streams and of technological dependency, between industries, sectors and classes, leads to an altogether different vision of how the economy works. Perhaps the best way to explain this is to list the principal differences.

The new vision can be called a 'general equilibrium' approach, if one likes. But it departs from the orthodox meaning of that phase by emphasizing the *interdependence of production*, rather than of markets; technical and institutional 'interlocks' —or their absence—rather than purely market relationships.

A second difference between the new approach and the old lies in the treatment of 'substitution'. In the old picture substitution is the law of life on both the supply and demand sides. In response to price changes, different patterns of goods and/or of factors will be chosen; when prices change, cheaper things will be substituted for more expensive in household budgets and industrial processes. Yet we all know this is unrealistic so far as industrial production is concerned; indeed, the availability of opportunities for substitution may itself be an index of development. Moreover, the conventional picture assumes that households and firms have *given* ends—the production of 'utility' or output respectively. It does not deal with the more important questions of introducing altogether new products and processes, changes which often alter the parameters of the system or perhaps even the consciousness of the society. Even within the narrow focus of the neo-Classical lens, however, many alleged cases of substitution really involve something quite different—technical progress, changes in the nature of the product, external effects on parameters of the system, and so on. Widespread possibilities for neo-Classical substitution must be a *special* case, and that is how the matter is treated in the new vision.

Third, the old vision treats the consumer as sovereign, and the effects of his choices enter into the determination of all major variables. This, of course, does not render the old vision incapable of discussing market power, producer sovereignty, or the 'new industrial state'. But, inevitably, such phenomena appear as special cases, limitations on the *general* principle of consumer sovereignty. In the new vision the consumer is cut down to size from the start. His preferences have little or *no* effect on prices and income distribution.

Fourthly, markets are not supposed naturally to be stable, or to engender optima (though, of course, in some cases they may). Prices are determined largely, and in simple models, wholly from the supply side. The choice of industrial techniques depends on prospective profits, which in turn depend largely on *aggregate* demand and the state of the labour market. Aggregate demand depends on business saving and investment plans, which in turn depend on a wide variety of factors, including the political climate, past growth rates, and 'animal spirits', none of which find much of a welcome in neo-Classical models. But aggregate demand is also influenced by, and influences, the distribution of income; indeed this relationship is central to the new picture, and provides a sharp contrast to the old.

A fundamental difference can be seen when we consider the *purposes* of the two visions. The basic constituents of the old vision are consumers and firms, agents whose optimising behaviour, individually or in the aggregate, the equations of the models describe. In particular, maximising behaviour is what the theory is all about, and the *object of the theory, by and large, is to predict such behaviour and its consequences*. But the circumstances in which behaviour takes place are taken for granted.

By contrast—and oversimplifying—the new vision is primarily interested in structure, in the patterns of dependency between established institutions, in how the system hangs together, and works or fails to work. The job of economic theory is to delineate the *blueprint* of the economic system, of the environment in which economic behaviour takes place. The basic constituents of theory are industries, sectors, processes or activities, defined in technological terms; so defined, the new vision's basic constituents normally will not coincide with 'decision-making' agencies. Neither the word 'household' nor the word 'firm', nor any synonym for either, appears in Sraffa's *Production of Commodities by Means of Commodities*, the basic work laying the foundation of the new paradigm. For decision-making, the prediction of behaviour of what *will* happen, is not the goal. The new vision is concerned to see how an economy keeps going, what is *supposed* to happen, and from that to discover what makes it break down, and what makes it develop into an economy of a different kind. These are seen as questions primarily addressed to the analysis of the system of production, and of the social relations surrounding production.

The central distinction between the two visions, then, lies in the treatment of production and distribution. For the traditional neo-Classical economist, production is a one-way street, running from primary 'factors' to 'final products'. Among the primary factors are land, labour, and, above all, *capital*, each receiving in competition a reward proportional, in some sense (depending on market circumstances) to its 'contribution'.

Not so in the new paradigm. The notion that the three traditional factors are on the same footing is discarded altogether. The great achievement of the Marginalist Revolution, as seen by its nineteenth-century proponents, namely the development of a unified theory applying to all three factors, is utterly dismissed. This can be seen nowhere so clearly as in the new conception of 'capital', in reality a revival of a point well understood before the Marginalists confused everything. 'Capital' has two meanings. On the one hand, it is property in the means of production, enabling owners of equal amounts of claims in these means to receive equal returns (given competitive conditions). In this sense it is a homogenous fund of value, capable of being embodied in different forms.

On the other hand, 'capital' also means produced means of production—that is, specific materials, tools, instruments, machines, plant and equipment, on which, with which, and by means of which, labour works. In this sense it is a set of heterogenous, disparate products. *Capital goods are not the same thing as capital.* 'Capital' is relevant to the analysis of the division of income among the members of society, but a non-specific fund has no bearing on production. 'Capital goods' are relevant to the study of production, but have no bearing on the distribution of income, since profit is earned and interest paid, on the *fund* (value) of capital invested, regardless of its specific form. 'Capital goods', specific instruments, can only be converted into a fund of 'capital' on the basis of a given set of prices for these instruments; but to know these prices we must already know the general rate of profit (in a reasonably competitive capitalist economy).[1] Hence the amount of 'capital' cannot be among the factors which set the level of the rate of profit. But in the orthodox, or neo-Classical theory the 'contribution' of 'capital' to *production* supposedly determines the demand for capital, which together with the supply determines the rate of profit. This must be rejected. No sense can be given to the 'contribution' to production of a *fund* of capital.

This is not to say that *saving and investment,* and their long-run consequences, are irrelevant to determining the rate of profits and relative shares. Quite the reverse; by eliminating the alleged 'contribution of capital' in production as an influence or determinant of distribution, we open the way for a theory of distribution based on the relation between the growth of spending, of capacity, and of the labour force, on the one hand;

1. This is perhaps the central issue in the recent dispute over capital theory between the 'two Cambridges', Cambridge, England, maintaining the view presented here, against Cambridge, Mass., which argued that the essential neo-Classical story could be developed in a 'heterogeneous-capital' model. Unfortunately, to do this, Cambridge, Mass. found that it had to assume conditions in which a simple Labour Theory of Value held! It is now widely agreed that neo-Classical capital theory is defective.

and on the market power available to the various parties, on the other. Unequal rates of inflation of money wages and prices necessarily imply changes in the relative shares going to capital and labour, as Keynes pointed out in the *Treatise on Money*. Inflation is partly a consequence of the ratio of demand to supply, but it also reflects relative market power. And here is where the rules of the game—the rules of property—come in. For property confers advantages, though not absolute ones, in the setting of prices and in bargaining for money wages. Exactly what these advantages are, how they work, by what kinds of forces—are among the questions which a theory of distribution should be able to answer.

In short, the new vision adopts a picture of the relation between production and distribution altogether distinct from that which has ruled the economists' roost since the Marginal Revolution. This, in turn, entails rejecting some widely used techniques of empirical analysis, in favour with both radical and straight economists. In particular, 'production function' studies, e.g. of technical progress, the contribution of education, the effects of discrimination, and of shares during growth, all involve a fatal flaw. For insofar as they proceed by assuming that a factor's *income share* indicates in any way its *productive power* at the margin, they are based on precisely the relationship which the new vision rejects.[2]

It thus seems that conventional theory, although it contains

2. Put this baldly, of course, seems an extraordinary assumption for anyone to make seriously. Given what we know about how our society works, if we read the newspapers (or the Valachi papers), we would never in our ordinary thinking expect to explain a change in the income of a group primarily by reference to a change in its marginal productivity. We would certainly think of demand and supply, and of income elasticity; these would provide the framework, within which bargaining, power plays, and politics would settle the final (or temporary) outcome. Marginal productivity might or might not come into it; just as it might or might not be measurable, but it would hardly be decisive. Is the shift in the income going to the top 5 per cent since 1960 to be seriously taken as reflecting an increase in their marginal productivity? Is the relative rise in professional income 1900–70, evidence of a long-term upward drift in their productivity at the margin? Yet, in spite of common sense and advanced theory, the production function studies, aggregate and individual, continue.

much of value and importance, contains a fatal flaw.[3] The neo-Classical theory of the general equilibrium of production, distribution and exchange holds that the payments in the *factor markets* are *exchanges* in the same sense as payments in the *product markets.* 'Distribution is the species of exchange', wrote Edgeworth, 'by which produce is divided between the parties who have contributed to its production.' Distribution, say the proponents of the new vision, is *not* a species of exchange; and capital *goods*, rather than capital, contribute to production. The ideological teeth begin to bite: an exchange, in equilibrium, means that *value equivalent is traded for value equivalent.* No exploitation there. But if distribution is *not* a form of exchange, then we must ask, Who Whom?

This catalogue of differences, and especially the last point, can be nicely illustrated by comparing two simple diagrams which visually summarize the two paradigms. The first, adapted from Samuelson and echoed in all major textbooks, is shown in Figure 1 and presents what might be called a same-level division of society.

Business and the public (producers and consumers), confront each other more or less as equals in the markets for both products and factors. (The equality is an overall one; there are some large or allied firms, some collective consumers.) Households demand final goods and services and supply the services of productive factors, in both cases in accord with what economists rather pompously call 'their given relative preference schedules', meaning what they like best. Businesses supply final goods and services according to their cost schedules in relation to the prices which consumers are prepared to pay, and demand the services of productive factors, according to their technical

3. This should be distinguished from the commonplace (though correct) criticisms that opportunities for substitution are not legion, that changes in techniques of production and consumption are time-consuming and costly, that information is hard to come by (and perhaps should be treated as itself a product!), that mobility is sluggish, foresight myopic, and expectations an irregular compound of habit and hope. These points will be readily admitted, for they merely indicate how far the actual world falls short of its own ideal type. The point of the present criticism is that the neo-classical ideal market economy is *not* a picture of how the economic system would work under ideal conditions, for it fundamentally misrepresents the relationship of distribution to exchange, whether conditions are 'ideal' or not.

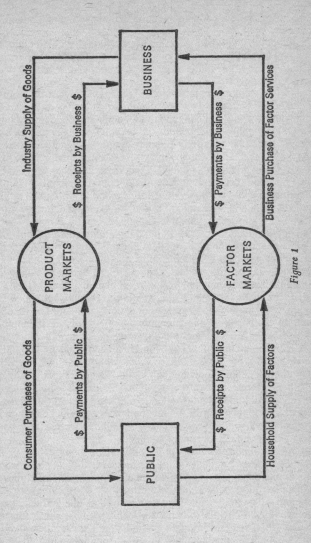

Figure 1

opportunities and needs in relation to consumer demand for products.

So goods and services flow counter-clockwise, while money flows clockwise. In each set of markets, *equivalents are traded for equivalents*, the value of goods and services flowing in one direction being just matched by the stream of revenue in the other. No exploitation is possible in competitive equilibrium. The value of household factor supplies just matches aggregate household demand and the output of goods and services by business just matches the value of productive services which business demands. This may seem to ignore the fact that households save and businesses invest, meaning that some final demand flows not from the Public but from Business. But that is easily allowed for. To finance this demand, Business must borrow Household savings, by supplying bonds which the public demands. Bonds are treated as a kind of good, flowing counter-clockwise, while loans join the stream of money flowing clockwise. These points enable the micro flow picture to be summed up as a macro flow picture, illustrating in the simplest way how macro rests on micro foundations.

Obvious objections to this economic schema can easily be raised. For instance, not all 'households' are on a par, since some *own* all the firms between them, while the rest merely *work for* the firms. Also the distribution of profit and similar income is not an exchange, since the only 'service' which the owner of a business in his capacity as owner, need supply in return for its profits is that of permitting it to be owned by him. (He does bear risks, of course, but so do the employees who will be out of their jobs in the event of failure.) Other objections were mentioned earlier in the charge that orthodox neo-Classicism ignores technological interdependences and institutional relationships, as the circular flow picture makes evident. Nowhere in it can one find social classes or any specific information about patterns of technical interdependence.

All these objections look at first like strong empirical problems which neo-Classicists should meet head on. In fact, however, the customary orthodox defence is oblique and of dubious validity. To the charge that their model rests on unrealistic assumptions, they reply that the *only* test of a model is the success of its predictions. So there is no *a priori* error in making unrealistic assumptions. Moreover 'simplifying assumptions' and 'theoretical constructs' are bound to be, in some sense, 'unrealistic' and there is no predicting without them. Unrealistic assumptions may therefore be warranted and the warrant is philosophical, positivism itself.

To these defences we will return. But first consider quite a different picture of capitalist society. Figure 2 epitomises the new approach, which, if the old is 'neo-Classical' could be dubbed 'Classical-Marxian'. It cannot be claimed that this is the only, or necessarily the best, distillation of an alternative picture from that tradition, but it will certainly serve to illustrate the contrasts.

To keep the diagram comparable, we retain the circle for the final goods market and the box standing for industry, though we shall interpret both quite differently. 'Households' and the 'factor market' disappear altogether. Instead we have a pyramid, representing the social hierarchy, divided into two parts: a small upper class of owners and a large lower class of workers. Owners own industry and receive profits; workers work for industry and receive wages. Workers consume, but do not (in this simplified model) save; owners both consume and (save in order to) invest.

Now consider the flows of goods and services and money payments. Labour is the only 'factor input'; other inputs are produced by industry itself, which is assumed to have access to land, mines, etc. (We are lumping landlords and capitalists together.) Hence we might expect to be able to value the total product in terms of labour, and though the mathematics is complicated, this can indeed be done, though not in all cases. The arrows running back and forth between factories represent inter-industry transactions, the exchanges between industries necessary to replace used-up means of production. The Net Social Product is sold for Total Receipts, and consists of all goods over and above those needed for replacement. These can be divided (for convenience) into Necessities, Luxuries and New Capital Goods.[4] Necessities go for Worker Consumption, Luxuries for Capitalist Consumption, and New Capital Goods are installed in the factories in return for Investment payments.

4. The traditional interest in classifying goods along lines such as these, largely abandoned in the face of positivist criticism—'these are just value judgements'—has been revived in the light of Sraffa's important and far-reaching distinction between basics, goods which enter directly or indirectly into the means of production of all goods, and non-basics.

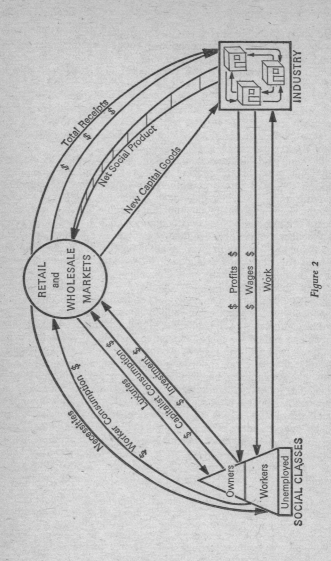

Figure 2

Hence, the national accounts work out:

> Total Receipts = Net Social Product = Wages + Profits = Wage Consumption + Capitalist Consumption + Investment Demand = Necessities + Luxuries + New Capital Goods.

From the point of view of Political Economy, however, the most important fact is that while wages are paid for work, and one can (and in some circumstances should) think of the wage bill, equal here to Worker Consumption, as reproducing the power to work, *profits are not paid for anything at all*. The flow of profit income is not an exchange in any sense, metaphorical or otherwise. The Samuelson diagram is fundamentally misleading; there is no 'flow' from 'household supply' to the factor market for capital. The *only* flow is the flow of profit income in the other direction. And this, of course, leads straight to that hoary but substantial claim that the payment of wages is not an exchange, either, or at any rate, not a fair one. For Wages plus Profits add up to the Net Social Product, yet Profits are not paid for anything, while wages are paid for work. Hence the work of labour (using the tools, equipment, etc., replacement and depreciation of which is already counted in) has produced the entire product. Is labour not therefore exploited? Does it not deserve the whole product?

The latter question opens Pandora's Box; as for the former, it all depends on what you mean.... What does certainly follow, however, is that distribution is *not* an exchange, profits are not paid *for* anything, and serve no essential economic function. This may not be exploitation but it shows clearly that no purely economic justification can be found for profits, interest, dividends, and the like.[5] Moreover, since the payment of profit is no exchange, there can be no equilibrium, in the usual sense.

5. Surely under both capitalism and market socialism profits serve the essential function of indicating where investment can most advantageously be directed. The *rate* of profit, similarly, serves to allocate productive resources between producing for current consumption and expansion for the future. There are two things wrong with this very common claim. First, (as sophisticated neo-Classical economists will quickly admit) the function of profits and the rate of profit as indicators requires merely that they be *calculated*; hence, in no wise justifies *paying* profits.

Calculated profit indicators are compatible with many different in-

A century-old school of thought, holding that our troubles come from the *excessive* profits sucked in by giant monopolies, and idolizing small competitive enterprise earning 'normal profits', is thereby undercut. There is no merit in 'normal profit', indeed there is no such thing. The issue for Political Economy is the Profit System itself, not its alleged abuse.

Figure 2 helps us to understand how the division of income comes about. Remember that the orthodox doctrine held that the distribution of income was determined in the factor market, by the marginal 'contribution' of factors in conjunction with their relative scarcity. Figure 2 makes it clear that income distribution interacts with all aspects of the economy, not just with the 'factor market'. This point can be made quite simply, though its consequences are far-reaching. Labour's share is given by the real wage times the amount of work. But the *real* wage is the *money* wage divided by an index of consumer goods prices. The money wage is set in the labour market, but prices are set in the final goods market. Labour's share, then, depends on *both* markets. Moreover, as the diagram shows, consumer demand depends on labour's share; the system is strongly interdependent in ways not found in orthodox teaching.[6]

This puts inflation in a new and clearer light. The standard approach is to distinguish 'demand-pull' inflation (originating in the final goods market) from 'cost-push' inflation (originat-

---

centive schemes (e.g. salary bonuses to managers of state-owned enterprises, moral incentives, etc.). Second, profit-based indicators are only one set among several. In a stationary economy, for example, the correct indicators to achieve maximum output would be based not on profits but on *labour values*! (Cf. Goodwin, Ch. 4.) In general, profit indicators alone are likely to be misleading; the rate and pattern of growth must also be considered in trying to identify the best investment plans. Even so, from the strict economic point of view, forgetting social complications, the best choices for maximizing consumption may differ from the best choices for maximizing growth. Once we allow for quality, the effect on the environment, etc., the variety of possible indicators becomes considerable.

6. This diagram also illustrates a proposition first discovered in the 1930s by the great Polish Marxist economist, Michel Kalechi, who independently and at the same time set forth the main propositions of the *General Theory*. Investment, I, is the change in the capital stock, written ΔK, where 'Δ' means 'change in', and comes entirely from savings out of profits. Let sp stand for the fraction of profits saved. So $\Delta K = sp\, P$, where P is profits. Divide both

ing in the factor market). Very few actual cases seem to fit either category. On the new approach this should come as no surprise, for the question has been wrongly posed. This issue is not where inflation originates, but how fast it proceeds in different markets. In Figure 1 it is natural to suppose that a price increase in the product market will be transmitted directly to the factor market and vice versa. Unless costs and prices rise together the circular flow cannot continue unimpeded. In Figure 2 it is evident that this is not so—costs and prices rising in the same proportion will be the special, limiting case. In all other cases the effect will be to raise or lower Profits. When wages rise faster than prices, there will be Profit Deflation; when prices rise faster than wages, Profit Inflation, to use the terminology suggested by Keynes in the *Treatise on Money*, his earlier major and now-neglected work. In all cases except the limiting one, then, inflation will affect income distribution and so aggregate demand and employment.[7]

What determines the relative rate of price and wage increases? The first answer, of course, must be 'supply and demand', and this is surely right. For example, large numbers of unemployed will tend to act as a drag on money wages. But the same balance of supply and demand may have a very different total *impact* on price in different circumstances, depending on market power, on the financial position of com-

---

sides by K, the capital stock. We then have $\frac{\Delta K}{K} = sp\frac{P}{K}$. But $\frac{\Delta K}{K} = g$, the

rate of growth, and $\frac{P}{K} = r$, the rate of profits.

Hence $g = sp\,r$, a simple formula connecting the growth rate and the profit

rate. Remembering that $\Delta K = I$, we also have $\frac{I}{sp} = P = rK$.

So, for a given technology *profits are higher and the growth rate lower the greater is the average propensity of the capitalist class to consume out of profits.* The extreme simplicity and great generality of this proposition, even now not widely known in the profession, are typical of the results obtained by the new approach.

7. An exactly parallel point should be made about the relative prosperity of different sectors during inflation. The relative rates of price and wage inflation will determine the relative changes in profits, which (on the assumption that most investment is financed by retained earnings) will set the relative growth rates. Thus inflation, except in the limiting case, will over the course of time bring about changes in the composition of the aggregate economy.

panies and unions, on the ability to make use of the law, or state agencies, to manipulate the press and the media, and so on. These considerations are preeminently ones of Political Economy, but they play an essential role in theory, for they determine the relative responsiveness of markets, and hence the relative speed of wage and price inflation.

We have now discussed the two paradigms. The neo-Classical one is far better known but we feel is significantly misleading. The new paradigm, by contrast, is clearly more realistic, and more capable of handling questions such as property and social class.

These claims are widely resisted, for the reasons mentioned. Conventional economists often contend that a paradigm cannot by 'misleading' in its representation of institutions *if it leads to models that predict well*. 'Realism' is not important; abstraction must take place, and a model can abstract from anything, so long as it performs well.

Such a defence is a methodological claim based on a, today, rather questionable philosophy of science. One response might be that neo-Classical models have not done very well on their chosen ground. Prediction has not been the greatest success of modern economics. But a more fundamental response would be to challenge the methodology itself. There is an intuitive appeal to the idea that a model of social institutions must be a good representation of things as they are at a given moment regardless of how they work out over time. It may be too much to demand of economics that it predicts what will happen. In modern industrial societies the economic system is too closely interlocked with other aspects of society to be isolated enough for effective tests. But to add *ceteri paribus* clauses simply tends to reduce predictions to vacuity. Instead, we must examine the definitions and assumptions of our models for their realism, and for the extent to which they incorporate the essentials. If they are realistic, the working of the model should mirror that of the economic system in relatively simple and abstract form. It should be clear from this that our case can be defended from the methodological objections of the Positivists.

The new approach is a coherent picture of the economy capable of providing technical analysis of a sophisticated nature.[8] But it has not been developed for its own sake, or

8. The picture can be very much improved as a representation of the modern economy by channelling Profits, not directly to

simply because it presents a better, more accurate picture of capitalism. It should be more fruitful, but the fruit should redden as it ripens. The new picture is intended precisely as *Political* Economics, as a guide to the criticism of the capitalist socio-economic system, and the objection to orthodox thinking was that in treating the distribution of income as a form of exchange it misrepresented the way the system works.

Orthodox economics tries to show that markets allocate scarce resources according to relative efficiency; political economics tries to show that markets distribute income according to relative power. It is good to know about efficiency, but in our world, it tends to be subservient to power.[9] By failing to appreciate this, and consequently failing also to accord the distribution of income between labour and capital a properly central role, orthodox economics has become cut off from the central economic issues of our time, drifting further into ever more abstract and mathematically sophisticated reformulations of essentially the same propositions. The heart of the matter is the concept of 'capital', and its relation to social class and economic power. When this is put right, as in the new paradigm, economic theory can once again speak to the critical issues of the day.

---

owners but to 'Wall Street', where Banks, Boards of Directors and Financial Institutions decide how much to retain, how much to invest, and how much to pay out in dividends. Then Capitalist Consumption will come out of Distributed Profits and Realized Capital Gains, and Savings will flow back to Wall Street in the form of bond and share purchases. This properly separates ownership and control, and shows the separation of financial and production decisions, the former dominating the latter. The model can also be modified to take account of worker savings, which, however, are empirically inconsequential.

9. Power, of course, is usually enhanced by efficiency, but the two are nevertheless quite distinct. Economic power ultimately rests on the ability to inflict a loss—the stick. A subsidiary form is the ability to bribe—the carrot. If economists paid as much attention to bribery and extortion as they do to marginal utility, we should be able to develop rough quantitative indices, by means of which one could sensibly discuss (and plan strategy to alter) the distribution of economic power in society.

6

History: the Poverty of Empiricism

GARETH STEDMAN JONES

History is the oldest branch of social studies and in Britain one of the most developed. In this essay Gareth Stedman Jones examines the main schools of history writing and the impact on them of the emergence of new types of social explanation. He argues that historians have been particularly prone to the empiricist delusion that the data they use are the sole basis of the generalizations they deduce. The task of producing the concepts adequate to historical explanation is abandoned in favour of the deceptive obviousness of chronological succession.

Gareth Stedman Jones is a Research Fellow of Nuffield College, Oxford. He is an editor of New Left Review *and author of* Outcast London *(OUP, 1971) a study of nineteenth-century London.*

A recent survey in the *Times Literary Supplement* suggested that the writing of history in England was on the verge of a renaissance. This is only another way of saying that the progress of British historiography in the last 100 years provides a spectacular case of arrested intellectual development, and conceptual poverty. British historians have largely remained impervious to the solutions put forward by Marxism, psycho-analysis, and classical sociology. Or else they have only glimpsed them through the blurred light of caricature and vulgarization. Thus the ingrained assumptions of British historical method have never been thoroughly shaken. The force of outside pressure has resulted in a few tactical concessions—the economic 'factor' has been conceded as important, real motives, it is admitted, are not always the same as those professed, and lately there have been hints of an arranged marriage between history and sociology. But the structure has remained intact. The result is as weird as if a Newtonian physicist were to come across Einstein, admit that relativity was probably a factor of some importance, and then attempt to carry on as before, under the impression that the occasional acknowledgement would absolve him from the necessity of further thought about it.

Positivism: facts and morals

The peculiar myopia of English historians goes back at least to the 1860s and 1870s, when history was first established as a subject worthy of academic study in English universities. At this time the main defining characteristic of academic history was a devout liberalism buttressed by a positivist methodology. The task of the historian in Ranke's much quoted dictum, was 'simply to show how it really was'—in other words to ascertain the facts. Historical facts were analogous to the facts of natural science: discrete, atomic and supremely indifferent to the position of the observer. What the natural scientist could reveal by the use of test-tube, microscope and experimental method, the historian could uncover through the use of archaeology, philology and painstaking textual criticism. Historians of the generation of Acton, Stubbs, Maitland, Gardiner and Bury undertook prodigious feats of factual production in the happy belief that soon all 'facts' would be uncovered and universal history would be completed.

In the original positivist programme, the collection of facts was to be followed by the framing of general laws comparable to those of Newtonian physics or, more relevantly, Darwinian biology. But the pronouncements of Comte were not greeted with enthusiasm by English historians, and Comte's main English disciple, Buckle, was execrated by Acton 'for submitting men and human actions to the crucible of induction'. Since, within the positivist framework, philosophy (and in particular the philosophy of history) was assumed to have been overthrown by natural science, therefore even 'Positivism' itself, in as much as it was a philosophy, could also be safely disregarded by British historians.

In place of dangerously speculative and scientifically unfounded general laws, the British historians substituted magisterial moral judgments. History, Thomas Arnold had stated in 1841, was a moral lesson. Over fifty years later, it was still possible for Acton to assert confidently that 'the inflexible integrity of the moral code is to me the secret of the authority, the dignity and the utility of history'. Yet in some unresolved way history was also a science. History was a science because it was composed of 'facts'. 'Facts' were events, and events resulted from the action of individuals producing them through the framework of institutions. All these were verifiable empirical realities, and once they had been established and confirmed, it was the task and duty of the historian to judge them. At its most elevated level therefore, history could attain the status of a scientific sermon.

It was probably for this reason that so much history was focused upon the Constitution and upon 'great men'. For non-sensible realities like class, mode of production or politically and culturally determined patterns of behaviour were not empirically verifiable. They could not simply be uncovered by the study of documents, and they did not afford the same straightforward criterion of moral pronouncement. Thus history was more conveniently interpreted as the interaction between great men and the institutions they created, modified, or resisted. As Charles Kingsley succinctly put it in his inaugural lecture as professor of history at Cambridge in 1861 : 'the new science of little men can be no science at all; because the average man is not the normal man, and never yet has been; because the great man is rather the normal man, as approaching more nearly than his fellows to the true "norma" and standard of a complete human character ... to turn to the mob for your theory of humanity is (I think) about as wise as to ignore the Apollo and the Theseus, and to determine the proportions of the human figure from a crowd of dwarfs and cripples'. As late as 1925, H. W. C. Davis, Regius professor at Oxford, attacked 'those self-styled social historians' who 'tell us that what we most need to know about any civilization in the past is what its poorer and more illiterate members thought and did ... our common humanity is best studied in the most eminent examples that it has produced of every type of human excellence'.

Liberty versus democracy

The positivistic adherence to the visible and immediately verifiable 'facts' of the past was reinforced by an almost unquestioned acceptance of the basic tenets of nineteenth-century English liberalism. Individuals were discrete, autonomous, and thus morally accountable for their actions. Superimposed upon this, were the optimistic assumptions implicit in the idea of progress. The central theme of history was seen to be the development of civil and religious liberty. This was fortunate, for England seemed to have been especially marked out by the hand of God for the execution of this divine mission. England's gift to the world had been the English Constitution. Stubbs and Freeman, their vision unblurred by mountainous erudition, traced its origins back to 'the dim recesses of German forests'. Gardiner and Macaulay carried its development through the 'puritan revolution' up to the 'glorious revolution' of 1688. Seeley argued its connection with the greatness of the British Empire and ordained its transmission throughout the globe. Of course Liberalism had no intrinsic relation to democracy—indeed it was predominantly hostile to it. This seriously disqualified the French Revolution which, in Lord Acton's words, had sacrificed liberty to equality, and in which the absolutism of the king had been replaced by the absolutism of the assembly. Thus the torch of Liberty remained firmly in the grasp of the Anglo-Saxons.

This Podsnapian ensemble was well suited to the social function of the teaching of history in late Victorian England. History, according to Freeman, was 'past politics', because, as Seeley put it, history was 'the school of statesmanship'. Statistically he was probably correct. By the first quarter of the century, it has been estimated that one third of the Oxford undergraduate population was reading history. Against a background of agricultural depression and the expansion of socially undemeaning posts in the imperialist administration, it is not surprising that three generations of undergraduates could accept without question Stubb's definition of the aim of history as 'the training of the judgment to be exercised in the moral, social and political work of life'. History was a 'humane' study, and 'humane' retained all its Renaissance and aristocratic connotations. Despite a growing professionalism expressed in the leaden scholarship of the *English Historical Review*, the historian was at pains not to alienate his socially privileged lay clientele. Even in 1928, Sir Maurice Powicke in his inaugural lecture as Regius professor at Oxford, was anxious not to draw any invidious distinctions between gentlemen and players: 'we want more country gentry and clergy,' he wrote, 'more ecclesiastical dignitaries, more school masters and mistresses, more lawyers, more public servants, more persons of leisure to be engaged in historical work'.

As a discipline, history occupied a prominent place in the culture of British imperialism. By the end of the nineteenth century it had almost superseded classics as a symbol of gentility. Combined with a smattering of the *idées reçues* of political economy, and perhaps with some of the missionary ardour of T. H. Green's philosophy of 'citizenship', history provided a more or less coherent rationale of British · capitalism and a triumphant justification of its imperial trophies in the years before 1914.

Intellectual revolution in Europe

The character of late nineteenth-century British historiography is fairly familiar to anyone who has browsed through a professorial inaugural lecture written in the last thirty years. There is nothing particularly surprising or exceptional about it. In the second half of the nineteenth century history as a positivistic accumulation of facts was cultivated as assiduously in France, Germany, or Italy as it was in England. Indeed in Germany under the domination of Ranke, Mommsen, and the heavyweight textual erudition of the Monumenta Germaniae Historica the process was carried much further. On the level of nationalist apologetic Froude and Seeley met their match in Sybel, Droysen, and Treitschke. In France, the work of Fustel de Coulanges, Lavisse, Aulard, Langlois and Seignebos proceeded upon the same methodological presuppositions that inspired Stubbs, Maitland, Acton, and Bury in England. French history could be justly defined in the words of its later critics as *histoire évènementielle* (narrative history).

But the similarity was not to last. Between the 1890s and the 1920s Europe experienced an intellectual revolution in the human sciences. The significance of the work of Freud, Weber, Durkheim, Pareto, Croce, Simmel, Dilthey, and Sorel for the study of history hardly needs comment. At the very least, it marked a decisive rejection of the more simplistic assumptions of mid-nineteenth-century positivist methodology, and raised history once more from the lowly idiographic status to which historians themselves had consigned it.

Significantly, England not only did not participate in this movement, it in fact remained virtually unaffected by it. The reasons for this well-insulated intellectual autarky are complex and as yet hardly investigated. To suggest that it may be attributed to the tenacity of the liberal-individualist tradition is really only to reformulate the question. A recent writer has claimed that five linked polarities dominated the thought of the founder of modern European sociology—community-society, authority-power, status-class, sacred-secular, alienation-progress. These were not novel themes. To some extent they reflected the thought of every country which had felt the impact of industrial capitalism and the French Revolution. They were, of course, in no sense foreign to English thought. In the guise of a cultural critique this dialectical anti-liberalism inspired the work of Burke, Coleridge, Carlyle, Newman, Ruskin, and Morris – to mention only the most prominent. The depth and strength of this tradition in English culture has been clearly portrayed in Raymond Williams's *Culture and Society*.

The impact of Marxism

Yet Williams depicts the period 1880-1920 as an 'interregnum' in this tradition. Why was it that a period of such great intellectual ferment in Europe should have coincided with three decades of the debility of anti-liberal English thought (whether conservative or socialist)? Undoubtedly the main reason lies in the momentous impact of Marxism upon the generation of European intellectuals who came to maturity in the 1880s and early 1890s. In France, the Ecole Normale, the seminary of the French intelligentsia, became a stronghold of socialism under the influence of Jaurès and Lucien Herr from the early 1880s. In Italy an entire generation of the intelligentsia fell under the sway of Marxism from the mid-1880s to 1900. In Germany an organized socialist intelligentsia dated back to the 1860s, and few thinkers were able to ignore it. For intellectuals, socialism generally meant historical materialism – its scientific exposition. The 1880s was the first decade in which Marx's works were widely read outside Germany, and the result was soon felt. Marxism was an overwhelming experience for a generation dissatisfied with the complacent philistinism of positivism. (Its effect might be compared to that of the later impact of Freud's thought upon a generation of intellectuals in Europe and America shaken by the Russian Revolution and the First World War.) Its testimony can be found in an army of works by

Pareto, Durkheim, Croce, Sorel, Michels, Weber, Sombart, Troeltsch, and Schumpeter, all examining, developing, or attacking Marxism as a system, and nearly all published in the years between 1895 and 1910. It might further be suggested that (with the possible exception of Durkheim) the most fruitful work of each of these writers was developed in reaction to Marxism and can be interpreted as a tortured counterpoint to Marxist propositions.

In England on the other hand, as Eric Hobsbawm has shown, Marx's work evoked little response. With the notable exception of Morris, Marxism was primarily interpreted as a useful weapon against Cobdenite *laissez-faire* ideology. Marx, inasmuch as he was read, was acknowledged as a great economic historian, and it was in this role that he influenced the work of liberals like Unwin and Hobson. What was either discounted or not perceived in Marxism, was the completeness of its rejection of all variants of liberal thought. Just as the Hegelianism of T. H. Green, through a peculiarly English osmosis, only resulted in producing alternative metaphysical foundations for liberal self-help ideology, so Marx's *Capital* was interpreted either as a useful compendium of arguments against the Manchester school, or else as a reinforcement of the aesthetic anti-capitalism of Ruskin and Morris. This tendency either to annex Marx to a previously formulated *parti pris*, or to treat him with benevolent contempt (Shaw and the Fabians) was due to two main reasons : first, the absence of any significant dissemination of socialist ideas (apart from the anodyne propositions of J. S. Mill) in the period from 1850 to 1880; second, the non-existence of an independent working-class party of any kind.

Strictly on utilitarian grounds, it had been argued up to the 1870s that the enfranchisement of the working class would produce a majority working-class party devoted to the redistribution of property, and 'the tyranny of the majority' over minority *élites*—and thus to the annihilation of culture. Yet contrary to the prophescies of Macaulay, Mill, Lowe, and Bagehot, the English working class hardly even began to think of organizing an independent party until at least two decades after the Second Reform Bill. The most well organized and articulate section of the working class, the skilled trade union movement, remained firmly under the hegemony of Gladstonian liberalism. The prospect of the seizure of power by a revolutionary working class seemed remote even after the appearance of widespread unemployment and the rise of New Unionism in the 1880s.

By European standards it was indeed remote. European intellectuals lacked the comforting spectacle of a working class dividing its loyalty between Mr Gladstone and Mr Disraeli. Police repression, anti-socialist legislation, the Commune, Boulanger, rightist groupings in church, army and administration, weak or discredited liberal parties, anarchist conspiracies, seigneurial domination in the countryside, and a huge peasantry—all these distinguished Europe from England. The strain upon positivistic liberalism was correspondingly greater. Classical utilitarian or rationalist explanations of social order were insufficient. The 'scientific' positivist assumptions were gradually submerged beneath the different but unanswered challenges of Marxism, irrationalism and romantic conservatism. It was from this philosophic maelstrom that modern sociology emerged.

INTELLECTUALS AND REFORM IN BRITAIN

In England, however, at least in the eyes of intellectuals, the working class constituted not so much a potential revolutionary threat as a 'social problem'; and the number of intellectuals who turned to, or passed through, socialism was comparatively few. Broadly there were three major approaches to the 'problem'. The first was a stately reaffirmation of the values of liberal individualism, stressing the role of philanthropy and education within a modified utilitarian framework. Its adherents included Marshall, Morley, Booth, A. J. Toynbee, and C. S. Loch. A second position, that of the Fabians and the Social Imperialists, attacked *laissez-faire* capitalism because of its inefficiency and waste. Its solution was greater state interference, comprehensive and 'disinterested' administration and more intensive colonial exploitation. From the confrontation of these groups there emerged a third solution. This accepted the necessity of some form of welfare state but moulded it in a liberal image (compulsory self-help); it was generally critical of imperialism, but not of capitalism as a whole. This 'new liberalism' ranged from Beveridge on the right, through Masterman and Hobhouse in the centre, to Hobson on the left.

Despite wide political and cultural differences, these heterogeneous groupings of intellectuals shared one common trait: the linking of social theory to detailed and concrete proposals for practical social reform. Unlike Germany and Italy, and to some extent France, there was no significant alienation of intellectuals from parliamentarist politics. This lack of any profound sense of estrangement from the bourgeois political arena powerfully sustained the liberal-individualist tradition at a moment when analogous legacies from enlightenment rationalism and positivism were being drastically challenged in Europe.

Uneven development

This unevenness of intellectual development is a crucial clue to the evolution of British historiography. In France Lucien Febvre and Marc Bloch were enthusiastic readers of *L'Année Sociologique*, and allied the high scholarly standards of Fustel de Coulanges with the insights of Marx, Weber, and especially Durkheim. Febvre himself noted in later years that Durkheim and Vidal de la Blache, the geographer, 'left an incomparably deeper mark upon historical studies at the beginning of the twentieth century than any specialists'. Elie Halévy, whose preoccupations in some senses were parallel to those of Weber, produced brilliant and so far unsurpassed interpretations both of utilitarianism and nineteenth-century England. Mathiez, and more particularly Lefebvre and Labrousse, heavily influenced by Marxism, transformed the study of the French Revolution through pioneer studies of the revolutionary crowd, food crises, and the pre-industrial harvest cycle. In Germany and Italy the onset of Nazism and Fascism arrested the transformation of history and its methodology. Nevertheless, the work of Meinecke, Croce, the Weberian school, and the brilliant insights of Gramsci bore ample testimony to the intellectual revolution that had preceded it.

In England, however, historians were unprepared for the shock of the First World War, and when the illusions of liberal England were suddenly shattered they were left in an intellectual void. The firm belief in progress with its positivist trappings was quickly dropped. J. B. Bury, professor of history at Cambridge, who had stated in 1903 that 'history is simply a science, no less and no more', repudiated this idea in 1916 in an essay significantly entitled, 'Cleopatra's nose'—a reduction of history to 'a chapter of accidents'. H. A. L. Fisher, an arch-liberal ideologue, concluded that history had no meaning after all. Herbert Butterfield was able to establish an awesome reputation on the basis of an insubstantial little pamphlet which warned the unwary against interpreting the past in the light of the present. At a more grandiose level, Toynbee, following Spengler, after applying the rather simplist concept of 'challenge and response' to twenty-one civilizations, confirmed the decline of the West, and advocated the establishment of some kind of syncretist religion to arrest the decay. Morale was so low that Toynbee's work was seriously discussed by historians, and if they rejected his conclusions it was more through an ingrained empiricist distrust of all theory, than any finer sense of discrimination.

In effect, despite the shipwreck of nineteenth-century positivist assumptions, the large majority of British historians made little attempt to reformulate their historical presuppositions. A polite veil of silence was drawn over the suggestion of a final and definitive factual history. But the method stuck. In the work of such representative inter-war historians as Powicke, Galbraith, Pickthorn, Neale, C. V. Wedgwood, G. N. Clarke, Basil Williams, Tamperley, and Trevelyan, there is more than enough to justify Hexter's comment, 'we do not terribly mind collecting historical data, but we detest thinking very hard about them'. There was still the assumption that the facts would somehow speak for themselves, and while a modest revaluation of Victorian historical interpretations was considered necessary and proper, the questions asked of the material did not radically differ. It is not surprising, for instance, that the existence of a flourishing school of English social anthropology aroused no interest among medieval historians, or that administrative historians should remain not merely uncurious but usually quite unaware of parallel sociological investigations into rationalization and bureaucracy.

Tawney and Namier

Against this depressing background it is understandable that Tawney and Namier could seriously be regarded as the 'Marx and Freud of English history'. What really distinguished them was not in fact breath-taking theoretical insights, or even a systematic conceptual system. It was rather that they were the first to be seriously influenced by the revolution in the human sciences that had taken place in Europe. Both were foreign to the dominant liberal academic tradition. Tawney's theoretical novelty stemmed from his application of Weber's religious sociology to English history. But the power of *Religion and the Rise of Capitalism* derived from a firmly held Christian social- ism which provided the basis for a dramatic reassertion of the romantic anti-capitalist tradition of Carlyle, Ruskin and Morris. Namier, on the other hand, as Carr has noted, came out of a purely European reactionary anti-liberal transition, which had no parallel in England. Significantly, Namier first came to Eng- land in the wake of Vilfredo Pareto whom he had heard lecture in Lausanne. Indeed it might be argued that Namier's major works owe more to Pareto's theory of *élites* than to Freudian psycho-analysis.

The influence of Tawney and Namier was widely acknow- ledged, and devoted bands of disciples soon enlisted behind their banners. But in both cases partisanship was of a peculiarly restricted kind. The major practical influence of Tawney was the foundation of the *Economic History Review*. Tawney did not tempt his followers to rush back to Weber; if anything he acted as the excuse for not reading Weber. Once again, what might have provided an avenue to a more broadly based and sociologically informed history, became a specialized discipline. It was not until nearly forty years later that Christopher Hill, in his study of *Society and Puritanism*, took up some of the broader issues that Tawney had raised. The case of Namier was similar. His works did not arouse any real concern with a systematic theory of *élites*, or even any serious integration of Freudian psycho-analysis into the study of history. For British historians Namierism generally meant a novel empirical method and an anti-intellectualist approach to politics—more akin to a Nietzschean revelation of the vulgar motive behind the elevated sentiment than to any developed Freudian theory. Instead of provoking study of the political sociology that had inspired Namier's work, his formulations were treated as a ready-made solution, a *Deus ex machina* that could be imposed upon any period that took the historian's fancy.

The demolition of Victorian historical assumptions left his- tory without a centre. Political and constitutional history had provided the main vertebra upon which the ambition of a uni- versal history had depended. After the First World War, what had been a solid marble block became a honeycomb. To politi- cal history was added economic history, administrative history, ecclesiastical history, army history, navy history, local history, entrepreneurial history, or agricultural history. No attempt was made to fuse this aggregate of specialist routines into a meaningful historical totality. That was left to the academic demi-monde of Toynbee and H. G. Wells. In its place there was a sort of gentleman's agreement that every branch of history was equal in the sight of God. Take-over bids were frowned upon and demarcation disputes were rare. The gallant attempt of Sir Karl Popper to save England from the pernicious vices of 'holistic thinking' was really so much wasted effort. English historians, with the clear conscience of a virtuous spinster, smugly cheered him on in his violent rejection of the blandishments of a chimerical seducer.

Labour history

The rise of soi-disant Marxism in the 1930s might appear to contradict this argument. But, in fact, its immediate impact upon the writing of history in England was rather slight. The adolescent fervour of the public school *enragé*, carried into history, resulted in a violent oscillation between stentorian economic determinism and the most abject humanitarianism. Its achievements were too trivial to challenge the pretensions of professional historians. In the absence of a serious Marxist philosophy in England, historians of the Left and even professed Marxists turned mainly to Tawney, Laski, Cole, and the pages of the *Economic History Review*. Instead of demolishing the fragmentation of historical study, they reinforced it. Political commitment produced 'labour history' and the diligent investigation of rent rolls. There was no revolution in theory. Cole and his followers applied much the same approach to the history of trade unions and labour movements that their predecessors had applied to the history of the constitution. At its worst it degenerated into antiquarianism, and at its most pernicious, in works like Francis Williams's *Magnificent Journey*, and B. C. Roberts's *History of the TUC*, it provided a sort of plebeian variant of the Whig theory of history.

The Cold War

The onset of the Cold War strengthened the forces of parochialism and fragmentation. A militant group of right-wing ideologues led by Professor Von Hayek and T. S. Ashton acted as a vigilante circle to expunge socialist incursions into historical interpretation. Its heroic mission was set by 'an international group of economists, historians and social philosophers who have for some years been meeting regularly to discuss the problems of the preservation of a free society against the totalitarian threat'. Its chosen field was the Industrial Revolution. Dismissing the accounts of contemporaries as loaded, discrediting the historical work of liberals like A. J. Toynbee and the Hammonds, and denying the traumatic social shock engendered by such a massive and rapid historical change upon any society, these Cold War crusaders rapidly narrowed the range of historical debate to a question that Mr Gradgrind would have understood. Did the real wages of the working class increase between 1790 and 1850? If they did, then the case for capitalism would have been proved. Other danger spots in history—the Civil War, the French and Russian Revolutions—were either reduced to manageable liberal proportions, or else deflated with a similar vulgar *panache*.

Counter-revolution was not only buttressed at the level of concrete historical research. At the level of historical theory, the spectre of 'historicism', never a very urgent threat in England, was flogged remorselssly by Popper, H. B. Acton, Berlin, and Talmon. Imprisoned within the narrow parameters of Cold War liberalism, the historian's conception of his subject had become trapped in a maze of archaic precepts. The extent of this ossification of constructive historical thinking can be shown in the contrast between two statements on the determination of human behaviour:

'History can only be reduced to a science by excluding individualism and personality.' If men are to be submitted to generalization, 'the first thing we must divest them of is personality, with all its distinctive characteristics, the chief of which is usually said to be the freedom of the will'.

'There is no historical thought properly speaking, save where facts are distinct not merely from fiction, but from theory and interpretation. . . . The discovery of new, terrifying impersonal forces may render life infinitely more dangerous, yet if they serve no other purpose, they do at any rate divest men of responsibility—from all those moral burdens which men in less enlightened days used to carry with such labour and anguish.'

The first statement was written by Lord Acton in 1858, the second by Sir Isaiah Berlin in 1954. The weary process of fact accumulation, plus or minus value judgment, remained unchanged in essentials. This bleak intellectual landscape afflicted Marxists as much as their opponents. Even to press home the most minimal theoretical point entailed a mountain of footnotes. Progressive historians wasted too much time attempting to convert heuristic concepts into the type of empirical statement that would be permissible within a liberal positivist framework.

Advances and retreats

The unfreezing of historical debate began some time after 1956. The important implications of Tawney's work, unheeded for over twenty years, were dramatically and ambitiously developed (in divergent directions) by Christopher Hill, Trevor-Roper, and Lawrence Stone. In work on the nineteenth century, two generations of left wing historians, constrained by academic hostility into the sometimes fruitful but often deadly byways of 'labour history', at last escaped the narrow confines of the subject. The work of Eric Hobsbawm and Edward Thompson has now established a serious history based upon Marxism and informed by psychology and sociology. Social history had seriously been defined by G. M. Trevelyan as history 'with the politics left out', and only slightly less absurdly by A. L. Rowse, as 'how society consumes what it produces'. Now a genuine social history was finally possible, over thirty years after it had been introduced in France. After years of exclusion from respectable academic and professional circles, the few historians who had produced really creative and important historical work in the 1940s and 1950s, Isaac Deutscher, E. H. Carr, and Richard Cobb, were begrudgingly acknowledged—partly through the necessity to diminish the enormous discrepancy between their home and foreign reputations.

Perhaps because of the leftish reputation of the majority of these historians, the more discerning of their orthodox rivals realized that in the fight against Marxism or its derivatives, the aid of bourgeois sociology would be more effective than the intellectual armoury of Bishop Stubbs. But the reaction of the majority of established historians was a feeling of confusion and terror at the prospect of having to master auxiliary disciplines. In addition, the abysmal standard of British Sociology made the task appear even more daunting. A brief spate of well-intentioned conferences produced a perfunctory academic *détente*. But the gains were to be counted not in novel orientations but in covering footnotes. Once again the inherited dogmas of the liberal individualist tradition were to act as an effective buffer against the invasion of sociology. G. R. Elton, a prominent Tudor historian, dismissed sociology because 'it was illegitimate to impose general theory on the facts; the historian was bound by his evidence'. His fierce denunciation of all new forms of knowledge was too candid to attract a large following. But what he was prepared to maintain openly and stridently, many were prepared to accept *sotto voce*.

Despite the optimism of the *Times Literary Supplement* there is no necessary reason why the 'new ways in history' should produce a permanent transformation of historical study. In the years since 1956, retrogressive paths in history have been quite as prominent as liberating influences. The recent promotion of administrative history, from Elton's *Tudor Revolution in Government* to MacDonagh's invention of the nineteenth century revolutionary bureaucrat, has laid the foundations of a growing academic industry distinguished mainly by conceptual archaism and reactionary apologetics. In economic history the recent discovery of 'quantification' and the computer, and the parallel concentration upon economic growth as the centre of all meaningful enquiry, threatens to narrow the scope of the subject still further. Its effect could be as deadening as that of the nineteenth-century discoveries of palaeography and textual criticism upon the study of political and constitutional history. Even some of 'the new ways of history' seem already to have been warped by the English historical climate. The influence of the *Annales* has finally been transmitted to England through the medium of the Cambridge school of historical demography—in the form of clumsy parody. The importation consists of a set of demographic techniques, and a magniloquent vocabulary (one of the less attractive features of French scholarship). But what in France, with the work of Goubert and Le Roi Ladurie, now forms one cornerstone of an attempt at total historical interpretation, in England is quickly becoming yet another form of historical specialization.

The truth is that British historians, with very few exceptions on the Left, have never aimed to construct historical totalities. Every attempt to reconstruct the structural foundations of history has been assimilated by dissolution into discrete specialisms.

This, indeed, was amply illustrated in the boldest native attempt to escape from ingrained methodological routines—that of Namier. It is no accident that Namier's most prominent self-styled disciple was A. J. P. Taylor. Fact accumulation, moralizing and liberal variants of the idea of progress—these were the blind alleys that Namier avoided. But this was not the lesson that his disciples drew from his work. Indeed if Taylor's work has any distinctive characteristics, it is precisely these. The only idea that he seems to have inherited from Namier without qualification is an obsessional anti-Germanism. Namierism had so little methodological impact upon the general approach to English history because it was not intrinsically strong enough to resist the massive weight of the English liberal tradition. After an initial panic, English empiricist historians simply transformed and remoulded it in their own image.

The dilemmas of moralism without progress

Nearly all the important accomplishments of English historians in the last seventy years have been achieved *against the grain*. In effect, promising developments have been hampered by, and ultimately suffocated beneath, a chronic structural malaise: what might be termed, for want of a better name, a dodo complex. In other words, British historians have been trapped in an extinct 'problematic', whose limits are the legacy of a tenacious and antique liberal individualism. This problematic first appeared in its critical form with the dismantling of the Whig interpretation of history. Fact accumulation plus moral judgment validated by the idea of progress no longer appeared satisfying or respectable. On the other hand, if this structure was really to be demolished, history would become vulnerable to the invasion of Marxism and sociology. Once the first flush of iconoclastic enthusiasm had cooled, the young Turks of English academic history realized that this possibility was intolerable. In 1944, Butterfield had already begun to recant. 'Those,' he wrote, 'who, perhaps in the misguided austerity of youth, wish to drive out that Whig interpretation ... are sweeping a room which humanly speaking cannot long remain empty. They are opening the doors for seven devils which, precisely because they are newcomers, are bound to be worse than this first.' 'Whig history,' he continued, 'was one of our assets ... it had a wonderful effect on English politics.'

In effect, the problem for English historians was that the idea of progress, which had underpinned the validity of their moral judgments, had now become hopelessly tainted as 'historicism'. Yet liberal-individualism itself had relied explicitly upon a form of historicism, in its halcyon days. Otherwise there would have been no meaning in history and no criterion of moral judgment. Relativism and 'the accidental view' could not provide the ultimate definition of history, for one of the uses of history has always been (in Western society at least) the creation of traditional mythologies attributing a historical sanctity to the present self-images of groups, classes, and societies. In the days of the Cold War, therefore, historians were torn between two separate assaults upon Marxism. On the one hand Popper and Berlin attacked 'historicism' as an illegitimate and immoral pursuit; on the other, a host of historians attempted to provide a sweeping historical predigree to 'Western values'. Imprisoned within this tragi-comic impasse, J. H. Plumb lamented in 1966 that it was nowadays impossible to re-infuse the idea of progress into liberal historiography without sliding into Marxism. His own attempt to interpret history once more as the unfolding of freedom, democracy, humanitarianism, toleration, and increasing material welfare confirmed his diagnosis.

'Fact' and 'theory'

The main opposition to world-weary liberal pessimism or wistful nostalgia has recently been led by E. H. Carr. In *What is History?* Carr launched a vigorous attack upon empiricism, pseudo-objectivism and the subordination of historical analysis to moral stricture. This fundamental work is undoubtedly the most penetrating critique of historical obscurantism to have come out of England in the last hundred years. Above all, Carr demolished the exhausted dichotomy between 'facts' and 'interpretations' which was the cornerstone of latter-day positivism. The liberal approach has always assumed that theory—'interpretations'—will emerge after the collection of facts : i.e. by induction. Under the sway of such a programme, it is not surprising that few English historians have ever reached the promised land of theory. Nor is it surprising that the few who did arrive were forced to employ such deceits and sleight of hand to get there, that they only succeeded in confirming the opinion of their more conventional colleagues that the pursuit of theory was always somehow at the expense of 'the facts', and as such beyond the responsibility of the historian. By the same token, they confirmed received notions—the uniqueness of the event, the free will and moral responsibility of the agent, and the role of accident.

The circularity of this debate stems from the positivism inherent in its definition of history. History was an objective thing. It was physically recorded in myriad bundles of archives from the Public Record Office to the local parish church. The task of the historian was to write it up. Theory would come, like steam from a kettle when it reached boiling point. The initial illusion is evident. Those who tried to create theory out of facts, never understood that it was only theory that could constitute them as facts in the first place. Similarly those who focused history upon the event, failed to realize that events are only meaningful in terms of a structure which will establish them as such.

Carr's critique at last disposed of some of these antique errors. His own formulations, however, may be criticized for one lingering concession to the 'problematic' of traditional liberal historiography. Carr attacked the notion that 'facts' and 'interpretation' are rigidly separable. Pointing out that all writing of history involves a selection from the sum of facts available, he demonstrated that any selection of facts obeys an implicit evaluative criterion. 'Facts' are thus inseparable from 'interpretations', which in turn are determined by 'values'. These values should, he argued, be grounded and verified by the immanent movement of history itself. Carr's own position—that this movement is essentially that of men's increasing control over nature and society, their environment and themselves—has an obvious relationship to that of the early Marx.

Concepts versus interpretations

This type of philosophy enables him to make an extremely effective attack on the liberal fact/value distinction in history; and yet in another way, his argument is still ultimately homologous to the old liberal idea of progress. For, as soon as it is conceded that there is such a thing as history in general, then it will be necessary to take up a position in an unreal debate—whether there is progress, and thus whether there is meaning and direction in history. But, as Louis Althusser has written, there is no such thing as history in general, there are only specific structures which have specific histories. In other words, there is no abstract thing called 'History' which bestows significance upon events in time; time is not a unitary flow that subsumes all classes, structures, and epochs within it. In effect the very notion of time must be reconstructed in every case. It is here that Carr tacitly opens the door to liberal historiography—for there is the implication that time itself will radiate the significance of any particular historical epoch, and that this will provide the key to the understanding of that age. This might seem a terminological quibble, but in fact it has important implications. In Carr's case, it leads him to pay very little attention to the construction of historical concepts. He simply states that the more sociological history becomes, the better it will be. But this is insufficient, since it assumes that there is a distinction between the two. In effect history is theory, and cannot logically be otherwise. It is the formulation of theoretical concepts with which to construct history that determines the greatness of the historian. It is significant that Carr's work omits any analysis or appraisal of the new methodological and theoretical approaches in recent international historiography. There is no reference for instance to the structural principles which inform such monumental works as Bloch's *Feudal Society* or Braudel's *Mediterranean in the Age of Philip II*. Yet it is precisely work like Braudel's which has subsequently produced a theoretical reconstruction in his essay on *Le Temps Historique*. For what is really central to the possibility of a new history, is not novel 'values' or 'interpretations' but the production of new concepts. It is no accident that Althusser has recently entitled a pioneering theoretical essay : 'Sketch of a *concept* of history.' It is within this debate—to which Lévi-Strauss, an anthropologist, has perhaps made the most important contribution, that the new 'problematic' of history lies today.

Individualist theory has provided a constant escape route from this necessity to reformulate historical concepts. Sir Karl Popper and his followers are about as enriching to a properly constituted historical science as Bishop Bossuet was to the historians of the Enlightenment. But whereas Bossuet was rapidly dispatched to oblivion, the leathery strength of nineteenth-century liberalism still exercises a jealous tutelage over English historical culture.

In the past, it provided the wrong answers to the prevalent

questions of the day. Today, the true problems are outside its universe altogether. For, as Lévi-Strauss has pointed out, history's only distinctive possession is a heterogeneous collection of chronological codes. Yet chronology only attains meaning as a method of formulating the historical character of structures. In a minimal sense at least, all great history is structural history. In England, this has never been acknowledged. The differential temporality of linked historical structures, has been obscured by the myth that all events are conjoined by the mere fact of continuous succession in time. The converse is equally true. Merely because parts of a social system are contemporaneous, they do not necessarily inhabit the same historical time. Only a theoretical practice which integrates these two fundamental axioms will seize the dialectic of any determinate historical development.

How is this new problematic to be established in the field of history? Precedent suggests that it will not result from the single-handed efforts of isolated individuals. As has been shown, the attempts of the past have all too easily been re-integrated into the dominant academic orthodoxy. Such well-weathered cultural bastions can only be undermined through combined assault. Socialist historians must form their own institutions, run their own journals, and stage their own debates without sliding into either sectarianism or eclecticism. They should not retreat into the safe pastures of labour history. They should not be content to chip away at the easily sacrificed protuberances of received historical interpretation. This will only trap them in the cosy humanitarian niche which liberal historians have always been all too happy to accord to them. They should instead establish the *theoretical* foundations of any history, they should advance into the structure and history of the ruling class, into the interpretation of the historical morphology of whole cultures. They should follow the example of perhaps the most successfully revolutionary group of modern historians—the *Annales* school. Like them, they should be aggressive and iconoclastic. Only vigorous intellectual imperialism and collective assault will make a mark. Otherwise the limp ghosts of long departed liberal mandarins will forever 'weigh like a nightmare on the brain of the living'.

Part Two

KEY PROBLEMS

7

Sociology: the Myth of Classlessness

J. H. WESTERGAARD

In the two decades following the Second World War there was a phenomenal growth in sociology; departments devoted to the subject multiplied and expanded in the universities and funds were available for research on an unprecedented scale. Most of those engaged in sociological theorizing in Britain and the United States during this period proclaimed their commitment to objectivity and value neutrality. Yet, as J. H. Westergaard demonstrates in this pioneering critique, the prevailing sociological analysis of all major issues of social structure, especially when concerned with the distribution of economic or political power, was misleading and contrary to the weight of evidence in sociological research. This essay was written in 1964: a postscript discusses developments since that date.

J. H. Westergaard is Reader in Sociology at the London School of Economics.

The years since the early 1950s have echoed with the claim that the old class structure of capitalism is steadily dissolving. The labels attached to that new order of society which is believed to be emerging from the ruins of the old—the 'welfare state', the 'affluent society', the home-centred society', the 'mass society', 'post-capitalism', and so on—have become the clichés of contemporary debate. Their variety and imprecision indicate some of the uncertainties of diagnosis and prognosis. Evaluations, too, have differed widely: reactions to the trends discerned range from triumph to despondency. But the descriptions offered of current trends generally have much in common: the assertion that the old sources of tension and class conflict are being progressively eliminated or rendered irrelevant; that the structure of contemporary Western societies is being recast in a mould of middle-class conditions and styles of life; that these developments signal 'the end of ideology'. Such notions in turn are infused with a sense of a social fluidity which is felt to falsify past characterizations of capitalism.

Yet arguments and evidence alike have often been taken for granted, rather than stated precisely and scrutinized carefully. Rhetoric has obscured both links and gaps in the chain of reasoning. Hunches, impressions, and assumptions have been given parity with facts. Minor changes have been magnified into major ones, uncertain indications into certain proof. Evidence consistent with several interpretations has been treated as if only one were possible. The labelling of trends has been extended into a labelling of sceptics as 'fundamentalists', their criticisms dismissed as the product of a psychological inability or unwillingness to recognize a changing reality. These are reasons enough for even a cursory review of the main themes and postulates of the fashionable interpretations of mid-twentieth-century capitalism and its allegedly dissolving class structure, as they have been formulated especially in Britain and the United States.[1]

Whatever their variations, these interpretations hinge on two basic assumptions. The first is that the substantive inequalities of earlier capitalism are both diminishing and losing their former significance. The second is that, for these or other reasons, radical dissent is progressively weakened as new pat-

1. The following are examples of literature up to the early 1960s, differing in approach and interpretation, in which the thesis is stated or implied that capitalism has been fundamentally transformed and that its class structure is being eroded or rendered innocuous: C. A. R. Crosland, *The Future of Socialism*, 1956; J. Strachey, *Contemporary Capitalism*, 1956; T. H. Marshall, *Citizenship and Social Class*, 1950; D. Butler and R. Rose, *The British General Election of 1959*, 1960; M. Abrams *et al.*, *Must Labour Lose?* 1960; F. Zweig, *The Worker in an Affluent Society*, 1961; R. Dahrendorf, *Class and Class Conflict in Industrial Society*, 1959; J. K. Galbraith, *American Capitalism*, 1956; D. Bell, *The End of Ideology*, 1961; K. Mayer, 'Diminishing Class Differentials in the United States', *Kyklos*, Vol. 12, No. 4, 1959; R. A. Nisbet, 'The Decline and Fall of Social Class', *Pacific Sociolog. Rev.*, Spring 1959. This is only a small, and in some respects haphazard, selection; but it illustrates varying expressions of a thesis which has been postulated, or simply assumed as self-evident, in a great deal of recent socio-political commentary.

terns of living and aspiration negate or cut across the older class-bound horizons and loyalties. Substantive inequalities are reduced, it is argued, by a continuous redistribution of wealth and the extension of economic security; by a growth in the numbers and importance of occupations in the middle ranges of skill and reward; by a progressive narrowing of the in-equalities of opportunity for individual advancement; and by a widening diffusion of power or influence. In so far as power remains concentrated, it no longer derives from the accumula-tion of private property, but from control over bureaucratic organizations of diverse kinds—public at least as much as pri-vate—in which authority is divorced from wealth. Thus two crucial dimensions of inequality no longer coincide.

In so far as inequalities remain in the chances of wealth, health, security, and individual advancement, these disparities lose their psychological (and, it is often implied, their moral) force as sources of conflict because, with steadily rising levels of living and a widening base of common rights of 'citizenship', their effects are confined to a continuously narrowing area of life. Analysis and speculation concerning the cultural, psycho-logical and political repercussions of these changes have, of course, focused primarily on the manual working class, whose homogeneity and distinctive character, it is argued, are being eroded. Among manual workers, according to one interpreta-tion, old loyalties of class are being replaced by new preoccu-pations with status: a former unity of industrial and political interest is dispelled by a growing sensitivity to invidious distinc-tions of social prestige and subtle variations in the styles of life, by which everyday patterns of social acceptance and rejection are symbolized. Alternatively, workers' aspirations are seen to focus more and more narrowly upon the home and the im-mediate family, a concern with material achievement pre-dominating that involves little or no concomitant preoccupation with the rituals of status or with the ideological orientations of class. In either version, loyalties of the world of work are replaced by loyalties of the hearth; the values and perspectives of the labour market are replaced by those of the consumers' market; a faith in collective action is replaced by a reliance on individual achievement or family security; in short, an ethos traditionally thought of as middle class is assumed to be spread-ing widely among manual workers. In addition, it is sometimes argued or implied, new dividing lines of cultural distinction or political tension are coming to the fore which bear no relation to the old divisions of economic class or social status: for instance, between adults and adolescents, the latter inhabiting a distinctive 'teen-age culture' of their own; between 'high-brows' or 'egg-heads' and the 'masses', irrespective of social position; between the old, the retired and those living on fixed incomes, on the one hand, and earners—employers and employees alike —on the other hand; between people in their role as producers and (somewhat schizophrenically, it would seem) in their role as consumers; between professionals and 'organization men' in both private and public administration; and so on.

The general tenor of these arguments is familiar; the balance within them between truth and falsehood, fact and speculation, plausibility and implausibility, much less so.

1. Inequalities of wealth

In its simplest form, the 'post-capitalist' thesis postulates a continuous tendency towards the reduction of inequalities in the distribution of income and wealth.[2] In particular, it is pointed out, incomes as recorded in the reports of tax authorities and official surveys have shown a fairly marked convergence towards the middle ranges since the late 1930s. This argument can be challenged on two major scores. The first, as critics both in Britain and the United States have emphasized, is that in part at least the reduction in measured income inequality merely reflects an increased use of devices to reduce the heavier tax liabilities of the wartime and post-war period. Such devices involve the conversion of real income into forms which escape normal rates of income tax—and which do not appear as income in the usual sources of information. There are no means of assessing the full amount of income which thus goes unrecorded. But since such devices are more readily available to those with relatively high incomes in general, and to private business in particular, the net result is an understatement of

2. The discussion in this section draws, *inter alia*, on the following analyses of trends in the distribution of income and wealth: for Britain, H. F. Lydall, 'The Long-term Trend in the Size Distribution of Incomes', *J. Royal Statist. Soc.*, series A, Vol. 122, No. 1, 1959; *idem, British Incomes and Savings*, 1955; *idem* and D. G. Tipping, 'The Distribution of Personal Wealth in Britain', *Bull. Oxford Univ. Inst. Statistics*, Feb. 1961; J. A. Brittain, 'Some Neglected Features of

income inequality in current data.[3] In fact, the few attempts made to adjust the data, in such a way as to make allowance for some of the distortions resulting from tax evasive devices, have indicated a much milder redistribution of effective income than usually assumed—and one confined largely or exclusively to the 1940s.

The second objection relates to this last point. Even when no allowance is made for the effects of tax evasion, such reduction in the inequality of incomes as can be traced in both British and American analyses is in the main a phenomenon of the Second World War and the years immediately around it. Signs of any consistent narrowing of income disparities in the recorded data during the decades before then are slight and uncertain; and if account is taken of the probability that means of tax evasion were further developed and more elaborately institutionalized in the 1950s, this last decade or so may well have witnessed a slight regression towards a distribution of effective income more unequal than in the 1940s. This may remain uncertain. But it is clear that such reductions of income inequality as have occurred are both limited in extent, and very largely the results of the special demands of the wartime economy and of policies introduced at or around the time of the war.

There are factors, it is true, which might be expected to make for a general, longer-term trend towards income equalization:

Britain's Income Levelling', *Amer. Econ. Rev.*, May 1960; J. L. Nicholson, 'Redistribution of Income in the United Kingdom', in C. Clark and D. Stuvel (eds.), *Income and Wealth: Series X*, 1964; R. M. Titmuss, 'The Social Division of Welfare', in his *Essays on the Welfare State*, 1958; T. Lynes, *National Assistance and National Prosperity*, 1962; for the United States, S. Kusnetz and E. Jenks, *Shares of Upper Income Groups in Income and Savings*, 1953; R. J. Lampman, *The Share of Top Wealth Holders in National Wealth, 1922–1956*; H. F. Lydall and J. B. Lansing, 'A Comparison of the Distribution of Personal Income and Wealth in the United States and Great Britain', *Amer. Econ. Rev.*, March 1959; G. Kolko, *Wealth and Power in America*, 1962; H. P. Miller, *Trends in the Incomes of Families and Persons in the United States, 1947 to 1960*, 1963; *idem, Rich Man, Poor Man*, 1964.

3. For a detailed examination of the variety of devices available for tax evasion in Britain, see R. M. Titmuss, *Income Distribution and Social Change*, 1962.

the decreased proportion of unskilled and casual workers in the labour force, as well as other changes in occupational structure; diminished pay differentials of skill, sex, and age; an increased progression in the rates of income tax. In the latter case, however, the redistributive effects are limited—perhaps indeed neutralized—by the continued importance of non-progressive forms of taxation, by the regressive operation of income tax allowances, and by the adoption of tax evasive devices.[4] In general, moreover, except in the 1940s the redistributive effects of these and other factors seem not to have been sufficient substantially to outweigh other long-run factors working in the opposite direction: among these, the increased proportion of old and retired people in the population, coupled with the fact that— at least in Britain—the incomes of retired people dependent on public support have barely kept up with general increases in income. This might seem to suggest a shift in the nature of income inequality—from disparities between classes and occupations to disparities between age groups. Indeed, such an interpretation is frequently implied, and fits in with the general thesis of a dissolving class structure. But it is essentially misleading. Poverty in old age is not a general phenomenon of the retired—but of those who in retirement have neither property income nor the proceeds of private (though tax-supported) pension schemes to rely on. The burden of poverty—on a contemporary definition of the term—has been shifted progressively into the tail-end of working-class and lower-middle-class life; but it remains a problem of those classes.

The inequality of incomes is thus maintained in part through differential access to fringe benefits and tax-free sources of income generally. Old disparities take on new forms appropriate to the corporate economy of the mid-twentieth century. But, despite a drop during the 1940s in the reported ratio of income from capital to earned income, property ownership remains a potent, direct source of income inequality; especially so, if regard is paid to effective rather than nominal income. And the distribution of private property remains strikingly

4. Some remarkable recent calculations suggest that, both in Britain and the United States, there may be hardly any progression in the proportionate incidence of all forms of taxation combined as between different levels of income. See Clark and Peters, 'Income Redistribution: Some International Comparisons', in Clark and Stuvel (eds.), op. cit. (footnote 2).

unequal. In Britain in the mid-1950s, two-fifths of all private property were estimated to be in the hands of only 1 per cent of the adult population, four-fifths in the hands of only 10 per cent. Concentration was still more extreme forty years earlier; but such diffusion as has taken place—and the estimate may overstate its extent—has only marginally affected the bulk of the population. Legal ownership of private corporate business is especially highly concentrated, four-fifths of all share capital being held by only 1 per cent of the adult population, and nearly all the rest by another 9 or 10 per cent. The concentration of private property in the United States is not quite so extreme— the result in part, no doubt, of a wide diffusion of home owner-ship and a rather larger surviving element of small-scale enter-prise, especially farming; but it is still very marked. In the middle 1950s, 1 per cent of the adult population owned a quarter of all private property. Moreover, the American figures show no substantial and consistent decline in the unequal distri-bution of property over time; and despite a slightly greater diffusion of shareholding, the concentration of legal ownership of private business corporations follows much the same general pattern as in Britain.[5]

Thus the argument that a continuous trend towards income equalization and a wide diffusion of property are dissolving the class structure of capitalist society can hardly be sustained. Nor, therefore, can any weakening of the 'radical conscious-ness' be attributed to such forces. This is not to say that the significance of the economic divisions characteristic of capital-ism remains unchanged. It is obvious that the much milder character of the trade cycle since the 1930s has reduced the insecurities of working-class life—even though the manual worker is still more exposed to the risk of short-time working and of redundancy, cyclical or technological, than others; and even though unemployment has increased since the early period after the war. The extension of general social services—while their redistributive effects are commonly exaggerated—has re-leased personal income for expenditure in other fields, shifting the effect of income differentials from the 'more essential' to the 'less essential' areas of consumption. Even so, such enlarge-ment of the basic rights of 'citizenship' has been neither an automatic nor a continuous process. In both Britain and

5. See also E. B. Cox, *Trends in the Distribution of Stock Owner-ship*, 1963; and the references in footnote 15.

the United States, it is essentially a phenomenon of the 1930s and the 1940s. The last decade and more have seen little or no extension of such policies: in Britain, indeed, regression in some respects; while in the United States measures introduced primarily during the New Deal have left vast areas of basic social security or insecurity—health and housing in particular —to the more or less unrestricted play of market forces, property interests, and private charity, in a manner reminiscent of the late nineteenth-century Britain.

The mitigation of the effects of inequality through an extension of citizenship rights and economic security has thus depended—as it does in the future—on the assertion of a 'radical consciousness'. Overall levels of living have, of course, also risen, as a consequence of forces of a more continuous and less directly policy-determined character: the long-run, though intermittent, upward trend in productivity; and (a factor often neglected) the spread of the small-family pattern, involving a curtailment of some of the traditional fluctuations in the economic cycle of the working-class family, and the shift of relative poverty largely to a single phase of the cycle, that of old age.

In short, inequalities of income and property have been only marginally reduced. But they operate in areas of expenditure increasingly removed from those of bare subsistence living, and against a background of generally rising average levels of real income. It may well be, therefore, that the persistent inequalities of wealth are coming to assume a different significance in the eyes of those who remain 'more unequal than others'. The visibility of economic inequality may diminish, obscured by past and prospective rises in the overall levels of living. Persistent disparities may be veiled, too, if their effects are felt increasingly late in life rather than in the early stages of a worker's career. Resentment may diminish, or change in character, as inequality is relevant more to the 'frills' of life than to essentials of survival.

Arguments to this effect are, in fact, implicit or explicit in a number of the more sophisticated versions of the 'post-capitalist' thesis. They point, not so much to a transformation of the economic structure of class as such, as to a transformation of the conditions relevant to the formation and direction of class consciousness: it is not the inequalities of class that have been reduced, but their 'transparency'. But in the shift from an economic and institutional analysis of class structure to a psychological analysis of class perceptions, assumptions are involved which are neither self-evidently true nor yet often enough made explicit. Of these, the most central—and a very simple one—is the premise that what the observer regards as 'frills' will also generally be so regarded. It cannot be realistically denied—though it may be forgotten—that 'standards' of living, in the sense of notions about what constitutes a tolerable or reasonable level of living, are not fixed, but tend to rise *more or less* concomitantly with actual levels of living. The logic of the 'post-capitalist' thesis then requires that this should be 'less' rather than 'more'. It implies the assumption, either that the rise in actual levels of living generally keeps one step ahead of, or on a par with, the rise in the standards or expectations which people set themselves; or that any discrepancy in the other direction will be insufficient to generate the degree of tension which in the past was a major component of political radicalism and industrial militancy. Indeed, the argument that class consciousness among working-class people is being progressively replaced by an increased concern with status, or by a 'home-centred' preoccupation with sheer material achievement, appears to postulate that any such excess of expectations over the level of living which can actually be achieved at any given time will provide, not a potential for social protest, but only an incentive for further individual effort within the limits of the existing economic and political order—a spur to efficient conformity.

Such postulates and assumptions, however, need much more explicit statement and concrete evidence than they have hitherto been given. Political trends in the post-war Western world are no proof of their accuracy; for those trends cannot be described simply in terms of a progressive reduction of class conflict; nor, in so far as they can, are they amenable to plausible explanation only in terms of the kind of arguments outlined above. Again, no proof is provided by the numerous studies, impressionistic observations and inspired conjectures which have pointed to heightened material aspirations and an increased adoption of 'middle-class' standards of living among workers. Doubt arises, not about the general truth of such observations, but about their interpretation. The notion that workers must somehow 'catch' middle-class values and orientations when they adopt spending habits that earlier were possible only for middle-class people is, of course, naïve in the extreme.[6] It is hardly necessary to belabour the point that the process by which the luxuries of yesterday become the necessities of today, and in turn are replaced by new luxuries, is a long-standing one, and one whose end does not seem in sight. What is important, however, is that the process may be changing its character —and not necessarily in the directions assumed in fashionable commentary. For it is arguable, indeed plausible, that the luxuries of today are increasingly widely seen as the necessities— not of tomorrow or a remoter future, but of today also; that the prerogatives of one class are increasingly demanded as the rights of all; in short, that the rate of increase in standards or expectations of living is accelerating faster than the rate of increase in actual levels of living. Ordinary standards of aspiration may to a growing extent be set by the levels in fact achieved only by the prosperous minority—through direct comparison, or under the impact of advertising and the mass media generally. Indeed, the dynamics of the contemporary capitalist economy requires such a sustained pressure for consumption, as the defenders of advertising are prone to stress.

If this is so, then the nature of the class structure is certainly changing. The character of individual classes as 'quasi-communities', as partially separate sub-cultures each with its own fairly distinctive set of norms, standards, and aspirations, will be loosening. Parochial, tradition-bound ceilings on hopes and demands in the various strata and groups of the working class will be in process of replacement by a common, 'middle-class' yardstick of material achievement. Though not a new phenomenon, the probable contemporary acceleration of the process is significant. This, in a sense, is precisely what the apologists for contemporary capitalism claim is happening; yet the conclusions they draw need by no means follow. Precisely opposite conclusions are equally, or even more, plausible. For while the common 'middle-class' yardstick is continually being raised, the levels of material achievement which it prescribes are perpetually, and by very definition, beyond the reach of the bulk of the population. The persistent economic inequalities thus

6. For a cogent critique of this and a number of other assumptions embedded in the postulate of working-class 'embourgoisement', see D. Lockwood, 'The "New Working Class" ', *European J. Sociology*, Vol. 1, No. 2, 1960; *idem* and J. Goldthorpe, 'Affluence and the British Class Structure', *Sociolog. Rev.*, Vol. 11, 1963.

guarantee a built-in tension between goals and the objective possibilities of achieving them. Whether tension is translated into political radicalism, or finds other forms of expression, is a separate question, and will be briefly discussed later. Its answer will depend in part on non-economic factors. But if the analysis is correct, it is clear that in at least one respect the potential for class conflict in contemporary capitalist societies, far from decreasing, may instead be growing.

2. Inequalities of opportunity

It is a major theme of much contemporary commentary that Western societies are becoming steadily more 'fluid'. Not only is it believed that economic and other distinctions between the social strata are getting blurred; but movement between the strata is assumed to be more frequent than before, the opportunity for such movement more equally distributed. The internal homogeneity, the external distinctiveness and the hereditary character of the working class are being weakened, so it is argued—as individuals increasingly acquire rather than inherit their class position; and as in any case the continuous growth in numbers of white-collar jobs provides new openings for upward social mobility. Assertions along these lines are common —even in general socio-political commentaries by social scientists who, in their role as technical specialists, must recognize the flimsiness of the evidence.[7]

For in fact the evidence flatly contradicts some of the formulations of this thesis; and it leaves others open to serious doubt. First, so far as can be seen, overall inequalities of opportunity for social ascent and descent have not been reduced in either Britain or the United States during this century—or, for that matter, in most other Western countries for which information is available. In comparison, for instance, with the son of a pro-

7. Among the studies on which the following discussion is based are: D. V. Glass (ed.), *Social Mobility in Britain*, 1956; N. Rogoff, *Recent Trends in Occupational Mobility*, 1963; articles in *Amer. Sociolog. Rev.* by E. Chinoy (April 1955), G. Lenski (Oct. 1958) and E. Jackson and H. J. Crockett (Feb. 1964); G. Carlsson, *Social Mobility and Class Structure*, 1955; K. Svalastoga, *Prestige, Class and Mobility*, 1959; S. M. Miller, 'Comparative Social Mobility' in *Current Sociology*, Vol. IX, No. 1, 1960; S. M. Lipset and R. Bendix, *Social Mobility in Industrial Society*, 1959.

fessional or a business executive, the odds against a manual worker's son achieving professional status, or just a middle-class job in general, have remained very much as they were at the turn of the century. More adequate data might alter the detailed picture, but hardly the general conclusion. Most of the evidence relates, of course, to the experience of people fairly well advanced in their careers—not to today's younger generation. But data on the distribution of educational opportunity in contemporary Britain, and on post-war trends of social mobility in the United States, do not suggest any prospect of striking changes in the future.[8]

Secondly, however, it may be argued that *relative* inequalities of opportunity between those born in different classes matter less than absolute chances of advancement; the absolute chance, say, which a working-class boy has of climbing out of the class in which he starts life. If changes in the occupational structure (or other changes) substantially increase such absolute chances of upward mobility—even if the same changes improve the career prospects of those born higher up the social scale, and relative opportunity thus remains as unequal as before—this could be significant in reducing the degree to which working-class status is, and appears to be, permanent and hereditary. In fact, shifts in occupational structure have occurred, and are still occurring, which could appear to justify some such expectations. The general consequences of these shifts need separate discussion. But their net effect on social mobility has been to increase upward movement no more than at most rather marginally. The evidence is patchy and not all of a piece. Nevertheless, there has been no sign of any marked expansion in the chances of climbing up the social scale.

This is not to say that the Western capitalist countries are 'closed' societies—Britain any more than the United States, despite the old stereotypes. There is a good deal of movement of individuals between the different strata, even though much of this movement covers fairly short distances in social space, involves shifts within either the manual or the non-manual group far more often than between them, and is characterized by sharp and persistent inequalities in the distribution of opportunities. The point is that, partially 'open' as they are,

8. See E. Jackson and H. J. Crockett, 'Occupational Mobility in the United States', *Amer. Sociolog. Rev.*, Feb. 1964; and the references in footnote 9.

these industrial societies have not become *more* open during this century. Factors which might have been expected to alter rates of mobility over time seem either to have been insignificant in effect, or to have cancelled each other out. Educational opportunities, for example, have been extended. But their extension, in large measure, has benefited all classes. Inequalities of educational opportunity remain marked—at the higher levels of education generally provided today in comparison with the past. The educational qualifications normally required at any given point of the occupational scale have simply been raised. It is true that the overall expansion of education has been accompanied by some reduction in the inequalities of educational opportunity. But this—a slow trend, so far as Britain is concerned, and one not noticeably accelerated after 1944—has occurred to a more limited degree than is usually assumed; so limited, that its consequences have evidently been roughly neutralized by concomitant restrictions on social mobility through channels other than the educational system.[9] These restrictions are often forgotten; but the increasing emphasis on the role of education in social recruitment is a direct reflection of them. In particular, with the professionalization, bureaucratization and automation of work, appointment to jobs in the middle and higher reaches of the occupational scale comes to depend more on school, college, and university qualifications than on personal qualities and experience acquired at work. The frequency of social mobility has not been significantly increased; but its incidence is steadily more confined to a single phase of the life cycle. If the individual is to be socially mobile,

9. See A. Little and J. H. Westergaard, 'The Trend of Class Differentials in Educational Opportunity in England and Wales'. *Brit. J. Sociology*, Dec. 1964. See also the various major special studies of the distribution of educational opportunity in post-war Britain: J. Floud *et al.*, *Social Class and Educational Opportunity*, 1956; R. K. Kelsall, *Report on an Enquiry into Applications for Admission to Universities*, 1957; Ministry of Education, Central Advisory Council, *Early Leaving*, 1954; *idem*, *15 to 18*, 1959–60 (Crowther report); Committee on Higher Education, *Higher Education: Report* and *Appendices I and II*, 1963; and especially, J. W. B. Douglas, *The Home and the School*, 1964. Cf. also D. V. Glass, 'Education and Social Change in Modern England' in M. Ginsberg (ed.), *Law and Opinion in England in the 20th Century*, 1959. For some United States data, see, e.g., D. Wolfle, *America's Resources of Specialized Talent*, 1954.

he must be so during his years of formal education: the chances of promotion or demotion, once he has entered on his adult working career, are almost certainly narrowing. The position of the adult manual worker—and to a growing extent, that of the routine grade clerical worker—becomes a more, not a less, permanent one.[10]

Nevertheless, it might be argued, this very change in the character of social mobility may alter people's perceptions of the chances of advancement. Mobility becomes more of an institutionalized process. The educational system is geared to it. Career opportunities become more predictable, as they come to depend more on a formalized kind of scholastic achievement. 'Elbows', 'string-pulling', connections and luck will matter less. In consequence, the chances of rising in the social scale may *seem* to be greater, even though they are not; and failure may be accepted with more resignation, if it is the result of a 'fair' process of selection. The argument, however, is double-edged. Failure may be the more unacceptable, if accepting it means to recognize one's intellectual 'inferiority'. Moreover, the very institutionalization of education as the royal road to success is likely to increase expectations to the point where they will come into conflict with the harsh reality of existing limitations on opportunity. There again, the question turns on psychological imponderables, about which very little is known. But there is good reason to believe that the demand for education is spreading well down the social scale. In part, indeed, this is a logical reaction to the growing importance of formal education as the main channel of social mobility: as the adult worker's hopes of promotion for himself become still more evidently unreal, aspirations focus instead upon the children's prospects. Be that as it may, such heightened recognition of the

10. Evidence suggesting a decline over time in the proportion of industrial managers or directors who reached their positions by promotion from low-grade clerical or manual jobs can be found for Britain in: Acton Society Trust, *Management Succession*, 1956; R. V. Clements, *Managers: a Study of their Careers in Industry*, 1958; C. Erickson, *British Industrialists: Steel and Hosiery, 1850–1950*, 1959. The Civil Service has shown increased recruitment of administrative class officials by promotion from the lower ranks (R. K. Kelsall, *Higher Civil Servants in Britain*, 1955), but is probably a special case. R. Bendix, *Work and Authority in Industry*, 1963, *inter alia* summarizes some American data on trends in the recruitment of industrial management.

importance of education is another example of a weakening of the old cultural distinctions between the classes. But precisely as workers increasingly share 'middle-class' aspirations for the education and future careers of their children, so the existing limitations and persistent inequalities of educational opportunity must result in the frustration of those aspirations as the common experience. Such frustration may be the harder to bear, because the condemnation of both parents and children to permanently inferior status is more final and irreversible than before.

The strength of the various factors involved is still unknown. The balance of probabilities, and the forms in which frustrated aspirations might find expression, are thus uncertain. Yet the conclusion stands that in this field, too, the potential for social protest is at least as likely to be growing as to be declining. Contemporary capitalism generates a tension between aspirations increasingly widely shared and opportunities which, by the very nature of the class structure, remain restricted and unequally distributed.

3. *Changes in occupational structure*

The share of white-collar jobs in total employment has been growing throughout this century. Commentators have often exaggerated the implications of this trend hitherto. They have tended to underplay the facts, for instance, that the very marked 'white-collar trend' in the United States in large measure has reflected a general shift from agricultural to urban employment; that the occupational composition of the male labour force has been very much less affected than that of the female labour force, within which 'white blouse' work has replaced domestic service as the dominant form of employment; and that the expansion of the 'tertiary sector' of the economy has increased the relative number, not only of white-collar jobs, but also to a small extent of non-domestic service jobs, many of them low-paid and demanding little skill. It is true, nevertheless, that shifts in occupational structure overall have involved a fall in the share of unskilled and casual work, and a rise in the share of both semi-skilled manual and various kinds of black-coated work.[11] Moreover, much of the commentary has

11. Shifts in occupational structure can be more accurately traced for the United States than for Britain; see, e.g. U S Bureau of Census,

been directed to the future rather than the past. Not only will the 'white-collar trend' continue for some time; but automation in industry is likely to produce a sizeable growth in the numbers of skilled workers and technicians, in place of that growth in the numbers of semi-skilled workers which in the past has been associated with the mechanization of industry and its conversion to conveyor-belt production. These prospects have been widely hailed as yet another source of capitalist social stability: a strengthening of the centre in place of 'polarization'.

There is, however, considerable room for doubt about such complacently enthusiastic interpretations.[12] The balance between the two trends—of automation, with its increased demand for skill and technical expertise, and of continuing mechanization of the older kind, with its increased employment of semi-skilled workers—is still uncertain, and may remain so for some time to come. The adoption of automation is likely to be a slow and uneven business. The relevant criteria, of course, will be profitability, not work satisfaction through 'job enlargement' for its own sake. Since capitalist economic organization provides no mechanisms for the sharing of gains and losses, resistance to automation from small business may be, and from trade unions will be, considerable. Labour resistance, indeed, is certain to grow if the American pattern of recent years spreads—the paradox of high unemployment rates persisting during a boom. There is a danger here for the working-class movement: of a division between those—the unskilled and workers in the declining industries—most affected by technological unemployment, and those whose labour is at a high premium in the changing

---

Occupational Trends in the United States, 1900–1950, 1958. Official British classifications of occupations have changed a good deal over time. But it is fairly clear that the approximate two-to-one ratio of manual to non-manual workers in the male population of 1951 represented only a rather limited relative decline of the manual element during this century. When the relevant later Census figures are available they may show some acceleration of the rate of decline. For one estimate of the growth of 'middle-class' occupations, see A. L. Bowley, *Wages and Income of the United Kingdom since 1860,* 1937.

12. The work of G. Friedmann includes admirably balanced and careful assessments of the implications of technological change for labour; see his *Industrial Society: the Emergence of the Human Problems of Automation,* 1955, and *The Anatomy of Work,* 1962.

market. But the unpredictability, and the potentially sweeping character, of the incidence and effects of automation may reduce that danger, if not eliminate it. Technological innovation thus generates tension of the very kind that, allegedly, is a matter of the past. And since the source of such tension is inherent in capitalist economic organization, it can only be overcome through extensive public intervention of the kind that, allegedly again, is a contemporary irrelevancy. If both the fruits and the sacrifices involved in automation are to be shared, they must be socialized : the case against private property and private economic control is underlined. Technological innovation may be inhibited, too, as it is at present, by shortages of skilled labour and technical expertise. But in so far as these shortages are overcome through extension of education and training, the premiums which the new skills can command in the labour market will diminish. Whether 'job enlargement' through automation will decrease political radicalism by increasing work satisfaction is unpredictable; for the relationship between work satisfaction and class consciousness remains as yet virtually unexplored. But in economic terms, any 'middle-class' potential of the new 'aristocracy of labour' rests on conditions in the labour market which happen now to be favourable, but which may well not continue to be so.

In general, the 'optimistic' evaluations of current and prospective shifts in occupational structure are based on a static view of the relative rewards, prestige and conditions associated with different occupations. Premiums for scarce skills are implicitly assumed to persist, even if the scarcity itself is unlikely to do so. White-collar work is implicitly assumed to retain its traditional status and characteristics, even though the expansion of such work is almost certainly also changing its traditional features. The rationalization, mechanization and perhaps even the partial automation of clerical work will accentuate the division between controllers and supervisors, on the one hand, and routine black-coated operatives, on the other. If so, the latter increasingly are reduced to the status of bureaucratic counterparts of the semi-skilled manual workers of industry. There has, no doubt, already been a long-standing trend in that direction, but a slow one. It is likely to be accelerated, and to gain greater significance, as the traditional compensation of routine clerical work disappears : that of a reasonable chance of

promotion. The forces which now tend to block previous channels of upward mobility for those who start their careers in
low-grade white-collar jobs have already been discussed.
Whether these and related changes will—at last—result in a
social and political identification of routine clerical workers
with the manual working class is a moot point. Their long
history of middle-class associations allows room for doubt.[13]
The changes in their status, conditions, and prospects could
produce other reactions—in particular circumstances, as recent
historical precedents suggest, considerably less pleasant ones.
The point remains that to interpret the continuing expansion
of white-collar work as a uniform strengthening of the 'stable'
middle strata of society is to apply a yardstick of decreasing
contemporary relevance.

4. *The distribution of power*

The controversy concerning the power structure of contemporary capitalism has revolved around two related conservative
theories. The first is that of the 'managerial revolution'—although the interpretations of this current in the post-war era
have carried few, if any, of the pessimistic overtones which
earlier were expressed in Burnham's book of that title.[14] The
second can be crudely categorized as the theory of 'countervailing power' or 'pluralism'. Each needs examination here,

13. D. Lockwood's *The Black-coated Worker: a Study in Class
Consciousness*, 1958, is an acute and elegant analysis of the roots of
white-collar workers' long-standing social and political separation
from the manual working class. See also C. W. Mills, *White Collar*,
1956.

14. Burnham, in *The Managerial Revolution*, 1941, drew in part on
earlier work suggesting a drift of business control into the hands of
salaried 'controllers': notably A. A. Berle and G. C. Means, *The
Modern Corporation and Private Property*, 1932. Evidence that the
formal divorce between ownership and control had been greatly
exaggerated was produced by the US Temporary National Economic Committee, especially in its *Monographs no. 29*, 1940, and *no.
30*, 1941. (See also, for Britain, P. S. Florence, *The Logic of British
and American Industry*, rev. ed., 1961.) The most sophisticated, and
at the same time 'optimistic', post-war British version of the thesis
of managerial control is C. A. R. Crosland, *The Future of Socialism*,
1956 (reproduced in cruder form in the Labour Party's policy
pamphlet, *Industry and Society*, 1957).

even though brevity demands some simplification of the arguments.

The theory of the managerial revolution in its post-war versions postulates that, with an increasing diffusion of stock ownership on many hands, effective control of corporate business is exercised by non-owning executives. Since the power of these 'managers' derives from their positions in the bureaucratic hierarchies of business, not from wealth, their interests and motives differ from those of the older owner-entrepreneurs. Their control will be directed less to profit maximization as such than to other purposes, which may conflict with profit maximization: the maintenance and growth of the corporations, as an end in itself; the interests of employees, customers, the public at large, as well as of shareholders. If there are dangers, these arise from the concentration of power common to all bureaucratic organization: they are unrelated to the distribution of private wealth. In any case, the controlling 'managers' form—not so much a new ruling class, as Burnham feared—but a profession whose ethic is one of service. So private enterprise has been tamed from within. Nationalization has become an irrelevancy, it is concluded—though this conclusion seems hard to square with the implication of the theory that private ownership, in the form of shareholding, no longer has any obvious function: profits distributed as dividends can be no incentive to managerial efficiency.

So much for the theory. In fact, however, this analysis glosses over the real nature of the distribution of legal ownership. For shareholders—themselves only a very small fraction of the total population—are sharply divided into the many with little and the few with much. It is true that diffusion has increased. The many own a somewhat higher, and the few a somewhat lower, proportion of total voting stock than in the past. But the distinction remains. Stock ownership is still very highly concentrated. And precisely because of diffusion, large stockholders —companies or individuals—need a diminishing share of the total to exercise effective influence on policy. Such influence need not be—and evidently often is not—exercised through direct participation in formal control. Instead, it may operate through a natural identity of interest between controllers and large stockholders. To assume such an identity of interest is not to resort to semi-metaphysical speculation. For the controllers—directors and top executives, in whose hands the major, strategic policy decisions lie—are, in fact, owners of large stockholdings themselves: the wealthiest shareholders of any identifiable groups in society. Their holdings may be distributed over a number of companies; their share of the voting stock in those corporations where they hold office is usually relatively small—though considerable in absolute terms. But it is hard to believe that, as wealthy stockholders, they voluntarily allow their policies to be dictated by considerations conflicting with those of long-run profit maximization. The contemporary formulations of management ideology certainly refer to the social responsibilities of corporate business—and no doubt do so without conscious hypocrisy. But there seems to be no evidence to suggest that the ultimate yardstick by which policies are determined, and 'social responsibilities' defined, is other than one of profit maximization. Policies are likely to be more efficiently and 'professionally' directed towards that end than was the case with the smaller-scale enterprise of classical nineteenth-century capitalism. Profitability may also be assessed over a longer time-span—as it doubtless is, too, by large shareholders and corporation executives alike, in comparison with small shareholders. But for an inherent conflict of interest between large shareholders and controllers there is no plausible case on the evidence. In societal perspective, the two overlap to the point of near-identity: private wealth is not divorced from private corporate power.[15]

But if capitalist enterprise has not been tamed from within, it may still have been tamed from without. Such a postulate is the crux of the theory of 'countervailing power' in its different

15. Evidence on these various points will be found, *inter alia*, in: P. S. Florence, *The Ownership, Control and Success of Large Companies*, 1961; H. Parkinson, *Ownership of Industry*, 1951; L. R. Klein *et al.*, 'Savings and Finances of the Upper Income Classes', *Bull. Oxford Univ. Inst. Statistics*, Nov. 1956; M. Barratt-Brown, 'The Controllers', *Universities and Left Rev.*, Autumn 1958; D. Villarejo, 'Stock Ownership and the Control of Corporations', *New University Thought*, Autumn 1961, Winter 1962; F. X. Sutton *et al.*, *The American Business Creed*, 1956; as well as in the references to property distribution given in footnotes 2 and 5 above. For general criticisms of the thesis of managerial control, see also, e.g. P. M. Sweezy, 'The Illusion of the Managerial Revolution', in his *The Present as History*, 1953; C. W. Mills, *The Power Elite*, 1957; R. Bellamy, 'Mr. Strachey's Guide to Contemporary Capitalism', *Marxist Qtly.*, Jan. 1957.

versions. Power, it is argued, is distributed among a variety of groups. The alignment of these groups with each other will shift from issue to issue. The result is a general, if not necessarily a static, balance of diffused power, in which no single set of interests is dominant. Bureaucratic rigidity, the 'iron law of oligarchy', may tend to separate leadership from rank and file within the individual groups and organizations; but such inequalities of power would cut across the traditional inequalities of class, property and wealth.[16]

It is clear that there is an element of truth in such a description. It should also be clear that the element is no more than the obvious: there is no *total* concentration of power in the hands of any single group. The 'theory' may provide something of a 'conceptual framework' for analysis of the distribution of power; it is no substitute for such analysis. For it leaves two crucial questions unanswered. First, how far do the various formally separate groups among which power is distributed represent in fact, not distinct and competing interests, but broadly similar interests in different institutional dress? Closer analysis may reveal, not a scattered diversity of influences, but

16. 'Pluralist' interpretations of the distribution of power, often in recent formulations accompanied by an idealization of the 'politics of consensus' (a concept which is virtually a contradiction in terms), have been most explicit in American socio-political analysis. See, e.g. J. K. Galbraith, *American Capitalism: the Concept of Countervailing Power*, 1956; D. Bell, *The End of Ideology* (new ed.), 1961; S. M. Lipset, *Political Man* (new ed.), 1963; and several 'pluralist' interpretations of, or commentaries on, the power structure of local communities, e.g. N. W. Polsby, *Community Power and Political Theory*, 1963; R. A. Dahl, *Who Governs?* 1961; E. C. Banfield, *Political Influence*, 1961; *idem* and J. Q. Wilson, *City Politics*, 1963. In Britain, somewhat similar assumptions and preoccupations have been expressed or implied, e.g. in C. A. R. Crosland, *The Future of Socialism*, 1956; S. E. Finer, 'The Political Power of Private Capital', *Sociolog. Rev.*, Dec. 1955, July 1956; *idem, Anonymous Empire*, 1958; R. T. McKenzie, *British Political Parties* (new ed.), 1964. Among general critiques, see, e.g. C. W. Mills, *The Power Elite*, 1957; T. Bottomore, *Elites and Society*, 1964; R. Presthus, *Men at the Top*, 1964; S. W. Rousseas and J. Farganis, 'American Politics and the End of Ideology', *Brit. J. Sociology*, Dec. 1963. See also the commentary by A. W. Kornhauser, ' "Power Elite" or "Veto Groups",' in S. M. Lipset and L. Lowenthal (eds.), *Culture and Social Character*, 1961.

a broad clustering of major sources of pressure. Secondly, once such major clusters of interests have been identified, at what point between them has the balance of power been struck? To answer these questions requires examination of the composition of the various *élites* and pressure groups in the main institutional fields of power, to establish the degree of identity between them in terms of social recruitment, everyday associations and politico-economic orientations. But it also requires direct examination of decisions made and policies executed. This in turn cannot—as is often assumed—be confined merely to establishing the outcome of conflicts between expressly formulated alternative policies and views: to seeing whether the ultimate decision in particular cases is closer to the explicit proposals of this or that party to the conflict. For those proposals themselves have been formulated within the limits of a 'realistic', tactical appraisal of the likely outcome, and within the limits of that institutionalization of conflict which is the essence of contemporary politics. Such institutionalization means that conflict is regulated through a series of compromises which define, not only the means and procedures of conflict, but also the area of conflict at any given time. Compromise thus enters into the initial determination of the limits of controversy: only a small band of the full range of alternative policies is effectively ventilated and disputed. Indeed, on some issues the band may be so narrow that decisions seem not to be 'made' at all—they just flow automatically from the 'climate of opinion' formed by the initial compromise. To determine the locus of power, therefore, one must examine the nature of that compromise itself: the location, within the full range of alternatives which represent the long-term, objective interests of the contending groups, of that narrower span of policy alternatives to which controversy is effectively, if perhaps temporarily, confined.

If these criteria are applied to contemporary Britain, it is clear that power is not in important respects diffused among a multitude of diverse interest groups, each with a distinct and separate identity. There is instead a clustering of power. The dominant grouping is that of a small, homogeneous *élite* of wealth and private corporate property—politically entrenched in the leadership of the Conservative Party; strongly represented in, or linked with, a variety of influential public and private bodies; assured of the general support of the press, if not at the overt political level of the publicly controlled mass media; its members sharing for a large part a common, exclusive educational background, and united by fairly close ties of kinship and everyday association. The broad contours of this *élite* are familiar from a good deal of recent research, the general similarity of which with pre-war evidence points to a strong degree of continuity. It is an *élite* which, while its economic base is that of financial and industrial capital, yet has its own uniquely British features, in part inherited from the agrarian-mercantile nobility and gentry of the pre-industrial era. It is neither a tightly closed group—indeed, much of its viability may derive from its absorptive capacity—nor a monolithically united one. But internal divisions remain generally confined to particular issues, and do not develop into major fissures of a durable kind. The challenge to its power comes, not from within its own ranks, but from outside. This is the challenge presented by the labour movement: other possible sources of challenge are either minor and impermanent, or tend to be absorbed into the labour movement as the only effective channel of opposition in the long run.[17]

The rise of labour—which, in distinct contrast to the dominant conservative group, has a socially heterogeneous political leadership, but a pretty homogeneously working-class mass support—has clearly imposed restraints upon the exercise of power by the primary *élite*. Since the war, especially, rights of property have been curtailed in certain fields, concepts of the public interest and of social welfare widened, areas of effective political conflict shifted leftwards, by comparison with the past. In very general terms these influences continue to operate whether or not the labour movement is in formal control of the government. The rightward swing in social and economic policy during most of the years of Conservative government 1951–64 has certainly not been negligible. But the fact that the larger part of the measures introduced by Labour after the war remain more or less intact—and that some of them would have been at least partly matched by Conservative measures, had Labour not won a majority in 1945—illustrates the limits imposed on the power of the main *élite* by the existence of a

17. A great deal of the relevant evidence can be found in W. Guttsman, *The British Political Elite*, 1963. See also, e.g. C. S. Wilson and T. Lupton, 'The Social Background and Connections of "Top Decision Makers",' *Manchester School*, Jan. 1959.

permanent opposition. Yet there is no 'equal' division of influence between the two groups. Labour remains in opposition even when, in constitutional terms, it forms the government. During the six years of its post-war Parliamentary majority to 1951, it continued to operate the existing machinery of government with few, if any, of such changes as radical policies would have required. Economic controls were exercised—as during the war—to a large extent through the agency of private business. Nationalization was confined to a limited, specialized and in part unprofitable field; it was implemeted with little coherent conception of the use of nationalized enterprise as an instrument of public policy; the membership of the boards was drawn in large measure from private business; and their responsibility to the government, Parliament and the public was left limited and ambiguous.[18] This is not to deny the very real achievements of the post-war Labour Government, or the genuine leftward shift which resulted. The point remains that the challenge presented by the labour movement has modified, but not radically curtailed, the power of the dominant *élite*, or the rights of private corporate property which are the economic source of that power. That this is largely the choice of the labour movement itself, the result of long-standing uncertainties of purpose on its part, does not alter the fact. The institutionalized compromise which characterizes the scene of political conflict has been drawn up at a point which still predominantly favours the interests of capital.

Those interests, however, are still more strongly favoured by the 'balance of power' in the United States. This is so evident that it might seem unnecessary to belabour the point. Yet it is a curious fact that support for the theory of countervailing power has been most strongly voiced by American commentators; and that a number of these in recent years have contrasted an allegedly 'pluralistic' pattern of diversified power in the United States with an '*élitist*' pattern in Britain where, it is argued, a concentration of power remains supported by wide-

18. On the exercise of economic controls by the post-war Labour Government, and on nationalization, see: A. A. Rogow, *The Labour Government and British Industry, 1945–50,* 1955; Acton Society Trust, *Studies in Nationalized Industry, 1950–53;* J. H. Smith and T. E. Chester, 'The Distribution of Power in Nationalized Industries', *Brit. J. Sociology,* Dec. 1951; C. Jenkins, *Power at the Top,* 1959; A. H. Hanson, *Parliament and Public Ownership,* 1961.

spread attitudes of deference to 'legitimate authority'.[19] That British social and political values include an element of such deference cannot be denied. But to use this element as the basis for a comprehensive characterization of the British scene, and a contrast with the American, involves the most flagrant absurdities. For to do so is to ignore the outstanding fact that in Britain the predominant power of private capital has been challenged by the labour movement, whose opposition finds institutionalized expression in the political as well as the industrial field. It is true that the effectiveness and radicalism of this challenge are weakened through a partial persistence of deference, in leadership and rank and file, to the forms and symbols of traditional authority. It is also true that the process by which the clash of interests has been institutionally limited involves a continual risk—as is evident today—of the reduction of the conflict between the parties to little more than a symbolic ritual. Even so, the challenge is there, as an actuality or as a potentiality which continues to colour British politics and condition the prospects of policy. This is so at least by comparison with the United States, where any such challenge is virtually absent from the political scene. The failure of the American labour movement to develop a permanent and coherent political arm is a well-known exception to the general pattern in the industrialized societies. Its causes have been long and widely debated.[20] Its effects are that the power of private property has been subjected to far fewer restrictions than generally elsewhere. This is evident, for instance, in such fields of everyday social welfare as housing, land use planning and medical care, where any measures proposed or adopted are conditioned by the initial assumption that entrenched rights of private ownership and private profit are sacrosanct to an extent inconceivable even to the conservative parties of most other advanced industrial capitalist societies. In so far as various

19. See, e.g. S. M. Lipset, 'The Value Patterns of Democracy', *Amer. Sociolog. Rev.*, Aug. 1963; H. H. Hyman, 'England and America: Climates of Tolerance and Intolerance', in D. Bell (ed.), *The Radical Right*, 1963; E. A. Shils, *The Torment of Secrecy*, 1956; R. R. Alford, *Party and Society*, 1963. The 'bible' of this school of interpretation of British politics appears to be W. Bagehot, *The English Constitution*, 1872.

20. See, e.g. D. D. Egbert and S. Persons (eds.), *Socialism and American Life*, 1952.

interests and pressure groups participate in, or make their voices heard in, the making of decisions and the formulation of policies, they do so only within the context of that initial assumption. Such is the extent of 'pluralism'. The compromise has been struck at a point as yet a good deal to the right of the 'balance of power' in Britain; and in such a way that, outside the field of 'civil rights' at least, effective political controversy and social criticism ranged in the 1960s over a still narrower span than in Britain. Indeed, it is a feature of the fashionable idealization of the 'politics of consensus'—American in origin—to elevate the restriction of effective political debate to a virtue. The presence in Britain of a political labour movement, and also within that of a semi-institutionalized left-wing minority, has, for all the inhibiting factors, kept the area of practical conflict, genuine debate, and tolerated nonconformity in long-term perspective more open than in the United States.

5. Class culture and class solidarity

Point for point the evidence underlines the same broad conclusion : the structural inequalities of capitalist society remain marked. Disparities of economic condition, opportunity, and power persist—modified, if at all, only within fairly narrow limits. There is no built-in automatic trend towards diminishing class differentials. But it does not necessarily follow that the persistent, objective lines of class division will also be, or continue to be, the lines within which consciousness of class takes shape or across which conflict occurs. That there need be no such neat correspondence is very clear from the example of the United States. It is the claim of many contemporary commentators that Britain, and Western Europe generally, are now going the way of North America in this respect. Among arguments in support of this claim are those which stress a lessened significance or visibility of inequality—as the old insecurities of working-class life are reduced or eliminated; as overall levels of living increase; as opportunities for individual social mobility, while not increased, become institutionalized through the system of formal education. The conclusion, as I have tried to show, in no obvious way follows from the facts. But other arguments have emphasized rather a general erosion of the cultural distinctiveness of working-class life, and of those features of the local environment from which, it is assumed, class consciousness among workers has traditionally derived its strength. Old loyalties to kin, locality and traditional patterns of life are on the wane; and so, it has been implied (especially in contributions to the debate from the 'new left'), the basis for class cohesion and political radicalism is dissipated. A 'sense of classlessness' or of middle-class identification replaces former values of solidarity.[21]

Though the evidence is far from adequate, there is no reason to doubt that in a number of respects working-class 'patterns of culture' are changing, and becoming less distinctive in the process. It seems reasonable to assume that those features of working-class life will be weakening which, in the past, were conditioned primarily by low absolute levels of living, extreme insecurity and marked local or social isolation. There are indications in that direction.[22] Class differentials in mortality, for example, seem to have been diminishing at certain points, or

21. These assumptions have often been made in an implicit, rather than an explicit, fashion. See, however, S. Hall, 'A Sense of Classlessness', *Universities and Left Review*, Autumn 1958 (also the criticism by R. Samuel, 'Class and Classlessness', *Universities and Left Review*, Spring 1959); F. Zweig, *The Worker in an Affluent Society*, 1961; D. Butler and R. Rose, *The British General Election of 1959*, 1960; R. Williams, *The Long Revolution*, 1961. In the background to this debate there have been such studies of, or commentaries upon, traditional working-class 'community' life as M. Young and P. Willmott, *Family and Kinship in East London*, 1957, and R. Hoggart, *The Uses of Literacy*, 1957. F. Pappenheim, *The Alienation of Modern Man: an Interpretation based on Marx and Tönnies*, 1959, is relevant to this debate at a much more abstract, general, and theoretical level. See also footnote 6.

22. Evidence for some of the following points will be found in: General Register Office, *Registrar General's Decennial Supplement for England and Wales, 1951: Occupational Mortality*, 1954, 1958; J. N. Morris and J. A. Heady, 'Social and Biological Factors in Infant Mortality,' *Lancet*, 12th Feb.–12th March, 1955; A. J. Mayer and P. Hauser, 'Class Differentials in Expectation of Life at Birth', in R. Bendix and S. M. Lipset, *Class, Status and Power*, 1953; D. V. Glass and E. Grebenik, *The Trend and Pattern of Fertility in Great Britain*, Royal Commission on Population Papers, Vol. 6, 1954; Census of England and Wales, 1951, *Fertility Report*, 1959; National Bureau Committee for Economic Research, *Demographic and Economic Change in Developed Countries*, 1958; R. Freedman *et al.*, *Family Planning, Sterility and Population Growth*, 1959; C. F. Westoff *et al.*, *Family Growth in Metropolitan America*, 1961.

assuming a more complex pattern than before, although the relative disparities in infant mortality in Britain have hitherto remained remarkably constant. Class differentials in fertility have recently narrowed substantially in the United States and some other countries. British data have so far shown only the most uncertain of hints of a similar change; but it seems plausible that it may occur here, too. Indeed, it is not inconceivable that the familiar gradient of fertility may be reversed. If working-class people increasingly adopt the same kind of material and educational aspirations as middle-class people, while persistent inequalities prevent them from realizing those aspirations, they may reduce the size of their families below the middle-class norm. There are signs of some such reversal in Norway, for example. Whatever the trends in fertility differentials, the absolute size of family has, of course, been considerably reduced in the working class, as it has in the middle class. This by itself has undoubtedly played a major part in transforming the general character of working-class family life. A traditional urban British pattern of fairly strong extended ties of kinship, coupled with a rather marginal domestic role for the man within the nuclear family, may well have been the result of material poverty and economic insecurity, the sharp fluctuations in the economic cycle of the family associated with high fertility, and local isolation of working-class communities. Though this pattern persists, it is giving way to one closer to contemporary middle-class family norms. This process seems more likely to be a long-standing secular trend, resulting from the reduced significance of the underlying causes, than the product primarily of post-war suburbanization, as has been suggested. But suburbanization has also been pointed to as part of a more general change in working-class residential distribution and conditions of life, to which wide significance has been attached. The closed, homogeneous, one-industry, one-class, one-occupation community, familiar from earlier industrialism, is no longer typical. Suburbs and new towns are taking the place of the old mining villages, textile districts, and dockside areas. And, through these and other changes, the street, the pub, the working-men's club are losing their importance as centres of local social contact, in a world where working-class families lead increasingly 'home-centred' lives.

There is as yet no certainty about the extent and pace of all such changes in working-class culture and environment. The main dispute, however, is not about the facts, but about their implications. Sweeping social and political deductions have been drawn, with gay abandon but little documentation. Not only has it become almost fashionable to deplore the dilution of traditional working-class culture *per se* – a reaction which reflects an odd, conservative nostalgia for a way of life moulded by insecurity, local seclusion, and crude deprivation, both material and mental. But this 'cultural dilution' has also, not infrequently, come to be equated with an alleged decline of class consciousness, and its replacement by narrow preoccupations of status and 'respectability' or by sheer apathy. No substantial evidence has been offered for this equation: it has been assumed, not proven. Underlying it, there is commonly a premise which deserves explicit examination. This is an assumption that the kind of working-class unity which finds expression in industrial, or more especially in political, action draws its nourishment from the simpler and more intimate loyalties of neighbourhood and kin. Consequently, it is postulated, as the latter are weakened so the former declines. The assumption is highly questionable. For it implies that the solidarity of class—which is societal in its sweep, and draws no nice distinctions between men of this place and that, this name and that, this dialect and that—is rooted in the kind of parochial solidarity which is its very antithesis. To doubt the implied identity between the two antitheses is not to deny that sectional loyalties of region and occupation have contributed in the past to the formation of wider loyalties of class; but the permanence of that contribution has depended upon a transcendence of the original narrow basis of solidarity. Thus the developing labour movement has in many cases drawn special strength from the workers of such locally cohesive, homogeneous communities as the mining valleys of Britain and the timber districts of Scandinavia (though not in this century, for instance, from the mill towns of Lancashire to any marked extent); and the industries located in communities of this kind are still characterized by a comparatively high incidence of strike action.[23] Yet, at the political level especially, the collective force of the labour movement grew precisely as the local isolation of these and other working-class communities declined. The two trends are not

23. See, e.g. C. Kerr and A. Siegel, 'The Inter-industry Propensity to Strike,' in A. W. Kornhauser *et al.*, *Industrial Conflict*, 1954.

just fortuitously coincidental, but logically related. For the growth of a nation-wide movement—uniting, say, miners of South Wales with shipyard workers of Clydeside and others throughout the country—entailed of necessity a widening of horizons, and the displacement (if not a total suppression) of local and sectional loyalties by commitment to a common aim, however uncertainly defined. In sociological jargon, the 'particularistic' ties of neighbourhood, kin, and regional culture provide no adequate basis for the maintenance of the 'universalistic' loyalties involved in class political action.

This historical widening of once parochial horizons also entailed the progressive abandonment of aims and aspirations restricted by static, traditional definitions. Past experience and purely local criteria no longer set the limits to individual or collective ambition. The standards of comparison by which workers judged their own condition and their children's future increasingly were raised, increasingly were shared, and increasingly reflected the conditions and prospects which industrial capitalism offered the more prosperous minority. Working-class adoption of 'middle-class' aspirations is thus no new phenomenon. Nor therefore can the process in its contemporary dress, or the general attenuation of traditional working-class culture of which it is part, be regarded as one which must necessarily induce social complacency and political paralysis. On the contrary, precisely because it involves an in-built discrepancy between common demands and the unequal distribution of means for their fulfilment, it provides a continuing potential for social protest; the more so, the more 'middle-class' demands become the norm.

6. Prospects for the future

To say that there is such a potential for social protest is not to say that it will necessarily be converted into active political radicalism. The absence of any significant socialist working-class movement in the United States, and the long-standing nature of the social perspectives with which this fact is associated, make any marked leftward trend there unlikely, at least for the present.[24] The prospects in Britain, and in Europe generally, are quite different, because labour and left-wing

24. E. Chinoy's *Automobile Workers and the American Dream*, 1955, is interesting in this context.

parties there provide an established channel for the political expression of social protest. Indeed, the debate of the 1950s onwards has been obscured, rather than illuminated, by the slapdash application of American analogies to the British political scene. It is of course possible here, too, that the sense of tension inherent in the contradiction between aspiration and opportunity may be dulled by overall 'affluence', by a general conviction that next year will bring what this year will not, or by such apparent complexity in the organization of society that the sources and mutual inter-connections of persistent inequalities became increasingly difficult to identify. But though this is possible, it is very far from certain. For one thing, our knowledge of the nature and interplay of the socio-psychological attitudes involved is virtually nil. What has passed for knowledge in the post-war debate has been little more than a series of disguised guesses and assumptions. Secondly, overall affluence cannot be taken for granted. On the contrary, the insecurities and the haphazard distribution of gains and sacrifices associated with the very processes of economic expansion, industrial change, and technological innovation seem likely to bring the structural inequities of the existing social organization into sharper relief in the future. Thirdly, recent political trends offer no proof one way or another, although they are often assumed to do so. For Labour's defeats at the polls in the 1950s reflect, not a decline in manual working-class support, but a falling-off in that minority support which the party draws from the non-manual strata of the population—these strata, in turn, forming a gradually increasing proportion of the electorate. According to the one published series of opinion surveys covering the entire period from the early 1940s on, manual working-class support for Labour, if anything, grew slightly in the 1950s by comparison with the previous decade.[25]

This, clearly, provides no confirmation of 'embourgoisement' and a faltering of political loyalties in the working class—though it is true that we need to know far more than we do about the underlying factors, and about any shifts of political orientation which may have taken place within particular subgroups of the two broad categories, manual and non-manual. There is room for varying deductions about immediate, short-term tactics. But it is indisputable that the Labour leadership's

25. R. R. Alford, *Party and Society*, 1963.

policy of 'softening' the image of the party to attract a larger middle-class vote has, so far at least, produced no firm, positive results. It can, of course, be argued that the image has still not been sufficiently 'softened'. It can also—and with greater plausibility—be argued that to pursue such a policy in conventional terms is to chase a will of the wisp. A competition with the Conservative Party is almost always likely to work in the latter's favour, if the terms of reference are those of 'legitimacy' of authority, 'respectability', and 'efficiency' within the general framework of the existing socio-economic structure; and the long-run effect may well be a political alienation of the established—so far stable, though not significantly increasing—basis of Labour support in the working class. Labour's effective survival depends upon its capacity both to maintain its present support, and to extend its strength into those sections of the population—whether manual or non-manual—who share much the same socio-economic situation as the bulk of Labour supporters, but have hitherto abstained or voted against the party. Neither aim can be achieved on a durable basis through promises of moderate reform, economic efficiency and 'dynamic' administration, however worthwhile each of these may be in itself. For the Conservative Party can generally—thought not at all times—compete successfully in these fields; and it has the added advantage—in the eyes of at least some of those critical marginal sections of the electorate whose permanent support Labour needs for its survival—of its aura of status and experience. In the long run the Conservatives are sufficiently flexible to adopt a number of moderate reform proposals for their own; to redefine criteria of economic efficiency; and even to discard some of the ritual mumbo-jumbo and gentlemanly amateurism inherited by British government and industry from the mid-nineteenth-century cultural compromise between nobility and bourgeoisie, in favour of practices more in tune with the demands of a late-twentieth-century capitalist economy. None of these involves any serious challenge to the established structure of power and property. By the same token, none will fundamentally affect the major, persistent inequalities which are inherent in that structure. It is those inequalities which offer the potential for a radical political programme; and which, because increasingly they characterize the condition of the lower 'middle' strata as well, provide the only durable basis for the maintenance and extension of Labour support. A successful extension of that support cannot be guaranteed. But there is no other way, if the criteria are those of long-term political strategy; and every justification for a genuinely socialist policy, if the criteria are those of a morality which rejects the validity of the structural inequalities of the present social order.

It may be said that the 1950s and early 60s have demonstrated an absence of sufficient popular support for a substantial leftward swing in policy. To attribute political moderation or apathy in this way to the Labour electorate rather than to the party leadership is to put the cart before the horse, or at least to argue from the unknown to the known. The end of the Labour Government of 1950 was the result, after all, of internal hesitations within the Cabinet and party officialdom. Since then—and the early 1960s are no exception—no sustained attempt has been made to present a policy of direct attack upon the established structure of power and property; to demonstrate the relevance of such a policy to the aim of substantially reducing the inequalities of condition, opportunity and human fulfilment which are inherent in that structure; to underline the pervasiveness and interconnections of those inequalities; or to relate them, their sources and the measures needed to tackle them to those issues of international relations, defence, economic aid, and domestic cultural policy with which they are enmeshed. Even proposals by themselves of a radical character, or with at least a radical overtone, have been put forward piecemeal and *ad hoc*. In short, there has been no coherent attempt to exploit the potential for effective social criticism. This failure must be seen as, at least in the first instance, the result of what has been called the institutionalization of class conflict. Labour's rise to an influence which falls a good way short of power, here as elsewhere, has of necessity involved large-scale organization, the bureaucratization of party and union structures and, more importantly, the establishment of a regularized *modus vivendi* with the opposing side.[26] These trends are neither avoidable nor deplorable in themselves. But they carry with them the risk that the *modus vivendi* becomes permanent rather than tem-

26. R. Miliband's *Parliamentary Socialism*, 1961, is an excellent account of the process by which the British labour movement's protest became 'institutionalized', and of Labour's early and generally willing acceptance of the limitations inherent in the process. See also *idem*, 'Socialism and the Myth of the Golden Past', in *The Socialist Register*, 1964.

porary, accepted by those who operate it as a virtue in its own right rather than a tactical step on the way. In consequence, the area as well as the means of political conflict is narrowed; and the responsiveness of the organizational machinery to the potentialities for change latent in the wider society is reduced. There has, as yet, in Britain been no total freezing of the *status quo*, no final and irreversible hardening of the bureaucratic arteries of the Labour movement. To that, the continued presence of the left-wing minority as a focus of dissent has contributed. But the danger grows that, unless channels of communication are kept reasonably free, and the leadership sensitive to interpretations of current and future needs other than those which derive directly from the day-to-day maintenance of the *modus vivendi*, the potential for radical social protest inherent in the persistent structural inequalities of the society may find no rational political expression. It may then instead, for example, produce a predominant pattern of resigned political indifference, coupled in unpredictable proportions with irrational surges of hostility towards large-scale organization as such; with epidemics of unofficial strike action, parochially oriented and uncoordinated; with a continuing element of juvenile gang crime and xenophobia; or with other manifestations of social tension—each unrelated to the others save through their common source, lacking the focus and direction of a common perspective and political purpose. This is possible; it must not be accepted as inevitable.

Postscript 1971

Realities have changed little since the early 1960s in respect of divisions of wealth and welfare, opportunity and power; but perceptions have. To note the persistence of inequalities in Western societies has become a commonplace of social observation. The simple equations current earlier are now no longer so readily taken for granted—the equation of technical innovation and economic growth with transformations of social structure; of rising affluence with mass quiescence; of ideological divisons only with the gaps between west, east, and the 'third world'. The notion that class is withering away is not dead; but it has been losing its status as self-evident truth. Its survival has required more subtle formulations than before; and some sections of centre and right-wing opinion have been inclined to abandon it, to recognize instead the tenacious hold of inequalities as welcome evidence of their inevitability and moral necessity.

It has clearly taken more than mere accumulation of contrary facts to shake the assumption of a steady erosion of inequalities. There were plenty of contrary facts all the time, and some heretics to point them out. But the facts did not speak loudly until the concomitant assumption of social harmony disintegrated. The climate of interpretation changed in the 1960s as a multiplicity of forces with no clear single source, no very coherent direction, but unmistakable cumulative impact, brought domestic tensions within Western societies once more into focus—the waning of the Cold War and its pressures to internal conformity; the escalation of hot war in south-east Asia; the assertion of civil rights and black power in America; a crumbling of central institutionalized control over industrial conflict in Britain and elsewhere; widespread student militancy; and the recurrence of sporadic 'direct action' outside the limits of conventional politics. In turn the change in climate encouraged the production of new evidence to dispel the complacent simplicities of 'post-capitalist' theory.

Thus increasingly elaborate research has driven home the wide range and continuity of inequalities of income and property. Attempts to estimate the total impact of public policy on real income distribution have become almost routine in Britain. They have confirmed the mainly neutral effect of taxation taken as a whole, the limited redistributive effect of social benefits taken as a whole, and the broadly unaltered pattern of overall income inequalities. Labour's tenure of office appears to have left the general picture much as it was before, with some signs that low incomes were tending to fall further behind. The only notable change in the relative position of individual groups seems to be the continued trend of decline for most male routine non-manual workers, now on average worse off than semi-skilled and often than unskilled manual workers in terms of crude earnings, though not in terms of hourly rates or probably as yet in terms of job security, perks, and prospects. Imperfections of basic data rule out detection of minor trends and variations. But it is clear that the predominant determinants of income distribution remain power and pull in the labour market, and property ownership, modified relatively little by public policy as currently pursued. Some new estimates of property ownership, using partly different assumptions and modes of calculation from earlier ones, have suggested a rather less intense concentration of wealth than otherwise indicated. But they have not altered the main features of the picture. The bulk of the population is excluded from property ownership of any substance—entirely from a share in the privately owned means of production. A certain loosening of the massive concentration of wealth in few hands probably indicates only a greater dispersal of capital among the families of the already rich, designed to reduce death duties, and a spread of petty property associated with increasing owner-occupation of housing. The general stability of economic inequalities in Britain seems broadly in line with trends in other Western countries, for example the United States. One international comparison is particularly interesting—that with Sweden, long hailed as the model of 'post-capitalism', combining high average affluence and strong economic growth with the welfare measures of a social democratic party entrenched in office since well before the Second World War. Welfare measures have certainly had effect; poverty and insecurity are of a distinctly lower order there compared, say, with Sweden's polar opposite among the most affluent capitalist societies, the United States; and the structure of the Swedish economy makes for a less marked concentration of capital than in America, let alone in Britain. But no general narrowing of inequalities of income or property ownership appears to have occurred in Sweden over the period since the 1940s; the proportion of the population living on low incomes has proved a good deal larger than had been assumed; and the premature termination of a major officially sponsored enquiry into the latter subject, for completion within government departments, has been widely attributed to ministerial embarrassment at its findings.[27]

27. Among the sources on which the references to Britain in this paragraph are based are: R. J. Nicholson, 'Distribution of Personal Income', *Lloyds Bank Review*, Jan. 1967; 'The Incidence of Taxes and Social Services Benefits in 1968', *Economic Trends*, Feb. 1970; A. J. Merrett and D. A. G. Monk, *Inflation, Taxation and Executive Remuneration*, 1967; A. R. Prest and T. Stark, 'Some Aspects of Income Distribution in the UK since World War II', *Manchester School*, Sept. 1967; A. B. Atkinson, *Poverty in Britain and the Reform of Social Security*, 1969; A. L. Webb and J. E. Sieve, *Income Distribution and the Welfare State*, 1971; G. Routh, *Occupation and*

'Poverty' has thus been rediscovered; and a good deal of recent research into the distribution of wealth and welfare has been associated with the attempt to map the contours of poverty. This definition of problems and objectives carries certain risks. The risks are those in the first instance of identifying, or seeming to identify, poverty as a distinct condition to be studied, and perhaps remedied, without reference to the larger organization of economy and society. It is true that much research on poverty today starts from premises which repudiate such an approach. Poverty is defined in relative, not in absolute terms, by reference to a more or less regularly rising average standard of living; and it arises, by that definition, from the general distribution of resources in society. Yet although this is a common starting point, its implications can fairly readily be forgotten. For to focus on poverty requires one to draw an arbitrary dividing line—sometimes, more reasonably, several alternative lines—to distinguish the 'poor' from the rest. Whatever precautionary statements accompany this, the effect can easily be to emphasize the specific to the neglect of the general. Poverty by contemporary definition in Britain, for

---

Pay in Great Britain 1906–60, 1965; reports on two large-scale national sample surveys of earnings according to occupation, *Employment and Productivity Gazette*, May 1969 and Dec. 1970; 'Low-paid Workers', *Incomes Data*, Aug. and Sept. 1970; J. E. Meade, *Efficiency, Equality and Ownership of Property*, 1964; J. R. S. Revell, 'Changes in the Social Distribution of Property', *Internat. Conf. of Econ. History*, Vol. 1, 1965; A. B. Atkinson, 'The Reform of Wealth Taxes in Britain', *Polit. Qtly.*, Jan.–March 1971 (special issue on taxation policy); *Inland Revenue Statistics*, 1970. A recent set of estimates suggesting a fairly marked fall in the share and rate of profits, A. Glyn and R. Sutcliffe, 'The Critical Condition of British Capital', *New Left Review*, March–April 1971, seems to require some reconciliation with the evidence from a wide range of sources on the relative constancy of patterns of income distribution. Some of the recent American evidence is referred to in S. M. Miller and P. Roby, *The Future of Inequality*, 1970. On the trends of income and property distribution in Sweden, see Swedish Department of Finance *Ägande och inflytande inom det privata näringslivet* (S.O.U. 1968:7); the main reports of the Swedish Low Income Enquiry, suspended in July 1971, are *Svenska folkets inkomster* (S.O.U. 1970:34), and *Den svenska köpkraftsfördelningen 1967* (S.O.U. 1971:39).

example, is concentrated among the old, the sick, the disabled, large families, 'fatherless' families, and families dependent on earners in low-income jobs. But if attention is focused on these categories, it takes more than just occasional statement of the point to remember that their conditions are extreme manifestations of the wider class-structured pattern of inequality in economy and society at large. All workers—manual and increasingly the routine non-manual—are vulnerable : liable to the hazards of poverty or near-poverty in old age, in sickness, on a change of family circumstances, on redundancy or short-time, in the later years of working life. Their vulnerability even in 'affluence' is quite different from the security which characterises middle- and upper-class life cycles, and which derives, not only from higher incomes, but from career patterns with cumulative increments, promotion prospects and fringe benefits; from possession or likelihood of inheritance of property, even on a limited scale; from material and other aid often available at critical points from relatives; from easier access to, and affinity in communication with, the supporting institutions of everyday life – educational, legal, social, administrative and health services.[28]

It is symptomatic that right-wing opinion has tended to absorb rather than reject the 'rediscovery of poverty'. One response has been to take the persistence of inequalities to prove their inevitability. The argument that contrasts of poverty and wealth

28. On 'poverty' in Britain and elsewhere, see *inter alia* B. Abel-Smith and P. Townsend, *The Poor and the Poorest*, 1965; P. Townsend, ed., *The Concept of Poverty*, 1970; K. Coates and R. Silburn, *Poverty: the Forgotten Englishmen*, 1970; and several of the studies listed in the previous footnote, e.g., (Atkinson 1969), Webb and Sieve (1971), D. Piachaud, 'Poverty and Taxation', in *Polit. Qtly.* (1971), Miller and Roby (1970), *Swedish Low Income Enquiry* (1970) including supplementary reports of the latter on special aspects. On inequalities of effective access to the law see, for Britain, e.g., B. Abel-Smith and R. Stevens, *In Search of Justice*, 1968, M. Zander, *Lawyers and the Public Interest*, 1968, and in respect of one particular field, O. R. McGregor *et al.*, *Separated Spouses*, 1971; W. G. Carson and P. Wiles, eds., *Crime and Delinquency in Britain*, 1971, includes several readings relevant to the differential application of the criminal law and law enforcement. On the unsettled issue of the use and availability of the British National Health Service, see M. Rein, 'Social class and the utilisation of medical care services', *Hospitals*, 1st July 1969 (cf. also *New Society*, 20th Nov. 1969).

have so diminished that there is little scope for redistribution looks thin when, for example, as one British estimate suggests, the share of total income going to the richest one per cent of the population may be of much the same order as that going to the poorest quarter or more. But by assuming the continuation of a market economy with private property as its central institution, it has seemed plausible to argue that no changes in the mix of taxes and benefits are likely to be able to break the stable pattern of inequality. That argument has received apparent reinforcement from the notion of poverty as a cultural condition, the product of collective incompetence and lack of initiative accumulating at the bottom of the socio-economic hierarchy and amenable at best to measures of cultural therapy. Structural economic change is then seen as neither relevant nor feasible. Characteristically, concepts of a 'culture of poverty' in this form have found favour mainly in the United States, a good deal less elsewhere. But research in Britain, for example, which has begun to throw some valuable light on the cultural differences between classes with which inequalities of educational opportunity are associated, is not entirely free of similar overtones, so long as it stops short of enquiring into the structural conditions by which distinctive patterns of 'subculture' may be explained. Nevertheless the dominant tendency of the right has been to assume that some redistribution is indeed necessary, and can be effected; and in proposing remedies, to concentrate precisely on 'the poor'. Suggestions current for the introduction of 'negative income tax', and new measures of the Conservative Government in Britain, have thus had as a common feature more substantial benefits at the bottom of the economic scale, coupled with encouragement of wider differentials for the rest. The philosophy—explicit in Conservative policy, but implicit already in parts of earlier Labour policy, including the scheme for pensions related to occupational earnings—is one that favours greater scope for market and property forces subject to bedrock provision; less emphasis on general redistribution and immunisation of significant areas of consumption and welfare from the effects of economic inequalities.[29]

29. A valuable critique of notions of a 'culture of poverty' is C. A. Valentine, *Culture and Poverty*, 1968. British studies of class cultural differences relevant to educational opportunity, referred to in the text, include work of, or in direct or indirect association with, B. Bernstein: see, e.g., W. Brandis and D. Henderson, *Social Class*,

The picture sketched earlier requires equally little modification in respect of substantive inequalities other than those relating to income, wealth, and security. Further evidence on social mobility in Britain and the United States has added to, but not altered, the essentials of previous indications. Despite a good deal of individual movement up and down the socio-economic scale, most of it short-distance and more of it than before channelled through educational institutions, the substantial inequalities of opportunity arising from social origin have hardly changed over a number of decades.[30]

Language and Communication, 1970, and D. Lawton, *Social Class, Language and Education*, 1968; cf. also B. Bernstein, 'A Critique of the Concept of "Compensatory Education"', in D. Rubinstein and C. Stoneman, eds., *Education for Democracy*, 1970. With respect to 'anti-poverty' policies, the main spokesman in Britain for increased 'selectivity' in welfare provision, greater general reliance on market mechanisms and some form of 'negative income tax' geared to these objectives has been the Institute of Economic Affairs; among its many publications see, e.g., A. Christopher *et. al.*, *Policy for Poverty*, 1970. An example of American contributions on the right wing of the debate, committed to a version of the 'culture of poverty' thesis and proposing remedies some of which are strongly reminiscent of the British 1834 Poor Law and the philosophy of the Charity Organisation Society, is E. C. Banfield, *The Unheavenly City*, 1970. P. Townsend *et al.*, *Social Services for all*, 1968, is a Fabian symposium including a number of discussions of 'selectivity' versus 'universalism' in welfare provision in Britain, while several recent specific policy proposals are examined in some detail in A. B. Atkinson, op. cit (1969). An interesting recent British discussion of social policy in general is R. A. Pinker, *Social Theory and Social Policy*, 1971.

30. The main recent contribution to research on social mobility is P. M. Blau and O. D. Duncan, *The American Occupational Structure*, 1967. No general study of social mobility in Britain has appeared since D. V. Glass, ed., op. cit. (1956); but as yet unpublished data from a national sample survey mainly concerned with other questions indicate no change in the overall pattern during the 1950s. OECD, Study Group in the Economics of Education, ed., *Social Objectives in Educational Planning*, 1967, includes contributions from a number of countries on socio-economic obstacles to equal educational opportunity. Data are not available to bring trends in this respect in Britain fully up to date; but information for one sector of education, the universities, indicates at most a very marginal shift in patterns of recruitment despite a large increase in the number of university places: U.C.C.A., *Statistical*

Power and its distribution remains as complex and elusive a subject for study as ever. But the component parts of 'post-capitalist' interpretations in this field have worn increasingly thin. There has been no evidence to strengthen the proposition of an emergent non-propertied managerial *élite* directing the private sector of the economy to aims other than long-term profit maximization. The use of public policy in support of private economic enterprise has become clearer and more articulated, not least in connection with counter-inflationary measures. Thus the crystallization of wage restraint in Britain under the Labour Government took as its premise the notion that trade unions have a prime responsibility to act as agents of industrial discipline *vis-à-vis* their members. That premise survives the possibly temporary translation of wage restraint policies into less direct forms under the Conservative Government; and it was among the main considerations which impelled both governments to propose legislation designed either to bring under institutional control, or to destroy, a secondary system of

---

Supplement to 6th Report, 1967/8, 1969. There has, of course, been an enormous literature on inequalities of opportunity, and general patterns of discrimination, relating to 'colour'. Relatively few of the British studies in this field, however, have related approaches and findings to the wider structure of stratification, or made even the point that black skin is just one addition to a series of socio-economic impediments to life chances in a class society. The disproportionate amount of research effort directed to this subject in isolation entails a risk, *inter alia*, of overemphasis in both interpretation and policy on one set of handicaps to individual achievement and 'citizenship' in an unequal society, to the neglect of the structure of inequality itself. Equality of opportunity is a very limited objective, and far less of a threat to the established order, than equality of condition: preoccupation with colour discrimination *per se*, like preoccupation with impediments to general social mobility *per se*, directs attention to the former rather than the latter. Among British studies which have in one way or another related the 'colour situation' to its larger context are, e.g., Ruth Glass, *Newcomers*, 1960, and 'Insiders-outsiders', *Transacts. 5th World Congress of Sociology*, Vol. 3. 1964; P. Foot, *Immigration and Race in British Politics*, 1965; J. Rex and R. Moore, *Race, Community and Conflict*, 1966; and several of the contributions to S. Zubaida, ed., *Race and Racialism*, 1970. A large and useful compendium of the output of the 'race relations' research industry is E. J. B. Rose *et al.*, *Colour and Citizenship*, 1969.

shop-floor bargaining and conflict which has emerged in partial autonomy of the central union hierarchies. Both the conduct of policy by the Labour Government within the limiting assumptions set by a predominantly private enterprise economy, and the incapacity of allegedly powerful unions and shop-floor organization to extract more than at most quite marginal changes in the position of labour, have provided new illustrations of the point that the 'locus of power' cannot be identified without examination of those terms of reference of institutionalized conflict which narrowly delimit areas and outcomes of disputes in advance. Power in such circumstances is more a matter of successfully excluding policy alternatives from consideration than of determining the choice of alternatives among those considered—to adopt the formulation of an American contribution to the debate, more of 'non-decision' making than of decision making. Postulates of a 'pluralistic' diffusion of power derive from a preoccupation with the latter at the expense of the former. They thus neglect that clustering of interests which enters into the initial delimitation of the effective range of conflict. Their political analysis is that of the 'inside dopester', the politician, bargainer or journalist who sees the daily tug of war at close range, but not the larger forces which predetermine what the tug of war is about.[31]

So on all these scores the assumption of a working class turning steadily 'middle class'—always an inference rather than the outcome of solid evidence—has lost plausibility. But with the front door closed to it, it has appeared again by the back door.

31. Two recent British books include useful reviews of evidence and arguments about the so-called 'managerial revolution'; J. Child, *The Business Enterprise in Modern Industrial Society*, 1969, and T. Nichols, *Ownership, Control and Ideology*, 1969. On the emergence of shop-floor bargaining and conflict in British industry, see, e.g., the *Report* of the Royal Commission on Trade Unions and Employers' Associations, 1968, and its *Research Papers* Nos. 1 and 10, 1966 and 1968. Among a number of contributions to the debate about power in the context of stratification, from various 'non-pluralist' perspectives, see, e.g., P. Bachrach and M. S. Baratz, *Power and Poverty*, 1970; G. W. Domhoff, *Who Rules America?*, 1967, and *The Higher Circles*, 1970; R. Miliband, *The State and Capitalist Society*, 1969; F. Parkin, *Class Inequality and Political Order*, 1971. Two restatements of the pluralist approach are R. A. Dahl, *Pluralist Democracy in the United States: Conflict and Consensus*, 1967, and A. M. Rose, *The Power Structure*, 1967.

In Britain, the persistence of marked structural inequalities has revived interest in the question why the contradiction between the promise and achievement of capitalism has failed to generate an effectively sustained radical challenge to the social order. Several recent contributions to the debate have shown a common element in their answers to this question, in application to the situation today and the prospects for tomorrow. That common element is an assertion that, without becoming 'bourgeois', critical sections of the contemporary working class are acquiring an orientation to life which provides no nourishment for collective radicalism. 'Affluence' does not produce identification with the 'middle classes'. But the conditions with which it is associated generate, so it is argued, a preoccupation with domestic matters and individual aspirations; a concern with limited and private achievement; a pragmatic conception of the possibilities of change, incapable of stretching much beyond the here and now. Rising aspirations may produce dissatisfaction; but the response will be fragmented in organization and narrowly circumscribed in objectives. Labour market and work place relations, in particular, will be a source of no more than localized conflict, directed essentially to raising wages. Earnings, current and prospective, are sufficient to deaden other sources of potential tension, and to make consumption and domestic concerns the central 'life interest' for many of today's and more of tomorrow's workers.[32]

As there are common assumptions in the various versions of this thesis, so there are also common weaknesses. The evidence on which these postulates are based is open to quite different,

32. The thesis of working-class 'privatisation', 'instrumentalism' and 'secularism', as outlined here, appears in various forms, and developed from different starting points, especially in J. H. Goldthorpe, D. Lockwood *et al.*, *The Affluent Worker* (3 vols.), 1968–9, R. T. McKenzie and A. Silver, *Angels in Marble*, 1968, and W. G. Runciman, *Relative Deprivation and Social Justice*, 1966. (A paper by F. Parkin, 'Working-Class Conservatives', *Brit. J. Sociology*, Sept. 1967, is also relevant in this context by virtue of its argument, *inter alia*, that changes in patterns of working-class residential settlement may be removing one of the barriers which in the past, according to the author, have helped to protect workers against penetration of the conservative ideology of 'official' society.) I have criticised these interpretations, along the lines summarised in the next paragraph, in 'The rediscovery of the cash nexus', *Socialist Register*, 1970.

and more plausible, interpretation. Class consciousness and class discontent in fact are far from absent in the *Weltanschauung* of the workers on which these studies have focused. There is not a coherent, let alone a revolutionary, ideology. But there is a firmly embedded 'quasi-ideology'; a sense of a shared condition as victims of injustice and exploitation; a critique directed at the social order at large, at wealth and big business, even at the Labour Party and the established trade unions for failing to serve those class interests from which they still derive their mass support. 'Domestic' and 'private' discontents, the tensions in particular which result from the contradiction between rising aspirations and continuing inequalities, do not therefore exist in an ideological vacuum, their common societal sources unrecognized. Nor is it plausible to draw a sharp line of division between home and work as rival centres of 'life interest' and social consciousness. If the wage packet increasingly is the only link that ties the worker to a grudging commitment to his work, to his bosses, and to society at large, that is a brittle strand, liable to wear thin or to snap when the dependability of earnings is threatened or pay rises fail to keep pace with rising demands. Recent work, in fact, has pointed precisely to the exposure and vulnerability of the 'cash nexus', though without either using the term or recognizing its implications. It is hardly an accident that the locus of industrial conflict in Britain has been shifting—outside control of the union hierarchies and the framework of tightly institutionalized bargaining, to the shop floor; from old industries characterized by the parochial solidarity of the 'isolated mass', to new industries of 'affluence'— motor manufacture in particular—where it is likely that the 'cash nexus' is especially exposed, through a conjunction of high monetary expectations on the part of workers with fluctuations of earnings and job security. In these circumstances, in particular, even industrial disputes formally confined to wages and immediaely related questions seem liable to bring wider issues of control, authority, and economic policy recurrently into focus.[33]

Industrial militancy, 'direct action', discontent may remain

33. Among studies of industrial relations and industrial conflict relevant to the last few points are, e.g. H. A. Turner, *et al.*, *Labour Relations in the Motor Industry*, 1967, J. E. T. Eldridge, *Industrial Disputes*, 1968, and T. Lane and K. Roberts, *Strike at Pilkingtons*, 1971.

fragmented. They do not of themselves constitute effective political radicalism. But the persistence of the structural inequalities of capitalism; the contradiction between these and rising expectations that tend to dissolve the former communal contraints of working-class culture, replacing old forms of solidarity by new ones more likely to be inspired by common objectives than by merely communal sentiments; the pressure on the 'cash nexus' as the single strand upon which everyday commitment to the established economic and social order depends—the combination of these carries with it an energy which, while it may continue to be dissipated, may also be released in a coherent and powerful radical impulse. The prospects remain open.

8

The New Capitalism

ROBIN BLACKBURN

Robin Blackburn discusses the thesis that the essential nature of capitalist society has changed. This essay investigates the theories of the managerial revolution and industrial society advanced by such writers as James Burnham, Ralph Dahrendorf and J. K. Galbraith.

Robin Blackburn is an editor of New Left Review *and is currently engaged in writing a book on Cuba.*

The traditional aim of socialist thought has been to become nothing less than the self-awareness of capitalist society. In a society profoundly ignorant of itself, it was the task of socialists to comprehend the principles on which the society worked. By discovering the real nature of capitalism, they were attempting to recapture an economic system that had escaped social control.

Today this intellectual task remains as formidable as ever, because capitalist society is by the law of its own nature in a continual state of restless transformation. The true character of capitalism has to be rediscovered by each new generation. And at this point it is necessary to ask whether capitalism has not changed so much since the classic period that we are now really confronted with an altogether different type of society. It is this possibility that I wish to examine. My conclusion will be that today we confront a radically new *form* of capitalism, but that the most novel features of neo-capitalism, far from mitigating or abolishing the fundamental contradiction of capitalism, rather pose this contradiction *in a purer and more dramatic manner*.

What defines capitalist society is its property system. Though private property has not been abolished in any legal sense, it is frequently argued that the private ownership of the 'means of production' has somehow been drained of real social significance. It is said that modern companies are controlled by professional managers with little reference to the interests of the 'capitalists' who formally own them. It is also claimed that the growth of Government intervention—through the creation of a public sector, welfare services and the introduction of economic planning—reduces still further the traditional importance of private wealth. The first transformation infuses industry with a new sense of social responsibility, the second ensures the supremacy of social justice. The two complementary theories provide an account of the economic structure of society which is comprehensive enough to provide an alternative to the traditional socialist account. The true political economy of the new capitalism may be less comforting than these theories suggest; at least a confrontation with them can enrich socialist theory itself.

The managers' revolution

In Britain, the view that capitalism has been overtaken by a managerial revolution is most systematically expounded in two books by C. A. R. Crosland, *The Future of Socialism* and *The Conservative Enemy*. It also appeared in the Labour Party document *Industry and Society* and in John Strachey's *Contemporary Capitalism*.[1] In the United States a variant of the managerialist thesis has recently been developed by J. K. Galbraith in his book *The New Industrial State*. The major point of reference for the prophets of the managerial revolution is the classic capitalism of the nineteenth century—and it is usually Marx's account of this classic model they invoke and contrast to their own analysis of the contemporary reality. In this classic

1. In most respects Strachey's book is more interesting than either of Crosland's works, but it does not provide such a good account of the managerial revolution. The most celebrated presentation of the theory is, of course, James Burnham's *Managerial Revolution*. Ralph Dahrendorf has restated the argument competently in his *Class and Class Conflict in Industrial Society*, relieving it of the wilder prognostications of Burnham. One can search in vain for any mention of the managerial revolution in most textbooks on management. Cf., for example, M. E. Stern: *Mathematics for Management*, 1963, but also E. S. Mason, 'The Apologetics of Managerialism', *Journal of Business*, January 1958.

epoch, the entrepreneur united in his person the functions of manager and owner. What has occurred since that date is what is called a 'decomposition of capital' with a consequent separation of ownership and control. Nowadays most large companies have a great many nominal owners—12,000 in the typical large British company. The theorists of the managerial revolution argue that it is impossible for all these owners to exercise any real control over the company they own. They are, in fact, forced to delegate this power to the paid managers of the company. These managers may have only a minimal shareholding in the company, or at any rate, a shareholding which only represents a tiny fraction of the total. These changes are reinforced by the increasing technical complexity of management which delivers still further power into the hands of the managers. Naturally, these changes in control lead, so the argument runs, to changes in company policy. According to optimistic variants of the theory there is an increasing emphasis upon the welfare of the company employees and a growing indifference to high dividends. The interest of the manager lies in harmonious work relations and in the long-term growth of the company, not in dividend maximization. Crosland summarizes his own version of the argument thus:

> Because ... the new managers do not have the same relation to private property as the old owners (though also for other reasons), there are significant differences in the nature of the profit goal and the degree of responsibility with which economic power is exercised. These differences constitute one feature of present-day, as opposed to capitalist, society.[2]

The reasoning behind these assertions can be shown to be fundamentally deficient in describing the character of *any* modern capitalist society, and even a corrected schema cannot be applied without further modification to the specifically British variant of modern capitalism. These deficiencies can be considered under the following three headings.

A. THE SOCIAL UNITY OF MANAGERS AND OWNERS

The sociological critique of the managerial revolution thesis is now fairly well established. In *The Power Elite*, for example,

2. *The Conservative Enemy*, p. 24.

Wright Mills showed that in the United States top managers could be closely identified with large shareholders. Ralph Miliband in *The State in Capitalist Society*, has recently developed and extended this critique on the basis of recent research into the relation between the economic elite and the dominant class in all the major advanced capitalist countries. One fact which all such research encounters is that those who actually direct and manage the modern capitalist enterprise are usually important shareholders in their own right even if they have much less than a controlling proportion of the shares in the company. Thus the most recent investigation of executive shareholding in the United States, based on a sample of over 180 corporations taken from the *Fortune* list of the 500 largest industrial concerns, concluded that 'The average expected dividends and capital gains from stockholdings earned by the chief executive officers in our sample amounted to $64,519 per year.'[3] An article in *Fortune* accompanying their list of the 500 largest industrial corporations for 1967 pointed out that: 'In approximately 150 companies in the current *Fortune* list, controlling ownership rests in the hands of an individual or of the members of a single family.' The author states that in arriving at this conclusion he used the 'conservative' criterion of 10 per cent stock ownership to decide when an individual or family was in a controlling position. He further insisted '... it is unrealistic to assume that because a manager holds only a small fraction of the company stock he lacks the incentive to drive up its profits. Chairman Frederick C. Donner, for example, holds only 0.017 per cent of G M U's outstanding stock, but it was worth about $3,917,000 recently.'[4] In Britain a survey of share-owning by the Oxford Institute of Statistics found that directors of companies held shares to an average of £28,000.[5] This was the *largest average holding* of all the groups about which information was available; the next largest group was that of titled persons with an average holding of worth nearly £14,000. Those directors or managers who have no important share holding are still likely to be tied to their owners by their social aspirations and values, by a respect for the institutions of

3. Robert J. Larner, *Management Control and the Large Corporation*, New York, 1970, p. 66.

4. R. Sheehan, 'Proprietors in the World of Big Business', *Fortune*, June 1967.

5. *Bulletin of the Oxford Institute of Statistics*, November 1955.

property and by a common social background.[6] However, as we shall see, capitalism has surer guarantees of managerial behaviour than these ideological bonds would in themselves provide.

B. ECONOMIC LOGIC OF THE MARKET

Marx himself never considered that the capitalist entrepreneur, in any real sense, *controlled* the economy as a whole, nor that any individual capitalist controlled, except in a very secondary sense, even his own enterprise. 'Capitalism subjects every individual capitalist to the immanent laws of capitalist production as external coercive laws. Competition forces him continually to extend his capital for the sake of maintaining it . . .'[7] In their daily actions men in a capitalist society produce and reproduce a certain type of economy; but this economy, which conditions the actions of the capitalist as well as of the worker, is not subject to *their command*.

Marx emphasised the *anarchy* of capitalist production. 'Anarchy' was used in a double sense. Firstly, it referred to the fact that the ultimate goal of capitalism as a system was the accumulation of capital and the making of profit, whereas the only goal of the socialist economy would be the satisfaction of human needs. Secondly, it referred to the fact that the actual mechanisms of the capitalist economy—the market system—were not subordinated to human control. This compounded anarchy afflicted the traditional capitalist economy with endemic imbalance—in particular, with the wild cycle of boom and slump. At the level of the enterprise the autonomy left to the entrepreneur was the ability to interpret, more or less successfully, the dictates of the market and to exploit, more or less successfully, the labour power he purchased. Thus, the workings of the law of value ensured that his enterprise could

6. A Young Fabian pamphlet reported that 64 per cent of the executives of the one hundred largest British companies went to Public Schools, and that 'at the growing points of power, in the large industrial firms, the influence of the Public Schools has been growing'. (H. Glennerster and R. Pryke, *The Public Schools*). This conclusion is supported by a study in *The Director*, January 1965, where it is revealed that over 75 per cent of directors in the age group 25–35 were at Public Schools compared with an overall average of 60 per cent.

7. Cf. *Capital*, Vol. I, Chap. 24, Section 3.

only survive if it corresponded to some demand effective within the market.[8] Moreover, he was constrained to supply that demand in a manner which yielded him a return on his capital that did not fall too far below the average. If he made a loss, he might find himself in the bankrupt's court or, at best, his capital would begin to dwindle and he would gradually cease to be a capitalist.

If this analysis was correct, then the 'control' of modern capitalist economies will only be different to the extent that the working of the law of value through the capitalist market has been modified. The market has been and is being modified considerably (some of the implications of this will be explored later), but the 'managerial revolution' is not an important modification of the market mechanism, if indeed it modifies it at all. Even at the enterprise level the initiative in the hands of the manager is to subordinate, with greater or less efficiency, his company to the changed market situation. That the modern manager 'controls' any more than the traditional entrepreneur is in this sense quite mistaken. The sanction of the take-over raid becomes under the new conditions a powerful deterrent to company policy not directed towards market demands. Sargent Florence writes:

> For a grasp of its movement and working as well as its structure, the capitalist free enterprise system may be pictured as a number of unit firms, great and small, floating or tossing in a 'sea of troubles'. Outside these firms there is the anarchy of the market. Though firms and industries are linked and inter-dependent—the input of one, the output of another—yet there is no authority set over them. Instead, there is competition (however imperfect), trade fluctuations, uncertain supplies and uncertain demands for which firms must produce in advance, investing in specialized capital still more in advance.... Apart from some peripheral control by the State and some auxiliary institutions and services, the main co-ordinating factor in this anarchy is through the price-mechanism.[9]

8. This *effective* demand reflects the existing distribution of wealth and income.

9. Sargent Florence, *Economics and Sociology of Industry*, pp. 119–20.

Improved methods of interpreting the market only make the manager's subordination to it more complete.

Crosland claimed, however, that the ultimate goals of profit-making and capital accumulation had been modified by increased social responsibility in those companies where ownership and control are most clearly separated. The only admissible evidence on this point would be observed differences in managerial behaviour. Too often the champions of the managerial revolution indulge in artibrary speculation about the *personal* motives of managers. The motives behind the decision of a manager may well be very complex and seemingly removed from economic calculations : he may desire to impress his wife or secretary, to further a personal vendetta, etc. But finally all these aims, by a sort of reduction of quality to quantity, will have to be mediated by the market; managerial decisions will have to be vindicated in market terms, as failure within the market will frustrate almost every kind of personal ambition and, indeed, threaten to deprive the manager of his managerial functions.

Moreover, it is by no means clear that the motives of the modern manager are so different from those of his predecessor. It is frequently claimed that the modern manager is growth-orientated : but was the idea of growth for its own sake, of capital accumulation instead of profit consumption, really so foreign to the nineteenth-century captain of industry? Marx himself certainly did not think so : 'Accumulate! Accumulate! That is Moses and all the prophets,' he wrote, explaining this capitalist commandment as follows :

> Fanatically bent upon the expansion of value, he (the capitalist) relentlessly drives human beings to production for production's sake, thus bringing about a development of social productivity and the creation of those material conditions of production which can alone form the real basis of a higher type of society, whose fundamental principle is the full and free development of every individual. . . . that which in the miser assumes the aspect of mania, is in the capitalist the effect of the social mechanism in which he is only a driving-wheel.[10]

Indeed, it is likely that in many cases the modern manager

10. Cf. *Capital*, Vol. I, Chap. 24, Section 3.

can *less* afford to ignore the need for profit distribution than the capitalist who manages his own firm. All studies agree that the manager of the modern company must allow for a certain minimum dividend even during the most inappropriate periods. By contrast such companies as Beaverbrook Limited, which was owner-managed, went for decades without any increase in dividends despite booming profits.

Turning to observable differences in behaviour between professionally managed and owner-managed firms, the two criteria most often cited by advocates of the managerial revolution are the extent of dividend distribution and the degree of concern shown for the welfare of the worker and the community. Where company paternalism is concerned, however, this can certainly not be claimed as an invention of those companies where ownership is divorced from management. To this day, the most striking examples of company concern for employee 'welfare' occur in the owner-managed concerns (in Britain, the chocolate companies; in Italy, Olivetti; in Japan, Matsushita). It is true that company paternalism is now more generally prevalent than before, but this is due to factors other than the simple rise of professionally-managed industry : for example, to the pressure of the trade unions and the greatly increased productivity of modern industry. Above all, the manager of both type of company today faces a shortage of skilled workers at a time when they are increasingly vital to the productive process. A multiplicity of fringe benefits and welfare schemes can become a market necessity, a device for tying the skilled worker to a particular factory. If, as is sometimes the case, company paternalism is too prodigal for its market situation, then the company will be weakened as a result. The recent takeover of an Olivetti division is a case in point.

As for dividend policy, the significance of the differences between owner-managed and professionally-managed firms is equally often misinterpreted. It is argued, for instance, that the tendency for manager-run companies to plough back profits and give smaller dividends is a visible mark of concern for growth. But the long-run operation of the market will ensure that if the manager does not distribute much of the profit to the shareholders then the rise in the value of the company brought about by re-investment of profits in the company will result in a rise of share values. These capital gains can be converted for the individual into (untaxed) current income. During certain periods this has been an attractive option given the prevailing tax structure. Some idea of how attractive this can be, is suggested by the fact that the average director's share-holding, worth £28,000 when the Oxford Institute survey was carried out over ten years ago, *would now be worth about £60,000 even if he has purchased no additional shares*.[11] The owner-managed company is less in a position to take advantage of escalation in share values—if share gains are realized to any extent (by selling company shares) then the owner-managers will gradually cease to be the dominant owners.[12] In other words, in a capitalist economy, growth can never be opposed as a goal to capital accumulation and profit-making.[13] On the one hand, growth will produce profits and more capital; on the other, the resources for expansion will tend to come from private or institutional capital which demands satisfactory returns.

If there is a difference between the logic of professionally-managed and owner-managed companies, it is that the former more exactly reflects the rationality of the market. The manager has less freedom to make decisions which answer to a purely personal whim or obsession. As professionally-managed companies come to dominate industry and commerce, artificial rigidities, preventing the free flow of capital in response to market pressures, disappear. Even where the new managers re-invest a very high proportion of the companies' profits, they must always estimate the 'opportunity cost' of such investments: that is, they must ensure that their return on capital compares satisfactorily with the return typical of the rest of

11. In *Contemporary Capitalism*, John Strachey says of the director that his 'motive is the acquisition of prestige and power rather than wealth', as if such goals were exclusive. The truth is that the achievement of a wide range of goals, including those of an altruistic nature, has to be mediated through success in capital accumulation.

12. To circumvent this, non-voting shares are sometimes issued, but they will only be bought if there is some prospect of good dividends.

13. Because growth is almost synonymous with capital accumulation, if one constructs a model of the firm 'growth-oriented and profit-oriented firms would respond in qualitatively similar ways to such stimuli as changes in factor price, discount rate, and excise and profit taxes.' Robert M. Solous in *The Corporate Economy*, ed. R. Marris and A. Wood, 1971, p. 341.

the economy. Growing expertise in management has thus had one consequence that might disconcert the proponents of the managerial revolution:

> The spread of budgeting in the business world has helped to re-establish and clarify the importance of the profit objective. A recent survey of more than four hundred companies established that more than 95 per cent of these engage in comprehensive planning for defined short-run profit objectives, and that of these about nine-tenths specify the objective concretely, in writing.[14]

The responsible modern manager will probably aim at a 'fair' profit rather than a short-term maximization, but in doing this he will neither be ignoring the pressures of the market nor be acting so differently from his nineteenth-century predecessors. Dividends cannot be too low or it will be difficult to attract share-buyers in future, and the 'responsible' manager will, presumably, wish to see a wide safety margin between his company and the take-over raid or the bankruptcy court. If he judges wrongly then these two regulators will ensure that resources are not deployed inefficiently in market terms. Of course, in some societies rather low profit levels can come to be tolerated in the name of caution, comfort and safety—this may often be the case in Britain today. But again the position of the manager is not necessarily relevant to this phenomenon—indeed one rather suspects that it would be precisely the ambience of the owner-managed family business that encourages such attitudes.

But within the international economy it is impossible to evade the operation of the market. Relative decline is the price of too much caution, tradition or comfort. In the decade of the fifties, the rate of profit in British industry fell by about one quarter; J. R. Sargent[15] has persuasively argued that this fact is directly related to technical stagnation and the decline of Britain's international industrial and trading position.

Many proponents of the managerialist thesis maintain that

14. Neil W. Chamberlain, *The Firm: Micro-economic Planning and Action*, 1962.

15. *Out of Stagnation*, Fabian Society, 1963. A fall in the rate of profit on capital does not mean that the *volume* of profits has declined—in fact it increased.

the large size of the modern corporation renders it virtually invulnerable to bankruptcy or take-over. The bankruptcy of Rolls-Royce in 1971, the travail of Penn Central or such routine events as the Greyhound Corporation's take-over of Armour in 1970, show that enterprises of very considerable size are by no means immune to these sanctions. Between 1964 and 1969 there were no fewer than 855 acquisitions of manufacturing or mining firms with assets of over $10 million in the United States.[16] Henry G. Manne has argued that such takeovers and the resulting 'market' for corporate control affords 'strong protection to the interests of vast numbers of small, non-controlling shareholders'.[17] Without fully accepting this picture of shareholder 'democracy' it is at least evident enough that competition among managers provides the owners with a real element of leverage over them. Although a typical large corporation today supplies about one half of the funds it needs for investment this by no means frees it from financial restraints or the fear of takeover. If it is to grow and compete satisfactorily that other half of its funds which it raises externally will be vital to it. If it raises a bank loan rather than issuing new shares this will in no way allow it to escape the necessary financial scrutiny. The lack of self-sufficiency of the modern corporation is evident enough from the fact of widespread interlocking directorships between financial and other industrial and commercial enterprises.[18] The existence of banking directors on the boards of industrial and commercial companies does not signal a return to the days of classical finance capital but it does demonstrate their dependence on proper financial criteria when issuing shares or raising credit.[19]

16. John Richard Felton, 'Conglomerate Mergers, Concentration and Competition', *American Journal of Economics and Sociology*, July, 1971.

17. Henry G. Manne, 'Mergers and the Market for Corporate Control', *Journal of Political Economy*, April, 1965.

18. The significance of interlocks between financial and non-financial corporations in the United States is examined by Paul Sweezy, 'Who Rules the Corporations?', *Monthly Review*, December, 1971.

19. Evidence on the growing indebtedness of US industrial corporations to the banks is supplied in Carol J. Loomis, 'The Lesson of the Credit Crisis', *Fortune*, 1971. The great extent of interlocking directorships between financial and non-financial corporations in the United States was revealed by the US House of Representatives,

To deny that a managerial revolution has occurred is not to refuse all significance to the facts on which the theory was based. One of the more significant changes which have occurred in the train of the so-called managerial revolution is a change in the forms of property income. What appears in one perspective as a 'decomposition' of capital appears in another as a more effective means for its accumulation. The retention and re-investment of profits by the modern company continually increase the value of its shares—and as capital gains they are untaxed or only lightly taxed. For this reason, as Professor Meade has pointed out:

> In the United Kingdom, there is a special reason why the figures of personal incomes derived from the Income Tax returns will seriously underestimate personal incomes from property. They exclude capital gains. But the increase in the value of companies' shares which is due to the accumulation of undistributed profits represents in effect a personal income of the shareholders which has been saved for them by the companies themselves.[20]

The question of the evidence for or against the managerialist thesis has always been a vexed one. From the beginning the managerialists have felt secure in the belief that all research pointed in the direction of a substantive separation of 'ownership' and 'control'. The simple fact that corporation executives were not the same people as the majority of controlling shareholders was solidly established by Adolf Berle and G. C. Means in 1934 in their work *The Modern Corporation and Private Property*. But as the discussion so far has sought to show, it is the interpretation of these facts which is in question, rather than the facts themselves. Indeed there is now a whole new body of evidence which quite undermines the theory of a managerial revolution and which tends to support the types of argument against it which I have outlined above. Thus a systematic comparison between owner-managed and professionally-managed

Report on Commercial Banks and their Trust Activities (the Patman Report).

20. J. E. Meade, *Efficiency, Equality and the Ownership of Property*. The disguised distribution of profits occurs not only as a consequence of capital gains but also through the distributing of extra shares in lieu of dividends (bonus issues, etc.). Cf. R. M. Titmuss, *Income Distribution and Social Change*, 1962.

corporations has been conducted by Robert J. Larner to discover what concrete differences in managerial behaviour can be observed between them. Basing his research on the *Fortune* list of the largest 500 non-financial corporations for 1963 he concludes:

> While the evidence indicates that control by management was the typical form of corporate control among the five hundred largest non-financial corporations of 1963, some of the behavioural consequences often associated with separation of ownership and control do not seem to have materialised. No fundamental differences in the level or stability of profit rates which might be attributed to management control were found.[21]

The explanation Larner offers for this throws light both on the arguments I have advanced above and on the managerialist speculations about the motives of managers:

> ... the system of financial incentives and rewards in large corporations makes executive compensation and income profit dependent, and thus effectively links the pecuniary interest of managers to the pecuniary interest of stockholders. There is indirect evidence in this study ... which indicates that executive remuneration and compensation are not closely related to the firm's growth, although, executive income, particularly the capital gains component, does have some positive relation to growth. Moreover, if the opportunity for capital gains was the principal financial incentive to maximise growth, then it seems that the owners, who by definition have larger stockholdings and therefore an even greater opportunity for capital gains, would have a stronger incentive to increase the rate of growth than managers.[22]

Larner gives some idea of the sort of managerial incentives involved when he reports that: '... of the firms in the sample which had bonus or incentive plans as part of their compensation of managers, every plan provided that the total bonus to be distributed among key executive personnel was to be based solely on the firm's earnings above some specified rate of profit.'[23]

21. *Management Control and the Large Corporation*, New York, 1970, p. 63.
22. Ibid., p. 64.
23. Ibid., p. 66.

Evidence from British business points in the same direction as Larner's investigation. Thus a study of the objectives of 25 large British companies based on replies to a searching questionnaire produced the following conclusion : 'None of the companies had any doubts that their primary objective was to be efficient and profitable and that being socially responsible would serve no useful purpose if it hindered these overall company goals.'[24]

A study of a sample of corporations in the North of England conducted by Theo Nichols arrives at the following judgment of the ownership control issue :

> We do not doubt that they (managers) have certain immediate economic interests which are in conflict with the maximization of shareholders' welfare. We do think, however, that in the long run moral, economic and legal considerations (and an as yet unascertainable mixture of all three) make it probable that they will satisfy shareholder expectations. There seems little reason to consider them, or the economic system they govern, as the manifestation of a 'post-capitalist' society.[25]

Critics of those who uphold the managerialist thesis have often complained that the managerialists have furnished precious little hard evidence that the professional manager acts in a significantly different way with respect to profit maximization than the owner-manager. Galbraith's *The New Industrial State* is particularly deficient in the substantiating material his argument requires. The evidence adduced by Larner, Shenfield and Nichols requires that the managerialists not only furnish some documentation for their own case but that they confront the now massive accumulation of research which undermines their whole approach to the question. Unless and until they do this convincingly the proponents of the managerial revolution theory will be the flat-earthers of economics and sociology.

C. THE DECOMPOSITION OF MANAGEMENT

Finally, the technical dimension of contemporary management must be considered. One of the claims of the managerial revolution is that the technical complexity of modern management is

24. Barbara Shenfield, *Company Boards*, London, 1971, p. 164.
25. Theo Nichols, *Ownership, Control and Ideology*, London, 1969, p. 153.

a major factor conferring autonomy on the managers who are professionally trained in skills that lay owners cannot hope to acquire. The truth today is that the whole trend of modern technology is tending to undermine the omnicompetence of the top manager. The 'decomposition of capital' is being followed by a 'decomposition' of the managerial function. Hardly had the manager been hailed as the executor of a successful revolution than, as a pure type, he began to disappear. For in modern industry, whole departments of specialists are entrusted with one or other managerial function (marketing, operations research, investment allocation, process control, etc.).

For Galbraith these different teams of specialists all belong to an entity known as the 'technostructure' which now exercises the power which formerly lay in the hands of the owners. Even top management is basically dependent on the expertise and advice of the technostructure: all it can do is choose between the narrow range of options which these experts produce. Galbraith is in fact still in pursuit of that elusive subject of the economic process which will explain all its inner workings. He rejects the concept of consumer sovereignty but only to embrace that of producer sovereignty. Examining the real workings of the capitalist economic system is much more arduous than simply attributing its major features to the passions or persuasions of some new elite.

If the decomposition of the managerial function is scrutinised then it soon becomes apparent that it is the very specialisation of the expert that constitutes the real limit on his power. The sphere of competence of the specialist is very strictly defined by his own particular skill. Rewards and sanctions descend downwards in a hierarchical manner inhibiting the development of group solidarity among those on the same level. We have seen that top management is constrained by the context of capitalist competition to maximise profits and to accumulate capital. The performance of each department can be evaluated in terms of its contribution to these overall goals. Increasingly sophisticated procedures in cost accounting enable top management to develop criteria for subordinating every aspect of company operations to financial control. The head office of a large corporation will employ an armoury of checking devices to ensure that its constituent divisions and departments contribute fully to the profit potential of the resources the corporation commands. Often competition between different divisions of the same corporation or the possibility of contracting out functions performed inside the corporation serve as a lever exercised by the head office over its outlying parts. Only in a company with most incompetent management will really important decisions about investment policy, product range, output, price, size of labour force, etc., escape proper central audit. The financial department will, of course, tend to have a decisive say in nearly all questions. However, the power residing with the financial expert is one which he derives from the context of the capitalist market itself and must exercise on behalf of the ultimate owners of the corporation.

The rise of the conglomerate corporation in the sixties showed how the problems of the 'pure' accumulation of capital had outgrown the boundaries of company organization based on a particular plant or even branch of industry. Nobody who charted the rise of the multi-product conglomerate and its subsequent vicissitudes could imagine that top management or the so-called 'technostructure' could stand in the way of capital's thirst for profit. The opening or closing of a plant, the hiring and firing of technicians of every type, must reflect finely calculated profit expectations. Any manager who ignores this imperils his own personal position and exposes his company to the competition of its rivals or to the predatory activities of the take-over expert.

It is the essence of capitalist organization that the 'dead' stored up labour of the past represented by capital dominates the living labour that propels the accumulation process forward. It is the company's task to organise as efficiently as possible the labour time that it has purchased. If each plant is to earn an adequate return on capital then the labour employed by it must be exploited as efficiently as possible. It is the task of management to so organize its plant that the value of what the workers produce exceeds by as much as possible the sum laid out in buying labour time and other factors of production. It is clear that this aim can only be achieved by maintaining an authoritarian structure within the factory, and throughout the company, which prevents either workers or technicians from controlling the productive organism of which they are the motor force. The labour of the worker or technician is purchased from him on an individual basis yet its power to create value resides in its collective, co-operative character. Capital reaps the reward of profit only because it insists on controlling and organising the fruits of organised, co-operative labour. As Marx puts it:

> 'Being independent of each other, the labourers are isolated persons, who enter into relations with the capitalist but not with one another. This co-operation begins only with the labour-process, but they have then ceased to belong to themselves. On entering that process they become incorporated with capital. As co-operators, as members of a working organism, they are but special modes of existence of capital. Hence the productive power developed by the labourer when working in co-operation, is the productive power of capital.
>
> The work of directing, superintending and adjusting becomes one of the functions of capital, from the moment that the labour under the control of capital, becomes co-operative .... The directing motive, the end and aim of capitalist production, is to extract the greatest possible amount of surplus value.'[26]

To imagine that the personnel manager, production manager or supervisor has any choice other than to extract surplus value as efficiently as possible from his labour force is quite absurd. That is to say that they seek to raise the value of what the worker produces as much as possible above the cost of hiring him. While the production managers are concerned with extracting profitable labour from the work-force, the marketing and sales managers are concerned with realising these profits by actually selling the goods the workers have produced. Harmonizing these different functions and bringing them into line with the financial criteria of an average or above average rate of return on capital is the job of top management. Within each of these functions there will be some room for the initiative of the particular managerial skill involved. But none of these agents of capitalist rationality are sovereigns of the economic process. In a more or less limited period of time they must all account for their actions in the only terms which count in the capitalist context: a good rate of return on capital.

Neo-capitalism and class struggle

The essential feature of neo-capitalism is not so much a modification of the internal structure of companies as a modification

26. *Capital*, Vol. 1, pp. 331, 333. I have discussed the mechanism of exploitation in *The Incompatibles*, R. Blackburn and A. Cockburn (eds), pp. 36–51.

of the national economic framework as a whole. In Britain the first really important intervention by the State in the national economy was produced by the exigencies of war production during the First World War. But State intervention only became generalized with the use of Keynesian techniques of regulating aggregate demand. This in itself was worth any number of managerial revolutions in its impact on the workings of a capitalist economy. This is hardly the place to explore the historical reasons for the introduction of Keynesian techniques into modern capitalism. This would require a separate study in itself. But it should be noted that the conventional view, that it was democratic pressure from a reformist labour movement which primarily induced the change, is far too simple. In effect, the explanation of why any given capitalist country adopted Keynesian techniques only acquires a true perspective when the *general history* of capitalism is considered. Such a general history is a necessary and much neglected dimension of analysis which should complement those so far discussed (the pure model and the particular instance). Thus it is possible to consider Fascism as a particular type of capitalist society—an 'ideal' model of this sort would be defined in terms of a particular political order and a given relation between classes, etc. On the other hand, an explanation of, say, German Fascism would have to provide a conjunctural sociology and history of Germany of the period before 1933. But in addition to this, although Fascism should certainly not be examined as if it were a stage through which all capitalist societies pass, it is useful to consider, for example, Nazism as an episode in the general history of capitalism. For one key consequence of this episode was the introduction of Keynesian techniques into the capitalist economies. Hitler, himself, was the first politician to successfully employ public expenditure as a means of generating full employment in the wake of the great depression.

Later it was the war against Hitler which brought full employment to the other capitalist countries. In 1938 there was more unemployment in the United States than there had been in 1933. The war succeeded where Roosevelt had failed in making Keynesian methods acceptable to American capitalism. Ever since, permanent preparations for war have played something like the same role. Even the placid social democratic experiment in neutral Sweden was under-pinned economically by Hitler's rearmament and war purchases. It is a comment on the fundamental irrationality of capitalism that the introduction of techniques for avoiding slumps owe more to the demented ambitions of Hitler than to the attempted reforms of Roosevelt. In our own day new advances in the structure of capitalism, in particular the introduction of indicative planning, were achieved under the mystical and nationalist banner of de Gaulle and not by the 'modernising' and 'reforming' régimes of Kennedy or Wilson. The significance of these must now be explored.

In the typical neo-capitalist economy, the ultimate goals of capitalism are not changed, but increasingly rational methods are employed to attain these goals—the accumulation of capital and the making of profits. Of course, the ultimate irrationality of these goals continually and endemically contaminates the 'rational' means being used to pursue them. The cycle of boom and slump is checked but other imbalances continually manifest themselves. In the last American recession, unemployment increased to over seven million; the loss of production even in boom years runs to many millions of dollars with some four million workers remaining permanently unemployed. Meanwhile, within the capitalist world as a whole, vast populations in the underdeveloped countries are pauperized by the anarchic movements of world commodity prices. Within nearly every advanced capitalist country itself, heavily populated regions are mysteriously condemned to stagnation and decay (N.E. England, Northern Ireland, Scotland, Massif Central, Southern Italy, Wallonia, Kentucky, etc.). Whole industrial sectors in each country are neglected or retarded and a persistent imbalance between public and private goods manifests itself. The relation of the capitalist economy to the natural environment is predominantly one of wasteful plunder in the pursuit of private profit: rivers are polluted, dust bowls are created, the air is contaminated and precious resources are squandered. The cluttered sprawl of most capitalist cities is a vivid testimony to the absence of any ultimate control over the workings of the system. But, despite all this, rationality of a kind is being, and has been, introduced. But a certain increase in the intelligibility of the capitalist system has been introduced at the same time.

It has been a main contention of Marxist writing that a socialist society would be distinctive above all in its *transparency*. Bourgeois society is essentially opaque. The movements of the economy remain obscure and unsuspected by even the most expert. In a socialist society men would restore to themselves that control over the society they create which capital has confiscated from them. A certain premonition of the transparency of socialist society seems to haunt neo-capitalism. It does this by giving added lucidity to the workings of the economy. Above all, it increases *the visibility of exploitation* produced by capitalist social relations.

Keynesian theory offers no solutions to the problems of growth and inflation; indicative planning and incomes policies are the new devices intended to meet these problems. In practice, neo-capitalist planning has mainly consisted in the exchange of information between the State and the big private companies and the harmonization of their plans.[27] The general effect is to enhance the instrumental 'rationality' of the process of capital accumulation.

The most critical field of State intervention in the advanced capitalist economy is that of incomes policies. The attempt to regulate the overall levels of profits and wages is potentially the most explosive development of all those which constitute the new form of capitalism. Marxists have often suggested that the real relations of production were in many ways much less visible in capitalist society than they had been in pre-capitalist societies. The serf could not fail to know that he actually gave a part of his labour time or his crop to his fuedal lord, whatever notions he might have held to justify this. By contrast, in the classic capitalist society the very anarchy and alienation of the productive process obscured the worker's vision of his relation to the capitalist—he knew that he was *bossed* but not necessarily that he was *exploited*. Joan Robinson has called the equations that express Marx's labour theory of value the most demagogic in all economic theory. But demagogic though they may be to the economist, to the layman they were abstract and complex. Rises in the *absolute* level of wages have obscured the remarkable fact that the relative shares of profits and wages have displayed a 'historical constancy' since the end of the nineteenth century (though periods of depression necessarily involve low profits).[28] The factor income of capital has usually

27. Cf. E. Mandel, 'Economics of Neo-Capitalism', *Socialist Register*, 1964.

28. N. Kaldor, *The Theory of Capital*, edited by F. Lutz and D. Hague, 1961. In 1938, the ratio of gross profits to all employment incomes (including directors' salaries) was 1 to 4.5, in 1952 it was again 1 to 4.5, in 1962 it was 1 to 4.8 (Cf. *Annual Abstract of Statis-*

withstood the assaults of organized labour.[29] It is this which suggests that the effectiveness of the labour movement as a 'countervailing power' is severely limited. Comparing different countries it can be seen that wage increases and the provision of welfare services are not uniquely correlated with the strength of the labour movement. Some notable forms of welfare provision have been created under the political influence of the labour movement (the health service in Britain, insurance and holidays in France, pensions in Sweden). But on the other hand certain spectacular recent increases in wages have occurred in countries where organized labour is comparatively weak (e.g. Japan). Capitalism contains an armoury of measures to combat labour's attempt to reduce the rate of exploitation: speed-up,

---

tics, 1956 and 1963). Of course there are other important forms of property income in addition to gross profits—namely rent and interest. The proportion of wages in the national income has fluctuated around 42 per cent. In 1948–51, it reached 43.4 per cent while by 1960–62 it was 42.0 per cent. However this decrease more or less corresponds to the decline of the working class as a proportion of the total population. In the late sixties the share of profits in the national income did decline significantly. The fall in profit levels must be mainly attributed to the generally depressed condition of British capitalism—to the extent it recovers so will profit levels.

29. The work of P. Sraffa suggests that in some ways wages may be no more than a partially predetermined variable in a capitalist economy (*Production of Commodities by Means of Commodities*, 1960; cf. also C. Napoleoni and F. Rodano in *Revista Trimestriale*, Nos. 1–4). If this is the case, it explains the need for an incomes policy. In guaranteeing a certain proportion of the national income to profit the capitalist system does not guarantee either the optimum amount of profit or the most satisfactory composition of that profit. Traditional trade union action may be unable to secure a sizeable increase in the return to labour; but its defensive struggles for money wages trigger off counter-tendencies (inflation, etc.) which disturb the balance between different types of capital and also adversely place a given capitalist nation *vis-à-vis* its competitors. 'The 'circularity' of the capitalist economy thwarts even the most resolute attempts to change it. For example, it is very difficult to prevent a 'corporation tax' being to some extent passed on to the consumer in higher prices. Similarly an increase in the so-called 'employers' contribution' to national insurance is rapidly absorbed as part of labour costs (see G. L. Reid and D. J. Robertson, *Fringe Benefits, Labour Costs and Social Security*, 1965).

'productivity deals', intensification of labour, inflation, tax increases, welfare cuts, etc. But if these measures have to be supplemented by an incomes policy the capitalist state will usually be driven to challenge the rights of organized labour.

In its classic phase the contrast between the income of labour and capital at a national level was much less tangible than the absolute increases in wages. Indeed, to this day, many union leaders appear to be under the impression that the relative position of wages and profits has somehow been fundamentally transformed. Classic capitalist society did, it is true, replace the particular and purely local confrontation of each feudal lord and his serfs by a social conflict involving a working class that was conscious of its national and even international identity. But although profits also had a universal existence, they did not have this in any way which was immediately perceivable by the popular consciousness. Instead of profits being apprehended as a global entity opposed to wages, there was a tendency only to denounce the fairly isolated cases of flagrant 'profiteering'. *The introduction of attempts to coordinate incomes unintentionally makes possible a return to something like the pre-capitalist visibility of exploitation but in a more universal context.*

In the 1960s nearly every European capitalist government sought to introduce some form of wages or incomes policy. This seemed the only way to contain inflation and prevent declining price competitiveness in international markets. Even though these attempts to control wages did not necessarily lead to a slower rate of increase of wage rates they were to be followed by increasingly militant economic class struggle. The strike statistics for these countries follow a rising curve after the mid-sixties reaching a peak in France in 1968, in Italy in 1969 and in Britain in 1970. There is, of course, no automatic connection between the attempt to introduce an incomes policy and a subsequent rise in the level of economic class struggle. The national level of wages and profits was regulated throughout the post-war period in Sweden without any such consequence. But Sweden at this time occupied a very strong position on the world market since its industries had not been destroyed by the war. Moreover a Social Democratic government was able to exploit this position to the advantage of the workers and ensure their loyalty to the capitalist system. In the more intense competitive climate of the sixties the scope for social democratic reformism was greatly reduced. In Britain even the close relationship between the Labour Party and the trade unions failed to produce a successful integration of the workers into the government's incomes policy. In France where the *'politique des revenues'* was implemented by an authoritarian government of the right the proletarian response was to prove historic. Though there were certainly many other reasons for the conflagration of May 1968, De Gaulle's attempt to control general wage levels was certainly a contributory factor. In the conditions prevailing in the capitalist world by the late sixties, few governments could avoid for very long some attempt to control wages: the Nixon measures of August 1971 are most significant in this respect since they came from a President who can have had no ideological prejudice in favour of capitalist planning.

In the long run, the confrontation between trade unions and the capitalist state which any attempt to control or plan incomes must involve can only bring into question the nature of capitalist social relations and the workings of capitalist political institutions. For a certain period the political implications of such a confrontation will not be understood by any working-class movement that is dominated by a purely trade unionist or reformist ideology. But whatever the stage of the political development of a given working-class movement, it is likely that the application of incomes policies will render more palpable the fundamental class antagonism between workers and capitalists, creating favourable conditions for intervention by revolutionary workers' organisations. Moreover, the sharp expression of class contradictions at a national and even international level also poses the question of the contradiction between the increasingly social nature of the forces of production and the still private character of appropriation via capitalist property relations. These two types of contradiction are likely to be most explosive where they coincide most clearly. *The modern working class with all its skills and its capacity for social co-operation is, after all, the vital component of the forces of production.* In the broader class struggles of an imperialist world challenged from without and divided within, capital finds that it can only maintain its economic position by weakening its political position. The more it seeks to contain its own contradictions the more it unifies and radicalises its real antagonist: a working class capable of destroying it because it is the bearer of a superior form of social co-operation.

9 The English Working Class

TOM NAIRN

The passage of the early English working class from revolt to political integration is often explained solely by Britain's ascendancy as the first major imperialist power. In this essay Tom Nairn focuses upon the political culture which British workers inherited from the British bourgeois class and argues that this was a crucial element in its domestication. Taking as his starting point Edward Thompson's pioneering and influential work The Making of the English Working Class *he seeks to demonstrate that 'history from below' must be complemented by a 'history from above'.*

Tom Nairn is an editor of New Left Review *and the author of* May 1968: The Beginning of the End (*U K, 1968*).

The English working class is one of the enigmas of modern history. Its development as a class is divided into two great phases, and there appears at first sight to be hardly any connection between them.

It was born in conditions of the utmost violence, harshly estranged from all traditional and tolerable conditions of existence and thrown into the alien, inchoate world of the first industrial revolution. Formed in this alienation by the blind energies of the new capitalist order, its sufferings were made more hopeless by the severest political and ideological persecution. From the outset it inspired fear by its very existence. In the time of general fear produced by the French Revolution, such dread and hostility became chronic, affecting the old ruling class and the new industrial bourgeoisie alike, and creating a climate of total repression. What was possible but revolt, in the face of this? Humanity, pulverized and recast in this grim mould, had to rebel in order to live, to assert itself as more than a mere object of history, as more than an economic instrument. The early history of the English working class is therefore a history of revolt, covering more than half a century, from the period of the French Revolution to the climax of Chartism in the 1840s.

And yet, what became of this revolt? The great English working class, this titanic social force which seemed to be unchained by the rapid development of English capitalism in the first half of the century, did not finally emerge to dominate and remake English society. It could not break the mould and fashion another. Instead, after the 1840s it quickly turned into an apparently docile class. It embraced one species of moderate reformism after another, became a consciously subordinate part of bourgeois society, and has remained wedded to the narrowest and greyest of bourgeois ideologies in its principal movements.

Why did this happen? It is important for us to try and understand why, for many reasons. But above all, because the difficulties confronting any socialist revolution in Britain today are as much the long-term product of this astonishing transformation as of any development in the ruling class or any evolution in the structure and techniques of capitalism.

The problem of the English working class cannot be separated from that of the growth of English bourgeois society as a whole —that is, it is one part of a wider enigma, and is normally obscured like everything else by those liberal mystifications the English have erected in honour of their past. We have a long way to go in penetrating this general obscurity. Nevertheless, one vital fact surely emerges and imposes itself upon any serious consideration of the origins of the English working class.

Given the time and circumstances of its birth, this class was fated to *repeat*, in certain respects, the historical experience of the English bourgeoisie itself.

The revolutionary period of the English bourgeoisie occurred early in the general evolution of capitalism, earlier than that of any equivalent class in a major country. Those urban and rural middle classes who made the Revolution of 1640 were pioneers of bourgeois development, advancing blindly into a new world. Such blindness was the price of being in the van. Although the English Revolution attempted like other revolutions to escape from the general blindness and chance of historical evolution in a conscious remaking of society, the attempt was inevitably crippled by the lack of the very materials for an adequate consciousness of this sort. The final destruction of English feudalism in the period 1640–60 took place long before the full flowering of bourgeois ideology. Initiating the cycle of bourgeois expansion in this way, the English middle classes could not hope to benefit from a new conception of the world that was itself produced in the course of the cycle and reached maturity at a later date. Hence, although they contributed powerfully to the Enlightenment their practical struggles were necessarily conducted in terms of a pre-Enlightenment philosophy, a religious world-view unequal to what was at stake, English Puritanism. This fact explains a large part of those aspects of the Revolution which appear to us as a failure: its profound *empiricism*, the patchwork of compromise and makeshift it ended in, and the resultant organic coalescence with the English *ancien régime*.

But economically, of course, the Revolution was not a failure. Out of the mercantile society which triumphed in it, capitalist forms of production arose with giant force, threatening in their turn the equilibrium of that society. Dependent for their inception upon a new race of free, disinherited labourers, these forms in their violent rise soon swelled this labour force into a major social class, an even greater potential threat to society, to the old patrician order of mercantilism and the new industrialism alike.

Thus, the first bourgeois class to occupy the centre of the world-historical scene engendered the first great proletariat. And the latter was inevitably forced into existence as far from the world-view it needed as the former had been. Any coherent and adequate proletarian ideology, the theory and practice of socialism, lay hidden in the future, the fruit of many struggles and debates in many countries. The English working class too was bound to grope its way in history.

To this central fact, the unavoidable darkness of its time, were added other constricting conditions derived from the peculiarities of English bourgeois development. The very precocity of the English bourgeoisie had, paradoxically, brought in its train a subsequent retardation of growth. 'The Revolutions of 1648 and 1789 were not *English* and *French* revolutions,' according to Marx, 'they were revolutions of a *European* pattern ... The Revolution of 1648 was the victory of the 17th century over the

16th century, the Revolution of 1789 the victory of the 18th century over the 17th century.'[1] The English bourgeoisie was to remain partly set within this pattern of the seventeenth century, it retains something of it even today. The conquests and prosperity of mercantile England, its emergence as one of the two world-powers, the great economic advance culminating in the Industrial Revolution—these were the real nerve and meaning of bourgeois development, its historical agency as creator of a new mode of production. Blind empiricism had opened the door to this triumph. Blind empiricism and its consequences were justified by it. The English bourgeoisie stood apart from the victory of the eighteenth century, isolated in a unique path of evolution, half innovator, half anachronism, bringing forth a new world from the very bowels of society while in heart and head it looked back to an older one. It was the most confident ruling class in modern history. What need did it have of the Enlightenment? It could take what it wanted from it, and produce its own limited, parochial Enlightenment in the shape of political economy and Utilitarianism. When the pattern of the eighteenth century finally erupted in 1789, it first greeted it, mistakenly, as a repetition of its own experience of the previous century, and then after realizing the mistake fought it to the death. This battle between the two great bourgeois revolutions crystallized all the peculiarities of English bourgeois development in a quite decisive way. Its estrangement from the central current of later bourgeois evolution was confirmed by this event, the insular destiny of its civilization.

The English working class was to be the principal victim of such estrangement. For the bourgeoisie, it was simply the accompaniment to a world economic hegemony, a natural form of consciousness and conduct, justified by practice, a national pride. For a century, nothing was to contradict this confidence. But from the beginning, the fortune of the bourgeoisie was the undoing of the working class; the former's characteristic mode of appropriation of the world was a characteristic mode of expropriation of the latter, a unique way of preventing it from appropriating the world in its turn.

The French Revolution was in general the practical realization of the Enlightenment, its translation into politics. Its most radical phase, the Jacobin dictatorship, was the realization

1. *The Bourgeoisie and the Counter-Revolution*, pp. 67–68, Selected Works, Vol. I.

of the most advanced and democratic conceptions of the Enlightenment, and was enacted by the only stratum of the bourgeoisie capable of pushing the Revolution to its limit, the petite bourgeoisie, in alliance with the workers, the peasants, and various dispossessed groups. The Jacobin ascendancy and Terror were what essentially distinguished the French Revolution from its great predecessor of the seventeenth century. The Jacobins of the English Revolution, the Levellers, had been defeated by Cromwell and his 'Girondins', the 'grandees', the forces of large landed and commercial property. But the French bourgeoisie, in its revolutionary struggle against the far more powerful and regressive French *ancien régime*, *needed* Jacobinism as the English had not. English feudalism and would-be absolution were swept away without the fire of Jacobinism.

Jacobinism, in one sense the apex of bourgeois progress, the most radical affirmation of its world-view, is nevertheless the most mixed of blessings in the future development of bourgeois society. Through it, capital comes into its inheritance by the active hegemony of classes destined to be expropriated by capital, it rises to dominance out of the herculean efforts and organized violence of its own future servants. But this origin is the worst of precedents for its own future stability. As the French bourgeoisie was to discover repeatedly in the nineteenth century, the great stamp imposed upon society by this critical experience—the noblest of all bourgeois achievements, a patrimony which it could not and cannot to this day fail to acknowledge—was also the never-ending source of its own weakness. It was a mark of Cain, perpetually visible as such to all the disinherited. While the bourgeoisie made a living museum of the revolutionary tradition, it remained a living inspiration, a promise surviving every defeat, to the masses.

Marx described this paradox of bourgeois development in the 'Communist Manifesto', claiming that the bourgeoisie—'in all its battles sees itself compelled to appeal to the proletariat, to ask for its help, and thus to drag it into the political arena. The bourgeoisie itself, therefore, supplies the proletariat with its own elements of political and general education, in other words it furnishes the proletariat with weapons for fighting the bourgeoisie.'[2] But in England the peculiar evolution of the bourgeoisie did *not* provide the English popular masses and the English proletariat with such a 'political and general education'.

2. *Communist Manifesto*, p. 43, Selected Works, Vol. I.

Not only had the English Revolution by-passed Jacobinism. The Revolution itself was buried in a morass of euphemism and misrepresentation, like some infantile trauma driven deep into the national subconscious. As a result, in this English bourgeois universe all appeared as 'locked fast as in a sort of family settlement; grasped as in a kind of mortmain for ever.'[3] The bourgeoisie, through its piecemeal entry on to the scene, was able to appropriate all the tradition of the dead generations and render it a living, oppressive, mystifying presence. What was written in the English sky, to correspond to the towering words of 1789, 'Liberté, Egalité, Fraternité'? The shamanism of the British Constitution, an assorted repertoire of (largely fake) antiquities, the poisonous remains of the once revolutionary ideology of Puritanism, and the anti-revolutionary invective of Edmund Burke.

The manufacturers, the new industrial bourgeoisie of the period 1789–1832, were certainly discontented with the old order, with the 'family settlement' inherited from 1688. They wanted a larger place in it, but not as the Third Estate had wanted its rights in France—that is, as an absolute necessity, a *sine qua non* of all further progress. They had already progressed so far that a revolutionary demand of this sort was ridiculous. A reform of the terms of the settlement was required, nothing more. Listen to the voice of their most rational and radical spokesman, expounding the characteristic English version of *'égalité'*: 'A single mistake in extending equality too far may overthrow the social order and dissolve the bonds of society,' mumbled Jeremy Bentham, 'Equality might require such a distribution of property as would be incompatible with security ... Equality ought not to be favoured, except when it does not injuriously affect security, nor disappoint expectations aroused by the law itself, nor disturb a distribution already actually settled and determined.'[4] It was too late for an English Jacobinism.

The English working class, therefore, was not only born far from socialism. This fact in itself, though inevitable, was not necessarily a fatal handicap. To proceed empirically is of no importance, if one can learn in time to do better—history is largely a tale of groping in the dark, a condition no person or

3. Edmund Burke, *Reflections on the Revolution in France* (Oxford Worlds' Classics Edition), p. 83.
4. *The Theory of Morals and Legislation*, pp. 119–29.

class can miraculously escape from. Not merely time, but a concrete combination of historical factors positively *separated* the English working class from socialism. It was, so to speak, deprived of a whole dimension of growth from the beginning. This privation was also, in the widest and most authentic sense, a *popular* one. That is, it concerned not simply the emergent proletariat, but the numerous closely-related strata of the 'people' out of which it emerged historically, and from which it was for long scarcely distinguishable: artisans and out-workers, the urban crowds of casual workers and workless, the petty bourgeoisie of small producers in town and country. These heterogeneous subordinate masses, pre-capitalist or half-capitalist in nature and outlook, were the potential social force behind Jacobinism. It is only through the early revolutionary radicalism of the bourgeoisie that they can dominate the historical scene, that the 'petty' bourgeoisie ceases to be in any sense 'petty' and assumes a transitory heroic rôle. Capital, by the relative ease with which it conquered and transformed English society, always kept these classes in subordination. The English petty bourgeoisie was deprived of the chance to play its heroic part in history. English radicalism was permanently reduced to a phenomenon of *protest*, burdened with an 'oppositional' mentality the very reverse of 'Jacobin' mentality, spasmodic in its appearances and, of course, infected with religious mania. This was the terrible negative 'education' inflicted on the English working class.

Alienated in this fashion from everything finest in bourgeois tradition, by the inner conditions of English social evolution, the masses suffered the *coup de grâce* from the new external conditions of the war against France from 1793 until 1815. Jacobinism became, not only something extraneous, but the face of an enemy, the object of patriotic hatred. National fervour became another weapon in the hands of the bourgeoisie, a reinforcement of its internal good fortune. English separateness and provincialism; English backwardness and traditionalism; English religiosity and moralistic vapouring; paltry English 'empiricism', or instinctive distrust of reason—all these features whch, seen in an abstractly comparative perspective, may appear as 'defects' or 'distortions' of bourgeois development in England, were in reality hammered together into a specific form of bourgeois hegemony during the infancy of the working class. The British Constitution, claimed Burke, 'works after the pattern of nature'. That is, it and all the rest were made to appear as merely parts of nature, and so inevitable—aspects of an English firmament, like the south-west wind and the rain, not so many forms of domination of capital.

The French bourgeoisie could only triumph by forging a double-edged sword, a weapon the working class could in its turn develop and use against its rulers. The German bourgeoisie, frustrated in its early development, consoled itself with an intellectual world of heroic proportions and intensity, a world out of which, in spite of its abstractness and spiritualism, the seminal ideas of socialism could come. But the English bourgeoisie, more fortunate, could afford to dispense with the dangerous tool of reason and stock the national mind with historical garbage. Capital did not have to resort to self-wounding excesses to establish its reign in England; it could hide behind the Bible, and make of practically everything 'national' an instrument, direct or indirect, of dominion.

Such was the cage of circumstances into which the English working class was bound to grow up. Such were the full, daunting dimensions of the alienation awaiting it, above and beyond the economic and human alienation which was the stuff of its daily life. From the beginning, a giant's task confronted it.

British socialists are fortunate indeed to possess the great account of the origins of the English working class which has recently appeared: Edward Thompson's *The Making of the English Working Class*.[5] Above all, because it concentrates attention upon what must be our primary concern, the rôle of the working class as maker of history. Engaged in constant polemic against vulgar determinism, Thompson insists that: 'The working class made itself as much as it was made',[6] and indicates how by the time of the Great Reform Bill in 1832 the working class had become an active influence whose 'presence can be felt in every county in England, and in most fields of life'.[7] The working class was not merely the product of economic forces, but also realized itself in 'a social and cultural formation' partly directed against the operation of these very forces. Thompson's book is essentially the history of this revolt.

The popular masses out of which the working class arose remained for generations attached to pre-industrial traditions,

5. Victor Gollancz, 1963.   6. Ibid., p. 194.   7. Ibid., p. 807.

their resistance to capitalism was also a reaching back towards this way of life, an attempt to recreate an ideal society of small, independent men controlling their own fate. The deepest sympathy with this aspect of popular sentiment is characteristic of Thompson's approach. Such aspirations were inevitably blotted out by the onward rush of capitalism, but were not for this reason unimportant or contemptible, and the author wants to 'rescue the poor stockinger, the Luddite cropper, the "obsolete" handloom weaver, the "utopian" artisan, and even the deluded followers of Joanna Southcott, from the enormous condescension of posterity . . .'[8] The slow, secular gestation of the first industrial revolution, the long phases of capital accumulation which opened the way to industrial capitalism, had created a rich, varied artisan culture with tenacious roots. During the period of formation of the working class, the most influential representative of this tradition was the journalist William Cobbett. Cobbett was typical in thinking of the misery and convulsion of the time as being an assault upon the immemorial rights of the 'free-born Englishman'. These rights, located in a mythical past, had to be defended and reasserted as a peculiarly English heritage. Thus, the traditions and never-ending retrospection of the ruling class were to be fought with an even deeper and more backward-looking traditionalism : radicalism was in essence the restoration of a kind of English golden age. This was 'the ideology of the small producers', as Thompson admits[9]. But he also insists upon the extent to which this sort of thinking was developed by the contact with the new proletarian public, and shows how its particular defensive strength was employed in the new situation. Even the Protestant dissident sects, in spite of their abject other-worldliness, had preserved a 'slumbering Radicalism'[10] with elements of resistance in it. In the conditions of the time, the new working class was desperately short of means of resistance. It has to utilize everything to hand, and posterity has no right to be condescending about the terrible limitations of what ensued, the crop of hybrid, even pathological, unions which the workers were saddled with.

Here, as so often, the author's sympathy and passion carry us to a real understanding of happenings; in his company, we penetrate beyond the level of more chronology, into real history, into an imaginative re-creation of the experience of the past. He is engaged in constant polemic with the academic 'ob-

8. Ibid., p. 12.   9. Ibid., p. 759.   10. Ibid., p. 30.

jectivity' which sees history as a relation of the 'facts', and the 'facts' as whatever can be expressed statistically. He tries consistently to grasp for us 'the quality of life' under the Industrial Revolution. This requires 'an assessment of the total life-experience, the manifold satisfactions or deprivations, cultural as well as material, of the people concerned'.[11] Only an imaginative effort of this sort brings us to the reality, the human dimensions of what happened. And it is in this sense that Thompson defends a 'classical' view of the period, as one of mass immiseration and suffering, against the empiricists who have maintained that, after all, it saw some rise in the standard of living. 'During the years between 1780 and 1840 the people of Britain suffered an experience of immiseration, even if it is possible to show a small statistical improvement in material conditions,' he points out, 'the process of industrialization was carried through with exceptional violence in Britain ... This violence was done to *human* nature.'[12] The fundamental curse of the era was the very thing which raised the standard of living—the new economic conditions of life, the new alienation of the work-process itself which 'casts the blackest shadow over the years of the Industrial Revolution'.[13]

Besides the romantic, backward-looking resistance to industrialization represented by Cobbett, the English people were presented with another ideology during the same years: that of Tom Paine. The English bourgeoisie had shut out the more revolutionary aspects of the Enlightenment. Paine did his best to make up for this. *The Rights of Man* and *The Age of Reason* are injections of pure Enlightenment rationalism, the militant and democratic optimism of a newer bourgeois world. Here was the authentic voice of an English Jacobinism, and Thompson reminds us how important it was: '... the main tradition of 19th century working-class Radicalism took its cast from Paine ... Until the 1880's it remained transfixed within this framework.'[14] But if this was so, could not Paine fill the lacuna left by the cramped intellectual development of the bourgeoisie, could not this tradition educate the working class into the aggressive egalitarianism the masters had no use for? The ruling class had abandoned Reason for a footling reasonableness—why could its subjects not appropriate the lost herit-

11. Ibid., p. 444.   12. Ibid., pp. 445–6.
13. Ibid., p. 446.   14. Ibid., p. 96.

age for themselves?

A book, however significant and popular, cannot itself permanently change and educate great masses of people. The presence and diffusion of the right ideas may be a necessary condition of advances in mass consciousness, but other conditions lie in the day-to-day awareness of people, their practical experience of reality. It is these which were decisive in this case. In considering what Thompson says on this theme, we approach the central nerve of his argument. 'Had events taken their "natural" course,' he observes, 'we might expect there to have been some show-down long before 1832, between the oligarchy of land and commerce and the manufacturers and petty gentry, with working people in the tail of the middle-class agitation. . . . But after the success of the *Rights of Man*, the radicalization and terror of the French Revolution, and the onset of Pitt's repression . . . the aristocracy and the manufacturers made common cause. The English ancien régime received a new lease of life. . .'[15] There was to be no second revolution in England. 'The only alliance strong enough to effect it fell apart; after 1792 there were no Girondins to open the doors through which the Jacobins might come.'[16] Another instalment of bourgeois revolution was only possible if a significant enough section of the substantial middle class wanted it, and was prepared to risk the 'alliance' in question. Only this could have disrupted the forces of property and weakened the régime enough to launch a revolution, providing the circumstances under which the petty bourgeoisie and workers might have obtained power. By themselves, the latter were incapable of generating a revolutionary situation, whatever ideas were in their minds. But it is situations, and action, the bite of experience, which crystallize ideas from the 'mind' into the nervous system itself, making of them a dominating reflex and redrawing the limits of consciousness. Perhaps this is truest of all in the case of revolutionary ideas, struggling as they are against the dense weight of most historical culture —and how few those critical situations are that can be turned into hinges of history in this way, 1789, 1917 or 1949! Hence, neither Paine nor any other revolutionary ideology could really penetrate and dominate the 'sub-political attitudes' of English subordinate classes. In several crucial passages, Thompson indicates what occurred instead.

The fundamental experience of the masses, in the period of

15. Ibid., p. 197.   16. Ibid., p. 178.

the making of the working class, was the very opposite of coherent, aggressive self-assertion. It was an experience of being driven into revolt, and finding every means of expression cut away, every channel hopelessly blocked, every friendly element neutralized. In this historical nightmare 'the revolutionary impulse was strangled in its infancy; and the first consequence was that of bitterness and despair'.[17] Psychologically, a sort of withdrawal was the only possibility, the turning-in of a whole class upon itself. Escape was possible solely on the level of fantasy : in what Thompson describes, eloquently, as the 'ritualized form of psychic masturbation' provided by the Methodist Revival, or in the even more demented vagaries of Joanna Southcott and other prophets. The chapters on the ghastly religious terrorism into which Puritanism had degenerated at this period are, indeed, among the most instructive and impressive things in the book.[18] 'In the decades after 1795 there was a profound alienation between classes in Britain, and working people were thrust into a state of *apartheid* whose effects ... can be felt to this day. . . . Segregated in this way, their institutions acquired a peculiar toughness and resilience. Class also acquired a peculiar resonance in English life : everything ... was turned into a battleground of class. The marks of this remain. . .'[19] Here was the result of the long, sporadic, ill-organized revolt of the proletariat, in the first generation of its existence: apartheid, apartness—within the new capitalist social order, whose laws supposedly abolished feudal ranks and levelled all relations to that of the business contract, the working class was beaten by repression almost into the condition of a feudal 'estate'. It was, so to speak, forced into a *corporative* mode of existence and consciousness, a class in and for itself, within but not of society, generating its own values, organizations, and manner of life in conscious distinction from the whole civilization round about it. Everywhere, the conditions of capitalism made of the worker something of an exile inside the society he supported. Only English conditions could bring about such total exile.

But it is, paradoxically, precisely in relation to insights such as this that one feels the limitation of *The Making of the*

17. Ibid., p. 177.
18. Ibid., see Ch. XI, *The Transforming Power of the Cross.*
19. Ibid., pp. 177 and 832.

English Working Class. We live in a society which, sociologically speaking, has been mainly working class for over a century. It is what it is, therefore, largely because of what the working class became, so that we must look with the most intense interest at any study of the formation of the class for clues as to this later evolution. There are many such hints in Thompson's book. But, exasperatingly, they remain hints. From his chosen period, 1789 to 1832, he looks backward in rich detail, describing popular traditions amply and appreciatively; while only occasional, almost incidental, remarks carry the reader forward in time to the maturity of the working class. This impression is aggravated by the inconclusive, even arbitrary, termination of the argument—the power of the work, the passion and enthusiasm animating it are such that one instinctively expects a more definite and sweeping conclusion. During the years of its terrible genesis, the English working class 'nourished, and with incomparable fortitude, the Liberty Tree. We may thank them for these years of heroic culture.' So the author ends. He is right, in their complacent embalming of the past the English have disfigured it, it is the duty, and the privilege, of socialists to rediscover and honour what deserves to be honoured, to make the past relive in the creative consciousness of the present. However, his study evokes other sentiments besides this gratitude, and Thompson has no words for them.

The formation of the English working class was a major tragedy. It was also one—and perhaps the greatest single—phase of *the* tragedy of modern times, the failure of the European working class to overthrow capital and fashion the new society that material conditions long ago made possible. The horrors of our time, Fascism and Stalinism, the agonizing problems of 'under-development' and the Cold War, are all products of this disastrous failure. If the working class of only one major industrial nation had succeeded, the course of history would have been radically changed. And did not the English working class seem destined to lead the way? With what confidence Marx wrote, in 1854, surveying its prodigious growth, its irresistible numbers, the overwhelming contrast between this leviathan and the bogus façades of Old England! 'In no other country . . . has the war between the two classes that constitute modern society assumed such colossal dimensions, such distinct and palpable features. But it is precisely from these facts that the working classes of Great Britain, before all others, are called to act as leaders in the great movement that must finally result in the absolute emancipation of Labour.'[20]

If, given the conditions of its origin, the English working class was bound to repeat to some extent the experience of the English bourgeoisie—should it not produce the first great and decisive working-class revolution, the equivalent of 1640 in proletarian terms?

But the basic existential situations of the working class and the bourgeoisie are entirely different, and beyond a certain point this difference invalidates the comparison. Whereas the bourgeoisie arises as the agent of a new mode of production within medieval society, as a 'middle' propertied class established securely upon this basis, the working class possesses no corresponding foundation within capitalist society. It has nothing outside itself, its own organization and consciousness. Hence, while the bourgeoisie was able to develop gradually, to transform the older order in stages as one kind of economic life fell apart before the piecemeal invasion of another, the working class cannot hope for the same sort of victory. In certain cases, the genesis of capitalism did bring about tremendous social tensions only resolvable by revolutions, in certain cases the bourgeoisie was compelled to evolve a pure, militant bourgeois consciousness as the weapon of its triumph—above all, in France. It was also possible for the bourgeoisie to transform society far more blindly and empirically, however, as the case of England shows —where 'empiricism' led to the most complete success of all, to the total subjection of society and economic domination of the world. And it is this kind of progress which is ruled out for the working class, and for socialism. Consciousness, theory, an intellectual grasp of social reality—these cannot occupy a subordinate or fluctuating place in the socialist transformation of society, no empirical and anti-ideology or trust in the 'natural' evolution of affairs can substitute for them.

Consequently, in order really to 'repeat' the pattern of English history, the working class had to become what the bourgeoisie had never been—what it had renounced, what it had found effective replacements for, what it desired *not* to be with all its force of instinct. That is, a class dominated by reason. To become a new hegemonic force, capable of dominating society in its turn, the English working class absolutely required a

20. 'Letter to the Labour Parliament', 1854, in *Marx & Engels on Britain*, p. 402.

consciousness containing the elements ignored by, or excised from, the consciousness of the English bourgeoisie.

This was the task that was completely, tragically, beyond the powers of the English working class. Nothing else was beyond its powers. In numbers, in essential solidarity and homogeneity, in capacity for organization, in tenacity, in moral and civil courage, the English working class was, and is, one of the very greatest of social forces. And it has always existed in one of the least militarized of bourgeois states. No external fetters could ever have withstood this colossus. It was held by intangible threads of consciousness, by the mentality produced by its distinctive conditions and experience.

One of the chief virtues of *The Making of the English Working Class* is the writer's insistence on the role of consciousness in finally determining the character of a class, and of class relations. The new 'collective self-consciousness' was, he claims, the 'great spiritual gain of the Industrial Revolution'.[21] The positive aspects of this consciousness, its brotherliness and mutuality, its sense of dignity and community, are clearly brought home to us. But its limitations are not clearly presented, although they are no less important, and have lasted just as long. 'If we have in our social life little of the traditions of *égalité*,' he says, 'yet the class-consciousness of the working man has little in it of deference.'[22] The 'apartness' of working class consciousness, however, *implies* a kind of deference—for it resigns everything else, the power and secret of society at large, to others, to the 'estates' possessing authority or wealth. A corporative mode of consciousness turns aside from everything not the 'natural' or 'proper' affair of the corporation or class, all that does not belong to 'its' own world. A real sense of social equality—foreign to the English bourgeoisie—renders such a consciousness utterly impossible, for its nerve is the conviction that everything social is the proper affair of everybody, once and for all. Hence, the imposition of this profoundly corporative outlook on the workers was a fundamental victory for the ruling orders. It is true indeed that the working class 'made itself, as much as it was made'—but not *freely*, rather along the lines laid down by the bitter experiences Thompson recounts so well, lines which partly turned this self-activity of the working class into the instrument of its own subjection. In the alienation from certain universal values of the bourgeoisie—

21. Thompson, op. cit., p. 830.   22. Ibid.

values vital to the further evolution of society—lay a particularism, an ideological parochialism fatal to all revolutionary ideas. Revolution is the rejection of all corporative attitudes in the name of a vision of man.

Yet this general reflection only conveys half of the tragedy, or half of the unique ascendancy the English bourgeoisie attained through it. The final bite of the process of formation of working-class consciousness lay in the *integration* of the latter into an entire system of false consciousness, each element in which supported every other. The workers could not be transformed into this peculiar, densely corporate type of class, while the bourgeois became 'citizens'. There could be no 'citizens' in English society. The bourgeoisie had to remain a 'middle class' —as if feudalism was still in full vigour!—the 'backbone of the nation' functioning under yet another 'estate', the 'upper class' or ruling class. To the particularism of the working class, there had logically to correspond a whole web of particularisms, the weird heterogeneity and pluralism of society as a whole in England. The English social world *had* to become a world of the inexplicably concrete, the bizarre, the eccentric individual thing and person defying analysis. Is this not the true historical sense of the quiet madness of England? Even such endearing, exasperating, Dickensian lunacy had its historical function— the function, so to speak, of not seeming to have any function or meaning.

The final success of the system in subordinating the working class can be gauged, perhaps, in terms of the sheer *impossibility* of a *real* 'apartheid' of one class. The working class could not in reality create such a separate world. The separate, inward-turned class-consciousness could not be uniquely a means of protection of the positive values and 'way of life' of the workers —it was bound to be also a specific vehicle of assimilation, whereby bourgeois ideas and customs were refracted downwards into the working class. The result was not a *naked* imitation of the middle class, but a kind of translation—the kind of working-class *caricature* of bourgeois ultra-respectability which puzzled and enraged Marx. The English working class transforms everything into its own corporative terms. Where in England can one find the perfect satirist's image of the bourgeois, if not among the older trade union leaders? But such mediate assimilation is more deadly than aping, precisely because it presupposes the self-activity of the class, because it reposes on a *genuine*, distinctly working-class consciousness.

Because of the intensive, apart character of working-class consciousness, no social or political doctrine ignoring the real economic position of the working class could grip it lastingly. It is possible to see the meaning of this, perhaps, if we recall Marx's observation on the French proletariat in its early days: 'The more developed and universal is the *political* thought of a people, the more the *proletariat*—at least at the beginning of the movement—wastes its forces on foolish and futile uprisings which are drowned in blood ... Their political understanding obscures from them the roots of their social misery, it ... eclipses their social instinct.'[23] The story of the English working class is almost the contrary of this. This is the kind of *bloody* tragedy it escaped, thanks to the lack of development, the non-universality, of its political thought. The social instinct of the English proletariat could not be eclipsed, it was firmly embodied in a distinct class consciousness. But neither could it be expressed, realized positively in a non-corporative vision of the world, under the conditions of the time. Hence, the workers tried first of all to solve their problems with the Utopian-corporative ideology of Owenite trade-unionism, an attempt to build a kind of socialism in and for the working class itself, ignoring the rest of society. When this was proved impossible, their attention and force were directed to the question of hegemony over society as a whole—but in the totally inadequate forms provided by Chartism, a simple radical-democratic programme dissociated from the 'social instinct' of the class. No force on earth would have defeated a social movement and ideology really expressing and rooted in the social instinct of the English working class, not even if the English ruling class had imported all the gendarmes in Prussia. But the defeat of Chartism was absolute, because it was not so rooted. After the collapse of the movement, the working class was thrown back necessarily into itself, and into a more moderate and timid form of corporate action, into the trade-unionism which remains its basis to this day.

Unable to really 'repeat' the world-building experience of the English bourgeoisie, from 1850 onwards the working class indulges in a *false* repetition of that experience, in a kind of mimesis of bourgeois evolution as the latter was seen and mis-represented by the bourgeoisie itself. It behaves *as if* the workers, in their turn, could transform society in their own image by a gradual extension of their influence, by an accumulation of reforms corresponding to the bourgeois accumulation of capital. Customarily, this development is ascribed to external factors: the long prosperity of British capitalism after mid-century, at the zenith of its power, or the imperialism which followed and permitted the ruling class to 'bribe' the workers still farther and make them conscious of their superiority to foreign exploited masses. But *The Making of the English Working Class* brings us to a vivid realization of the *internal* history that gave to such factors their true meaning and effects. It adds, or begins to add, a missing dimension to the history of the working class and of 'British Socialism'.

What could have made a difference, what could have prevented the fatal, closed evolution springing from the conditions Thompson describes? The temptation some will feel is to answer in one short, eloquent word: Marxism. Was not this the coherent, universal, hegemonic ideology of socialism alone corresponding to the social instinct of the English working class? But the word has only to be raised for the false simplicity of the answer to be obvious. The ideas of Marx penetrated the consciousness of the English workers less than anywhere else, when they eventually arrived on the scene.

The dialectical contradiction made evident by the failure of Marxism among English workers consists in this: the very type of intense class-consciousness which preserves a fundamental authenticity of reflex and attitude—the prerequisite, the best guarantee of socialism—also conceals and renders inaccessible this vital area of awareness, beneath a carapace of dead matter. This carapace, the product of generations of the static, vegetative culture of working class 'apartheid', with all its parochialism and elements of mimesis, cannot be split merely by the annunciation of Marxist ideas. Marxism is the product of the confluence and rethinking of all the major currents of bourgeois thought—it is the child of the Enlightenment and of German philosophy, as well as of English political economy. And in it, the ideas of classical economics assume a quite new significance and resonance. England, the home of political economy, is also historically estranged from the Enlightenment and German philosophy—consequently, in England Marxism encounters an environment in a sense estranged from, unaffected by, impervious to the very sources of Marxism itself, in spite of the national reverence for political economy.

This fact, together with the immense accumulation of historical peculiarities in England, on the level of the social superstructures and on the level of class consciousness and class relations, meant that Marxism as much—in the form of the commonly diffused basic schemes of 'vulgar Marxism'—was bound to be more or less *meaningless*. Presented in this fashion —as a kind of revealed truth on a plate—it could not possibly make fruitful contact with the actual experience and consciousness of the working class. If it could not enter into consciousness in this way, how could it change consciousness?

To put the matter in another way, very schematically: the characteristic of the English working class was its alienation from bourgeois reason, and an objective necessity for its self-realization was the overcoming of this alienation. Hence, Marxism—which, of course, in content offered the possibility of just this—could only be absorbed in England through a truly gigantic process of thought, an intense and critical activity capable of compensating and remedying the deprivation. Marxism, to be effective, had to be the means whereby the working class threw off the immense, mystifying burden of false and stultifying consciousness imposed on it by English bourgeois civilization. To be this, it had to be thought out organically in English terms as an unmystified consciousness of English history and society. But this was a prodigious cultural task. And in Victorian England there was no radical, disaffected intelligentsia to even undertake it.

All working-class movements, all socialist movements, need 'theory'. The problem of consciousness and the changing of consciousness is always a crucial one. But in England, as Edward Thompson's book shows us, from the beginning the question assumed quite special acuteness, due to the special form of bourgeois hegemony in England and the special, distorted forms of consciousness this hegemony largely depended on. The problem was, to create theory in an environment rendered impervious to rationality as such; to create the intense rational consciousness and activity which were the necessary pre-requisites of revolution in this society of totemized and emasculated consciousness, to generate the intellectual and emotional force capable of exploding the omnipresent weight of the tradition of the dead generations. The English working class, immunized against theory like no other class, by its entire historical experience, *needed* theory like no other.

It still does.

10

The History of US Imperialism

GARETH STEDMAN JONES

Many illusions about the historical development of the United States derive from a failure to appreciate its underlying continuity. The non-territorial nature of US imperialism during some important periods obscured this fact and allowed many historians to represent the United States as a champion of national liberation.

Since the Russian Revolution, the rulers of America have been increasingly concerned to justify their imperial system against revolutionary attack. They have employed two constant methods to maintain their domination. The first has been physical—the proliferation of US bases, the mobility of the American fleet, the alertness of the marines, the manoeuvrings of the CIA, the bribery of friendly politicians. All this is well known. The second method has been ideological: the construction of a mythological, non-communist, non-socialist, and even non-nationalist road to political independence for the countries of the Third World. To woo the aspiring politicians of these new states, the United States has offered them the model of the 'American Revolution' of 1776. It was on this basis that Franklin Roosevelt considered that the United States was uniquely equipped to advise India on the road to independence, and it was again on the basis of this claim that Eisenhower felt entitled to ditch his Anglo-French imperialist allies at the time of the Suez crisis in 1956. America, in the estimation of her ruling politicians, was the first ex-colony, and so was uniquely equipped to steer a benevolent course through the stormy waters of post-war decolonization.

Of course, one embarrassing feature of this otherwise roseate

vista was America's own imperial record—as a colonial power.[1]
For it was impossible to deny that the Spanish-American war
of 1898 had resulted in the acquisition of Puerto Rico and the
Philippines, or that Hawaii had been annexed to the metropolitan power. To circumvent these difficulties, a large school of
official historians has attempted to provide satisfactory legal-
istic or at least non-economic explanations for America's unexpected lapse into the colonialism associated with the Old
World. With as much ingenuity as their self-imposed myopia
would permit, the historians came up with a satisfactory solution. The notorious Monroe doctrine was a defensive reaction
against the colonial ambitions of European powers. Its purpose
was simply to provide the necessary defensive bulwarks behind
which the new nation could be consolidated. According to one
official historian, nineteenth-century American leaders 'were at
most only incidentally concerned with real or imagined interests abroad'. The events of the 1890s had no precedent. They
were 'an aberration'. America lurched into an empire in a fit
of absent-mindedness—'it had greatness thrust upon it'. A
Schumpeterian explanation was advanced for the Spanish-
American War. Incursions into the Caribbean and the Philip-

1. This study is intended as an interpretative essay. It makes no
pretensions to original historical research, and draws heavily upon
recent work by American historians. The study of imperialism is
of crucial importance for all socialists. Yet the discussion among
those politically committed to the struggle against imperialism has
so far lacked any serious historical or sociological dimensions. While
orthodox historians tend to ignore the subject entirely and to stress
the historical uniqueness of each nation state, the Left has tended
to treat imperialism as an undifferentiated global product of a
certain stage of capitalism. This lacuna is not merely of academic
interest, since it has frequently led to political misjudgements or
chauvinist delusions. In the United States for instance it sometimes
leads to a tacit acceptance of the 'manifest destiny' of the United
States newly clothed in revolutionary proletarian garb. In recent
years the origins and dominant historical trajectory of US imperialism have for the first time come under serious scrutiny from
American historians. Yet the results of this important research seem
to have been neglected by theorists of imperialism (for the latest
example, see the otherwise excellent exchange between Nicolaus
and Mandel in *New Left Review*, No. 59). This essay is a provisional
attempt to trace out and interpret some of the main themes that
emerge from this discussion and thus give a schematic shape to the
historical specificity of modern American imperialism.

pines were not in any sense determined by real economic interests, but were the result of the machinations of the cheap yellow press. The war was necessary to satisfy the frenzied and hysterical emotions of the people. The United States was forced to intervene to prevent new colonial incursions into the American hemisphere. America had not engaged in a determined war of economic expansion but had reluctantly assumed the Anglo-Saxon burden of helping backward peoples forward to liberty and democracy.

This official interpretation of the background to twentieth-century American power has been skilfully elaborated in hundreds of volumes replete with an apparent apparatus of scholarship. For the most part, these legends have taken the form of a knowing or unknowing confusion between imperialism and colonialism. The *invisibility* of American imperialism when compared with the territorial colonialism of European countries,[2] has been internalized by its historians to such an extent, that with a clear conscience they have denied its very existence.[3] Whether this has been the result of State Department gold or simple inability to grasp conceptual distinctions, the end product has been the same: it has meant, in the words of Barrington Moore, astute propaganda but bad history and bad sociology.[4]

Until recently alternative interpretations put forward by radical or socialist critics have scarcely been more satisfactory. While official historians have celebrated the American ascent to world power either in terms of beneficent and inexorable manifest destiny or else in terms of an unavoidable geopolitical logic of power, radical critics have tended to see American history as a progressive betrayal of the ideals and possibilities of a lost golden age: Beard's triumph of *personalty* (mobile capital)

2. For an intelligent discussion of the political form of US imperialism and its relationship with the Cold War, see Ronald Aronson, 'Socialism: the Sustaining Menace', and Robert Wolf 'American Imperialism and the Peace Movement', *Studies on the Left*, No. 3, 1966.

3. The word imperialism was not used in its modern sense until the beginning of the twentieth century when Hobson made the concept well known. Marx's use of the term had nothing to do with its Hobsonian or Leninist connotations, but referred to the adventuristic foreign policy of Napoleon III.

4. Barrington Moore Jr., *Social Origins of Dictatorship and Democracy*, 1966, pp. 112–13.

over *realty* (agrarianism).[5] In the heroic epoch of simple agrarians and small entrepreneurs, according to C. Wright Mills, 'a free man, not a man exploited, and an independent man, not a man bound by tradition, here confronted a continent and, grappling with it, turned it into a million commodities'.[6] America was a country unburdened by a feudal or militaristic past and unmarred by the social and religious strife of Europe; but the foundation of an independent America contained a promise that its subsequent history failed to fulfil. David Horowitz could write in 1965: 'When America set out on her post-war path to contain revolution throughout the world, and threw her immense power and influence into the balance against the rising movement for social justice among the poverty-stricken two-thirds of the world's population, the first victim of her deeds were the very ideals for a better world—liberty, equality and self-determination—which she herself, in her infancy, had done so much to foster.'[7]

In recent years the work of William Appleman Williams has also tried to break away from conventional patriotic fantasies.[8] Williams has rejected the myth of a golden age and laid bare the deep national historical roots of American imperialism. Nevertheless, for all its virtues, Williams's work has remained imprisoned in a similar idealistic-moralistic problematic. Williams's argument is best understood as a response to the Turner thesis which associated American democracy with the existence of an expanding frontier to the West.[9] According to Turner, 'whenever social conditions tended to crystallize in the East, whenever capital tended to press upon labour or political restraints to impede the freedom of the mass, there was this gate of escape to the free conditions of the frontier. These free lands promoted individualism, economic equality, freedom to rise,

5. Beard's interpretation of the American Revolution is to be found in *An Economic Interpretation of the Constitution of the United States*, 1913, and *Economic Origins of Jeffersonian Democracy*, 1915.

6. C. Wright Mills, *White Collar*, 1951, p. 12.

7. David Horowitz, *From Yalta to Vietnam—American Foreign policy in the Cold War*, 1969, p. 426. The author has, of course, changed his position considerably since writing this book.

8. William Appleman Williams, *The Contours of American History*, 1961; and see also, *The Tragedy of American Diplomacy*, 1957.

9. F. J. Turner, *The Frontier in American History*, 1920 (republished essays).

democracy.' Williams turns this thesis on its head. According to Williams, American history can be seen as the compound of two conflicting themes.[10] The first of these themes has been the conception of a corporate Christian Commonwealth based upon the ideal of social responsibility; the second has been the untrammelled individualism based upon the ideals of private property. In Williams's eyes, the expanding westward frontier which in the twentieth century became metamorphosed into a global American imperialism has always been the dominant means by which Americans have evaded the possibility of building a genuine democracy, of constructing the true Christian Socialist Commonwealth which has always remained immanent in American history. Thus American history is not basically seen as the product of the struggle and interaction of classes within a particular social formation, but of the clash between '*weltanschauungs*'. The development of American imperialism is seen not so much as the result of the inner logic of capitalist development, but rather as the product of a conscious evasion. Like Hobson before him, Williams seems to envisage the possibility of a modified American capitalism shorn of its unnecessary imperialist outworks, and asks whether the ruling class of corporation capitalism has 'the nerve to abandon the frontier as Utopia' and 'to turn its back on expansion as the open door of escape'.

Despite these shortcomings, however, Williams's work possesses one major virtue: it shows expansionism to have been a consistent theme running throughout American history from its very beginning. On the basis of his work and that of his followers, it is possible to raise more adequately the problem of the specificity of American imperialism. Discussion among Marxist and Socialist writers has tended to concentrate perhaps too insistently upon the analysis of imperialism as a global stage of capitalist development. Such discussion has generally neglected the subsidiary but nevertheless crucial problem of the relationship between the historical determinants of a particular social formation and the specific mode of imperialist domination engendered by it.

Twentieth-century American imperialism may be said to have been characterized by two distinctive features which have clearly differentiated it from other imperialist systems. These are:

10. Williams, *Contours*, p. 481.

1. Its *non-territorial* character. Unlike the mode of imperialism employed by the British, French, German, Italian, or Japanese, American imperialism has generally been characterized by its non-possession of a formal colonial empire. In this sense, official historians are partially correct when they speak of the Spanish-American war as 'an aberration'. The acquisition of Puerto Rico and the Philippines was a deviation, not as official historians have thought from an otherwise peaceful and non-expansionist American history, but rather from the typical economic, political, and ideological forms of domination already characteristic of American imperialism.

The twentieth-century American empire, in intention at least, has been *an invisible empire*. American imperialism has been characterized by the concealment of American imperial interests behind a shield of supranational or inter-governmental organizations—the League of Nations, the UN, the World Bank, the Marshall Plan, the OAS, the Alliance for Progress. Secondly, it is noticeable that the United States has attempted to evade formal political control even when client governments have nakedly relied upon American military and political power—South Vietnam, South Korea, Taiwan, and certain Latin American states (the classical example is Cuba after the Platt Amendment).

2. Its possession of a *formally anti-imperialist* ideology. The twin bases upon which this ideology rests are firstly the self-image of the United States as the first ex-colony, and secondly the creation and constant reproduction of a theory of 'Communist aggression' which has justified 'defensive' interventions on the part of the United States in the interests of 'freedom' and the territorial integrity of independent states. Thus the Cold War, the creation of NATO, the proliferation of United States bases throughout the world, the Bay of Pigs, and the United States intervention in Vietnam are generally seen by official United States ideologues as part of an anti-imperialist crusade, as a struggle to contain Communist aggrandisement.

Until recently American imperialism and the Cold War have been treated even by the Left as two separate subjects. This conceptual apartheid has resulted in economic reductionism in the one case and psychologistic interpretations in the other. The intention of this essay is to examine the development of American imperialism from the moment of the formation of the United States as an independent political entity to the epoch of the First World War and the Russian Revolution. It is hoped that this tentative sketch will provide some of the elements necessary to resolve the question : *how far the characteristic modern form of American imperialism is a product of the Cold War, and how far it is an independent product resulting from the particularity of American historical development.*

1. The American 'Revolution': struggle for a national imperialism

The claim that American independence was the result of an anti-colonial revolution will bear little examination. Modern industrial imperialism is a mode of economic and social domination characteristic of capitalism at a mature stage of development. The question of political sovereignty has ultimately been contingent to the practice of this type of imperialism. Modern anti-colonial revolutions have been revolts against social systems based upon foreign exploitation, in which the national question could only be resolved by a social revolution.

A comparison between this specific system of oppression and the colonial status of North America under the mercantile system would reveal only the most meaningless and abstract resemblances. The truly colonized and exploited peoples were not the White American settlers, but the Indians and the Black slaves. The American 'Revolution', far from procuring their liberation, tightened their chains of dependence, and in the case of the Indians, accelerated the speed of their extermination.[11] While the mercantile system may have inhibited certain forms of industrial production in the thirteen colonies and was to become the source of some administrative and fiscal inconvenience, this was marginal beside the impetus given to indigenous capital accumulation through the development of the triangular trade, and the advantages conferred by a ready supply of slaves for the plantation economies and the provision of military protection against the Indians. The essential fact is that white settlers in North America were partners in English

11. Thomas Jefferson, one of the founding fathers, expressed the dominant attitude to the Indians—or at least of those who did not wish to exterminate them outright. He was glad 'to see the good and influential individuals among the Indians in debt; because we observe that when these debts get beyond what the individuals can pay, they become willing to lop them off by a cession of land.'

mercantile imperialism, and not its victims. They were no more part of some pre-industrial *damnés de la terre* than are white Rhodesian planters or Hong Kong merchants today. The white settlers accepted the English mercantile system until they were strong enough to do without it. The purpose of American independence, as John Adams put it in 1774, was the formation of 'an independent empire'.

If it is difficult to categorize the American War of Independence as anti-imperialist, it is equally difficult to describe the American 'Revolution' as a bourgeois revolution, or indeed as a social revolution of any kind. While most historians have agreed that the internal struggle between different social groups was quite secondary to the national war of independence, some have nevertheless attempted to draw analogies with the French Revolution.[12] Advocates of this position point to the immediately fiscal origins of both struggles, draw attention to the separation of church and state and go on to compare the confiscation of French *emigré* lands with the confiscation of Tory estates, the destruction of feudalism in France with the abolition of quit rents and entails in America, the Declaration of Independence with the Oath of the Tennis Court. While of course it would be absurd to deny the important detonating effects of the American Revolution abroad,[13] such analogies only highlight the immense difference between the two movements. Unlike the French Revolution, the American Revolution produced no clearcut contest between social classes, but tended to divide allegiances across class lines. Secondly, the American Revolution was virtually untouched by any social challenge from below. A radical alliance between the subordinate classes failed to emerge. Small subsistence farmers in the interior—the nearest thing to an American peasantry—failed to make significant contact with artisans in the towns. The spectre of slave revolt exercised a major subterranean influence upon the course of the American Revolution. The promise of freedom in exchange for loyalism provoked large-scale waves of slave desertions near the British lines. But slaves did not participate in the struggle as a coherent political force and found few allies in the classes above them. The leadership of the

12. Richard B. Morris, *The American Revolution Reconsidered*, 1967, ch. 2 discusses the possibilities of such an interpretation.

13. See R. R. Palmer, *The Age of Democratic Revolution*, 2 vols. 1959.

movement for national independence and the construction of a new Constitution ended, as it had begun, in the hands of a coalition of slave-owning agrarian capitalists in the South and mercantile capitalists in the North-East. Thirdly, it may be argued that a bourgeois revolution, by definition, must entail a radical change in anterior forms of property relationship. It would be difficult to argue that the American Revolution produced any such transformation. Feudal vestiges such as entails and quit rents had long been rendered meaningless by American conditions, and their abolition was most ardently supported by the supposedly 'feudal class'—indebted Southern planters in need of a more fluid market in land. The real seeds of future conflict lay in the uneasy coexistence between a form of capitalism based upon free labour and a form of capitalism based upon slavery, within a single polity still in the process of expansion. But in the Revolutionary period, this fundamental tension was overridden by the sectional conflict between the large scale capitalist property-owning class as a whole (including commercial farmers, Northern merchants *and* Southern slave owners) and indebted subsistence farmers in the interior: a struggle which reached its climax in 1787–8 with Shay's Rebellion and the making of the Constitution. As Staughton Lynd writes, 'the United States Constitution represented, not a triumph of capitalism over a landed aristocracy ... but a compromise or coalition between men of wealth in the cities and men of wealth on the land.'[14]

The United States was then already structurally an imperialist state at the moment of its foundation. The foundation of the United States was in no sense an anti-imperialist or even an anti-colonial revolution. If anything the American Revolution accelerated the development of American imperialism by freeing westward expansion from the controls imposed by the British. Westward expansion and settlement at the expense of the Indians was eventually to secure the United States the crucial advantage of possessing the largest single domestic market in the world. But already at the time of the Revolution, its political advantages were realized. The famous Turner thesis was understood from the beginning by the more sophisticated American politicians. Madison, for instance, in his Federalist Papers, clearly understood the purpose of the frontier

14. Staughton Lynd, 'Beyond Beard' in *Towards a New Past*, ed. Barton J. Bernstein, 1970, p. 53.

—for by the almost indefinite provision of cheap land further and further to the West, the dangers of class warfare resulting from unequal distribution of property, could be postponed. Just as an expanding internal frontier in Sweden had resulted in relatively weak instruments of feudal domination, so it was hoped that the Western frontier would act as the self-perpetuating safeguard of property and democracy in America.

2. Two forms of expansion—prelude to the Civil War

Even at the beginning of the nineteenth century, Americans were looking beyond the West, in their fantasies of a new world Empire. A Kentuckian boasted in 1810, for example, 'that his countrymen were full of enterprise' and 'although not poor, are greedy after plunder as ever the old Romans were. Mexico glitters in our eyes—the word is all we wait for.'[15] The war of 1812 with England possessed many elements of a war of inter-imperialist competition. It was certainly hoped that Canada would be conquered, and some Congressmen pressed for an invasion of Florida and Cuba, while others suggested that the war offered a legitimate excuse for finishing off the Indians. The famous Monroe Doctrine was also a much more expansionist statement than conventional American historians will admit—by keeping Europeans away from territorial footholds in the Americas, the field would be left open for American economic predominance.[16] As Henry Clay, Monroe's contemporary, predicted, in half a century North Americans in relation to South America 'would occupy the same position as the people of New England do to the rest of United States'.

But there were basic limits to the rate of expansion in the first half of the nineteenth century. The most obvious of these was the as yet inadequate development of the forces of production. America, at least before the 1840s,[17] could not be described as an industrialized country. A second reason was the necessary time spent in Western expansion. American historians who speak complacently of the absence of the settler-type col-

15. Quoted in Williams, *Contours*, p. 184.

16. For a good discussion of the significance of the Monroe Doctrine in the nineteenth century, see R. W. Van Alstyne, *The Rising American Empire*, 1960.

17. The turning point comes in the late 1830s. See Douglass C. North, *The Economic Growth of the United States 1790–1860*, 1961.

onialism characteristic of European powers merely conceal the fact that the whole *internal* history of United States imperialism was one vast process of territorial seizure and occupation. The absence of territorialism 'abroad' was founded on an imprecedented territorialism 'at home'. A third reason was the growing conflict between North and South. Here also the basic issue was Western expansion. The effect of the English industrial revolution was to give an enormous boost to the slave-based cotton crop economy of the South.[18] Slavery was certainly not in danger of dying a natural death as an economic anachronism. In the case of cotton, slavery was an efficient method of production, and as a dynamic sector of the economy slave-based cotton production was moving west in the South just as small independent farmers producing cereals were moving west in the North. The most productive cotton crop areas moved from the Eastern seaboard into Alabama and Mississippi—and after 1840 into Texas.[19] This had politically explosive implications because it threatened to upset the balance that had been established between the relative number of slave and free states.

The problem had existed in embryo since the 1790s when the 1790 census had threatened the South with numerical minority and consequent loss of influence over the direction of the Federal government. But it had been hoped at that time that the South could make up its losses by gains in the West. By the 1820s open conflict was only narrowly averted by a compromise which established Missouri as a slave state in exchange for Maine as a free state. In the 1830s the South was more ominously threatened by the 'transportation revolution' which progressively undermined the economic basis of the traditional alliance of South and West (via the Mississippi and New Orleans) by connecting the West with the North-East. By the 1840s the problem had become menacing. President Polk came into power in 1845 determined upon a course of aggressive expansion. His aim was to take Oregon, Texas, and California. In a strident war against Mexico he captured Texas and California, but decided to deal with the British and compromise over Oregon. The

18. In the 1830s cotton represented two-thirds of the total value of American exports and remained well over half until the Civil War.

19. For an excellent early discussion of the migratoriness of cotton production, see Karl Marx and Frederick Engels, *The Civil War in the US*, International Publishers, 1937, pp. 58–71.

result was recrimination from the North and the West over the supposed betrayal of Northern interests. After much conflict a compromise was made in 1850, establishing California as a free state and leaving Texas unallocated for competition. It was the determination of the North and West to break down this compromise that led to Civil War.

The competition between two different forms of production in some respects slowed down the rate of United States expansion—for it was liable to lead to the same forms of conflict as those raised by Western expansion itself. This problem had already been posed in the 1820s. When Adams became President in 1826, he suggested a conference of the newly established Spanish American Republics. 'As navigators and manufacturers,' he wrote, 'we are already so far advanced upon a career which they are yet to enter, that we may for many years after the conclusion of the war maintain with them a commercial intercourse, highly beneficial to both parties.' Southerners strongly objected, for this implied a blow at their conception of empire. Many of them wanted Cuba as a new slave territory. Southern expansion, in other words, would have necessitated *territorial* expansion. Similarly Southerners resented the importation of ideas of *laissez-faire* liberal democracy into American foreign policy, whose purpose was to benefit Northern manufacturers, and which implied a threat to slave-owning society. As industrial capitalism took more and more hold in the North, articulate Southerners emphasized more and more their 'preindustrial' traits—courtesy, grace, cultivation, the broad outlook versus money-grubbing. Their ambitions for Cuba remained. They had assumed with John Quincey Adams that the laws of political gravitation would push Cuba inevitably into the arms of the United States. But this did not happen. By the 1850s the South was becoming increasingly impatient with 'the apple that refused to fall from the tree'. Southerners attempted to persuade Spain to sell the island and when this did not work, they issued the Ostend Manifesto proclaiming their right to take it. The Manifesto was quickly disclaimed by Northerners in Washington. It was not that expansion was unpopular, but rather that Northerners were not prepared to sanction the expansion of the slave economy.

The Civil War was also a necessary precondition of a fully developed American imperialism in a second sense. For the War can justly be described in the words of Barrington Moore, 'as the last revolutionary offensive on the part of urban or bourgeois capitalist democracy'.[20] Industrialization itself had of course, started well before the War. In fact its pace had been rapidly increasing since 1837. What the War accomplished was the removal of the political and institutional fetters upon industrial capitalism. Legislation passed by the Northern-dominated War Congresses included measures for stronger central banking, high tariffs to protect new industries, a contract labour law to provide a steady flow of cheap immigrant labour, the Homestead Act to gain the support of the West and Federal assistance for internal improvements (the granting of generous loans and free land to build rail links between the industries of the East and the farms of the West, thus unifying the domestic market). It is instructive to compare this legislation, as Moore has done, with the planters' programme of 1860: Federal enforcement of slavery, no high protective tariffs, no subsidies nor expensive tax-creating internal improvements, no national banking and currency system. The extent to which the Plantation Economy had imposed fetters upon the emancipation of capital and the scale of the Northern capitalist victory after the Civil War are both evident.

3. The triumph of bourgeois imperialism

From the 1840s, Eastern Capitalists had begun to show increasing interest in overseas economic expansion, especially in the supposedly vast China market, and in such areas as California and Hawaii, which were seen as stepping stones to it. But they had lacked the legislative power to enforce their policies. In the period after 1870 these empire builders succeeded because the Civil War had given them the political power to implement their plans. The territorial colonialism of Southerners, primarily interested in the extension of the plantation system, was finally superseded by the bourgeois empire of Northerners primarily interested in overseas economic control as an outlet for profitable investment and surplus commodities. The control of policy-making by industrialists and financiers was a pre-condition to the creation of a new commercial empire in its two chief spheres—South America and the Far East.

Indeed it might be argued that the rapidly increasing rate of industrialization, triggered by victory in the Civil War, made

20. Moore, op. cit., p. 112.

such an empire not only possible but also necessary. As efficient machines produced more and more industrial and agricultural goods, consumption could not maintain the pace. The resulting deflation 'needed only the impetus derived from the failures of large banks or Wall Street firms to push the whole economy into full scale depression'.[21] Of the twenty-five years after 1873, half were years of depression: 1873–8, 1882–5 and 1893–7. If the general price index is figured as 100 in 1873, then it fell to 77 in a few years, in the 1880s it again fell from 87 to 76 and again from 78 in 1890 to 71 in 1894. The break in the 1880s was particularly sharp, since agricultural prices fell when good European crops combined with still greater American wheat production. Industrial prices followed suit. Between 1880 and 1884 business failures tripled to almost 12,000 annually.

The result of these cataclysmic depressions was to accelerate cartelization and concentration of ownership. Speaking of the 1873 panic Andrew Carnegie, recollected, 'so many of my friends needed money, that they begged me to repay them. I did so and bought out five or six of them. That was to give me my leading interest in the steel business.' The depression of 1883 similarly allowed him to purchase the Homestead steel plant. Out of this expanded plant came vast amounts of steel, much of which sought foreign markets in the 1890s because of insufficient demand at home. Simultaneous to this process, the rate of foreign investment continued to expand until it reached 3 billion 300 million dollars in 1899. This capital accumulated from the profits of the American industrial revolution was reinvested in new machinery and plants, but an increasing volume also flowed into Latin America, Canada, and Asia.

The problem of foreign outlets was even more intense for the agricultural sector. With the opening of vast new lands in 1855 and the progress of farm mechanization, production soared way beyond home needs—and sometimes world needs. The result was a sharp decline in prices—and an increase in farm bankruptcies. At the beginning of the Reconstruction period it was thought that the lands of the West would provide limitless opportunities for another 100 years. Even the semi-desert areas, it was claimed, would soon be made profitable by ploughing,

21. Walter LaFeber, *The Empire—An Interpretation of American Expansion 1860–98*, 1963, p. 8. This is the best detailed examination of American expansion in the second half of the nineteenth century, and the factual material in this section is largely taken from it.

settlement, and the planting of trees. Taking such promises literally, farmers, cattlemen, and speculators settled more land in 30 years than they had in the previous 300.[22] In the 1880s this dream turned into a nightmare—the fall of prices and the exhaustion of bad soil made the land barely sufficient for subsistence. Between 1888 and 1892 half the population of Western Kansas left their farms in search of new opportunities. But the end of the frontier had already been reached. This had another important consequence—for by 1886 the American railroad system had been more or less completed: 200,000 men had been employed on railroad construction, who were now forced to find other jobs. Similarly iron makers were now forced to find markets, having increased their output enormously between the 1860s and the 1880s.

The three major depression periods coincided with outbreaks of industrial violence perhaps unmatched in other capitalist countries of the period—the railway strike of 1877, the Chicago Haymarket riot of 1886, and the Pullman Strike and Coxey's march of the unemployed upon Washington in the 1890s. Madison's prediction that class war would follow the closing of the frontier seemed to be coming true.

The aftermath of the Civil War thus produced an economic substructure that impelled a fully-fledged modern imperialism. The victory over the Southern planters ensured that the nature of imperial expansion would not generally follow the European pattern of formal political domination over vast colonial areas —except within the borders of the United States itself. There was no prominent military-agrarian class vying for proconsular employment.[23] The new American empire was to be a strictly bourgeois product. It would both solve the problem of surplus disposal and reduce discontent at home. The open class conflict unleashed by the industrial depressions from the 1870s to the 1890s swung the vast majority of the anxious middle class behind a policy of informal but careful planned economic domination in Asia and Latin America.

The lines of this new policy were prophesied with remarkable accuracy by William Seward, Republican Secretary of State at

22. LaFeber, op. cit., p. 20.
23. See Joseph Schumpeter, *Imperialism and Social Classes*. The development of American Imperialism is perhaps the most decisive refutation of his argument.

the end of the 1860s.[24] Seward understood that the primary objective of expansion would no longer be territorial, once the economy had been more industrialized. He considered that commercial expansion would now be the key to making America 'the master of the world'. The new commercial empire would no longer need territory for colonization, which in Seward's view raised the danger of a standing army; it only needed certain land bases to protect the flow of trade and investment. The key to this new world empire was to be Asia. As early as 1853, he had warned of the growing competition there. France, England, and Russia, he wrote, are the great rivals. 'Watch them with jealousy, and baffle their designs against you . . . you are already the great continental power of America. But does that content you? I trust it does not. You want the commerce of the world. This must be looked for on the Pacific. The nation that draws most from the earth and fabricates most, and sells the most to foreign nations, must be and will be the great power of the earth.'

In 1867 Seward purchased Alaska. This was far from a white elephant. It was designed to sandwich British Columbia between American territory and thereby, Seward hoped, increase the pressure upon Canada to join the United States. More important, however, it established what he called a 'drawbridge between America and Asia'. Seward regarded Alaska as the Northern protected-flank in his aim to dominate the Pacific. The Southern flank would be ensured by an American controlled Panama Canal. In the centre would be California and Hawaii. In pursuit of this policy Seward promoted the American representative in Hawaii to Minister Resident in 1863, and four years later tried to prepare the islands for the hug of annexation by pulling the country into a reciprocity treaty. This was vetoed by the Senate, but he was successful in annexing the Midway Islands 1,200 miles west of Hawaii in 1867. The importance of these islands was not their intrinsic economic value, but their crucial position as safe coaling stations for American ships.

In the late 1860s and early 1870s there was little widespread interest in Seward's policy, but with the onset of depression in the 1870s, and the only fitful prosperity of the 1880s and 1890s, the necessity of empire became more apparent. In the depression of the 1870s, the new Secretary of State negotiated a treaty

24. For a discussion of Seward's strategy see Williams, op. cit., p. 318 et seq.

with Hawaii, and moved more actively towards control of Latin America. The United States intervened in Cuba and Venezuela, and encouraged investment in the South of Mexico—a move to secure more surely the projected line of the Panama canal. The 1873 revolution in Cuba destroyed many Spanish and Cuban planters by forcing them to sell their remaining holdings to pay debts. American capital entered the island in large quantities when the expansion of European beet sugar production drove down prices and bankrupted inefficient growers, who sold out cheaply. As the *North American Review* boasted in 1888, this species of ownership gave Americans the financial fruits without political responsibilities. A few years later, there was systematic penetration of American capital into Mexico. With the ending of railroad construction in the United States a group of capitalists moved across the border and obtained Mexican government subsidies of two million dollars and concessions for the construction of five major railways. The victory of Northern capitalism in the Civil War had meant the triumph of a policy of high tariffs. One factor which differentiated British and American imperialism in the last half of the century was the American exploitation of tariffs as an instrument of informal empire. This mode of domination in South America increasingly took the form of the reciprocity treaty. Using the high all-round protective tariff as a bargaining counter, Frelinghuysen, then U S Secretary of State, negotiated this form of treaty with Mexico, Cuba, Puerto Rico, Santo Domingo, Salvador, and Colombia. In return for a virtually free entrance for American manufactures, he reduced the tariff on certain imported raw materials—thus increasing the subordination of Latin American states to the U S economy. As he himself explained, reciprocity in the case of the Caribbean islands, 'brings the islands into close commercial connection with United States and confers upon us and them all the benefits that would result from annexation were that possible'.

The expansion of the frontier by trade into South America and the Pacific in the 1880s and early 1890s was increasingly associated with the idea of an ever expanding commercial frontier which would alleviate discontent at home. Frederick Turner in the 1890s produced his famous frontier thesis of American Democracy. His ideas heavily influenced both Theodore Roosevelt and Woodrow Wilson (who considered himself to be carrying Turner's ideas into practice). Turner regarded

commercial expansion as the magic escape route from his otherwise depressing conclusions. The march to the Pacific would
not stop at the shore line. Turner saw the necessity of continued expansion, and for strong government support of enter-
prising capitalists. 'Once fully afloat on the sea of world wide
economic interests', he wrote, 'we shall develop political interests. Our fisheries dispute furnishes one example; our Samoan
interests another; our Congo relations a third. But perhaps most
important are our present and future relations with South
America, coupled with our Monroe doctrine. It is a settled
maxim of international law that the government of a foreign
state whose subjects have lent money to another state may
interfere to protect the right of bond-holders, if they are endangered by the borrowing state.'

Turner was not alone in his idea of the necessity of developing
the new frontier. Similar ideas were put forward with much
force in the best-selling works of Josiah Strong, the Protestant
missionary. Strong stressed the political significance of the disappearance of public lands. Many expect revolution, warned
Strong, and the Christian church was all that stood in the way.
Strong's writings cast an interesting light on the frequent assertion by academic historians, that missionary activity bore no
relation to economic interest. According to him, the Anglo-
Saxon with his two virtues of civil liberty and spiritual Christianity would move down on Mexico and Central America,
out upon the islands of the sea, over Africa and beyond, and
'can anyone doubt that the result of this competition of races
will be the survival of the fittest?' The expansion of Anglo-
Saxon Christianity would also solve the fundamental problems
of overproduction. Noting that 'steam and electricity have
mightily compressed the earth', so that 'our markets are to be
greatly extended', he commented, 'commerce follows the missionary ... a Christian civilization performs the miracle of
loaves and fishes, and feeds its thousands in a desert'. Missionary
activity encouraged native peoples to adopt Western habits and
Western dress, thus missionary and trader were in perpetual
alliance.

By the 1890s, there was a growing consensus among business
men and politicians that further expansion was necessary to
avert economic depression. This policy had been implicit in
the 1880s, when Congress sanctioned a large increase in naval
spending. There was opposition to territorial expansion in non-

contiguous areas. It was argued that colonialism of this kind would lead to the dangers that had brought down the Roman Empire—through the necessity of large standing armies and an increasingly strong military caste. But there was no disagreement about the wisdom of informal methods of domination. This much is illustrated by the role of President Cleveland who is popularly recorded in American history books as a fervent anti-colonialist. The Brazilian Revolution of 1894–5 threatened the growing American trade with that country. Vigorous pressures for intervention were made by Standard Oil and W. S. Crossman and Brothers. As a result, Cleveland ordered the navy to intervene to check the rebels, and it was kept on duty off Rio for a further year to check any further danger to American property. Cleveland's attitude to British interference in Venezuela was similarly vigorous. England was forced to back down, since, as Secretary of State Olney claimed, 'Today the United States is practically sovereign on this continent, and its fiat law upon the subjects to which it confines its interposition.' Henry Cabot Lodge remarked, in a significant reformulation of the Monroe doctrine: 'The doctrine has no bearing on the extension of United States, but simply holds that no European power shall establish itself in the Americas or interfere with American governments.'

4. The advent of the Spanish-American War

It was the fierce depression of the 1890s that set America on the final path towards war with Spain. When the depression burst in 1893, there was a considerable body of business opinion that attributed the slump in trade to incorrect monetary policy. But the attempt of the Cleveland Administration to provide a monetary cure for the crisis made little difference. The result was a growing agreement that the crisis was one of overproduction and the lack of markets. This consensus was expressed by McKinley in 1895: 'No worthier cause than the expansion of trade can engage our energies.... We want our markets for our manufactures, and agricultural products.... We want a foreign market for our surplus products.... We want a reciprocity which will give us foreign markets for our surplus products, and in turn that will open our markets to foreigners for those products which they produce and we do not.' The National Association of Manufacturers took up this cause enthusiastically, and were particularly keen on entry into the fabled Asian market. In Japan and Korea it met with some success. Japan doubled her imports of cotton in 1895, and Americans gained substantial contracts in shipbuilding. In Korea, Horace Allen, a missionary who was also the economic secretary of the American legation, was able to gain the concession of the Un San mines, the richest gold mines in the Far East. Allen then reorganized the Korean Cabinet so that pro-Japanese elements were unable to oppose the grant and persuaded the Korean government to institute the death penalty for Japanese traders copying American goods in the area. Accompanying this thrust of finance and manufacture in the Far East was an intensified missionary effort in the area. One missionary stated his role bluntly in the *Congregationist Magazine*: 'If I were asked to state what would be the best form of advertising (in China) for the great American Steel Trust or Standard Oil or Baldwin Locomotives.... or Singer Sewing machine ... I should say take up the support of one or two dozen mission statio⎺ Despite such sterling efforts, however, US imperialism fo⎺ stiff competition from Japan, Russia, England, and Franc⎺ China. Because of the collusion of other powers, American capitalists lost the chance to finance China's war indemnity to Japan, and thus the railroad concession that went with it. Anxiety about the Chinese market played a considerable part in determining the annexation of the Philippines in the Spanish–American war.

In 1895 there was a further Cuban revolution directed against Spain. The causes of discontent in the island were in fact a direct result of the Reciprocity Treaty negotiated with the United States. A new American tariff in 1895 had eliminated the privileged position of Cuba in the American sugar market, and plantations were consequently forced to discharge hands. In the Revolution that followed considerable damage was done to Cuban-American property. Powerful US corporations launched a campaign for intervention in the island. Initial support for the revolution changed into a demand for intervention to support moderate and conservative elements in Cuba. At the same time businessmen who did not have assets to defend and who had hitherto opposed the War, considered that the situation was creating an atmosphere of business uncertainty, and that intervention was necessary to stablize the situation so that domestic recovery and Asian expansion could proceed uninterrupted. The causes of the War were quite blatantly stated in a note from the American Government to Spain. It read: 'The extraordinary, because direct and not merely theoretical or sentimental, interest of the US in the Cuban situation cannot be ignored. ... Not only are our citizens largely concerned in the ownership of property and in the industrial and commercial ventures ... but the chronic condition of trouble causes disturbance in the social and political conditions of our own peoples. ... A continuous irritation within our borders injuriously affects the normal functions of business, and tends to delay the condition of prosperity to which this country is entitled.'

The war proceeded very much along the lines prophesied by Seward forty years before. Hawaii and the Philippines were annexed as necessary stepping stones to the penetration of China. The annexation of the Philippines aroused opposition because it seemed to be the first step towards a European type of colonialism, which entailed a growing military sector and increased taxes. But such was not McKinley's original intention. All that was initially needed was an adequate naval base. It was the Filipino rebellion against US occupation, that made annexation an unfortunate necessity. In Cuba itself, this necessity was averted by a resolution from Senator Platt of Connecticut, to the effect that the government and control of the island would be left in the hands of its people, subject only to a restriction of its relations with foreign powers, a limit on the national debt, support for American actions, and the provision of bases. This was a decidedly better solution than the Puerto Rican annexation, since it maintained effective control without the threat of immigration to racist sentiment.

The War itself was only a prelude to an attempt to make a full-scale economic penetration of Asia, and particularly China. The Secretary of State in 1899 issued a demand for equal access and fair treatment for American economic power in China. A further note asserted America's direct interest in maintaining the territorial and administrative integrity of that country. These Open Door notes were America's characteristic contribution to the practice of imperialism.[25] It was not akin to

25. The State Department historians deny any fundamental connection between the Open Door Notes and the practice of American imperialism. See, for example, George Kennan, *American Diplomacy 1900–50*, 1952.

British imperial policy in the period. London's version of the policy acknowledged spheres of interest whereas the United States demanded absolute equality of treatment. Convinced of the necessity to expand and yet wanting to avoid the pitfalls of a formal colonial empire (with the consequent necessity of war against rivals), the United States employed the strategy of the Open Door to exploit its growing economic power.

The depression of the 1890s had a further important consequence for the changing practice of American imperialism: the growing domination of finance capital over industrial capital. Significantly, Rockefeller became a financier, while older giant capitalists like Carnegie sold out and retired. In the depression the great majority of industrial capitalists became temporarily dependent on finance capital, like that represented by the house of Morgan. Banks, like Morgan and Rockefeller, were able to control the vast capital assets tied up in life insurance companies in addition to the security and profits derived from industrial plants such as Standard Oil and U S Steel. The conflict between finance and industrial capital had certain repercussions on the character of the American empire. Since poor countries had to have money to buy American exports of goods and services, they had to accumulate it, either by increasing their export of raw materials or else by borrowing it from abroad. The result was what Taft referred to as 'dollar diplomacy'. Backward countries needed capital, but financiers needed government help at home in order to attract capital from the great number of individual savers who were unfamiliar and doubtful about the security of such overseas investment. This made financiers particularly keen to win firm guarantees of repayment from debtor nations.

5. The maturation of the U S imperial system

With the Open Door policy, the implementation of dollar diplomacy, and the seizure of the Panama Canal zone from Colombia, the main infra-structure of the early US imperialist system was completed. Theodore Roosevelt produced the final metamorphosis of the Monroe doctrine when he declared, 'I regard the Monroe doctrine as being equivalent to the open door in South America.' He went on to assure each Latin American nation that it could count on the friendship of the United States, if it 'acted with reasonable efficiency and decency in social and political matters' and 'if it keeps its orders and pays its obligations'. If nations behaved they would enjoy prosperity, if not they would be punished by American intervention.

This system was to be exemplified in the American treatment of Cuba.[26] A revolt in 1917 immediately evoked protests from the resident American business community, and as a matter of course the Marines were sent in. State Department historians claim that this intervention was necessitated by the danger of German activity in the island—but not surprisingly have produced no evidence to support this assertion. The purpose of intervention was to restore political stability and thus create conditions for profitable business activity. As part of this stabilization policy, General Enoch Crowder was appointed to supervise a new electoral code, and oversee the elections of 1920. Crowder proceeded to draw up six necessary qualifications for a Cuban president and member of the Cuban cabinet. The first condition was stated to be 'a thorough acquaintance with the desires of the US government', and the sixth condition was 'amenability to suggestions which might be made to him by the American Legation'. At the instance of the house of Morgan, Crowder was appointed ambassador to Cuba, although it had hitherto been illegal for a soldier to hold a diplomatic post. A bank loan to the Cuban government by Morgan was endorsed by the American Government, and timid attempts by the Cuban Government to raise revenue by a 4 per cent profits tax were satisfactorily replaced by a 1 per cent sales tax. Although particularly blatant, this episode was a typical product of the heavy involvement of American finance capital in South America.

Conventionally, historians tend to contrast the swashbuckling crudity of dollar diplomacy by Roosevelt and Taft with the high-minded idealism, 'the legalistic-moralistic approach to international problems' associated with Wilson, and the arbitration movement.[27] The contrast between Roosevelt and Wilson is presented as one between the 'realist' and the 'moralist'. While Roosevelt is seen as the wielder of the 'big stick' and creator of the Great White Fleet, Wilson is seen as the fierce

26. See Robert F. Smith, *The United States and Cuba: Business and Diplomacy 1917–60*, 1960, ch. 1.

27. For a critique of this approach see Lloyd C. Gardner, 'American Foreign Policy 1900–21: a second look at the realist critique of American Diplomacy' in Bernstein, op. cit., pp. 202–31.

critic of dollar diplomacy, the hammer of the trusts and the naïve champion of world peace. In this context, much is made of Wilson's repudiation of the Taft-backed International Banking Consortium as evidence of Wilsonian moralism. This is a misunderstanding, however. Wilson did not oppose loans to China as such, he merely opposed loans in which the American banking group could not have the controlling interest. As he explained to the bankers, he intended the United States to 'participate and participate very generously in the opening to the Chinese and to the use of the world of the almost untouched and perhaps unrivalled resources of China'. He kept his word by exempting expanding corporations from anti-trust legislation, and providing the legislative encouragement that the financiers desired.

In fact Woodrow Wilson provided twentieth-century American imperialism with its most coherent and self-righteous defender. As as early adherent of the Turner frontier thesis,[28] Wilson defined the nation's natural politico-economic development and its prosperity as a function of westward expansion.[29] With the end of the continental frontier, expansion into world markets with the nation's surplus economic goods and capital was, in his view, indispensable to the stability and prosperity of the economy. It was also no more than a natural development in the life of any industrial nation, and in no way morally invidious; for in his view, the nation's economic expansion was a civilizing force that carried with it principles of democracy and Christianity, bonds of international understanding and peace. Given superior American industrial efficiency, the United States would assume supremacy in the world's markets, provided artificial barriers to her economic expansion were eliminated. Accordingly, Wilson admired and championed Hay's Open Door policy and advocated vigorous government diplomacy to attain these ends. In a speech in 1921, he stated: 'If we are not

28. For the defects of the Turner thesis, see Clarence H. Danhof, 'The Economic Validity of the Safety Valve Doctrine', in Coats and Robertson, *Essays in American Economic History*, 1969, pp. 219–27, and Stephen Thernstrom, 'Urbanisation, Migration and Social Mobility in Late 19th Century America' in Bernstein op. cit., pp. 158–76.

29. For a discussion of Wilsonianism see Williams, op. cit., p. 411, *et seq*; Gardner, op. cit.; Martin J. Sklar, 'Woodrow Wilson and the Political Economy of Modern US Liberalism', *Studies on the Left*, No. 3, 1960.

going to stifle economically, we have got to find our way out into the great international exchanges of the world.... The nation's irresistible energy has got to be released for the commercial conquest of the world.' As a policy for achieving this he advocated a strong mercantile marine, a downward revision of the tariff and laws encouraging American overseas banking. Wilson's beliefs about universal peace were inextricably linked with his commercial philosophy.

Wilson hoped to stay out of the First World War and then dominate the peace settlement as the undisputed economic master of the world. He nevertheless feared the commercial threat of Germany and hated its military-dominated government. In addition prominent finance houses like Dupont and Morgan provided economic support to the Allied war effort. Wilson's war aims were genuinely expressed in his rules for the League of Nations. For there was no fundamental incompatibility between the ambitions of American imperialism and the sermonizing tones of the Covenant. There, like the Ten Commandments, were the principles of American economic expansion—the open door, the freedom of the seas, the prohibition of territorial changes except in accordance with the wishes of the inhabitants, compromises between advanced powers and underdeveloped territories that ensured the economic expansion of the former, and a political system of control which would be dominated by the United States, Britain, France, and Japan.

This grandiose bourgeois evangelism was upset by the very cupidity of the capitalist system, which Wilson had so idealized. In October 1917, his scheme was threatened by the accomplishment of the Bolshevik Revolution.[30] Wilson's position on socialism had been unambiguous. The President's thought, records his official biographer, 'disclosed itself as antipathetic to unsettled political conduct and to revolution as a method of government'. Such a philosophy had formed the justification for his extensive interventions in Haiti, Nicaragua, the Dominican Republic, and in the Mexican Revolution. Wilson, in his own words, had set about 'to teach the South American Republics to elect good men' and to establish a government in Mexico 'under which all contracts and business and concessions

30. For an account of the politics of American counter-revolutionary intervention in Russia, see Appleman William's essay in Horowitz (ed), *Containment and Revolution*, 1967.

will be safer than they have been'.

Despite his announcement that he 'stood resolutely and ab-solutely for the right of every people to determine its own destiny and its own affairs', Wilson wasted little time on deciding that the Bolsheviks constituted an exception to his principle of self-determination. By defining the Bolsheviks as German agents, the task of self-justification was made relatively simple. It was not moral scruple that prevented Wilson from making a swift and effective intervention in Russia, nor even the dictates of the war with Germany, for Wilson made the decision to intervene with American troops before the Germans were stopped short in the second battle of the Marne. What prevented proper intervention by the Pacific imperialist powers was their expansionist greed and mutual suspicions. America could not afford to leave the Manchurian railway in the control of the Japanese, and was more concerned to prevent covert Japanese expansion in China and Siberia at the expense of American economic interests, than to make an all-out attack on Bolshevism. Here Wilson made a massive but characteristic mistake. The eventual result of this local imperialist squabble was, of course, Pearl Harbour and the Pacific War.

6. Conclusions

Several critical factors differentiated America from European imperialist powers in the nineteenth century. America lacked a powerful militarily-oriented aristocracy, was free from the land hunger which sustained European colonial settlement and was exceptionally well-endowed in necessary raw materials. The Northern victory in the Civil War ensured the emergence of a bourgeois non-territorial imperial system whose primary rationale was initially not the supply of raw materials but the provision of markets for American goods and outlets for Ameri-can capital. By the beginning of the twentieth century, the basic structure of the American imperial system had been com-pleted. The growth of this system had neither been anomic nor indiscriminate. American power from the beginning had been concentrated upon Latin America and the Far East. These areas were guaranteed by the two classic statements of American imperialism—the Monroe Doctrine and the Open Door Note.

At the end of the ninteenth century it seemed that American ambitions in these two areas were soon to be completely fulfilled. In the previous half century, the main obstacle to American economic expansion had been the entrenched positions already occupied by the British. By the turn of the century, however, the balance of economic power had shifted. British economic hegemony in South America had begun to give way before the encroachments of American capital. For Americans this shift was symbolized by the settlement of the Venezuelan dispute in 1895. Traditional hostility or suspicion towards Britain was increasingly replaced by the idea of an Anglo-American partnership which would smooth the transition between the Pax Britannica and the Pax Americana.[31] This would allow the United States all the fruits of imperial control without its concomitant fiscal and military burdens. America had no need of a formal colonial empire but could increase her imperial power simply by relying upon her superior economy.[32] Just as early British imperialism had honeycombed the Portuguese empire while protecting its formal structure, so a similar special relationship might be established between the United States and the British Empire. The United States could afford to move from the crude territorial expansionism of Polk to a peaceful and ordered world governed by due respect for property and the Open Door. Just as British industrial supremacy had produced the pacifism of John Bright, so American industrial supremacy was to produce the sanctimonious moralism of Woodrow Wilson and the League of Nations.

It was increasingly evident, however, in the years before 1914, that America's economic power would not go unchal-

31. See LaFeber, op. cit., pp. 313–18.
32. The United States was probably the most self-sufficient country in the world in this period. Nevertheless in 1910 America was the world's third largest trader. US exports only constituted 4–5 per cent of GNP in the years before 1914. Her main imports were capital and labour. In 1914 foreign investment in the US constituted 7.2 billion dollars, while US investment abroad constituted 3.5 billion dollars. This balance was almost exactly reversed during the First World War. The semi-autarkic nature of the US economy in the nineteenth century might at first sight contradict an economic interpretation of the rise of US imperialism. In the period 1870–1900 the population increased by 97 per cent, and home consumers consumed 90 per cent of US total production. By 1898, however, this 10 per cent amounted to 1 billion dollars worth and was heavily concentrated in iron, steel, textiles and agricultural machinery—precisely the industries which pushed hardest for overseas expansion.

lenged. America's reservation in the Far East was increasingly threatened by Japan in the years after the Russo-Japanese war, while the rise of German 'militaristic' imperialism might pose a threat to American penetration of Eastern Europe and the Middle East. Moreover, in the second decade of the century, a yet more ominous phenomenon appeared in the shape of indigenous movements against imperialism under the banner of nationalism or socialism. The Chinese Revolution of 1911, the Mexican Revolution and then the Russian Revolution posed a drastic threat to the ideology of Wilsonism.

Wilson's League of Nations was therefore conceived both as a means of securing American imperial supremacy without recourse either to formal colonial empire or to inter-imperialist warfare, and secondly as a means of building a Holy Alliance of industrial powers to hold down the rebellious forces of the underdeveloped world. It envisaged the consolidation of an informal American empire in which each dependent country would be tied to the United States on the model of the Platt amendment. As is well known, Wilson's proposal of the League was rejected by the American electorate after the war. What had been devised as an inexpensive means of securing the permanence of the Open Door international order had begun to appear like an open-ended commitment to police the globe in the defence of non-essential interests. It would be a mistake, however, to interpret the rejection of the League as a retreat to a naïve isolationism. The American ambition to establish an Open Door world remained unchanged. But in the 1920s it was considered possible to achieve this end without the dangerous organizational commitments implied by the League.[33] The Washington Conference of 1921 was designed to lay down Open Door rules for the Far East and to ensure that Japan remained a subordinate imperialist partner in an Anglo-American domain. The Kellog-Briand Pact and the Lausanne Conference, together with the Dawes plan, similarly employed American economic power to ensure the extension of the Open Door principle into Europe, the Middle East and Africa. The contradiction between the industrial supremacy of the United States after the First World War and its limited interventions in world politics was more apparent than real.

33. For an account of American manoeuvres to expand the Open Door in the inter-war period, see, R. F. Smith, 'American Foreign Relations, 1920–42', in Bernstein, op. cit., pp. 232–62.

The Great Depression and the coming of the Second World War, however, brought to an end this prospect of informal economic domination. The collapse of the world market brought with it an intensified struggle between the established imperialist powers (USA, Britain, France) and aspirant contenders (Germany and Japan). The massive unemployment and growing social discontent in America expressed itself once more, as in the 1890s, in an intensified search for new export markets and the protection of existing preserves. The American objective of penetrating the British Empire through the Open Door was made difficult by the establishment of Imperial Preference in the Ottawa agreement. But the worse sufferers were Germany and Japan. Japanese goods were systematically excluded from the British Empire, from the United States and from American dependencies.[34] Given the structure of her imperial system, the United States thus had little option later but to participate both in the European and in the Pacific Wars. For the rise of Japanese militarism posed a threat to the Open Door in Asia, while the possibiltiy of the German domination threatened to close down markets in Europe and to encroach upon American preserves in Latin America. When France collapsed and Britain seemed on the verge of defeat in 1940–1, however, America was in a strong position to prop up the tottering British empire on her own terms.[35] In return for American aid, the British were forced to accept completely the rules of the Open Door and to modify the Ottawa agreements to allow American economic penetration. With the undermining of British imperialism, the collapse of Germany and the imposition of an American diktat on Japan, the United States assumed its

34. For an account of Anglo-US economic suffocation of Japanese imperialism as a major cause of the Pacific War, see Noam Chomsky, 'The Revolutionary Pacifism of A. J. Muste', *American Power and the New Mandarins*, 1969, pp. 130–77.

35. Roosevelt told his son at the outbreak of the Second World War: 'It's something that's not generally known, but British bankers and German bankers have had world trade pretty well sewn up in their pockets for a long time ... Well, now, that's not so good for American trade, is it? ... If in the past German and British economic interests have operated to exclude us from world trade, kept our merchant shipping down, closed out this or that market, and now Germany and Britain are at war, what should we do?' Quoted in Smith, op. cit., p. 252.

long-anticipated place as the undisputed leader of world capitalism.

It should thus be clear that there has been considerable continuity both in ideology and in political form between the American imperialism that developed in the second half of the nineteenth century and the American imperialism that has manifested itself since 1945. The ideology and political expression of American imperialism in the century before 1914 was shaped by the exigencies of inter-imperialist struggle. Americans before the First World War had no reason to disguise their plans and methods of economic domination. This was because they did not consider their form of imperialism to constitute imperialism. It did not not occur to 'liberals' like Wilson or the dollar diplomatists who preceded him, that investment in and ownership of other nations' raw materials, transport, industry and financial apparatus constituted an imperialist form of exploitation. Imperialism to them meant British and European style territorial expansion and monopolistic spheres of interest held down by large and threatening military castes. Exploitation meant exorbitantly profitable concessions gained by undue influence over government officials—in short the supposed 'unfair practices' which in the liberal mythology of domestic progressivism, distinguished the unhealthiness of the trust from the healthiness of the corporation.

Open Door expansion, on the other hand, appeared to them unproblematically as a natural division of labour between industrialized and agrarian nations; it meant mutually beneficial business relationships and trade; it meant the assumption by the United States of its natural place in the world economy through the elimination of 'artificial' impediments to the operation of the laws of competitive commerce. In the words of President Truman, 'the Open Door policy is not imperialism, it is free trade.'

The October Revolution of 1917 traumatized American imperialism, because it proved that it was possible to carry through a successful socialist and anti-imperialist revolution. After its initial attempt to put down the Revolution by force, the United States ostracized the Soviet Union in the clear expectation that a régime at such variance to domestic and international liberal practice was doomed to collapse. But it did not collapse and managed to survive in defiance of all the social-darwinist laws which Wilson believed to govern international relations.[36] The subsequent survival of the Chinese, Korean, Vietnamese and Cuban revolutions has only confirmed this frightened sense of bewilderment. Yet functionally Communism is also 'the sustaining menace'. For not only does it provide the rationale for massive defence expenditure (A B Ms), but it also breathes new life into the official anti-imperialist mythology.

American imperialism has also tried to preserve its original non-territorial character. The mythology of American 'advisers', even when they number tens of thousands, and the cover operations of the C I A testify to this. But efforts to preserve the informal empire during the past quarter of the century have been progressively undermined by the very success of American capitalism in encroaching upon rival imperial systems. In the Second World War the United States flattened the imperial pretensions of Japan, contributed to the collapse of Germany and seriously undermined the economic viability of British imperialism. Faced by the threat of anti-imperialist movements in these moribund colonial systems, the United States has been to an increasing extent forced to fill the vacuum and bear the military and financial costs. The result has been a strange reversal of roles. While the Americans police the world and bear a high proportion of the infra-structural costs of the defence of the international capitalist system, Germany and Japan—only lightly burdened by defence costs—have expanded dramatically under the American military umbrella and now compete in American markets. The 'invisible empire' of the United States has disappeared, and in its place stands a conspicuous military machine raining destruction upon Vietnam. The old American fear of the professional soldier has been largely realized by the consequent growth of the military-industrial complex. History has turned full circle. The territorialism so despised by the bourgeois empire builders of the North is now being practised on a massive scale throughout the world by a Southern-dominated[37] standing army.

36. Wilson advocated a gospel of efficiency. He concluded an address to businessmen on expansion in 1912 with the words, 'I do not wish to make the analysis tedious. I will merely ask you, after you go home, to think over this proposition; that what we have been witnessing for the past 100 years is the transformation of a Newtonian Constitution into a Darwinian Constitution.' Quoted in Gardner, op. cit., p. 212.

37. See Morris Janowitz, *The Professional Soldier*, 1960, ch. 3.

11

The Problem of the Capitalist State

NICOS POULANTZAS

In his book The State in Capitalist Society (*London, 1969*), *Ralph Miliband presented a systematic and documented account of the nature of class power in bourgeois democracies. In this exchange Nicos Poulantzas and Ralph Miliband debate the important questions of method and substance which the book raised for Marxist theory.*

Nicos Poulantzas teaches political theory at the Sorbonne and is the author of Political Power and Social Class (*U K, 1972*).

Ralph Miliband's recently published work, *The State in Capitalist Society*,[1] is in many respects of capital importance. The book is extremely substantial, and cannot decently be summarized in a few pages: I cannot recommend its reading too highly. I will limits myself here to a few critical comments, in the belief that only criticism can advance Marxist theory. For the specificity of this theory compared with other theoretical problematics lies in the extent to which Marxist theory provides itself, in the very act of its foundation, with the means of its own internal criticism. I should state at the outset that my critique will not be 'innocent': having myself written on the question of the State in my book *Pouvoir Politique et Classes Sociales*,[2] these comments will derive from epistemological positions presented there which differ from those of Miliband.

First of all, some words on the fundamental merits of Miliband's book. The theory of the State and of political power has, with rare exceptions such as Gramsci, been neglected by Marxist thought. This neglect has a number of different causes, related to different phases of the working-class movement. In Marx

1. Weidenfeld and Nicolson, London, 1969.
2. Maspero, Paris, 1968.

himself this neglect, more apparent than real, is above all due to the fact that his principal theoretical object was the capitalist mode of production, within which the economy not only holds the role of determinant in the last instance, but also the dominant role—while for example in the feudal mode of production, Marx indicates that if the economy still has the role of determinant in the last instance, it is ideology in its religious form that holds the dominant role. Marx thus concentrated on the economic level of the capitalist mode of production, and did not deal specifically with the other levels of such as the State : he dealt only with these levels through their *effects* on the economy (for example, in the passages of *Capital* on factory legislation). In Lenin, the reasons are different : involved in direct political practice, he dealt with the question of the State only in essentially polemical works, such as *State and Revolution*, which do not have the theoretical status of certain of his texts such as *The Development of Capitalism in Russia*.

How, by contrast, is the neglect of theoretical study of the State in the Second International, and in the Third International after Lenin, to be explained? Here I would advance, with all necessary precautions, the following thesis : the absence of a study of the State derived from the fact that the dominant conception of these Internationals was a deviation, *economism*, which is generally accompanied by an absence of revolutionary strategy and objectives—even when it takes a 'leftist' or Luxemburgist form. In effect, economism considers that other levels of social reality, including the State, are simple epiphenomena reducible to the economic 'base'. Thereby a specific study of the State becomes superfluous. Parallel with this, economism considers that every change in the social system happens first of all in the economy and that political action should have the economy as its principal objective. Once again, a specific study of the State is redundant. Thus economism leads either to reformism and trade-unionism, or to forms of 'leftism' such as syndicalism. For, as Lenin showed, the principal objective of revolutionary action is *State power* and the necessary precondition of any socialist revolution is the destruction of the bourgeois State apparatus.

Economism and the absence of revolutionary strategy are manifest in the Second International. They are less obvious in the Third International, yet in my view what fundamentally determined the theory and practice of 'Stalinist' policy, dominant in the Comintern probably from 1928, was nevertheless the same economism and absence of a revolutionary strategy. This is true both of the 'leftist' period of the Comintern until 1935, and of the revisionist-reformist period after 1935. This economism determined the absence of a theory of the State in the Third International, and this *relation* (economism/absence of a theory of the State) is perhaps nowhere more evident than in its analyses of fascism—precisely where the Comintern had most need of such a theory of the State. Considerations of a concrete order both confirm and explain this. Since the *principal symptoms* of Stalinist politics were located in the relations between the State apparatus and the Communist Party in the U S S R, symptoms visible in the famous Stalin Constitution of 1936, it is very comprehensible that study of the State remained a forbidden topic *par excellence*.

It is in this context that Miliband's work helps to overcome a major lacuna. As is always the case when a scientific theory is lacking, bourgeois conceptions of the State and of political power have pre-empted the terrain of political theory, almost unchallenged. Miliband's work is here truly *cathartic*: he methodically attacks these conceptions. Rigorously deploying a formidable mass of empirical material in his examination of the concrete social formations of the U S A, England, France, Germany or Japan, he not only radically demolishes bourgeois ideologies of the State, but provides us with a positive knowledge that these ideologies have never been able to produce.

However, the procedure chosen by Miliband—a *direct* reply to bourgeois ideologies by the immediate examination of concrete fact—is also to my mind the source of the faults of his book. Not that I am against the study of the 'concrete': on the contrary, having myself relatively neglected this aspect of the question in my own work (with its somewhat different aim and object), I am only the more conscious of the necessity for concrete analyses. I simply mean that a precondition of any scientific approach to the 'concrete' is to make explicit the epistemological principles of its own treatment of it. Now it is important to note that Miliband nowhere deals with the Marxist theory of the State as such, although it is constantly implicit in his work. He takes it as a sort of 'given' in order to reply to bourgeois ideologies by examining the facts in its light. Here I strongly believe that Miliband is wrong, for the absence of explicit presentation of principles in the order of exposition of a scientific discourse is not innocuous : above all in a domain like the theory of the State, where a Marxist theory, as we have seen, has yet to be constituted. In effect, one has the impression that this absence often leads Miliband to attack bourgeois ideologies of the State whilst placing himself on their own terrain. Instead of *displacing* the epistomological terrain and submitting these ideologies to the critique of Marxist science by demonstrating their inadequacy to the real (as Marx does, notably in the *Theories of Surplus-Value*), Miliband appears to omit this first step. Yet the analyses of modern epistemology show that it is never possible simply to oppose 'concrete facts' to concepts, but that these must be attacked by other parallel concepts situated in a different problematic. For it is only by means of these new concepts that the old notions can be confronted with 'concrete reality'.

Let us take a simple example. Attacking the prevailing notion of 'plural élites', whose ideological function is to deny the existence of a ruling class, Miliband's reply, which he supports by 'facts', is that this plurality of *élites* does not exclude the existence of a ruling *class*, for it is precisely these élites that constitute this class:[3] this is close to Bottomore's response to the question. Now, I maintain that in replying to the adversary in this way, one places oneself on his ground and thereby risks floundering in the swamp of his ideological imagination, thus missing a scientific explanation of the 'facts'. What Miliband avoids is the necessary preliminary of a *critique of the ideological notion of élite* in the light of the scientific concepts of Marxist theory. Had this critique been made, it would have been evident that the 'concrete reality' concealed by the notion of 'plural élites'—the ruling class, the fractions of this class, the hegemonic class, the governing class, the State apparatus—can only be grasped if the very notion of élite is rejected. For concepts and notions are never innocent, and by employing the notions of the adversary to reply to him, one legitimizes them and permits their persistence. Every notion or concept only has meaning within a whole theoretical problematic that founds it: extracted from this problematic and imported 'uncritically' into Marxism, they have absolutely uncontrollable effects. They always surface when least expected, and constantly risk clouding scientific analysis. In the extreme case, one can be unconsciously and surreptitiously contaminated by the very

3. Miliband, pp. 24 ff. and 47.

epistemological principles of the adversary, that is to say the problematic that founds the concepts which have not been theoretically criticized, believing them simply refuted by the facts. This is more serious: for it is then no longer a question merely of external notions 'imported' into Marxism, but of principles that risk vitiating the use made of Marxist concepts themselves.

Is this the case with Miliband? I do not believe that the consequences of his procedure have gone so far. It nevertheless remains true that, as I see it, Miliband sometimes allows himself to be unduly influenced by the methodological principles of the adversary. How is this manifested? Very briefly, I would say that it is visible in the difficulties that Miliband has in comprehending social classes and the State as *objective structures*, and their relations as an *objective system of regular connections*, a structure and a system whose agents, 'men', are in the words of Marx, 'bearers' of it—*träger*. Miliband constantly gives the impression that for him social classes or 'groups' are in some way reducible to *inter-personal relations*, that the State is reducible to inter-personal relations of the members of the diverse 'groups' that constitute the State apparatus, and finally that the relation between social classes and the State is itself reducible to inter-personal relations of 'individuals' composing social groups and 'individuals' composing the State apparatus.

I have indicated, in an earlier article in *New Left Review*, that this conception seems to me to derive from a *problematic of the subject* which has had constant repercussions in the history of Marxist thought.[4] According to this problematic, the agents of a social formation, 'men', are not considered as the 'bearers' of objective instances (as they are for Marx), but as the genetic principle of the levels of the social whole. This is a problematic of *social actors*, of individuals as the origin of *social action*: sociological research thus leads finally, not to the study of the objective co-ordinates that determine the distribution of agents into social classes and the contradictions between these classes, but to the search for *finalist* explanations founded on the *movitations of conduct* of the individual actors. This is notoriously one of the aspects of the problematic both of Weber and of contemporary functionalism. To transpose this problematic of the subject into Marxism is in the end to admit

4. 'Marxist Political Theory in Great Britain', *New Left Review*, No. 43.

the epistemological principles of the adversary and to risk vitiating one's own analyses.

Let us now consider some of the concrete themes of Miliband's book in the light of this preamble.

1. The false problem of managerialism

The first problem which Miliband discusses, very correctly, is that of the *ruling class*, by way of reply to the current bourgeois ideologies of *managerialism*. According to these ideologies, the contemporary separation of private ownership and control has transferred economic power from entrepreneurs to managers. The latter have no interest as owners in the strict sense, and hence do not seek profit as their aim—in other words, profit is not a motivation of their conduct, but growth, or development. Since the ruling class is here defined by the quest for profit, and this quest no longer characterizes the directors of the economy, the ruling class itself no longer exists: we are now confronted with a 'plurality of élites', of which the managers are one. What is Miliband's response to this?[5] He takes these ideologies literally and turns their own arguments against them: in fact, managers do seek profit as the goal of their actions, for this is how the capitalist system works. Seeking private profit, they also make up part of the ruling class, for the contradiction of the capitalist system according to Marx, Miliband tells us, is 'the contradiction between its ever more social character and its enduringly private purpose'.[6] While not excluding the existence of some managerial goals relatively different from those of owners, Miliband considers managers as one among the distinct economic élites composing the ruling class.

I consider this a mistaken way of presenting the problem. To start with, the distinctive criterion for membership of the capitalist class for Marx *is in no way* a motivation of conduct, that is to say the search for profit as the 'aim of action'. For there may well exist capitalists who are not motivated by profit, just as there are non-capitalists (the petty-bourgeoisie in small-scale production, for instance) who by contrast have just such a motivation. Marx's criterion is the objective place in production and the ownership of the means of production. It should be remembered that even Max Weber had to admit that what defined the capitalist was not 'the lure of gain'. For Marx, profit

5. Miliband, op. cit.   6. Miliband, p. 34.

is not a motivation of conduct—even one 'imposed' by the system—it is an objective category that designates a part of realized surplus value. In the same way, the fundamental contradiction of the capitalist system, according to Marx, is not at all a contradiction between its social character and its 'private purpose', but a contradiction between the socialization of productive forces and their *private appropriation.* Thus the characterization of the existing social system as capitalist in no way depends on the motivations of the conduct of managers. Furthermore : to characterize the class position of managers, one need not refer to the motivations of their conduct, but only to their place in production and their relationship to the ownership of the means of production. Here both Bettleheim and myself have noted that it is necessary to distinguish, in the term 'property' used by Marx, formal legal property, which may not belong to the 'individual' capitalist, and *economic property or real appropriation*, which is the only genuine *economic power*.[7] This economic property, which is what matters as far as distribution into classes is concerned, still belongs well and truly to *capital*. The manager exercises only a functional delegation of it.

From this point of view, the managers as such do not constitute a distinct fraction of the capitalist class. Miliband, basing himself on the non-pertinent distinction of motivations of conduct, is led to consider the managers a distinct 'economic élite'. By doing so, he not only attributes to them an importance they do not possess, but he is prevented from seeing what is important. For in effect, what matters is not the differences and relations between 'economic élites' based on diverging aims, but something of which Miliband says virtually nothing, *the differences and relations between fractions of capital*. The problem is not that of a plurality of 'economic élites' but of fractions of the capitalist class. Can a Marxist pass over in silence the existent differences and relations, under imperialism, between comprador monopoly capital, national monopoly capital, non-monopoly capital, industrial capital, or financial capital?

7. Bettleheim, *La Transition vers l'Economie Socialiste*, and Poulantzas, *Pouvoir Politique et Classes Sociales*, pp. 23 ff.

2. *The question of bureaucracy*

The next problem that Miliband selects for discussion, again correctly, is that of the relation between the ruling class and the State. Here too Miliband's approach to the question is to provide a direct rebuttal of bourgeois ideologies. These ideologies affirm the *neutrality* of the State, representing the general interest, in relation to the divergent interests of 'civil society'. Some of them (Aron, for example) claim that the capitalist class has never truly *governed* in capitalist societies, in the sense that its members have rarely participated directly in the government; others claim that the members of the State apparatus, the 'civil servants', are neutral with respect to the interests of social groups. What is the general line of Miliband's response to these ideologies? Here too he is led to take up the reverse position to these ideologies, to turn their argument against them. He does so in two ways. First of all he establishes that the members of the capitalist class have in fact often directly participated in the State apparatus and in the government[8]. Then, having established the relation between members of the State apparatus and the ruling class, he shows (*a*) that the *social origin* of members of the 'summit' of the State apparatus is that of the ruling class, and (*b*) that *personal* ties of influence, status, and milieu are established between the members of the ruling class and those of the State apparatus.[9]

I have no intention of contesting the value of Miliband's analyses, which on the contrary appear to me to have a capital *demystifying* importance. Yet however exact in itself, the way chosen by Miliband does not seem to me to be the most significant one. Firstly, because the *direct* participation of members of the capitalist class in the State apparatus and in the government, even where it exists, is not the important side of the matter. The relation between the bourgeois class and the State is an *objective relation*. This means that if the *function* of the State in a determinate social formation and the *interests* of the dominant class in this formation *coincide*, it is by reason of the system itself: the direct participation of members of the ruling class in the State apparatus is not the *cause* but the *effect*, and moreover a chance and contingent one, of this objective coincidence.

8. Miliband, pp. 48–68.
9. Ibid., pp. 69–145, especially 119 45.

In order to establish this coincidence, it would have been necessary to make explicit the role of the State as a specific instance, a regional structure, of the social whole. Miliband, however, seems to reduce the role of the State to the conduct and 'behaviour' of the members of the State apparatus.[10] If Miliband had first established that the State is precisely *the factor of cohesion of a social formation and the factor of reproduction of the conditions of production of a system* that itself determines the domination of one class over the others, he would have seen clearly that the participation, whether direct or indirect, of this class in government *in no way changes things*. Indeed in the case of the capitalist State, one can go further : it can be said that the capitalist State best serves the interests of the capitalist class only when the members of this class do not participate directly in the State apparatus, that is to say when the *ruling class* is not the *politically governing class*. This is the exact meaning of Marx's analyses of nineteenth-century England and Bismarckian Germany, to say nothing of Bonapartism in France. It is also what Miliband himself seems to suggest in his analyses of social-democratic governments.[11]

We come now to the problem of the *members of the State apparatus*, that is to say the army, the police, the judiciary and the administrative bureaucracy. Miliband's main line of argument is to try to establish the relation between the conduct of the members of the State apparatus and the interests of the ruling class, by demonstrating either that the social origin of the 'top servants of the State' is that of the ruling class, or that the members of the State apparatus end up united to this class by personal ties.[12] This approach, without being false, remains descriptive. More importantly, I believe that it prevents us from studying the specific problem that the State apparatus presents; *the problem of 'bureaucracy'*. According to Marx, Engels and Lenin, the members of the State apparatus, which it is convenient to call the 'bureaucracy' in the general sense, constitute a specific *social category*—not a class. This means that, although the members of the State apparatus belong, by their class origin, to different classes, they function according to a specific internal unity. Their class origin—*class situation*—recedes into the background in relation to that which unifies them—their *class position* : that is to say, the fact that they belong precisely to the State apparatus and that they have as their *objective function*

10. Ibid., pp. 68–118.   11. Ibid., pp. 96 ff.   12. Ibid., pp. 119–45.

the actualization of the role of the State. This in its turn means that the bureaucracy, as a specific and relatively 'united' social category, is the 'servant' of the ruling class, not by reason of its class origins, which are divergent, or by reason of its personal relations with the ruling class, but by reason of the fact that its internal unity derives from its actualization of the objective role of the State. The totality of this role itself coincides with the interests of the ruling class.

Important consequences follow for the celebrated problem of the *relative autonomy* of the State with respect to the ruling class, and thus for the equally celebrated question of the relative autonomy of the bureaucracy as a specific social category, with respect to that class. A long Marxist tradition has considered that the State is only a simple tool or instrument manipulated at will by the ruling class. I do not mean to say that Miliband falls into this trap, which makes it impossible to account for the complex mechanisms of the State in its relation to class struggle. However, if one locates the relationship between the State and the ruling class in the social origin of the members of the State apparatus and their inter-personal relations with the members of this class, so that the bourgeoisie almost physically 'corners' the State apparatus, one cannot account for the relative autonomy of the State with respect to this class. When Marx designated Bonapartism as the 'religion of the bourgeoisie', in other words as characteristic of *all* forms of the capitalist State, he showed that this State can only truly serve the ruling class in so far as it is relatively autonomous from the diverse fractions of this class, precisely in order to be able to organize the hegemony of the whole of this class. It is not by chance that Miliband finally admits this autonomy only in the extreme case of fascism.[13] The question posed is whether the situation today has changed in this respect: I do not think so, and will return to this.

3. The branches of the State apparatus

Miliband's approach thus to a certain extent prevents him from following through a rigorous analysis of the State apparatus itself and of the relations between different 'branches' or 'parts' of this apparatus. Miliband securely establishes that the State apparatus is not only constituted by the government, but also

13. Ibid., p. 93.

by special branches such as the army, the police, the judiciary, and the civil administration. Yet what is it that governs the *relations* between these branches, the respective importance and the relative predominance of these different branches among themselves, for example the relation between parliament and the executive, or the role of the army or of the administration in a particular form of State? Miliband's response seems to be the following:[14] the fact that one of these branches predominates over the others is in some way directly related to the 'exterior' factors noted above. That is to say, it is either the branch whose members are, by their class origin or connections, nearest to the ruling class, or the branch whose predominance over the others is due to its immediate 'economic' role. An example of the latter case would be the present growth of the role of the army, related to the current importance of military expenditure.[15]

Here, too, I cannot completely agree with Miliband's interpretation. As I see it, the State apparatus forms an *objective system* of special 'branches' whose relation presents a *specific internal unity* and obeys, to a large extent, *its own logic*. Each particular form of capitalist State is thus characterized by a particular form of relations among its branches, and by the predominance of one or of certain of its branches over the others: liberal State, interventionist State, Bonapartism, military dictatorship or fascism. But each particular form of capitalist State must be referred back, *in its unity*, to important modifications of the relations of production and to important stages of class struggle: competitive capitalism, imperialism, state capitalism. Only *after* having established the relation of a form of State as a unity, *that is as a specific form of the system of State apparatus as a whole*, with the 'exterior', can the respective role and the mutual internal relation of the 'branches' of the State apparatus be established. A *significant* shift in the predominant branch in the State apparatus, or of the relation between these branches, cannot be *directly* established by the immediate exterior role of this branch, but is determined *by the modification of the whole system of the State apparatus and of its form of international unity as such*: a modification which is itself due to changes in the relations of production and to developments in the class struggle.

14. Ibid., pp. 119 ff.
15. Ibid., pp. 130 ff.

Let us take as an example the present case of the *army* in the advanced capitalist countries. I do not think that the 'immediate' facts of the growth of military expenditure and increasing inter-personal ties between industrialists and the military are sufficient to speak of a *significant* shift of the role of the army in the present State apparatus: besides, in spite of everything, Miliband himself is very reserved in this matter. In order for such a shift to occur, there would have to be an important modification of the form of State as a whole—without this necessarily having to take the form of 'military dictatorship'—a modification which would not be due *simply* to the growing importance of military expenditure, but to profound modifications of the relations of production and the class struggle, of which the growth of military expenditures is finally only the *effect*. One could thus establish the relation of the army not simply with the dominant class, but with the totality of social classes—a complex relation that would explain its role by means of a shift in the State as a whole. I believe that there is no more striking evidence of this thesis, in another context, than present developments in Latin America.

4. *The present form of the Capitalist State*

Can we then speak in the present stage of capitalism of a modification of the form of the State? I would answer here in the affirmative, although I do not believe that this modification is necessarily in the direction of a preponderant role of the army. Miliband also seems to give an affirmative reply to the question. How does he situate this present modification of the form of State?[16] If the relation between the State and the ruling class is principally constituted by the 'interpersonal' relations between the members of the State apparatus and those of the ruling class, the only approach that seems open is to argue that these relations are now becoming increasingly intense and rigid, that the two are practically interchangeable. In effect, this is just the approach which Miliband adopts. The argument seems to me, however, merely descriptive. Indeed, it converges with the orthodox communist thesis of *State monopoly capitalism*, according to which the present form of the State is specified by increasingly close inter-personal relations between the monopolies and the members of the State apparatus, by the 'fusion

16. Ibid., especially pp. 123 ff.

of State and monopolies into a single mechanism'.[17] I have
shown elsewhere why and how this thesis, in appearance ultra-
leftist, leads in fact to the most vapid revisionism and reformism.[18] In fact, the present modification of the form of State
must mainly be sought and studied not in its simple effects,
which are besides disputable, but in profound shifts of the
articulation of economy and polity. This modification does not
seem to me to alter the relative autonomy of the State which
at present, as J. M. Vincent has recently noted in connection
with Gaullism,[19] only assumes different forms. In brief, the
designation of any existent State as the pure and simple agent
of big capital seems to me, *taken literally*, to give rise to many
misinterpretations—as much now as in the past.

5. The ideological apparatuses

Finally there is one last problem which seems to me very important, and which will provide me with the occasion to go
further than I have done in my own work cited above. I wonder
in effect if Miliband and myself have not stopped half-way on
one critical question. This is the role of *ideology* in the functioning of the State apparatus, a question which has become especially topical since the events of May–June 1968 in France. The
classic Marxist tradition of the theory of the State is principally
concerned to show *the repressive role of the State*, in the strong
sense of organized physical repression. There is only one notable
exception, Gramsci, with his problematic of hegemony. Now
Miliband very correctly insists in long and excellent analyses
(*The process of legitimization*, I, II, pp. 179–264) on the role
played by ideology in the functioning of the State and in the
process of political domination: which I have tried to do from
another point of view in my own work.

I think however that, for different reasons, we have both
stopped half-way: which was not the case with Gramsci. That
is to say, we have ended by considering that ideology only
exists in ideas, customs or morals without seeing that ideology
can be embodied, in the strong sense, in *institutions*: institutions which then, by the very process of institutionalization,

17. See the acts of the colloquy at Choisy-le-Roi on 'State Monopoly Capitalism' in *Economie et Politique*, Special Number.

18. Poulantzas, op. cit., pp. 297 ff.

19. *Les Temps Modernes*, August-September, 1968.

belong to the system of the State whilst depending principally on the ideological level. Following the Marxist tradition, we gave the concept of the State a *restricted* meaning, considering the principally repressive institutions as forming part of the 'State', and rejecting institutions with a principally ideological role as 'outside of' the State, in a place that Miliband designates as the 'political system', distinguishing it from the State.[20]

Here is the thesis I would like to propose: the system of the State is composed of *several apparatuses or institutions* of which certain have a principally repressive role, in the strong sense, and others a principally ideological role. The former constitute the repressive apparatus of the State, that is to say the State apparatus in the classical Marxist sense of the term (government, army, police, tribunals and administration). The latter constitute the *ideological apparatuses of the State*, such as the Church, the political parties, the unions (with the exception of course, of the *revolutionary* party or trade union organizations), the schools, the mass media (newspapers, radio, television), and, from a certain point of view, the family. This is so whether they are *public* or *private*—the distinction having a purely juridicial, that is, largely ideological character, which changes nothing fundamental. This position is in a certain sense that of Gramsci himself, although one he did not sufficiently found and develop.

Why should one speak in the plural of the State ideological apparatuses, whilst speaking in the singular of the State repressive apparatus? Because the State repressive apparatus, the State in the classic Marxist sense of the term, possesses a very rigorous internal unity which directly governs the relation between the diverse branches of the apparatus. Whilst the State ideological apparatuses, by their principal function—ideological inculcation and transmission—possess a greater and more important autonomy: their inter-connections and relations with the State repressive apparatus appear, by relation to the mutual connections of the branches of the State repressive apparatus, vested with a greater independence.

Why should one speak of *State* ideological apparatuses; why should these apparatuses be considered as composing part of the State? I will mention four principal reasons:

1. If the State is defined as the instance that maintains the cohesion of a social formation and which reproduces the condi-

20. Miliband, pp. 50 ff.

tions of production of a social system by maintaining class domination, it is obvious that the institutions in question—the State ideological apparatuses—fill exactly the same function.

2. The condition of possibility of the existence and functioning of these institutions or ideological apparatuses, under a certain form, is the State repressive apparatus itself. If it is true that their role is principally ideological and that the State repressive apparatus does not in general intervene *directly* in their functioning, it remains no less true that this repressive apparatus is always present behind them, that it defends them and sanctions them, and finally, that their action is *determined* by the action of the State repressive apparatus itself. The student movement, in France and elsewhere, can testify to this for schools and universities today.

3. Although these ideological apparatuses possess a notable autonomy, among themselves and in relation to the State repressive apparatus, it remains no less true that they belong to the same system as this repressive apparatus. Every important modification of the form of the State has repercussions not only on the mutual relations of the State repressive apparatus, but also on the mutual relations of the State ideological apparatuses and of the relations between these apparatuses and the State repressive apparatus. There is no need to take the extreme case of fascism to prove this thesis : one need only mention the modifications of the role and relations of the Church, the parties, the unions, the schools, the media, the family, both among themselves and with the State repressive apparatus, in the diverse 'normal' forms through which the capitalist State had evolved.

4. Finally, for one last reason : according to Marxist-Leninist theory, a socialist revolution does not signify only a shift in *State power*, but it must equally *'break'*, that is to say radically change, the State apparatus. Now, if one includes ideological apparatuses in the concept of the State, it is evident why the classics of Marxism have—if often only in implicit fashion—considered it necessary to apply the thesis of the 'destruction' of the State not only to the State repressive apparatus, but *also to the State ideological apparatuses*: Church, parties, unions, school, media, family. Certainly, given the autonomy of the State ideological apparatuses, this does not mean that they must all be 'broken' in homologous fashion, that is, *in the same way* or *at the same time* as the State repressive apparatus, or that any one of them must be. It means that the 'destruction'

of the ideological apparatuses has *its precondition* in the 'destruction' of the State repressive apparatus which maintains it. Hence the illusory error of a certain contemporary thesis, which considers it possible to pass here and now, to the 'destruction' of the university in capitalist societies, for instance. But it also means that the advent of socialist society cannot be achieved by 'breaking' only the State repressive apparatus whilst maintaining the State ideological apparatuses intact, taking them in hand as they are and merely changing their function.

This question evidently brings us closer to the problem of the *dictatorship of the proletariat* and of the *cultural revolution*: but I have the feeling that it takes us farther from Miliband. I do not, however, want to enter here into the problem of the political conclusions of the Miliband's book, in which he shows himself very—too—discreet: the question remains open. I will end by recalling what I said at the beginning: if the tone of this article is critical, this is above all proof of the interest that the absorbing analyses of Miliband's work have aroused in me.

Reply to Nicos Poulantzas

RALPH MILIBAND

Ralph Miliband is Senior Lecturer in Politics at the London School of Economics. Since 1964 he has edited an annual review The Socialist Register *and is author of* Parliamentary Socialism (*UK, 1962*) *and* The State in Capitalist Society (*UK, 1969*).

I very much welcome Nicos Poulantzas's critique of *The State in Capitalist Society* in the last issue of *New Left Review*: this is exactly the kind of discussion which is most likely to contribute to the elucidation of concepts and issues that are generally agreed on the Left to be of crucial importance for the socialist project, yet which have for a very long time received altogether inadequate attention, or even no attention at all.

While some of Poulantzas's criticisms are, as I shall try to show, unwarranted, my purpose in the following comments is only incidentally to 'defend' the book; my main purpose is rather to take up some general points which arise from his review and which seem to me of particular interest in the investigation of the nature and role of the state in capitalist society. I hope that others may be similarly provoked into entering the discussion.

1. The problem of method

The first such point concerns the question of method. Poulantzas suggests that, notwithstanding the book's merits (about which he is more than generous) the analysis which it attempts is vitiated by the absence of a 'problematic' which would adequately situate the concrete data it presents. In effect, Poulantzas taxes me with what C. Wright Mills called 'abstracted empiricism', and with which I myself, as it happens, tax pluralist writers.[1] Poulantzas quite rightly states that 'a precondition of any scientific approach to the "concrete" is to make explicit the epistemological principles of its own treatment of it'; and he then goes on to say that 'Miliband nowhere deals with the Marxist theory of the state as such, although it is constantly implicit in his work' (p. 69). In fact, I quite explicitly give an outline of the Marxist theory of the state[2] but undoubtedly do so very briefly. One reason for this, quite apart from the fact that I have discussed Marx's theory of the state elsewhere,[3] is that, having outlined the Marxist theory of the state, I was concerned to set it against the dominant, democratic-pluralist view and to show the latter's deficiences in the only way in which this seems to me to be possible, namely in empirical terms. It is perfectly proper for Poulantzas to stress the importance of an appropriate 'problematic' in such an undertaking; and it is probably true that mine is insufficiently elucidated; but since he notes that such a 'problematic' is 'constantly implicit in my work', I doubt that my exposition is quite as vitiated by empiricist deformations as he suggests; i.e. that the required 'problematic' is not absent from the work, and that I am not therefore led 'to attack bourgeois ideologies of the State whilst

1. *The State in Capitalist Society*, p. 172.
2. Ibid., pp. 5, 93.
3. 'Marx and the State' in *The Socialist Register*, 1965.

placing [myself] on their own terrain' (p. 69).

Poulantzas gives as an example of this alleged failing the fact that, while I maintain against pluralist writers the view that a plurality of élites does not exclude the existence of a ruling class (and I do in fact entitle one chapter 'Economic Elites and Dominant Class') I fail to provide a critique of the ideological notion of élite and do therefore place myself inside the 'problematic' which I seek to oppose. Here too, however, I doubt whether the comment is justified. I am aware of the degree to which the usage of certain words and concepts is ideologically and politically loaded, and indeed I provide a number of examples of their far from 'innocent' usage;[4] and I did in fact, for this very reason, hesitate to speak of 'élites'. But I finally decided to do so, firstly because I thought, perhaps mistakenly, that it had by now acquired a sufficiently neutral connotation (incidentally, it may still have a much more ideological ring in its French usage than in its English one); and secondly because it seemed, in its neutral sense, the most convenient word at hand to suggest the basic point that, while there do exist such separate 'élites' inside the dominant class, which Poulantzas describes by the admittedly more neutral but rather weak word 'fractions', they are perfectly compatible with the existence of a dominant class, and are in fact parts of that class. He suggests that the 'concrete reality' concealed by the notion of 'plural élites' can only be grasped 'if the very notion of élite is rejected' (p. 70). I would say myself that the concrete reality can only be grasped if the concept of élite is turned against those who use it for apologetic purposes and shown to require integration into the concept of a dominant or ruling class: i.e. there *are* concepts of bourgeois social science which can be used for critical as well as for apologetic purposes. The enterprise may often be risky, but is sometimes legitimate and necessary.

However, the general point which Poulantzas raises goes far beyond the use of this or that concept. In fact, it concerns nothing less than the status of empirical enquiry and its relationship to theory. In this regard, I would readily grant that

4. e.g. 'Governments may be solely concerned with the better running of "the economy". But the descriptions of systems as "the economy" is part of the idiom of ideology, and obscures the real process. For what is being improved is a *capitalist* economy; and this ensures that whoever may or may not gain, capitalist interests are least likely to lose' (op. cit., p. 79. Italics are original).

The State in Capitalist Society may be insufficiently 'theoretical' in the sense in which Poulantzas means it; but I also tend to think that his own approach, as suggested in his review and in his otherwise important book, *Pouvoir Politique et Classes Sociales*, a translation of which into English is urgently needed, errs in the opposite direction. To put the point plainly, I think it is possible, in this field at least, to be so profoundly concerned with the elaboration of an appropriate 'problematic' and with the avoidance of any contamination with opposed 'problematics', as to lose sight of the absolute necessity of empirical enquiry, and of the empirical demonstration of the falsity of these opposed and apologetic 'problematics'. Poulantzas declares himself not to be against the study of the 'concrete': I would go much further and suggest that, of course on the basis of an appropriate 'problematic', such a study of the concrete is a *sine qua non* of the kind of 'demystifying' enterprise which, he kindly suggests, my book accomplishes. After all, it was none other than Marx who stressed the importance of empirical validation (or invalidation) and who spent many years of his life in precisely such an undertaking; and while I do not suggest for a moment that Poulantzas is unaware of this fact, I do think that he, and the point also goes for Louis Althusser and his collaborators, may tend to give it rather less attention than it deserves. This, I must stress, is not a crude (and false) contraposition of empiricist versus non- or anti-empiricist approaches: it is a matter of emphasis—but the emphasis is important.

2. *The objective nature of the State*

Poulantzas's critique of my approach also underlies other points of difference between us. But before dealing with these, I should like to take up very briefly what he calls 'the false problem of managerialism'. Managerialism *is* a false problem in one sense, not in another. It is a false problem in the sense that the 'motivations' of managers (of which more in a moment) are not such as to distinguish the latter in any fundamental way from other members of the capitalist class: i.e. he and I are agreed that the thesis of the 'soulful corporation' is a mystification. But he also suggests that I attribute to the managers 'an importance they do not possess' (p. 72). This seems to me to underestimate the significance of the 'managerial' phenomenon in the internal organization of capitalist production (which, incident-ally, Marx writing a hundred years ago, did not do).[5] Poulantzas for his own part chooses to stress 'the differences and relations between fractions of capital'. But while these *are* important and need to be comprehended in an economic and political analysis of contemporary capitalism I would argue myself that the emphasis which he gives to these differences and relations may well obscure the underlying cohesion of these various elements—and may well play into the hands of those who focus on these differences in order to deny the fundamental cohesion of the capitalist class in the conditions of advanced capitalism.

More important, however, Poulantzas also suggests that I attach undue importance, indeed that I am altogether mistaken in attaching *any* importance to the 'motivations' of the man-agers. Thus, 'the characterization of the existing social system as capitalist in no way depends on the motivations of the con-duct of the managers ... to characterize the class position of managers, one need not refer to the motivations of their con-duct, but only to their place in production and their relation to the ownership of the means of production' (p. 71). I think myself that one must refer to both not because managerial 'motivations' are in themselves critical (and Poulantzas is mis-taken in believing that I think they are)[6] but precisely in order to show why they are not. By ignoring them altogether, one leaves a dangerous gap in the argument which needs to be put forward against managerialist apologetics. This is why, I take it, Baran and Sweezy, for instance, devote a good deal of atten-tion to 'business behaviour' in their *Monopoly Capital*.

5. In fact, *his* formulations may go rather further than is war-ranted : 'A large part of the social capital is employed by people who do not own it and who consequently tackle things quite dif-ferently than the owner' (*Capital*, Moscow, 1962, III, p. 431). 'This is the abolition of the capitalist mode of production within the capitalist mode of producton itself, and hence a self-dissolving contradiction, which *prima facie* represents a mere phase of transi-tion to a new form of production' (Ibid., p. 429).

6. e.g. 'Like the vulgar owner-entrepreneur of the bad old days, the modern manager, however bright and shiny, must also submit to the imperative demands inherent in the system of which he is both master and servant; and the most important such demand is that he should make the 'highest possible'' profits. Whatever his motives and aims be, they can only be fulfilled on the basis of his success in this regard.' (*The State in Capitalist Society*, p. 34.)

I

This issue of 'motivations' also arises, in a much more significant and far-reaching way, in connection with what I have
called the state élite and its relation to the ruling class. Poulantzas notes that, in order to rebut the ideologies which affirm
the neutrality of the state, I bring forward evidence to show
that members of that class are themselves involved in government, and also show the degree to which those who man the
command posts of the various parts of the state system are,
by social origin, status, milieu (and, he might have added, ideological dispositions) connected with the ruling class. But, he
also adds, this procedure, while having a 'capital *demystifying*
importance',[7] is 'not the most significant one' (p. 72). His reason
for saying this is so basic that I must here quote him at some
length: 'The relation between the bourgeois class and the
State is an *objective relation*. This means that if the *function*
of the State in a determinate social formation and the *interests*
of the dominant class in this formation *coincide*, it is by reason
of the system itself' (p. 73).[8] Similarly, the members of the state
apparatus 'function according to a specific internal unity. Their
class origin—*class situation*—recedes into the background in
relation to that which unifies them—their *class position*: that
is to say, the fact that they belong precisely to the State apparatus and that they have as their *objective function* the actualiza-
ation of the role of the State. The totality of this role coincides
with the interests of the ruling class' (pp. 73–4).[9]

I should like to make two comments about this. The first
and less important is that Poulantzas greatly under-estimates
the extent to which I myself do take account of the 'objective
relations' which affect and shape the role of the State. In fact,
I repeatedly note how government and bureaucracy, irrespective of social origin, class situation and even ideological dispositions, are subject to the structural constraints of the system.
Even so, I should perhaps have stressed this aspect of the matter
more.

But however that may be, I believe—and this is my second
point—that Poulantzas himself is here rather one-sided and that
he goes much too far in dismissing the nature of the state élite
as of altogether no account. For what his *exclusive* stress on
'objective relations' suggests is that what the state does is in
every particular and at all times *wholly* determined by these
'objective relations': in other words, that the structural con-

7. Italics in text.   8. Italics in text.   9. Italics in text.

straints of the system are so absolutely compelling as to turn those who run the state into the merest functionaries and executants of policies imposed upon them by 'the system'. At the same time, however, he also rejects the 'long Marxist tradition (which) has considered that the State is only a simple tool or instrument manipulated at will by the ruling class' (p. 74). Instead, he stresses 'the relative autonomy of the state'. But all that this seems to me to do is to substitute the notion of 'objective structures' and 'objective relations' for the notion of 'ruling' class. But since the ruling class is a dominant element of the system, we are in effect back at the point of total subordination of the state élite to that class; i.e. the state is not 'manipulated' by the ruling class into doing its bidding: it does so autonomously but totally because of the 'objective relations' imposed upon it by the system. Poulantzas condemns the 'economism' of the Second and Third Internationals and attributes to it their neglect of the state (p. 68). But his own analysis seems to me to lead straight towards a kind of structural determinism, or rather a structural super-determinism, which makes impossible a truly realistic consideration of the dialectical relationship between the state and 'the system'.

For my own part, I do believe that 'the state in these class societies is primarily and inevitably the guardian and protector of the economic interests which are dominant in them. Its "real" purpose and mission is to ensure their continued predominance, not to prevent it.'[10] But I also believe that within this 'problematic', the state élite is involved in a far more complex relationship with 'the system' and with society as a whole than Poulantzas's scheme allows; and that at least to a certain but definite and important extent that relationship is shaped by the kind of factors which I bring into the analysis and which Poulantzas dismisses as of no account.

The political danger of structural super-determinism would seem to me to be obvious. For if the state élite is as totally imprisoned in objective structures as is suggested, it follows that there is *really* no difference between a state ruled, say, by bourgeois constitutionalists, whether conservative or social-democrat, and one ruled by, say, Fascists. It was the same approach which led the Comintern in its 'class against class' period fatally to under-estimate what the victory of the Nazis would mean for the German working-class movement. This is an ultra-left devia-

10. *The State in Capitalist Society*, p. 265.

tion which is also not uncommon today; and it is the obverse of a right deviation which assumes that changes in government, for instance the election of a social-democratic government, accompanied by some changes in the personnel of the state system, are sufficient to impart an entirely new character to the nature and role of the state. Both are deviations, and both are dangerous.

It is the same sort of obliteration of differences in the forms of government and state which appears in Poulantzas's references to the 'relative autonomy' of the state. He suggests that Marx designated Bonapartism as the 'religion of the bourgeoisie', and takes Marx to mean that Bonapartism was 'characteristic of *all* forms of the capitalist state' (p. 74).[11] I stand to be corrected but I know of no work of Marx which admits of such an interpretation; and if he had said anything which did admit of such an interpretation, he would have been utterly mistaken. For in any meaningful sense of the concept, Bonapartism has *not* been characteristic of all forms of the capitalist state—rather the reverse. What Marx did say was that Bonapartism in France 'was the only form of government possible at the time when the bourgeoisie had already lost, and the working class had not yet acquired, the faculty of ruling the nation'.[12] It is perfectly true that all states are in some degree 'autonomous', and Poulantzas misreads me when he suggests that I 'finally admit this autonomy only in the extreme case of Fascism' (p. 74).[13] What I do say is that Fascism is the extreme case of the state's autonomy in the context of capitalist society, which is not at all the same thing—and that between the kind of autonomy which is achieved by the state under Fascism, and that which is achieved by it under the conditions of

11. Italics in text.

12. 'The Civil War in France', in *Selected Works* (Moscow, 1950), Vol. I, p. 469.

13. It is, incidentally, this recognition on my part of the 'relative autonomy' of the state which leads me, *inter alia*, to suggest that Poulantzas also misreads me when he states that my analysis 'converges with the orthodox communist thesis of *State monopoly capitalism*, according to which the present form of the State is specified by increasingly close inter-personal relations between the monopolies and the members of the State apparatus, by the "fusion of State and monopolies into a single mechanism"' (p. 71). In fact, I think this scheme to be *simpliste* and explicitly question its usefulness (*The State in Capitalist Society*, p. 11. n. 2).

bourgeois democracy, there is a large gulf, which it is dangerous to underestimate. This scarcely leads me to an apotheosis of bourgeois democracy. It leads me rather to say that 'the point of the socialist critique of "bourgeois freedoms" is not (or should not be) that they are of no consequence, but they are profoundly inadequate, and need to be extended by the radical transformation of the context, economic, social and political, which condemns them to inadequacy and erosion.'[14]

3. *The ideological institutions*

Poulantzas's references to the sections of my book devoted to ideology also raise points of great substance. He suggests that both he and I 'have ended by considering that ideology only exists in ideas, customs and morals without seeing that ideology can be embodied, in the strong sense, in *institutions*' (p. 76).[15] I myself must plead not guilty to the charge. What he, again most generously, calls my 'long and excellent analyses' of the subject largely focus precisely on the institutions which are the purveyors of ideology, and on the degree to which they are part and parcel, as institutions, of the general system of domination—and I do this in relation to parties, churches, pressure groups, the mass media, education, and so on. What value my analyses may have lies, I think, in my attempted demonstration of the fact that 'political socialization' *is* a process performed by institutions, many of which never cease to insist on their 'un-ideological', 'un-political' and 'neutral' character.

The much more important point is that Poulantzas suggests that these institutions 'belong to the system of the State' and he proposes the thesis that this system of the state 'is composed of *several apparatuses or institutions* of which certain have a principally repressive role, and others a principally ideological role', and among these he lists the Church, political parties, unions, the schools, the mass media and, from a certain point of view, the family (p. 77).[16]

I am extremely dubious about this. I suggest in *The State in Capitalist Society* that the state is increasingly involved in the process of 'political socialization' and that it plays, in certain respects, an extremely important role in it.[17] But I also think that, just as it is necessary to show that the institutions men-

14. Ibid., p. 267.   15. Italics in text.   16. Italics in text.
17. *The State in Capitalist Society*, pp. 183 ff.

tioned earlier *are* part of a system of power, and that they are, as Poulantzas says, increasingly linked to and buttressed by the state, so is it important not to blur the fact that they are not, in bourgeois democracies, part of the state but of the political system. These institutions *are* increasingly subject to a process of 'statization'; and, as I also note in the book, that process is likely to be enhanced by the fact that the state must, in the conditions of permanent crisis of advanced capitalism, assume ever greater responsibility for political indoctrination and mystification. But to suggest that the relevant institutions are actually part of the state system does not seem to me to accord with reality, and tends to obscure the difference in this respect between these political systems and systems where ideological institutions are indeed part of a state monopolistic system of power. In the former systems, ideological institutions do retain a very high degree of autonomy; and are therefore the better able to conceal the degree to which they do belong to the system of power of capitalist society. The way to show that they do, is not to claim that they are part of the state system, but to show how they do perform their ideological functions outside it; and this is what I have tried to do.

Finally, Poulantzas notes that my book says very little by way of 'political conclusions'. If by 'political conclusions' is meant 'where do we go from here?' and 'how?', the point is well taken. I have no difficulties in suggesting that the aim of socialists is to create an 'authentically democratic social order, a truly free society of self-governing men and women, in which, in Marx's phrase, the state will be converted "from an organ superimposed upon society into one completely subordinate to it" '.[18] But this obviously raises very large and complex questions which I did not believe it possible to tackle, let alone answer with any kind of rigour, at the tail-end of this particular book.

18. Ibid., p. 277.

Part Three
ALTERNATIVES

12 Karl Marx's Contribution to Historiography

E. J. HOBSBAWM

In this essay E. J. Hobsbawm investigates the very different uses which successive generations of historians have made of Marx. Whereas in the past it was thought that the defining character- istic of Marxist history was a stress on the economic factor there is now a progressive discovery of other dimensions of the Marxist method, especially Marx's concern to locate the complex structural dynamic of every social formation. While the new emphasis does not cancel out the old it does reveal it to have been partial and one-sided.

E. J. Hobsbawm is Professor of Modern History at Birkbeck College, London University. He is the author of Industry and Empire *(UK, 1968),* The Age of Revolution *(UK, 1963) and* Labouring Men *(UK, 1965).*

The nineteenth century, that age of bourgeois civilization, has several major intellectual achievements to its credit, but the academic discipline of history which grew up in that period, is not one of them. Indeed, in all except the techniques of research, it marked a distinct step back from the often ill-docu- mented, speculative and excessively general essays in which those who witnessed the most profoundly revolutionary era— the age of the French and Industrial Revolutions—attempted to comprehend the transformation of human societies. Academic history, as inspired by the teaching and example of Leopold von Ranke and published in the specialist journals which de- veloped in the latter part of the century, was correct in opposing generalisation insufficiently supported by fact, or backed by un- reliable fact. On the other hand it concentrated all its efforts on the task of establishing 'the facts' and thus contributed little to history except a set of empirical criteria for evaluating certain kinds of documentary evidence (e.g. manuscript records of events involving the conscious decisions of influential individuals) and the ancillary techniques necessary for this purpose.

It rarely observed that these documents and procedures were applicable only to a limited range of historical phenomena, because it uncritically accepted certain phenomena as worthy of special study and others not. Thus it did not set out to concentrate on the 'history of events'—indeed in some countries it had a distinct institutional bias—but its methodology lent itself most readily to chronological narrative. It did not by any means confine itself entirely to the history of war, politics and diplomacy (or, in the simplified but not untypical version taught by schoolmasters concerning kings, battles and treaties), but it undoubtedly tended to assume that this formed the central body of events which concerned the historian. This was history in the singular. Other subjects could, when treated with erudition and method, give rise to various histories, qualified by descriptive epithets (constitutional, economic, ecclesiastical, cultural, the history of art, science or philately, etc.). Their connection with the main body of history was obscure or neglected, except for a few vague speculations about the *Zeitgeist* from which professional historians preferred to abstain.

Philosophically and methodologically academic historians tended to demonstrate an equally striking innocence. It is true that the results of this innocence coincided with what in the natural sciences was a conscious, though controversial, methodology which we can loosely call positivism, but it is doubtful whether many academic historians (outside the Latin countries) knew that they were positivists. In most cases they were merely men who, just as they accepted a given subject-matter (e.g. politico-military-diplomatic history) and a given geographical area (e.g. western and middle Europe) as the most important, also accepted, among other *idées reçues*, those of popularised scientific thought, e.g. that hypotheses arise automatically from the study of 'facts', that explanation consists of a collection of chains of cause and effect, the concepts of determinism, evolution, etc. They assumed that, just as scientific erudition could establish the definitive text and succession of the documents which they published in elaborate and invaluable series of volumes, so it would also establish the definitive truth of history. Lord Acton's *Cambridge Modern History* was a late but typical example of such beliefs.

Even by the modest standards of the human and social sciences of the nineteenth century, history was therefore an extremely, one might almost say, a deliberately, backward discipline. Its contributions to the understanding of human society, past and present was negligible and accidental. Since the understanding of society requires an understanding of history, alternative and more fruitful ways of exploring the human past had, sooner or later, to be found. The subject of this paper is the contribution of Marxism to this search.

One hundred years after Ranke, Arnaldo Momigliano summed up the changes in historiography under four heads:[1]

1. Political and religious history had declined sharply, while 'national histories look old-fashioned'. In return there had been a remarkable turn towards social-economic history.

2. It was no longer usual, or indeed easy, to use 'ideas' as an explanation of history.

3. The prevalent explanations were now 'in terms of social forces', though this raised in a more acute form than in Ranke's day the question of the relation between the explanation of historical events and explanation of individual actions.

4. It had now (1954) become difficult to speak of progress or even meaningful development of events in a certain direction.

The last of Momigliano's observations—and we quote him as a reporter of the state of historiography rather than as an analyst —was probably more likely to be made in the 1950s than in earlier or later decades, but the other three observations plainly represent old-established and lasting trends in the anti-Rankean movement within history. From the middle of the nineteenth century, it was noted as long ago as 1910[2] the attempt had been made to substitute a materialist for an idealist framework in it, thus leading to a decline in political, the rise of 'economic or sociological' history: no doubt under the increasingly urgent stimulus of the 'social problem' which 'dominated' historiography in the second half of that century.[3] Plainly, it took rather longer to capture the fortresses of university faculties and schools of archives, than enthusiastic encyclopaedists supposed.

1. 'One Hundred Years after Raske', in *Studies in Historiography*, London, 1966.
2. *Encyclopaedia Britannica*, 11th edition, article 'History'.
3. *Enciclopedia Italiana*, article 'Storiografia'.

By 1914 the attacking forces had occupied little more than the outlying posts of 'economic history' and historically oriented sociology, and the defenders were not forced into full retreat—though they were by no means routed—until after the Second World War.[4] Nevertheless, the general character and success of the anti-Rankean movement is not in doubt.

The immediate question before us is, how far this new orientation has been due to Marxist influence. A second question is, in what way Marxist influence continues to contribute to it.

There can be no doubt that the influence of Marxism was from the start very considerable. Broadly speaking, the only other school or current of thought aiming at the reconstruction of history, which was influential in the nineteenth century, was positivism (whether spelled with a small or large initial letter). Positivism, a belated child of the eighteenth-century Enlightenment, would have won our admiration in the nineteenth century. Its major contribution to history was the introduction of concepts, methods and models from the natural sciences into social investigation and the application of such discoveries in the natural sciences as seemed suitable, to history. These were not negligible achievements, but they were limited ones, all the more so as the nearest thing to a model of historical change, a theory of evolution patterned on biology or geology, and drawing both encouragement and example after 1859 from Darwinism, is only a very crude and inadequate guide to history. Consequently the historians inspired by Comte or Spencer have been few, and, like Buckle or even the greater Taine or Lamprecht, their influence on historiography was limited and temporary. The weakness of positivism (or Positivism) was that, in spite of Comte's conviction that sociology was the highest of the sciences, it had little to say about the phenomena that characterize human society, as distinct from those which could be directly derived from the influence of non-social factors, or modelled on the natural sciences. What views it had about the human character of history were speculative, if not metaphysical.

The major impetus for the transformation of history therefore came from historically oriented social sciences (e.g. the

4. Indeed, for several years after 1950 they mounted a fairly successful counter-offensive, encouraged by the favourable climate of the cold war, but also perhaps by the inability of the innovators to consolidate their unexpectedly rapid advance.

German historical school in economics), but especially from Marx, whose influence was acknowledged to be such that he was often given credit for achievements which he did not himself claim to have originated. Historical materialism was habitually described—sometimes even by Marxists—as 'economic determinism'. Quite apart from disclaiming this phrase, Marx would certainly also have denied that he was the first to stress the importance of the economic basis of historical development, or to write the history of humanity as that of a succession of socio-economic systems. He certainly disclaimed originality in introducing the concept of class and class struggle into history, but in vain. '*Marx ha introdotto nella storiografia il concetto di classe*' wrote the *Enciclopedia Italiana*.

It is not the purpose of this paper to trace the specific contribution of Marxist influence on the transformation of modern historiography. Evidently it differed from one country to another. Thus in France it was relatively small, at least until after the Second World War, because of the remarkably late and slow penetration of Marxist ideas in any field into the intellectual life of that country.[5] Though Marxist influences had by the 1920s penetrated to some extent into the highly political field of the historiography of the French Revolution—but, as the work of Jaurès and Georges Lefebvre shows, in combination with ideas drawn from native traditions of thought—the major reorientation of French historians was led by the *Annales* school, which certainly did not require Marx to draw its attention to the economic and social dimensions of history. (However, the popular identification of an interest in such matters with Marxism is so strong, that the *Times Literary Supplement* has only recently[6] put even Fernard Braudel under Marx's influence). Conversely, there are countries in Asia or Latin America in which the transformation, if not the creation, of modern historiography can almost be identified with the penetration of Marxism. So long as it is accepted that, speaking globally, the influence was considerable, we need not pursue the subject further in the present context.

It has been raised, not so much in order to establish the fact that Marxist influence has played an important part in the modernisation of historiography, as in order to illustrate a major difficulty in establishing its precise contribution. For, as

5. Cf. George Lichtheim, *Marxism in Modern France*, 1966.
6. 15 February, 1968.

we have seen, the Marxist influence among historians has been identified with a few relatively simple, if powerful, ideas which have, in one way or another, been associated with Marx and the movements inspired by his thought, but which are not necessarily Marxist at all, or which, in the form that has been most influential, are not necessarily representative of the mature thought of Marx. We shall call this type of influence 'vulgar-Marxist', and the major problem of analysis is to separate the vulgar-Marxist from the Marxist component in historical analysis.

To give some examples. It seems clear that 'vulgar-Marxism' embraced in the main the following elements:

1. The 'economic interpretation of history', i.e. the belief that 'the economic factor is the fundamental factor on which the others are dependent' (to use R. Stammler's phrase); and more specifically, on which phenomena hitherto not regarded as having much connection with economic matters, depended. To this extent it overlapped with

2. The model of 'basis and superstructure' (used most widely to explain the history of ideas). In spite of Marx and Engels' own warnings and the sophisticated observations of some early Marxists such as Labriola, this model was usually interpreted as a simple relation of dominance and dependence between the 'economic base' and the 'superstructure'; mediated at most by

3. 'Class interest and the class struggle.' One has the impression that a number of vulgar-Marxist historians did not read much beyond the first page of the Communist Manifesto, and the phrase that 'the (written) history of all hitherto existing societies is the history of class struggles'.

4. 'Historical laws and historical inevitability.' It was believed, correctly, that Marx insisted on a systematic and necessary development of human society in history, from which the contingent was largely excluded, at all events at the level of generalization about long-term movements. Hence the constant preoccupation of early Marxist writers on history with such problems as the role of the individual or of accident in history. On the other hand this could be, and largely was, interpreted as a rigid and imposed regularity, e.g. in the succession of socio-economic formations, or even a mechanical determinism which sometimes came close to suggesting that there were no alternatives in history.

5. Specific subjects of historical investigation derived from Marx's own interests, e.g. in the history of capitalist development and industrialization, but also sometimes from more or less casual remarks.

6. Specific subjects of investigation derived not so much from Marx, as from the interest of the movements associated with his theory, e.g. in the agitations of the oppressed classes (peasants, workers), or in revolutions.

7. Various observations about the nature and limits of historiography, derived mainly from (2) and serving to explain the motives and methods of historians who claimed to be nothing but impartial searchers after truth, and prided themselves on establishing simply '*wie as eigentlich gewesen*'.

It will at once be obvious that this represented, at best, a selection from Marx's views about history and at worst (as quite often with Kautsky) an assimilation of them to contemporary non-Marxist—e.g. evolutionist and positivistic—views. It will also be evident that some of it represented not Marx at all, but the sort of interests which would naturally be developed by any historian associated with popular, working-class and revolutionary movements, and which would have been developed even without the intervention of Marx, e.g. a preoccupation with earlier examples of social struggle and socialist ideology. Thus in the case of Kautsky's early monograph on Thomas More, there is nothing particularly Marxist about the choice of the subject, and its treatment is vulgar-Marxist.

Yet this selection of elements from, or associated with, Marxism, was not arbitrary. Items 1–4 and 7 in the brief survey of vulgar-Marxism made above, represented concentrated charges of intellectual explosive, designed to blow up crucial parts of the fortifications of traditional history, and as such they were immensely powerful. Perhaps more powerful than less simplified versions of historical materialism would have been, and certainly powerful enough in their capacity to let light into hitherto dark places, to keep historians satisfied for a considerable time. It is difficult to recapture the amazement felt by an intelligent and learned social scientist at the end of the nineteenth century, when encountering the following Marxist observations about the past: 'That the very Reformation is ascribed to an economical cause, that the length of the Thirty Years' War was due to economic causes, the Crusades to feudal land-hunger, the evolution of the family to economic causes, and that Descartes' view of animals as machines can be brought into relation with the growth of the Manufacturing system.'[7] Yet those of us who recall our first encounters with historical materialism may still bear witness to the immense liberating force of such simple discoveries. However, if it was thus natural, and perhaps necessary, for the initial impact of Marxism to take a simplified form, the actual selection of elements from Marx also represented a historical choice. Thus a few remarks by Marx in *Capital* on the relation between Protestantism and capitalism, were immensely influential, presumably because the problem of the social basis of ideology in general, and of the nature of religious orthodoxies in particular, was a subject of immediate and intense interest.[8] On the other hand some of the works in which Marx himself came closest to writing as a historian, e.g. the magnificent *Eighteenth Brumaire*, did not stimulate historians until very much later; presumably because the problems on which they throw most light, e.g. of class-consciousness and the peasantry, seemed of less immediate interest.

The bulk of what we regard as the Marxist influence on historiography has certainly been vulgar-Marxist in the sense described above. It consists of the general emphasis on the economic and social factors in history which have been dominant since the end of the Second World War in all but a minority of countries (e.g. until recently West Germany and the United States), and which continue to gain ground. We must repeat that this trend, though undoubtedly in the main the product of Marxist influence, has no special connection with Marx's thought. The major impact which Marx's own specific ideas have had in history and the social sciences in general, is almost certainly that of the theory of 'basis and superstructure'; that is to say of his model of a society composed of different 'levels' which interact. Marx's own hierarchy of levels or mode of their interaction (insofar as he has provided one)[9] need not be accepted

7. J. Bonar, *Philosophy and Political Economy*, 1893, p. 367.
8. These remarks were to give rise to one of the earliest penetrations of what is undoubtedly a Marxist influence into orthodox historiography, namely the famous theme on which Sombart, Weber, Troeltsch, and others were to play variations. The debate is still far from exhausted.
9. One must agree with L. Althusser that his discussion of the

for the general model to be valuable. It has, indeed, been very widely welcomed as a valuable contribution even by non-Marxists. Marx's specific model of historical development—including the rôle of class conflicts, the succession of socio-economic formations and the mechanism of transition from one to the other—have remained much more controversial, even in some instances among Marxists. It is right that it should be debated, and in particular that the usual criteria of historical verification should be applied to it. It is inevitable that some parts of it, which are based on insufficient or misleading evidence, should be abandoned; for instance in the field of the study of oriental societies, where Marx combines profound insight with mistaken assumptions, e.g. about the internal stability of some such societies. Nevertheless it is the contention of this paper that the chief value of Marx for historians today lies in his statements about history, as distinct from his statements about society in general.

The Marxist (and vulgar-Marxist) influence which has hitherto been most effective, is part of a general tendency to transform history into one of the social sciences, a tendency resisted by some with more or less sophistication, but which has unquestionably been the prevailing one in the twentieth century. The major contribution of Marxism to this tendency in the past has been the critique of positivism, i.e. of the attempts to assimilate the study of the social sciences to that of the natural ones, or the human to the non-human. This implies the recognition of societies as systems of relations between human beings, of which the relations entered into for the purpose of production and reproduction are primary for Marx. It also implies the analysis of the structure and functioning of these systems as entities maintaining themselves, in their relations both with the outside environment—non-human and human—and in their internal relationships. Marxism is far from the only structural-functionalist theory of society, though it has good claims to be the first of them, but it differs from most others in two respects. First, it insists on a hierarchy of social phenomena (e.g. 'basis' and 'superstructure'), and second, on the existence within any society of internal tensions ('contradictions') which counteract

---

'superstructural' levels remained much sketchier and inconclusive than that of the 'basis'.

the tendency of the system to maintain itself as a going concern.[10]

The importance of these peculiarities of Marxism is in the field of history, for it is they which allow it to explain—unlike other structural-functional models of society—why and how societies change and transform themselves; in other words, the facts of social evolution.[11] The immense strength of Marx has always lain in his insistence on both the existence of social structure and its historicity, or in other words its internal dynamic of change. Today, when the existence of social systems is generally accepted, but at the cost of their a-historical, if not anti-historical analysis, Marx's emphasis on history as a necessary dimension is perhaps more essential than ever.

This implies two specific critiques of theories prevalent in the social sciences today.

The first is the critique of the mechanism which dominates so much of the social sciences, especially in the United States, and draws its strength both from the remarkable fruitfulness of sophisticated mechanical models in the present phase of scientific advance, and the search for methods of achieving social change which do not imply social revolution. One may perhaps add that the wealth of money and of certain new technologies suitable for use in the social field, which are now available in the richest of the industrial countries, make this type of 'social engineering' and the theories on which it is based, very attractive in such countries. Such theories are essentially exercises in 'problem-solving'. Theoretically, they are extremely primitive, probably cruder than most corresponding theories in the nineteenth century. Thus many social scientists, either consciously or *de facto*, reduce the process of history to a single change from 'traditional' to 'modern' or 'industrial' society, the 'modern' being defined in terms of the advanced industrial countries, or even of the mid-twentieth-century United States, the 'traditional' as that which lacks 'modernity'. Operationally this single large step can be sub-divided into smaller steps, such as those of Rostow's Stages of Economic Growth. These models eliminate

10. It need hardly be said that the 'basis' consists not of technology or economics, but 'the totality of these relations of production', i.e. social organization in its broadest sense as applied to a given level of the material forces of production.

11. Obviously the use of this term does not imply any similarity with the process of biological evolution.

most of history in order to concentrate on one small, though admittedly vital, span of it, and grossly oversimplify the mechanisms of historical change even with this small span of time. They affect historians chiefly because the size and prestige of the social sciences which develop such models, encourage historical researchers to embark on projects which are influenced by them. It is, or should be, quite evident that they can provide no adequate model of historical change, but their present popularity makes it important that Marxists should constantly remind us of this.

The second is the critique of structural-functional theories which, if vastly more sophisticated, are in some respects even more sterile inasmuch as they may deny historicity altogether, or transform it into something else. Such views are more influential even within the range of influence of Marxism, because they appear to provide a means of liberating it from the characteristic evolutionism of the nineteenth century, with which it was so often combined, though at the cost of also liberating it from the concept of 'progress' which was also characteristic of nineteenth-century thought, including Marx's. But why should we wish to do so?[12] Marx himself certainly would not have wished to do so: he offered to dedicate the *Capital* to Darwin, and would hardly have disagreed with Engels' famous phrase at his graveside, which praised him for discovering the law of evolution in human history, as Darwin had done in organic nature. (He would certainly not have wished to dissociate progress from evolution, and indeed specifically blamed Darwin for making it into its merely accidental by-product.)[13]

The fundamental question in history is how humanity developed from the earliest tool-using primate to the present. This implies the discovery of a mechanism for both the differentiation of various human social groups, and the transformation of one kind of society into another, or the failure to do so. In certain respects, which Marxists and common sense regard as crucial, such as the control of man over nature, it certainly implies unidirectional change or progress, at least over a suffi-

12. There are historical reasons for this rebellion against the 'revolutionary' aspect of Marxism, e.g. the rejection—for political reasons—of the Kautskyan orthodoxies, but we are not here concerned with these.

13. 'Marx to Engels', 7.8.1866, *Werke*, t. 31, p. 248.

ciently long time-span. So long as we do not suppose that the mechanisms of such social development are the same as or similar to those of biological evolution, there seems to be no good reason for not using the term 'evolution' for it.

The argument is, of course, more than terminological. It conceals two kinds of disagreements : about the value-judgment on different types of societies, or in other words, the possibility of ranking them in any kind of hierarchical order, and about the mechanisms of change. Structural-functionalisms have tended to shy away from ranking societies into 'higher' and 'lower', partly because of the welcome refusal of social anthropologists to accept the claim of the 'civilized' to rule the 'barbarian' because of their alleged superiority in social evolution, and partly because, by the formal criteria of function, there is indeed no such hierarchy. The Eskimo solve the problems of their existence as a social group[14] as successfully in their own way as the white inhabitants of Alaska; some would be tempted to say, more successfully. Under certain conditions and on certain assumptions, magical thinking may be as logical in its way as scientific thinking and as adequate for its purpose. And so on. These observations are valid, though they are not very useful insofar as the historian, or any other social scientist, wishes to explain the specific content of a system rather than its general structure.[15] But in any case they are irrelevant to the question of evolutionary change, if not indeed tautologous. Human societies must, if they are to persist, be capable of managing themselves successfully, and therefore all existing ones must be functionally adequate; if not, they would have become extinct, as the Shakers did for want of a system of sexual procreation or outside recruitment. To compare societies in respect of their system of internal relations between members is inevitably to compare like with like. It is when we compare them in respect

14. In the sense in which Lévi-Strauss speaks of kinship systems (or other social devices) as a 'coordinated ensemble, the function of which is to insure the permanency of the social group' (Sol Tax, ed., *Anthropology Today*, 1962, p. 343).

15. 'It remains true ... even for a properly revitalized version of functional analysis, that its explanatory form is rather limited; in particular, it does not provide an explanation of why a particular item *i* rather than some functional equivalent of it, occurs in system *s*.' Carl Hempel, in L. Gross, ed., *Symposium on Social Theory*, 1959.

of their capacity to control outside nature that the differences leap to the eye.

The second disagreement is more fundamental. Most versions of structural-functional analysis are synchronic, and the more elaborate and sophisticated they are, the more they are confined to social statics, into which, if the subject interests the thinker, some dynamizing element has to be introduced.[16] Whether this can be done satisfactorily is a matter of debate even among structuralists. That *the same analysis* cannot be used to explain both function and historic change, seems widely accepted. The point here is not that it is illegitimate to develop separate analysis models for the static and the dynamic, such as Marx's schemas of simple and extended reproduction, but that historical enquiry makes it desirable for these different models to be connected. The simplest course for the structuralist is to omit change, and leave history to someone else, or even, like some of the earlier British social anthropologists, virtually to deny its relevance. However, since it exists, structuralism must find ways of explaining it.

These ways must either, I suggest, bring it closer to Marxism, or lead to a denial of evolutionary change. Lévi-Strauss' approach (and that of Althusser) seem to me to do the latter. Here historical change becomes simply the permutation and combination of certain 'elements' (analogues, to quote Lévi-Strauss, to genes in genetics), which, in the sufficiently long term, may be expected to combine in different patterns and, if sufficiently limited, to exhaust the possible combinations.[17] History is, as it were, the process of playing through all the variants in an endgame of chess. But in what order? The theory here provides us with no guide.

Yet this is precisely the specific problem of historical evolu-

16. As Lévi-Strauss puts it, writing of kinship models, 'If no external factor were affecting this mechanism, it would work indefinitely, and the social structure would remain static. This is not the case, however; hence the need to introduce into the theoretical model new elements to account for the diachronic changes of the structure.' Loc. cit., p. 343.

17. 'Il est clair, toutefois, que c'est la nature de ce concept de "combinaison" qui fonde l'affirmation ... que le marxisme *n'est pas un historicisme* : puisque le concept marxiste de l'histoire repose sur le principe de la variation des formes de cette "combinaison".' Cf. *Lire le Capital*, t. II, p. 153.

tion. It is of course true that Marx envisaged such a combination and recombination of elements or 'forms' as Althusser stresses, and in this as other respects was a structuralist *avant la lettre*; or more precisely, a thinker from whom a Lévi-Strauss (by his own admission) could, in part at least, borrow the term.[18] It is important to remind ourselves of an aspect of Marx's thought which earlier traditions of Marxism undoubtedly neglected, with a few exceptions (among which, curiously, must be numbered some of the developments of Soviet Marxists in the Stalin period, though these were not wholly aware of the implications of what they were doing). It is even more important to remind ourselves that the analysis of the elements and their possible combinations provides (as in genetics) a salutary control on evolutionary theories, by establishing what is theoretically possible and impossible. It is also possible—though this question must remain open—that such an analysis could lend greater precision to the definition of the various social 'levels' (basis and superstructure) and their relationships, as Althusser suggests.[19] What it does not do is to explain why twentieth-century Britain is a very different place from neolithic Britain, or the succession of socio-economic formations, or the mechanism of the transitions from one to the other, or, for that matter, why Marx devoted so much of his life to answering such questions.

If such questions are to be answered both the peculiarities which distinguish Marxism from other structural-functional theories, are necessary: the model of *levels*, of which that of the social relations of production are primary, and the existence of internal contradictions within systems, of which class con-

18. R. Bastide, ed., *Sens et usage du terme structure dans les sciences sociales et humaines*, 1962, p. 143.

19. 'On voit par là que certains rapports de production supposent comme condition de leur propre existence, l'existence d'une *superstructure* juridico-politique et idéologique, et pourquoi cette superstructure est nécessairement *spécifique* ... On voit aussi que certains autres rapports de production n'appellent pas de superstructure politique, mais seulement une superstructure idéologique (les sociétés sans classes). On voit enfin que la nature des rapports de production considérés, non seulement appelle ou n'appelle pas telle ou telle forme de superstructure, mais fixe également le *degré d'efficace* délégué à tel ou tel niveau de la totalité sociale.' Loc. cit., p. 153.

flict is merely a special case.

The hierarchy of levels is necessary to explain why history has a *direction*. It is the growing emancipation of man from nature and his growing capacity to control it, which makes history as a whole (though not every area and period within it) 'oriented and irreversible', to quote Lévi-Strauss once again. A hierarchy of levels not arising on the base of the social relations of production would not necessarily have this characteristic. Moreover, since the process and progress of man's control over nature involves changes not merely in the forces of production (e.g. new techniques) but in the social relations of production, it implies a certain order in the succession of socio-economic systems. (It does not imply the acceptance of the list of formations given in the *Preface* to the *Critique of Political Economy* as chronologically successive, which Marx probably did not believe them to be, and still less a theory of universal unilinear evolution. However, it does imply that certain social phenomena cannot be conceived as appearing in history earlier than others, e.g. economies possessing the town-country dichotomy before those which lack it.) And for the same reason it implies that this succession of systems cannot be ordered simply in one dimension, technological (lower technologies preceding higher) or economic (*Geldwirtschaft* succeeding *Naturalwirtschaft*), but must also be ordered in terms of their social systems.[20] For it is an essential characteristic of Marx's historical thought that it is neither 'sociological' nor 'economic' but both simultaneously. The social relations of production and reproduction (i.e. social organization in its broadest sense) and the material forces of production, cannot be divorced.

Given this 'orientation' of historical development, the internal contradictions of socio-economic systems provide the mechanism for change which becomes development. (Without it, it might be argued that they would produce merely cyclical fluctuation, an endless process of de-stabilising and re-stabilising; and, of course, such changes as might arise from the contacts and conflicts of different societies.) The point about such internal contradictions is, that they cannot be defined simply as 'disfunctional' except on the assumption that stability and permanence are the norm, and change the exception; or even on the more naive assumption, frequent in the vulgar social

20. These may, of course, be described, if we find this useful, as different combinations of a given number of elements.

sciences, that a specific system is the model to which all change aspires.[21] It is rather that, as is now recognized much more widely than before among social anthropologists, a structural model envisaging only the maintenance of a system is inadequate. It is the simultaneous existence of stabilising and disruptive elements which such a model must reflect. And it is this which the Marxist model—though not the vulgar-Marxist versions of it—has been based on.

Such a dual (dialectical) model is difficult to set up and use, for in practice the temptation is great to operate it, according to taste or occasion, either as a model of stable functionalism or as one of revolutionary change; whereas the interesting thing about it is, that it is both. It is equally important that internal tensions may sometimes be reabsorbed into a self-stabilizing model by feeding them back as functional stabilizers, and that sometimes they cannot. Class conflict can be regulated through a sort of safety-valve, as in so many riots of urban plebeians in pre-industrial cities, or institutionalized as 'rituals of rebellion' (to use Max Gluckman's illuminating phrase) or in other ways; but sometimes it cannot. The state will normally legitimize the social order by controlling class conflict within a stable framework of institutions and values, ostensibly standing above and outside them (the remote king as 'fountain of justice'), and in doing so perpetuate a society which would otherwise be riven asunder by its internal tensions. This is indeed the classical Marxist theory of its origin and function, as expounded in *Origin of the Family*.[22] Yet there are situations when it loses this function and—even in the minds of its subject—this capacity to legitimate and appears merely as—to use the phrase of Thomas Morus—'a conspiracy of the rich for their own benefit', if not indeed the direct cause of the miseries of the poor. This contradictory nature of the model can be obscured by pointing to the undoubted existence of *separate* phenomena

21. One may add that it is doubtful whether they can be simply classified as 'conflicts', though insofar as we concentrate our attention on social systems as systems of relation between people, they may normally be expected to take the form of conflict between individuals and groups or, more metaphorically, between value-systems, roles, etc.

22. Whether the state is the only institution which has this function, has been a question that much preoccupied Marxists like Gramsci, but need not concern us here.

within society representing regulated stability and subversion: social groups which can allegedly be integrated into feudal society, such as 'merchant capital' and these which cannot, such as an 'industrial bourgeoisie', or social movements which are purely 'reformist' and those which are consciously 'revolutionary'. But though such separations exist, and where they do, indicate a certain stage in the development of the society's internal contradictions (which are *not*, for Marx, exclusively those of class conflict),[23] It is equally significant that the same phenomena may, according to the situation, change their functions; movements for the restoration of the old regulated order of class society turning (as with some peasant movements) into social revolutions, consciously revolutionary parties being absorbed into the *status quo*.[24]

Difficult though it may be, social scientists of various kinds (including, we may note, animal ecologists, especially students of population dynamics and animal social behaviour) have begun to approach the construction of models of equilibria based on tension or conflict, and in doing so draw nearer to Marxism and further away from the older models of sociology which regarded the problem of order as logically prior to that of change and emphasized the integrative and normative elements in social life. At the same time it must be admitted that Marx's own model must be made more explicit than it is in his writings, that it may require elaboration and development, and that certain vestiges of the nineteenth-century positivism, more evident in Engels' formulations than in Marx's own thought, must be cleared out of the way.

We are then still left with the *specific* historical problems of the nature and succession of socio-economic formations, and the mechanisms of their internal development, and interaction.

23. G. Lichtheim (*Marxism*, 1961, p. 152) rightly points out that class antagonism plays only a subordinate part in Marx's model of the break-up of ancient Roman society. The view that this must have been due to 'slave revolts' has no basis in Marx.

24. As Worsley, summarizing work along these lines put it 'change within a system must either cumulate towards structural change of the system, or be coped with by some sort of cathartic mechanism,' 'The Analysis of Rebellion and Revolution in Modern British Social Anthropology', *Science and Society*, XXV, 1, 1961, p. 37. Ritualization in social relations makes sense as such a symbolic-acting out of tensions which might be otherwise intolerable.

These are fields in which discussion has been intensive since Marx,[25] not least in the past decades, and in some respects the advance upon Marx has been most striking.[26] Here also recent analysis has confirmed the brilliance and profundity of Marx's general approach and vision though it has also drawn attention to the gaps in his treatment, particularly of pre-capitalist periods. However, these themes can hardly be discussed even in the most cursory form except in terms of concrete historical knowledge; i.e. they cannot be discussed in the context of the present colloquium. Short of such a discussion I can only assert my conviction that Marx's approach is still the only one which enables us to explain the entire span of human history, and forms the most fruitful starting point for modern discussion.

None of this is particularly new, though some of the texts which contain the most mature reflections of Marx on historical subjects, did not become available until the 1950s, notably the *Grundrisse* of 1857-8. Moreover, the diminishing returns on the application of vulgar-Marxist models, have in recent decades led to a substantial sophistication of Marxist historiography.[27] Indeed, one of the most characteristic features of contemporary western Marxist historiography is the critique of the simple, mechanical schemata of an economic-determinist type. However, whether or not Marxist historians have advanced substantially beyond Marx, their contribution today has a new importance, because of the changes which are at present taking place in the social sciences. Whereas the major function of historical materialism in the first half-century after Engels' death was to bring history closer to the social sciences, while avoiding the oversimplifications of positivism, it is today facing the rapid historization of the social sciences themselves. For want of any help from academic historiography, these have in-

25. Cf. the great quantity of research and discussion on oriental societies, deriving from a very small number of pages in Marx, of which some of the most important—those in the *Grundrisse*—were not available until fifteen years ago.

26. E.g. in the field of pre-history, the work of the late V. Gordon Childe, perhaps the most original historical mind in the English-speaking countries to apply Marxism to the past.

27. Compare, for instance, the approaches of Dr Eric Williams' *Capitalism and Slavery*, 1964, a valuable and illuminating pioneer work, and Prof. Eugène Genovese, to the problem of American slave societies and the abolition of slavery.

creasingly begun to improvise their own—applying their own characteristic procedures to the study of the past, with results which are often technically sophisticated, but, as has been pointed out, based on models of historic change in some respects even cruder than those of the nineteenth century.[28] Here the value of Marx's historical materialism is great, though it is natural that historically minded social scientists may find themselves less in need of Marx's insistence on the importance of economic and social elements in history than did the historians of the early twentieth century; and conversely might find themselves more stimulated by aspects of Marx's theory which did not make a great impact on historians in the immediately post-Marxism generations.

Whether this explains the undoubted prominence of Marxian ideas in the discussion of certain fields of historically oriented social science today, is another question.[29] The unusual prominence at present of Marxist historians, or of historians trained in the Marxist school, is certainly in large part due to the radicalization of intellectuals and students in the past decade, the impact of the revolutions in the Third World, the break-up of Marxist orthodoxies inimical to original scientific work, and even to so simple a factor as the succession of generations. For the Marxists who reached the point of publishing widely-read books and occupying senior positions in academic life in the 1950s were often only the radicalized students of the 1930s or 1940s, reaching the normal peak of their careers. Nevertheless, as we celebrate the 150th anniversary of Marx's birth and the centenary of the *Capital*, we cannot but note—with satisfaction if we are Marxists—the coincidence of a significant influence of Marxism in the field of historiography, and a significant number of historians inspired by Marx or demonstrating, in their work, the effects of training in the Marxist schools.

28. This is particularly obvious in fields such as the theory of economic growth as applied to specific societies, and the theories of 'modernization' in political science and sociology.

29. The discussion of the political impact of capitalist development on pre-industrial societies, and more generally, of the 'prehistory' of modern social movements and revolutions, is a good example.

13

Marx and the Critique of Political Economy

NORMAN GERAS

In this essay Norman Geras explores the critique of political economy that Marx developed in Capital *and the crucial role of the concept of 'fetishism' in this critique. Geras insists that when Marx criticized the 'fetishism of commodities' he was referring both to ideological mystification and to substantive domination.*

Norman Geras is Lecturer in Government at Manchester University.

'Vulgar economy ... everywhere sticks to appearances in opposition to the law which regulates and explains them. In opposition to Spinoza, it believes that "ignorance is a sufficient reason" ' (I, 307).[1] '... Vulgar economy feels particularly at home in the estranged outward appearances of economic relations ... these relations seem the more self-evident the more their internal relationships are concealed from it' (III, 797). '... The philistine's and vulgar economist's *way of looking at things* stems ... from the fact that it is only the direct *form of manifestation* of relations that is reflected in their brains and not their *inner connection*' (Marx to Engels, 27 June 1867). 'Once for all I may here state, that by classical Political Economy, I understand that economy which, since the time of W. Petty, has investigated the real relations of production in bourgeois society, in contradistinction to vulgar economy, which deals with appearances only' I, 81). 'It is the great merit of classical economy to have destroyed this false appearance and illusion ... this personification of things and conversion of production relations into entities, this religion of everyday life ... nevertheless even the best

1. References to *Capital* give the volume number (Roman) and the page number (Arabic) of the edition published by Lawrence and Wishart, London, 1961-2. The letters of Marx and Engels can be found in the *Selected Correspondence* (Moscow n.d.).

spokesmen of classical economy remain more or less in the grip of the world of illusion which their criticism had dissolved, as cannot be otherwise from a bourgeois standpoint, and thus they all fall more or less into inconsistencies, half-truths and unsolved contradictions' (III, 809).

In this manner does Marx, on many occasions, specify the distance separating vulgar economy from classical political economy, and *a fortiori* from his own critique of the latter, providing us at the same time with a conception of the minimum *necessary* condition to be satisfied by any work aspiring to scientific status : namely, that it uncover the reality behind the appearance which conceals it. The intention of this article is to deal with a group of problems (in particular, the problem of fetishism) related to Marx's formulations of this requirement and to the systematic recurrence of its appropriate terminology—appearance/essence, form/content, illusion/reality, phenomena/hidden substratum, form of manifestation/inner connection, etc. It should, however, be made clear at the outset that scarcely anything is said about the development of Marx's views on these questions, hence about the relation between the *Economic and Philosophical Manuscripts* of 1844 and *Capital*; and, about the relationship between Hegel and Marx, nothing at all. Thus the process of Marx's intellectual formation and development is set to one side, and these problems are considered only as they emerge in *Capital* itself, at the interior of what is a more or less finished, more or less coherent structure of thought.

The theoretical foundation of Capital

If we begin, then, with what I have called the minimum necessary condition of Marx's science, this methodological requirement to which he assigns an exceptional importance, the first question which arises is as follows : what is its theoretical foundation? What establishes its necessity? At all events, it is hardly an arbitrary construction on Marx's part. The text of *Capital* provides us with two kinds of answer. In one, it is revealed as the common requirement of *any* science.

'... a scientific analysis of competition is not possible before we have a conception of the inner nature of capital, just as the apparent motions of the heavenly bodies are not intelligible to any but him, who is acquainted with their real motions, motions which are not directly perceptible by the senses' (I, 316).

'That in their appearance things often represent themselves in inverted form is pretty well known in every science except Political Economy' (I, 537).

'. . . all science would be superfluous if the outward appearance and the essence of things directly coincided' (III, 797).

In such passages Marx presents the conceptual distinction between appearance and reality as a form of *scientificity as such*, by notifying us that the method he is applying in political economy is simply a general requirement for arriving at valid knowledge, one which he has taken over from the other sciences where it has long been established. Taken on its own, this answer is not entirely satisfactory. It makes of Marx's primary methodological injunction—to shatter the obviousness of immediate appearances—an abstract procedural rule which must form part of the equipment of every science, regardless of the content of that science, of the nature of its object of study. Taken on its own, this answer does not yet specify why it is appropriate to extend the methods of astronomy to the subject matter of political economy. For this reason we put it in parenthesis for the moment, though it should be borne in mind since it will be reconsidered at a later stage of the argument.

We proceed to Marx's second answer which is of a different order altogether from the first. This answer is, of course, contained in the doctrine of fetishism. For the latter specifies those properties of Marx's object of study itself which imperiously *demand* that appearances be demolished if reality is to be correctly grasped. It analyses the mechanisms by which capitalist society necessarily appears to its agents as something other than it really is. The notion of fetishism raises quite complex problems, which will be developed presently, but even now it should be clear that we have in this second answer a theoretical foundation for the distinction, essence/appearance, and its variations, which was lacking in the first. The relation between methodological injunction and object of study is no longer one of externality, as is the case with an abstract rule applicable to any content whatsoever. It is, rather, what may be termed a *relation of adequacy* between object and method, the character of the latter being determined by the structure of the former. It is because there exists, at the interior of capitalist society, a kind of internal rupture between the social relations which obtain and the manner in which they are experienced, that the scientist of that society is confronted with the necessity of constructing reality against appearances. Thus, this necessity can no longer be regarded as an arbitrary importation into Marx's own theoretical equipment of something he merely extracted from other pre-existing sciences. And the passages quoted at the beginning of this paper are seen to lead, by a short route, to the heart of the notion of fetishism.

It is enough to consult any standard commentary on Marx to see that this notion is not free from ambiguity or confusion, and, to some extent, this is also true of Marx's own exposition in the first chapter of *Capital*. It seems necessary, therefore, to adopt an analytic procedure, in an attempt to isolate different aspects of the concept and to examine them separately, even if such a procedure runs the risk of fragmenting what Marx conceived to be a unified phenomenon. For, if it enables us to clarify the aspects, taken separately, the chances of understanding their relations to one another, that is to say, of reconstituting them as a whole, are thereby enhanced. An initial distinction, one which is clear enough, between two aspects of fetishism is provided by the text of *Capital* itself: '... a definite social relation between men ... assumes, in their eyes, the fantastic form of a relation between things' (I, 72).

'... their own social action takes the form of the action of objects, which rule the producers instead of being ruled by them' (I, 75).

In capitalist society the phenomenon of fetishism imposes itself on men (*a*) as mystification and (*b*) as domination. Clearly the two aspects are intimately related, inasmuch as men are in no position to control, rather than submit to, social relations which they do not correctly understand. And that they are so related is reflected in subsequent literature on the subject where they are normally run together. Thus Garaudy writes: 'The relations between men take on the appearance of relations between objects ... Things rule the men who have created them.' And Sweezy: '... the real character of the relations among the producers themselves is both distorted and obscured from view ... the world of commodities has, so to speak, achieved its independence and subjected the producers to its sway.'[2] How-

2. Roger Garaudy, *Karl Marx: the Evolution of his Thought*, London, 1967, p. 125; Paul Sweezy, *The Theory of Capitalist Development*, London, 1946, p. 36. Cf. also George Lukács, *Histoire et Conscience de Classe*, Paris, 1960, pp. 110–13 and Sidney Hook, *Towards the Understanding of Karl Marx*, London, 1933, p. 162.

ever, for the reasons stated, I intend as far as possible to maintain the distinction, and to treat mystification and domination
separately, taking the latter first although the former is more
directly pertinent to the problem of appearance and reality and
also more problematic. No discussion of fetishism can ignore
this feature of domination altogether, and it may perhaps be
appropriate to clear it out of the way.

The role of alienation in Capital

What we have to deal with here is not domination in general
but a historically specific form of domination. It differs, for
example, from the relations of 'personal dependence' which
Marx identifies as characteristic of the European middle ages
(I, 77), and this for two reasons: whereas there the domination
is undisguised, under capitalism it is concealed; secondly, and
more to the point here, it is precisely an *impersonal* kind of
domination exercised by the totality of economic relations over
all the agents of capitalist society, embracing also the capitalist
whose overriding interest is the extraction of as much surplus
labour as possible from the worker. He too cannot be held
'responsible for relations whose creature he socially remains'
(I, 10; Preface to the First German Edition). It is unnecessary
to rehearse all the aspects of this impersonal domination—
the independence of the production process *vis-à-vis* the producers, the past labour of the worker confronting him as a
hostile power in the shape of capital, the instruments of labour
employing the worker rather than vice versa, the drudgery
and stupefaction of work, and so on. All these are comprised by
the concept of alienation. However, in *Capital* this is a historical
concept of alienation. Its social and historical premises are
precisely economic relations based on the production and exchange of commodities.

This is brought out clearly in the following passages: 'The
owners of commodities ... find out, that the same division of
labour that turns them into independent private producers,
also frees the social process of production and the relations of
the individual producers to each other within that process, from
all dependence on the will of those producers, and that the
seeming mutual independence of the individuals is supplemented
by a system of general and mutual dependence through or by
means of the products' (I, 107–8).

Political Economy 'has never once asked the question why labour is represented by the value of its product and labour-time by the magnitude of that value. These formulae, which bear it stamped upon them in unmistakable letters that they belong to a state of society, in which the process of production has the mastery over man, instead of being controlled by him, such formulae appear to the bourgeois intellect to be as much a self-evident necessity imposed by Nature as productive labour itself' (I, 80–1).

Here, the roots of the phenomena grouped under the term alienation, are located in specific social relations, and not in the fact that there is an ideal essence of man, his 'species-being', which has been negated or denied. And this is the difference that separates *Capital* from certain passages in the *Economic and Philosophical Manuscripts*,[3] even though there, too, Marx deals with such features of capitalist society as the domination of the worker by his product and the stultifying character of his work.[4] In place of a concept of alienation founded on an essentialist anthropology, we have one tied to the historical specificity of forms of domination.

To this extent, those discussions of fetishism which simply take for granted the complete unity between the *Manuscripts* and *Capital*,[5] are of dubious value, conflating as they do two concepts of different theoretical status. And when Lukács, in his discussion of fetishism, speaks of one-sided specialization 'violating the human essence of man' (op. cit., p. 128), he is guilty of the same conflation. On the other hand, Althusser has proposed a reading of fetishism in which, of the two aspects that have been distinguished, namely, mystification and domination, only the former is treated. The notion of men being dominated by their own products has vanished (almost) without trace. Such an interpretation demands, of course, that the concept of fetishism be regarded as entirely unrelated to, and independent of, that of alienation,[6] and the latter is accordingly

3. T. B. Bottomore ed., *Karl Marx: Early Writings*, London, 1963, pp. 126–8.

4. Ibid., pp. 122–5.

5. E.g. Garaudy, op. cit., pp. 52–63 and 124–7.

6. J-C. Forquin, 'Lecture d'Althusser' in *Dialectique Marxiste et Pensée Structurale*, special number of *Les Cahiers du Centre d'Etudes Socialistes*, 76–81, February-May, 1968, p. 27.

dismissed as 'ideological' and 'pre-Marxist'.[7]

In this reading Althusser is guilty, in the first place, of violating the text of *Capital*, as the following passages make clear : '... the character (*Gestalt*) of independence and estrangement (*entfremdet*) which the capitalist mode of production as a whole gives to the instruments of labour and to the product, as against the workman, is developed by means of machinery into a thorough antagonism' (I, 432).

'Since, before entering on the process, his own labour has already been alienated (*entfremdet*) from himself by the sale of his labour-power, has been appropriated by the capitalist and incorporated with capital, it must, during the process, be realised in a product that does not belong to him (*in fremdem Produkt*)' (I, 570–1).

'Capital comes more and more to the fore as a social power, whose agent is the capitalist. This social power no longer stands in any possible relation to that which the labour of a single individual can create. It becomes an alienated (*entfremdete*), independent, social power, which stands opposed to society as an object, and as an object that is the capitalist's source of power' (III, 259).

And even were the term 'alienation' altogether absent, there are enough passages where the *concept*, and all the phenomena it embraces, are presented, to invalidate Althusser's reading of *Capital* on this point.[8]

However. it is not only a question of the validity of the interpretation of Marx. There are serious theoretical consequences as well. For in Althusser the concept of alienation, as that form of domination engendered by capitalist relations of production, is replaced—and here is its surviving trace—by the notion of men as the mere functionaries, or bearers (Träger), of the relations of production which determine their places and their functions.[9] What Marx regards as a feature specific to *capitalist* relations of production, Althusser articulates as a *general* proposition of historical materialism. Thus de-historicizing the concept of alienation in a manner quite strange for a

7. Louis Althusser, *For Marx*, London, 1969, p. 239.

8. For example 1 : 112, 310, 360–1, 422–3, 645. There is an excellent discussion of the relation between the *Manuscripts* and *Capital* in Ernest Mandel, *La Formation de la Pensée Economique de Karl Marx*, Paris, 1967, pp. 151–79.

9. 'The Object of Capital', in *Reading Capital*, London, 1970, p.180.

Marxist author (for how is this different from the fault of the classical political economists who regard commodity production as eternal?) he makes it impossible to comprehend, from his perspective, those passages in which Marx anticipates a future social formation where, precisely, men will control their relations of production, rather than be controlled by them, where they will, therefore, cease to be mere functionaries and bearers. We shall see later on that Althusser commits an exactly parallel error in relation to the other aspect of fetishism, mystification. For the moment it is sufficient to observe that, in his legitimate anxiety to be done with the anthropological concept of alienation, he throws out the historical concept as well, de-historicizing it in a 'new' way.

The reality of value relations

Returning now to the problem of essence/appearance and the mystificatory aspect of fetishism, it will be well to make a secondary distinction: between (*a*) those appearances, or forms of manifestation, in which social relations present themselves and which are not mystificatory or false *as such*, inasmuch as they do correspond to an objective reality; they become mystified only when regarded as products of nature or of the subjective intentions of men; and (*b*) those appearances, or forms of manifestation, which are quite simply false, illusions in the full sense, corresponding to no objective reality. This distinction governs what follows. (Unless, therefore, it is made explicit, the term 'appearance' should not be taken to mean 'mere, i.e. false, appearance'. The same goes for the word 'form'.) And it is a helpful one to the extent that it enables one to avoid the kind of confusion into which many accounts of fetishism fall, and of which the following passage by Karl Korsch is an example: 'The value relations appearing in the exchange of the products of labour as "commodities" are essentially not relations between things, but merely an imaginary expression of an underlying social relation between the human beings who co-operate in their production. Bourgeois society is just that particular form of the social life of man in which the most basic relations established between human beings in the social production of their lives become known to them only after the event, and even then only in the reversed form of relations between things. By depending in their conscious actions upon such imaginary concepts, the members of modern "civilized" society are really, like the savage by his fetish, controlled by the work of their hands.'[10]

While there is much here that is unobjectionable (e.g. value relations as the product of social relations, men dominated by their own creations), it is incorrect to describe value relations as imaginary. As I shall try to show, Marx does not do so. Such a description is dangerously close, though Korsch manages to keep his distance, to a purely subjectivist explanation of fetishism, of the kind given by Berger and Pullberg when, in an article on the sociology of knowledge, they formulate the following stupefying definition: '... alienation is the process by which man forgets that the world he lives in has been produced by himself.'[11] What they themselves 'forget' is that, if forgetfulness were all that was involved, a reminder should be sufficient to deal with the constituent problems of alienation.

How is it then with Marx? What is in question at the moment are the following forms of manifestation: that labour is represented by the value of its product, labour-time by the magnitude of that value, and social relations by the value relations between commodities. For Marx, neither values nor value relations are imaginary. They are not illusory appearances, but *realities*. This point cannot be emphasized too strongly. It represents a first step towards understanding what is involved in fetishism. Thus he writes: '... the labour of the individual asserts itself as a part of the labour of society, only by means of the relations which the act of exchange establishes directly between the products, and indirectly, through them, between the producers. To the latter, therefore, the relations connecting the labour of one individual with that of the next appear, not as direct social relations between individuals at work, but as *what they really are*, material relations between persons and social relations between things' (I, 73. My emphasis).

It is in the light of this statement that the ambiguous footnote which occurs shortly afterwards should be interpreted: 'When, therefore, Galiani says: Value is a relation between persons ... he ought to have added: a relation between persons expressed as a relation between things' (I, 74).

10. Karl Korsch, *Karl Marx*, New York, 1963, p. 131.
11. P. Berger and S. Pullberg, 'Reification and the Sociological Critique of Consciousness', *New Left Review*, No. 35, January-February, 1966, p. 61.

This means, not that a relation between persons takes on the illusory appearance of a relation between things, but that where commodity production prevails, relations between persons really do take the form of relations between things. This is the specific form of capitalist social relations; other societies, both pre- and post-capitalist, are characterized by social relations of a different form. A moment's consideration of the defining relations of capitalist society—capitalist/worker, producer-of-/consumer-of-commodities—is enough to verify this. For the capitalist, the worker exists only as labour-power, for the worker, the capitalist only as capital. For the consumer, the producer is commodities, and for the producer the consumer is money. Althusser is therefore correct to insist that the social relations of production are not, and are not reducible to, simple relations between men.[12] And the reply of one of his critics—that they are, but mediated by things[13]—is not so much a counter-statement as a restatement of the same thing. It should, however, be borne in mind that the objects, namely commodities, the value relations between which are the form taken by capitalist social relations, are social and not natural objects.

It is just because these value relations are neither imaginary nor illusory but real, that Marx is able to make the following judgment: 'The categories of bourgeois economy . . . are forms of thought expressing *with social validity* the conditions and relations of a definite, historically determined mode of production, viz., the production of commodities' (I, 76. My emphasis).

At the same time Marx describes these forms of thought as absurd. But what kind of absurdity is it? 'When I state that coats or boots stand in a relation to linen, because it is the universal incarnation of abstract human labour, the absurdity of the statement is self-evident. Nevertheless, when the producers of coats and boots compare those articles with linen, or, what is the same thing, with gold or silver, as the universal equivalent, they express the relation between their own private labour and the collective labour of society in the same absurd form' (I, 76).

It is the absurdity not of an illusion, but of reality itself, and to this extent it is an absurdity which is true.

12. 'The Object of Capital', op. cit., p. 174.
13. S. Pullberg, 'Note pour une lecture anthropologique de Marx' in *Dialectique Marxiste et Pensée Structurale*, op. cit., p. 145.

The social reality behind fetishized relationships

Having insisted on the *reality* of value, and of the objective form taken on by capitalist social relations, the form, that is to say, of a relation between objects, we further specify them by emphasizing that they are *social* realities. This determination Marx himself makes quite clear: 'If ... we bear in mind that the value of commodities has a purely social reality, and that they acquire this reality only in so far as they are expressions or embodiments of one identical social substance, viz., human labour, it follows as a matter of course, that value can only manifest itself in the social relation of commodity to commodity' (I, 47).

'... the coat, in the expression of value of the linen, represents a non-natural property of both, something purely social, namely, their value' (I, 57).

Further, by a third specification, it is necessary to recognize value and the objective form of social relations as *historically specific* social realities, and not just social realities in general. From this, three important conclusions are to be derived.

1. The distinctions, form/content, appearance/essence, retain their significance for the analysis and explanation of these realities, but on condition that the first term of each opposition is not taken to be synonymous with illusion. Because the forms taken by capitalist social relations, their modes of appearance, are historically specific ones, they are puzzling forms, they contain a secret. The reasons why social relations should take such forms, rather than others, are not self-evident. It requires a work of analysis to discover them, to disclose the secret, and, in doing this, it reveals the contents of these forms and the essence of these appearances. At the same time, the content explains the form, and the essence the appearances, which cease thereafter to be puzzling. But this must not be regarded as a journey from illusion to reality. It is rather a process of elucidating one reality by disclosing its foundation in and determination by another. Thus the form of value (viz., exchange-value) and the object character of social relations is not dissolved or dissipated by Marx as an illusion, but its content is laid bare: the individuals working independently and producing use-values not for direct consumption but for exchange. It is the commodity form itself which is responsible for the enigma (I, 71), and its solution therefore requires an analysis of that form.

Similarly, Marx uncovers the content of surplus-value by indicating its source in the surplus labour-time of the worker. He
thus discovers *its* secret. Bourgeois political economy, itself
unable to hit upon this secret, except in the New World (I, 774)
and, even there, without drawing the necessary conclusions,
takes the only other road open to it. It de-historicizes value and
surplus-value, makes of them products of nature, and, in parallel
fashion, regards the impersonal and objective form of capitalist
social relations as an entirely natural state of affairs. It thus
transforms the properties possessed by commodities, capital,
etc., qua *social* objects, into qualities belonging *naturally* to
them as things. *This* is the root and beginning of the mystification of fetishism.

2. It is not that something imaginary has been endowed with
the quality of reality. The mechanism of mystification consists
in the collapsing of social facts into natural ones. In this way,
the value form is fetishized. This is expressed most clearly
by Marx in a passage in the second volume, where he refers
to: '... the fetishism peculiar to bourgeois Political Economy,
the fetishism which metamorphoses the social, economic character impressed on things in the process of social production
into a natural character stemming from the material nature of
those things' (II, 225).

There is, however, no shortage of examples of Marx observing
this metamorphosis in relation to particular features of capitalist
society. Thus he writes of the productive power of social labour:
'... co-operation begins only with the labour-process, but they
[i.e. the workers] have then ceased to belong to themselves ...
Hence, the productive power developed by the labourer when
working in co-operation, is the productive power of capital ...
Because this power costs capital nothing, and because, on the
other hand, the labourer himself does not develop it before his
labour belongs to capital, it appears as a power with which
capital is endowed by Nature' (I, 333).

And of money: 'What appears to happen is, not that gold
becomes money, in consequence of all other commodities expressing their values in it, but, on the contrary, that all other
commodities universally express their values in gold, because
it is money ... These objects, gold and silver, just as they come
out of the bowels of the earth, are forthwith the direct incarnation of all human labour. Hence the magic of money' (I, 92).[14]

14. Cf. I, 57–8.

And of interest-bearing capital: 'It becomes a property of money to generate value and yield interest, much as it is an attribute of pear-trees to bear pears' (III, 384).

Now, it is in order to undo the mystifying effects of this metmorphosis that Marx insists: '. . . capital is not a thing, but rather a definite social production relation, belonging to a definite historical formation of society, which is manifested in a thing and lends this thing a specific social character' (III, 794).[15]

The demystification is achieved by means of a denaturation. But this is not the same thing as a de-objectification. Pending the destruction of bourgeois society, capital remains an objective form, a social object, whose content and essence are accumulated labour, which dominates the agents of that society, and it must be comprehended as such.

It should further be noted that the *false* appearances to which the fetishization of forms gives rise are yet 'something more and else than mere illusions.'[16] By this I mean that they are not attributable simply to a failure of perspicacity on the part of the social agents, to some act of 'forgetfulness', with its source in purely subjective deficiencies. In every case where Marx presents us with an example of fetishization, he goes to great pains to indicate the roots and *raison d'être* of the resulting illusions in the reality itself. Briefly, most, though not all, of his indications can be subsumed under the following general kind of explanation: in capitalist society, the social relations between the producers take the form of objective qualities belonging to their products, namely, commodities; there is nothing, however, in the commodity which indicates that these qualities which it actually possesses as a commodity (say, money) do not belong to it as a thing (gold); the collapse into nature is therefore itself perfectly 'natural', i.e., comprehensible. If then the social agents experience capitalist society as something other than it really is, this is fundamentally because capitalist society *presents itself* as something other than it really is. As Maurice Godelier has put it: 'It is not the subject who deceives himself, but *reality* which deceives *him*.'[17]

3. We have seen that one type of mystification consists of

15. Cf. I, 766.

16. Henri Lefebvre; *The Sociology of Marx*, London, 1968, p. 62.

17. M. Godelier, 'System, Structure and Contradiction in *Capital*', *Socialist Register*, 1967, p. 93.

reducing the social objectivity of the forms of capitalist relations to a natural objectivity. This mystification is fetishism. However, Marx also exposes a second type of mystification, one which involves a reduction of these forms, in the opposite direction, from social objectivity to social *subjectivity*. This occurs when they are declared to be imaginary, fictional forms. While this is not fetishism, indeed, may be regarded as an over-reaction against it, it is nevertheless a mystification: 'The act of exchange gives to the commodity converted into money, not its value, but its specific value-form. By confounding these two distinct things some writers have been led to hold that the value of gold and silver is imaginary ... But if it be declared that the social characters assumed by objects, or the material forms assumed by the social qualities of labour under the regime of a definite mode of production, are mere symbols, it is in the same breath also declared that these characteristics are arbitrary fictions sanctioned by the so-called universal consent of mankind. This suited the mode of explanation in favour during the 18th century. Unable to account for the origin of the puzzling forms assumed by social relations between man and man, people sought to denude them of their strange appearance by ascribing to them a conventional origin' (I, 90–1).

Thus, the fact that the material forms of capitalist social relations are not natural ones, does not deprive them of their objectivity, that is to say, of their character of being objects, which become independent *vis-à-vis* the social agents, dominate them according to their own laws, and cannot be ascribed to human subjectivity, either as their source or as their explanation. Such an ascription, whether it be seen as an agreement—convention, consent, social contract—or as a failure of consciousness—act of forgetting, lack of insight, trick of the imagination—has this theoretical consequence: it spirits away the uncontrolled, and fundamentally uncontrollable, character of these objects, these forms of capitalist social relations. For, in the first case, it is sufficient to undo the agreement, make new agreements, work out new conventions, in order to handle the contradictions of capitalism. Marx is plunged into liberal political theory or its poorly disguised variant, social-democratic reformism. In the second case, a new act of consciousness, a reappropriation of the world in thought, serves the same purpose. Marx is plunged into Hegel.

Pure appearance: the wage form

I have dealt, so far, with those forms of capitalist social relations, those modes of appearance in which they present themselves, which are not illusory as such, but are subject to two
kinds of transformation which render them mystificatory: they
are fetishized, i.e. grounded in nature, or given an idealistic
explanation. I come now to the forms which are illusory in the
full sense, appearances which are *mere* appearances. First and
foremost here, because it is an illusory form which is itself the
source of a number of other illusions, is the wage form. In
this, the value of labour-power is transformed in such a way
that it takes on the (false) appearance of the value of labour. It
'thus extinguishes every trace of the division of the working-
day into necessary labour and surplus-labour, into paid and
unpaid labour' (I, 539). Which is to say, it conceals the *essential*
feature of capitalist relations, namely, exploitation. The latter
is based on the difference between the value of labour-power,
for which the capitalist pays in order to use it for a given time,
and the greater value which the same labour-power in operation
creates during that time. But since, in the wage form, what
appears to happen is that the capitalist pays, not for the labour-
power, but for the labour, the inequality of the exchange is
falsely disguised as an equal exchange.

Those passages where Marx refers to the difference between
the value of labour-power and the value it creates as 'a piece
of good luck for the buyer, but by no means an injury to the
seller' (I, 194), and where he denies that 'the seller has been
defrauded' (I, 585), must therefore be regarded as having a
provisional and double-edged character. On the one hand, it is
indeed the case that capitalist exploitation is not fundamentally
based on the individual capitalist cheating his workers; according to all the laws of commodity production, the worker does
get paid for the full value of the commodity he sells. On the
other hand, these laws themselves entail an injury and a
fraud much greater than individual cheating, the unconscious
injury and defrauding of one class by another. The provisional
character of the original statements is, therefore, made plain:
'The exchange of equivalents, the original operation with which
we started, has now become turned round in such a way that
here is only an apparent exchange ... The relation of exchange subsisting between capitalist and labourer becomes a

mere semblance appertaining to the procss of circulation, a mere form, foreign to the real nature of the transaction, and only mystifying it' (I, 583).

Here, the analysis of the form which reveals the content, the penetration of the appearance which discloses the essence, *is* a journey from illusion to reality. The same goes for another of the appearances to which the wage form gives rise : namely, the appearance that the worker disposes of his labour-power according to his own free will. This is a mere appearance, an illusion, whose reality is that the worker is forced to sell his labour-power. Thus, the transition from the sphere of circulation, that 'very Eden of the innate rights of man [where] alone rule Freedom, Equality, Property and Bentham' (I, 176), to that of production which reveals 'that the time for which he is free to sell his labour-power is the time for which he is forced to sell it' (I, 3o2) This transition is one from illusion to reality : '. . . in essence it always remains forced labour—no matter how much it may seem to result from free contractual agreement' (III, 798).

However, two precisions are required at this point.

1. I have said that these analyses which refer us from the appearance (equal exchange, free labour) to the essence (unequal exchange, forced labour), are at the same time journeys from illusion to reality. They are also, it is clear from the above, transitions from the process of circulation to the process of production. But the circulation process is no illusion. What we are dealing with here are illusions arising *in* and *during* the circulation process by contrast with the realities uncovered by an analysis of the production process. This precision is important, because it is at all costs necessary to avoid dissolving the various 'levels' of the social totality, by regarding them all as mere forms of manifestation of one essential level, and thus depriving them of their specific efficacy. It is the attempt to theorize this necessity in the concept of 'over-determination' that is Althusser's real contribution to contemporary Marxist discussion.[18] Nor is it simply a question here of the relation between the circulation and production processes. As Marx makes clear, from these semblances of the sphere of circulation there arises a whole ideological superstructure: 'This phenomenal form [i.e. the wage form], which makes the actual relation invisible, and, indeed, shows the direct opposite of that relation,

18. 'Contradiction and Overdetermination' in *For Marx*, op. cit.

forms the basis of all the juridical notions of both labourer and capitalist, of all the mystifications of the capitalist mode of production, of all its illusions as to liberty, of all the apologetic shifts of the vulgar economists' (I, 540).

The Marxist critique of the illusions pertaining to this superstructure equally does not deprive it of its positive reality.

2. The decisive factor, which makes possible the discovery in the production process of the essence of the false appearances of circulation, consists in this : that, in moving from circulation to production, the analysis moves from the consideration of relationships between individuals to that of the relations between classes, of which the former are a function. Only this change of terrain can demystify the appearances. Its importance will be dealt with at a later stage of the argument.

The wage form, then, unlike the value form, corresponds to no objective reality. Marx is quite unequivocal on this point and attempts to give it special emphasis : '. . . "value of labour" . . . is an expression as imaginary as the value of the earth' (I, 537).

'. . . "price of labour" is just as irrational as a yellow logarithm' (III, 798).

And yet this illusory form is not one that is easily seen through or dissipated. Marx gave notice of this when he described as one of the three new elements of *Capital* his discovery of the irrationality of the wage form (Marx to Engels, 8 Jan. 1868). But he also says it explicitly in *Capital* : 'These imaginary expressions arise, however, from the relations of production themselves' (I, 537).

'. . . the price of labour-power . . . inevitably appears as the price of labour under the capitalist mode of production' (III, 801).

'If history took a long time to get at the bottom of the mystery of wages, nothing, on the other hand, is more easy to understand than the necessity, the *raison d'être*, of this phenomenon' (I, 540).

Like the illusions of fetishism discussed above, the illusion of the wage form is opaque and tenacious, because here as there it is a case of reality deceiving the subject rather than the subject deceiving himself. This is the way the value of labour-power *presents itself*. And Marx analyses some of the mechanisms of the process—e.g. changes of wages corresponding with the changing length of the working day; 'price of labour' does not seem more irrational than 'price of cotton', exchange-value and use-value being intrinsically incommensurable magnitudes any-way (I, 540–1). In this, as in the earlier case, what Marx tells us is that capitalist society itself is characterized by a quality of opacity, so that *it* creates the necessity of a methodology which will penetrate the appearance to uncover the reality, and then, by a reverse course, so to speak, demonstrate why this reality should take on such an appearance.

Science and ideology: the Althusserian Disjunction

But, at all events, this opacity is a historically specific one. For Marx, different types of social relations are characterized by different degrees of opacity and transparency, and capitalism itself creates the historical possibility of a society where 'the practical relations of everyday life offer to man none but per-fectly intelligible and reasonable relations with regard to his fellowmen and to Nature' (I, 79). A socialist society would then be one where the social relations are not concealed or distorted by mystificatory ideologies. But here the notion that the distinc-tion, essence/appearance, is a form of scientificity as such recurs in the shape of a problem. For, if the relations of a socialist society will be transparent, then surely this distinction will be unnecessary to the science of that society, and should be under-stood, like value and surplus-value, as part of that conceptual apparatus necessary to the analysis of capitalism; and not, like, say, forces and relations of production, as one of the concepts which Marxism brings to the analysis of any social formation. Marx's first specification of the theoretical status of the distinc-tion is then further called into question.

In this connection it is not irrelevant to observe that, in much the same way as he de-historicizes the concept of alienation, Althusser obliterates the historical specificity of capitalist opacity in his thesis that, for Marx, even a communist society would not be without its ideology (and ideology in the Marxist sense, i.e., involving false consciousness).[19] Again it is not only the interpretation of Marx that is in question. There are serious theoretical consequences. What becomes, for example, of the notion of the proletariat taking cognizance of its real situation in capitalist society in the act (process, praxis) of abolishing it; of its comprehending the real mechanisms of capitalist ex-ploitation, and revolting against them to create a society in

19. *For Marx*, p. 232; *Reading Capital*, p. 177.

which, among other things, it will be neither exploited nor mystified? What, in short, becomes of the notion of class consciousness? It has vanished literally without trace. In its place appears the radical disjunction (a new 'coupure', this) between the theory, the scientific knowledge, of socialist intellectuals and the ideology of the masses. Thus, Althusser speaks of categories appropriate for the ideological struggle but deficient for the purposes of theory,[20] and of Marxism as a science which produces new forms of ideology in the masses.[21] The unity between the theory of the theoreticians and the practice of the class is broken and one is left with nothing other than a variant of hostile bourgeois caricatures of Leninism : the political leaders use their knowledge to manipulate the consciousness of the masses. Once again, there is a legitimate concern at the bottom of this false position : the concern to preserve the specificity of theoretical practice. There is, after all, some distance between the consciousness of even the most revolutionary worker and the science of Marx or Lenin. But it is a distance and not a rupture. Further, it is the distance of a dialectical relationship, because traversed in both directions. The scientific theory is brought to bear on the consciousness of the class, but the consciousness of the class also directs and provides orientation for the theory. If this unity is sundered, it becomes difficult to distinguish the Marxist theory of political struggle from a theory of manipulation.[22] Perhaps for this reason, Althusser has more recently permitted himself some more adequate formulations of the relation between theory and class, ones precisely which lay emphasis on the ability of the proletariat to comprehend its objective position, and thus liberate it from the postulated eternal subjection to ideology.[23] What is questionable is whether such formulations can be rendered coherent with the theoretical structure he had previously elaborated, or whether, on the other hand, to defend them and give them foundation, he will be forced to abandon his positions one after another.

The source of Althusser's error is that he read in *Capital* only a theory of the *raison d'être* of mystification, a theory which, to

20. *For Marx*, p. 199.
21. *Reading Capital*, p. 131.
22. J-C. Forquin, op. cit., p. 31.
23. Louis Althusser, 'Avertissement aux lecteurs du livre I du *Capital*', in *Le Capital*, Livre I, Garnier-Flammarion, Paris, 1969, p. 25.

be sure, is there. But in this reading he failed to perceive what is also there, a theory of the conditions and possibility of demystification. The latter is, perhaps, less developed than the first, and this primarily because *Capital* terminates abruptly as Marx takes up the consideration of classes—'Vingt lignes, puis le silence'.[24] Yet it is plain enough. Speaking of the way in which exploitation is concealed by the circulation process, Marx goes on : 'To be sure, the matter looks quite different if we consider capitalist production in the uninterrupted flow of its renewal, and if, in place of the individual capitalist and the individual worker, we view them in their totality, the capitalist class and the working class confronting each other. But in so doing we should be applying standards entirely foreign to commodity production' (I, 586).

The matter looks quite different : the appearance of a relation of equality between individuals gives way to the reality of collective exploitation. And this is achieved by an analysis of the *essential* relations of capitalist society, i.e. the class relations. But it is not only theoretical analysis which has this effect. The *political struggle of the working class* is an exact duplication. Here, not the analyst, but the organized working class applies 'standards entirely foreign to commodity production'. *It* ceases to consider the relation of individual capitalist to individual worker and views them 'in their totality' by actually confronting the capitalist class as a whole. By doing so it penetrates the false appearances of bourgeois ideology. This in no sense invalidates Marx's proposition that the workers are inevitably mystified so long as, and to the extent that, they remain trapped within bourgeois relations of production. For, this is so. But the proletariat does not escape these relations of production only on the day of the socialist revolution. It begins to move outside them from the moment it engages in organized political struggle, since the latter involves the adoption of a class position, this criterion entirely foreign to commodity production, and the refusal any longer to think exclusively in terms of relations between individuals. For this reason, the 'structuralist' notions of the revolution as rupture (Althusser) or limit (Godelier) are less precise than the notion of revolution as praxis (with, to be sure, its ruptural point). And the full force of Rosa Luxemburg's insistence on the demystifying effects of mass political struggle becomes

24. *Reading Capital*, p. 193.

evident. At the same time, the Althusserian disjunction between the consciousness of the masses and that of the theoretician is shown to lack foundation. The integral relation between the two is based on the fact that the theoretician takes up, in analysis, the same positions as the masses adopt in political struggle; though, of course, this should not be understood as a reduction of the sort 'theory is practice'.

The above passage from Marx also introduces another dimension of the distinction, essence/appearance, one which has been emphasized, above all, by Herbert Marcuse.[25] As we have seen, all the concepts with which Marx specifies the essential relations of capitalist society have a basically cognitive function. They make possible a knowledge of reality in opposition to the false evidences of immediate appearances. But, if, in order to do this, and in the process of doing it, they refer us to 'standards entirely foreign to commodity production', then they are at the same time critical concepts. Thus, the concept of surplus-value not only permits a comprehension of the mechanisms of capitalist exploitation. By laying bare the division of the working-day into necessary and surplus labour-time, it envisages a state of affairs in which there is no exploitation. It contains 'an accusation and an imperative'.[26] However, this critical function of the concepts must not be understood as a mere taking up of positions, or moralizing. If they fail in their cognitive function, then they are useless in their critical one. When Marx clearly takes his distance from 'that kind of criticism which knows how to judge and condemn the present, but not how to comprehend it' (I, 505), he informs us that the essential concepts derive what validity they have not from their particular moral stance (relativism), but from the fact that they permit a coherent organization of appearances and an explanation of their source such as no other concepts can provide. This is, indeed, the criterion which validates these concepts. As Marcuse has expressed it: 'If the historical structure ... postulated as "essential" for the explanation ... makes it possible to comprehend causally the situation both in its individual phases as well as in terms of the tendencies effective within it, then it is really the essential in that manifold of appearances. This determina-

25. Herbert Marcuse, *Reason and Revolution*, New York, 1963, pp. 258, 295–6, and 321.

26. Herbert Marcuse, 'The Concept of Essence' in *Negations*, London, 1968, p. 86.

tion of essence is true; it has held good within the theory.'[27]

It remains to make explicit that in *Capital* the distinction between essence and appearance is, as well as everything else, a distinction also between the totality and its parts. Each single relationship or fact is an appearance whose full meaning or reality is only articulated by integrating it theoretically within its total structure. This has already been seen with regard to the light thrown on individual relationships by a consideration of the relations between classes.

But it applies more generally. I confine myself to certain 'pairs' of facts, treated by Marx in his chapter on machinery and modern industry. Machinery is the most powerful instrument for lightening labour; its capitalist employment leads to greater exploitation and domination. Science and technology make huge and unprecedented strides under capitalism; but at the expense of the workers' physical and intellectual powers. Modern machinery shatters the petrified forms of the division of labour creating the need for variability of functions and, thus, for a less one-sided, more rounded, development of the worker; under the anarchic conditions of capitalism, however, the worker lives and experiences this tendency as insecurity of employment and suffering. These pairs of facts are actually contradictions. As such, they represent tendencies which are neither simply progressive, nor simply regressive, because *contradictory*. The essence which explains them, and deprives them of all appearance of contingency, is the central contradiction between forces of production, the increasing productive power of social labour, on the one hand, and relations of production, the continued private appropriation of surplus-value, on the other. They partake of this central contradiction and, as partial facts, are only properly comprehended in relation to the social totality which they and it inhabit.

27. Ibid., p. 74.

14

The Unknown Marx

MARTIN NICOLAUS

In this essay Martin Nicolaus argues that the Grundrisse, *the outline of a critique of political economy which Marx wrote in preparation for* Capital, *marks a crucial but neglected phase in the development of Marx's thought. In this work Marx discusses the impact of automation on social relations and anticipates the central contradiction that will confront the capitalist mode of production as the role of labour power is increasingly reduced in the production process. In unravelling the consequences of Marx's analysis Nicolaus maintains that the* Grundrisse *provides a framework for investigating the class forces at work in contemporary capitalist society which most Marxists have misunderstood.*

When he assessed his intellectual career in 1859, Karl Marx condemned to deserved obscurity all of his previous works but four. *The Poverty of Philosophy* (1847) first set forth the decisive points of his scientific views, although in polemical form, he wrote; and he implied that the same description applied to the *Manifesto of the Communist Party* (1848), a *Speech on Free Trade* of the same year, and an unfinished series of newspaper articles entitled *Wage-Labour and Capital*, published in 1849. He made no mention of the *Economic-Philosophical Manuscripts* (1844), *The Holy Family* and the *Theses on Feuerbach* (1845), and he referred to the manuscript of *The German Ideology* (1846) without naming its title as a work which he and Engels gladly abandoned to the mice.[1] Three years before his death, when

---

1. Cf. the *Preface* of the *Critique of Political Economy*. With one exception, I have used the *Werke* edition of Marx's and Engels' writings, published by Dietz, Berlin, from 1962 to 1967; but I have

he received enquiries regarding the eventual publication of his complete works, he is reported to have answered dryly, 'They would first have to be written.'[2]

Marx, then, viewed most of the early works which have so aroused the enthusiasm of contemporary interpreters with scepticism bordering on rejection, and was painfully conscious towards the end of his life that the works which he had presented or was ready to present to the public were mere fragments.

The publication of the Grundrisse

Only once in his life did he speak with a tone of achievement and a sense of accomplishment about one of his works. Only once did he announce that he had written something which not only encompassed the whole of his views, but also presented them in a scientific manner. That occasion was in the *Preface* to the *Critique of Political Economy* (1859), a work which also remained merely a fragment, due to difficulties with its publisher. Only two chapters of the *Critique* reached the public, but their content, while of importance, hardly justified the claims implicitly made for them in their *Preface*. The *Preface* outlines a whole world-view, a set of scientific doctrines which explains the movement of history in its sociological, political, and economic dimensions, and demonstrates how and why the present organization of society must collapse from the strain of its internal conflicts, to be replaced by a higher order of civilization. The published chapters, however, demonstrate no such breadth, nor is the ultimate emergence of a new order clearly derivable from their content. They deal, rather, with fairly technical economic questions, and promise a long, arduous road with no clearly visible goal. What, then, was Marx talking about in the *Preface*? Was he making claims for theories he had not yet constructed, for ideas he had not yet written down?

Until 1939, this question remained largely a mystery. The

---

quoted the English titles and supplied my own translations. The *Preface* appears in *Werke*, Vol. 13, pp. 7–11 (W13: 7–11). An English translation can be found in Marx-Engels, *Selected Works*, Vol. I, pp. 361–5.

2. Quoted in Maximilien Rubel, *Karl Marx, Essai de Biographie Intellectuelle*, Marcel Rivière, Paris, 1957, p. 10.

bold generalization made in the *Preface* could be traced back to equally bold but equally general statements in *The Poverty of Philosophy* and in the *Manifesto*; the volumes of *Capital* contain some echoes, again polemical and general. But it was difficult, if not impossible, to derive from the extant portions of *Capital* the answers to the most important question which the *Preface* announces as theoretically solved, namely the question of how and why the capitalist social order will break down. Thus Rosa Luxemburg wrote her *Accumulation of Capital* (1912) precisely for the purpose of filling this most important gap in Marx's unfinished writings,[3] thereby throwing gasoline on a fiery intra-party dispute which still flickers today. Why the manuscript on the basis of which Marx wrote the *Preface* of 1859 remained buried until the outbreak of the Second World War remains a mystery still; but in any case, in 1939 the Marx-Engels-Lenin Institute in Moscow brought out of its files and published an enormous volume containing Marx's economic manuscripts from the years 1857–68. A second volume followed two years later; and in 1953 the Dietz publishing house in Berlin republished the two volumes in one. Entitled by the editors *Grundrisse der Kritik der Politischen Okonomie (Rohent-wurf)*—Fundamental Traits of the Critique of Political Economy (Rough Draft)—and published together with important extracts from Marx's notebooks of 1850–51, this work at long last permits an examination of the material of which the generalizations in the *Preface* are the distillate.[4]

The *Grundrisse* has not been ignored since its publication, but neither has it been appreciated for its full importance. Assessed initially as interesting material for a reconstruction of the genesis of *Capital*, the work long vegetated in the Marxologists' underground.[5] Eric Hobsbawm introduced a fraction of it, chiefly the historical passages, as *Pre-Capitalist Economic Form-*

3. Cf. Paul Sweezy, *The Theory of Capitalist Development*, Monthly Review Press, New York, 1942, p. 202.

4. Marx, *Grundrisse der Kritik der Politischen Okonomie (Rohent-wurf)*, Dietz, Berlin, 1953, and Europäische Verlagsanstalt, Frankfurt. Hereafter cited as *Grundrisse*. Excerpts published in a Rowohlt paperback, Marx : *Texte zu Methode und Praxis* III, hereafter cited as R.

5. Maximilien Rubel, 'Contribution à l'histoire de la genèse du "Capital",' in *Revue d'Histoire économique et sociale*, II, 1950 p. 168.

ations in 1965.[6] Of late, isolated excerpts have appeared in the works of André Gorz and Herbert Marcuse.[7] Together, these seem to have sharpened the appetite of a growing body of intellectuals, in the amorphous New Left especially, for a closer look at this hitherto unknown but obviously important work. A French translation of the first part of the whole has finally appeared this year, but readers who remain imprisoned within the English language will have to wait.[8] No definite plans for an English translation have been made public.

All the same, the work is of epochal significance. The fruits of fifteen years of economic research, the best years of Marx's life, are contained in these pages. Marx considered it not only a work which overthrew the central doctrines of all previous political economy, but also the first truly scientific statement of the revolutionary cause.[9] Although he could not know it at the time, it was to be the only work in which his theory of capitalism from the origins to the breakdown was sketched out in its entirety. However obscure and fractured, the *Grundrisse* may be said to be the only truly complete work on political economy that Marx ever wrote.

Marx's focus on the market

The *Grundrisse* is a summit at the end of a long and difficult climb. Marx had published the first of what he considered his scientific works, the *Poverty of Philosophy*, a decade before; and he did not publish the first volume of *Capital* until a decade after. To understand the significance of the *Grundrisse*, it will be necessary to survey briefly the economic writings which preceded it.

Immediately after the completion of his critique of Hegel's

6. Lawrence and Wishart, London, and International Publishers, New York.

7. André Gorz, *Strategy for Labor*, Beacon Press, Boston, 1967, pp. 128–30; Herbert Marcuse, *One-Dimensional Man*, Beacon Press, Boston, 1964, pp. 35–6.

8. Karl Marx, *Les Fondements de la Critique de l'Economie Politique* (*Grundrisse*), 2 vols., Editions Anthropos, Paris, 1967.

9. *Grundrisse*, p. xiii; cf. also Marx to Engels, January 14th, 1858: 'I am getting some nice developments. For instance, I have thrown over the whole doctrine of profit as it has existed up to now.' *Selected Correspondence*, London and New York, 1942, p. 102.

philosophy of law, in which he had concluded that the anatomy of society was not to be found in philosophy, Marx began to read the political economists. In this project he was preceded and no doubt also guided by the young Engels, who had published his *Umrisse zu einer Kritik der Nationalökonomie* in Marx's and Ruge's *Deutsch-Französischen Jahrbücher* for the same year, 1844. Engels argued in this article that the development of the bourgeois economy for the last century, as well as the development of the economic theory which corresponded to it, could be summarized as one long, continuous, and increasingly outrageous affront to all fundamental principles of morality and decency, and that if a rationally ordered, moral economic system were not immediately installed, then a monstrous social revolution must and ought to occur shortly. The brunt of Engels' attack was directed at what he considered the fundamental principle of the bourgeois economy, namely the institution of the *market*. All moral bonds in society have been overthrown by the conversion of human values into exchange-values; all ethical principles overthrown by the principles of competition; and all hitherto existing laws, even the laws which regulate the birth and death of human beings, have been usurped by the laws of supply and demand. Humanity itself has become a market commodity.[10]

With one significant difference, this line of reasoning was taken up and developed by Marx throughout his economic writings from 1844 to 1849. The difference is that (as is plain from his 1844 *Manuscripts*) Marx immediately rejected the one-sided moralism of Engels' critique to relace it with a dialectical basis. He threw out the categorical imperatives which lurked beneath the surface of Engel's paper. Competition and the market, he wrote, were not so much an affront to morality as rather a fragmentation and surrender of the developmental potentialities inherent in the human species. Within the society based on private property, the products of human labour belong not to the labourer for his own enjoyment; rather, they become the property of alien persons and are used by them to oppress him. The clearest symptom of this fact, Marx wrote, is that the labourer does not produce the things most useful to him, but instead the things which will fetch the highest exchange-value

10. Engels, 'Umrisse zu einer Kritik der Nationalökonomie', W1: 499–524, and as an appendix to Marx, *Economic-Philosophical Manuscripts*, trans. Milligan, London and New York.

for their private owner. Thus the process of material creation becomes fractured into segments, and the product itself becomes fractured into use-value and exchange-value, of which the latter alone is important. 'The consideration of *division of labour* and *exchange* is of the greatest interest, since they are the *perceptible, alienated* expression of human *activity* and *capacities* . . . .'[11] In sum, from an entirely different philosophical starting-point, Marx arrived at the same critical perspective as Engels, namely that the crux of bourgeois society was to be found in competition, supply and demand, the market; that is, in its system of *exchange*.

The notion of alienation (as an economic category) also contained within it the seeds of a different insight, but one which did not rise to prominence until the *Grundrisse*, as will be seen. Meanwhile, however, Marx continued along with the majority of his radical intellectual acquaintances to sharpen his attack on the sovereignty of competition. His polemic against Proudhon (*The Poverty of Philosophy*) reveals him in sharp disagreement with that self-declared luminary on almost every point of economics and philosophy, including especially every issue relating to the institutions of exchange and competition in bourgeois society, except one: that competition is basic.[12] If the bourgeoisie abolishes competition to replace it with monopoly, it thereby only sharpens the competition among workers. In the *Manifesto* Marx writes: 'The essential condition for the existence, and for the sway of the bourgeois class, is the formation and augmentation of capital; the condition for capital is wage-labour. Wage-labour rests exclusively on competition between the labourers'.[13] From which Marx concludes that if the workers can, by forming associations, eliminate the competition among themselves, then 'the very foundation on which the bourgeoisie produces and appropriates products' will be cut out from under its feet. In Marx's *Speech on Free Trade*, the same theme recurs: if industrial development slumps, workers will be thrown out of jobs and their wages must fall; if industry

11. The 1844 Manuscripts are only to be published in a supplementary volume of the *Werke* edition. The reference here is from the Bottomore translation in Marx, *Early Writings*, London, 1963, p. 187.

12. W4: 161 and *Poverty of Philosophy*, London and New York, p. 149.

13. W4: 474 and Marx-Engels, *Selected Works*, I, p. 45.

grows, the workers will enjoy a momentary up-swing, only to be cast down again when machinery replaces them.[14] Here as in *Wage-Labour and Capital*, Marx's 'law' that wages must always tend towards the absolute minimum necessary to keep the worker barely alive is derived straightforwardly from the principles of supply and demand, with the additional assumptions that the supply of the labour commodity must always tend to exceed demand.[15] We find here occasional hints of insight that other processes are at work also, but the only systematically worked-out doctrines are those which analytically derive the future course of capitalist development and the role of the working class within it from the competitive mechanism, from the expected shape of the market for the commodity, labour. The economics of commodity exchange and of money formed Marx's chief study.

From competition to production

The first and most important thing that needs to be made clear about the place which the *Grundrisse* occupied in Marx's intellectual development is that it represents a critique of all of those earlier ideas. 'Critique' does not mean 'rejection', rather in this case it means, penetration to a deeper level. The great advance which the *Grundrisse* represents in Marx's thinking lies in its rejection, on grounds of superficiality, of the thesis that the market-mechanism is a motivating, causal, or fundamental factor; and in its recognition that the market is merely a device to co-ordinate the various individual moments of a process far more fundamental than exchange. While Marx's earlier economics had centred around the movement of *competition*, in the *Grundrisse* he analyses systematically, and for the first time in his work, the economics of *production*.

Before we examine the text more closely, a few examples may be in order for the sake of gaining an overview.

1. The most obvious and most easily traceable difference between pre- and post-1850 economic theory in Marx is a shift in terminology. Before, Marx consistently refers to the commodity which the worker offers for sale as 'labour', and makes explicit that this commodity is exactly like any other com-

14. W4: 455 and *Poverty of Philosophy*, pp. 215–16.
15. W6: 397–423 and *Selected Works*, I, pp.. 79–105; see also W6: 535–56.

modity. If one sees bourgeois society exclusively as a system of markets, this definition is true enough. In the *Grundrisse* and thereafter, however, Marx arrives at the view that labour is not a commodity like any other, that labour in fact is unique, and that the commodity which the worker sells must be called 'labour-power'. In later re-editions of the earlier economic works, Marx and Engels duly alter the terminology to correspond to the new view, and in various prefaces state their reasons for so doing, and the importance of the change.[16]

2. In the earlier economic writings, the course of capitalist development is derived analytically, as noted, from the projected motion of supply and demand. Compare this with Marx's flat statement at several occasions in *Capital* that the mechanisms of competition 'show everything backward'[17] and the analytic deductions made from supply and demand alone are superficial, in fact, contradictory to the hidden but essential core-processes of capitalist production and accumulation. The intellectual foundations for these later statements in *Capital* are laid in the *Grundrisse*.

3. Finally, a general overview of the analytic progress which the *Grundrisse* represents can be gained by tracing Marx's attitude towards Ricardo, especially towards Ricardo's theory of the surplus. At the time of his first encounter with Ricardo and the surplus in 1844, Marx noted only that the emphasis Ricardo lays on the surplus proves that profit, not human beings, is the chief concern of bourgeois economics, and that this theory is the ultimate proof of the *infamy* to which political economy has sunk.[18] In the *Poverty of Philosophy* (1847), Ricardo is treated with somewhat more respect, and Marx quotes at length from the English socialist Bray, who uses the Ricardian surplus-theory to prove the exploitation of the working class. Yet Marx quotes Bray not in order to emphasize the fundamental importance of this theory, but merely to criticize certain deductions derived from it.[19] Likewise, in *Wage-Labour and Capital*, Marx simply states the Ricardian thesis that the product of labour is worth more than the reproduction of the labourer, but without analys-

16. See notably Engels' preface to the 1891 re-edition of *Wage-Labour and Capital*, W6: 593–9 and *Selected Works*, I, pp. 70–8.

17. *Capital*, III, W25: 219. English translation, London and New York, 1962, p. 205.

18. Quoted in Rubel, *Biographie Intellectuelle*, p. 119.

19. W4: 98–105 and *Poverty of Philosophy*, pp. 69–79.

ing it further.[20] He is clearly aware at this point of the *existence* of a surplus, but he is clearly not conscious of the enormous implications for economic theory of this fact; the theory, in short, is not central to his analysis, but co-exists passively together with, and in the shadow of, the dominant supply and demand analysis. When he began his economic studies all over again from the beginning in 1850, however, Marx plunged directly into Ricardo and spent at least the next two years absorbing Ricardo in detail. His notebooks and excerpts from this period, which are appended to the text of the *Grundrisse* by the editors, show that Ricardo's surplus theory then began to reveal its implications for Marx, and that he concentrated his attention upon it.[21] Finally, in the *Grundrisse* itself, although Marx criticizes Ricardo at several points, he treats him with a great amount of respect and calls him the 'economist *par excellence* of *production*.'[22] This gradual shift of attitude corresponds to, and reflects, Marx's growing awareness of the importance of the theory of surplus value, on which Marx begins to base his entire theory of capitalist accumulation in the *Grundrisse*.

Like any exercise in comparative statics, these before/after examples may give rise to the mistaken idea that the application of Ricardian concepts changed Marx overnight from a supply-demand theorist into a surplus-value accumulationist. The change, to be sure, was much more gradual; there are elements of the surplus theory, as we have said, scattered in the early works, and the later works by no means assert the unimportance of the competitive mechanism, quite the contrary. These subtleties should not obscure the fact that a qualitative breakthrough beyond the surface of market-based analysis took place, and that this breakthrough is the chief analytic problem with which the *Grundrisse* is concerned.

The social bond of money

Although gnomic in detail, the larger structure of the *Grundrisse* text moves consistently towards the solution of clearly defined problems. After a brilliant, unfinished Introduction—which cannot detain us here—the work consists of two chapters,

20. W6: 409–10 and *Selected Works*, I, pp. 91–2.
21. See *Grundrisse*, pp. 787–92, 829.
22. *Grundrisse*, p. 18 and R: 20.

the first dealing with money (pp. 32–149) and the second, much longer, with capital (pp. 150–764). The latter is subdivided into three parts, dealing respectively with production, circulation, and the transformation of surplus value into profits. The problems and issues with which the text deals, however, are not so narrowly economic as the chapter-headings might imply. Here as elsewhere, but perhaps more clearly here than elsewhere, Marx's 'economics' is also and at the same time 'sociology' and 'politics'. The first chapter immediately makes this clear.

On one level, the chapter on money is a polemic against the monetary-reform scheme then newly proposed by Alfred Darimon, a follower of Proudhon and therefore a bitter opponent of Marx. On a somewhat less superficial level, it is merely a treatise on money, and can be read as the first draft of Marx's developed monetary theory as it appears in the *Critique*. Its most important aspect, however, is its sociological and political critique of a society in which money is the predominant medium of exchange. Under what historical circumstances can money become the abstraction of exchange-values, and exchange-values become the abstraction of all forms of exchange? What social preconditions must exist in order that money may function as a nexus between individuals engaged in exchange-relations? What are the social and political consequences of this form of the exchange-relation? What larger forms of social organization correspond to this molecular constellation of individuals engaged in private transactions? These are the problems with which Marx is concerned, just as Sombart, Weber, Simmel and Tönnies about a half-century later investigated the effects of money-exchange on societal bonds. Marx writes:

The convertibility of all products and activities into exchange-values presupposes the dissolution of all fixed personal (historic) relations of dependence in production, and presupposes the universal dependence of all producers on one another. The production of every individual is dependent on that of all the others, and the conversion of his product into articles for his consumption has become dependent on the consumption of all the others. Prices *per se* are old; exchange, likewise; but the growing determination of prices by production cost and the increasing role of exchange among all relations of production are things which first develop, and continue to develop more fully, within bourgeois society, the society of free competition. Relegated by Adam Smith in true 18th-century fashion to the prehistoric period, these developments are in truth the product of history.

This reciprocal dependence can be seen in the ever-present need to exchange, and the fact that exchange-value is the universal medium. The economists express this as follows: everyone pursues his private interest and only his private interest, and thus without knowing or willing it, everyone serves the private interests of all. the general interests. The point here is not that, in following his private interests, everyone attains the totality of private interests, namely the collective interest. One could as well conclude from this abstract slogan that everyone reciprocally blocks the interests of the others, so that, instead of a general affirmation, this war of all against all produces a general negation. The point is rather that private interest is itself already a socially determined interest, which can be attained only within certain socially ordained conditions and with socially given means, and which is therefore dependent on the reproduction of these conditions and means. It is the interest of a private person; but its content and the form and means of its realization are set by social conditions independently of the individual.

This universal reciprocal dependence of individuals who are [otherwise] indifferent to one another forms their social bond. This social bond is expressed in *exchange-value*....
An individual exercises power over the actions of others, he lays a claim to social wealth, in so far as he possesses *exchange-value*, *money*. He carries his social power and his bond with society in his pocket....

Every individual possesses social power in the form of an object, a thing. Take away from this thing its social power, and this power over persons must be invested in persons.

Relations of personal dependence ... are the first forms of social organization, in which human productive powers are but little developed, and only in isolated points. Personal independence, based on dependence on *things*, is the second great form, which for the first time allows the development of a system of universal social exchange, universal relations, universal needs, and universal wealth. Free individuality, based on the universal development of individuals and on their joint mastery over their communal, social productive powers and wealth, is the third stage. The second creates the pre-conditions of the third.[23]

Here we see the interpenetration of economic, social and political categories clearly developed. Whatever Marx may have had to say about the specific fluctuations of monetary value, or about the effects of metallism or paper currency, is of minor importance to his system of ideas compared to the fundamental thesis, here expressed, that money is an object which expresses a certain type of historically produced relationship among human beings. Money is a *social bond*; that is, it links together and reciprocally governs the most diverse activities of otherwise isolated individuals. He who possesses this objectified social bond can dominate the activities of others; he represents the social bond *per se* and can thus act in the capacity of the representative of the generality, the collectivity, to govern the activities of individuals within the society.

The equal exchange that reproduces inequality

So far, Marx's analysis of money formulates more sharply and more clearly the ideas about alienated exchange developed by him in the *Manuscripts* of 1844. In a brief transitional section which introduces the chapter on capital, however, Marx progresses a significant step beyond the earlier analysis. He no longer stops short at this point to bewail the alienation of individuals from each other and from themselves, which are results of bourgeois exchange-relations, but goes on to inspect this form of social relationships in historical and political perspective. Basic here is the comparison of bourgeois relations with feudal relations. After all, the revolutionary rise of the bourgeoisie did bring with it the political emancipation of the individual from the bonds of statutory domination, and did change the polity from a closed chain of inborn privilege and serfdom into an open market place of free-contracting adults. No longer is the worker bound for life to his overlord, nor are there statutes to empress from the labouring classes a steadily growing secular tithe. The merchant who sells and the housewife who buys loaves of bread; the entrepreneur who buys and the worker who sells hours of labour—all are free persons freely engaged in the free exchange of equivalents. This is a line of

23. Ibid., pp. 74–6 and R : 36–8.

argument which the socialists of Marx's time, at least in his estimation, could not systematically refute. While the socialist damned the competitive society, the market relation and the cash nexus, the bourgeois ideologists were only too happy to reply by praising these very conditions as the basis of political freedom.[24]

> In these simple forms of the money-relation, all the immanent contradictions of bourgeois society appear extinguished, and that is why bourgeois democrats take refuge within them . . . to justify the existing economic relationships. In truth, so long as a commodity or labor is seen only as an exchange-value, and the relations between them are seen only as exchange-relations, as equilibration of these exchange-values, then the individuals, the subjects between whom this process takes place, are merely partners in exchange. There is absolutely no formal difference between them. . . . Each subject is a partner in exchange; that is, each has the same relation to the other as the other has to it. Thus, as subjects of exchange, this relationship is one of *equality*. It is impossible to find a trace of distinction, much less of contradiction among them, not even a mere difference. Furthermore, the commodities which they exchange are, as exchange-values, equivalents; or at least count as equivalents. (There could at most be subjective error in their reciprocal appraisal, and in so far as one individual gained an advantage over another, *this would not be in the nature of the social function which brings them together*, for this function is identical for both, and within it they are equal. It would rather be the result of natural cleverness, persuasion, etc, in short, a result of the purely individual superiority of one individual over another. . . .) Thus if one individual accumulates wealth and the other does not, neither is doing it at the expense of the other. . . . If one becomes poorer and the other richer, it is of their own free will, and proceeds in no way out of the economic relation, the economic situation in which they meet.[25]

The argument which Marx is here putting into the mouth of an imaginary bourgeois antagonist is a telling one. For if it is true

24. 'The analysis of what free competition really is, is the only rational answer to its glorification by the middle-class prophets or its damnation by the socialists.' Ibid., p. 545 and R: 198.

25. Ibid., pp. 153, 158, and R: 47, 53.

that the labourer, in selling labour, and the capitalist, in paying wages, are engaged in the reciprocal exchange of commodities having equal value—i.e. if their exchange is an exchange of equivalents—then the capitalist class structure is only coincidentally related to the capitalist economic system. The rich get richer not because of any inherent, structural necessity, but only by the accident of superior judgment and persuasiveness. Nor is the historic existence of the capitalist class economically accounted for by saying that the worker does not receive full value in exchange for his labour. If that were the case, if the capitalist paid the labourer less than an equivalent for his labour, then the capitalist could gain only to the extent that the labourer lost, but no more. The capitalist as buyer and the worker as seller of labour could disadvantage one another only to the degree that two nations engaged in foreign trade can; if one consistently pays the other less than full value, one can grow richer and the other poorer, but the total wealth of both together can be no greater at the end than at the beginning of their intercourse (or so the mercantilists believed). It is evident that such a process could not continue for long or on a large scale; soon the disadvantaged party must become extinct. The problem which must be solved is: how can it be that the worker does receive the full exchange-value for his commodity, and nevertheless there exists a surplus from which the capitalist class lives? How is it that the worker is *not* cheated *in* the wage-contract, and is nevertheless exploited? What is the source of surplus value? That is the question to which Marx addresses himself in the first hundred pages of the chapter on capital.

The emergence of surplus value

After a systematic review of earlier forms of capital (merchant capital or money capital), and after placing the problem in proper historical focus, Marx summarizes the analysis by condensing the process of capitalist production into two fundamental components, two basic elements:

1. The labourer gives his commodity, labour, which has a use value and a price like all other commodites, and receives in exchange a certain sum of exchange values, a certain sum of money from the capitalist.

2. The capitalist exchanges labour itself, labour as value-creating activity, as productive labour; that is, he exchanges the productive force which maintains and multiplies capital, and thereby becomes the productive and reproductive force of capital, a force belonging to capital itself.[26]

On inspection, the first exchange-process appears plainly comprehensible; Marx says simply that the labourer gives labour and receives wages in exchange. But the second process does not appear to be an exchange at all; even its grammar is one-sided, asymmetrical. That is precisely the point, Marx writes. In an ordinary exchange transaction, what each of the parties does with the commodity each receives is irrelevant to the structure of the transaction itself. The seller does not care whether the buyer uses the commodity acquired for productive purposes or not; that is his private affair and has no economic relevance for the process of exchange pure and simple. In the specific case of the 'exchange' between labour and wages, however, the use to which the buyer of labour puts his purchase is of the utmost importance to him not only in his private capacity, but in his capacity as *homo oeconomicus*. The capitalist gives wages (exchange-value) for the use of labour (for its use-value) only in order to convert this use-value into further exchange-value.

Here ... the use-value of the thing received in exchange appears as a specific economic relation, and the specific use to which the thing bought is put forms the ultimate purpose of both processes [1 & 2 above]. Thus, the exchange between labour and capital is already formally different from ordinary exchange; they are two different processes. ... In the exchange between labour and capital, the first act is an exchange and can be classified entirely as ordinary circulation; the second process is qualitatively different from exchange, and to have called it exchange at all was a misuse. This process is the direct opposite of exchange; it is an essentially different category.[27]

After several digressions, Marx then examines this 'essentially different category' at length. Approaching the question via the distinction between the use-value and the exchange-value of the labour commodity, he notes that the exchange-value of labour is determined by the value of the goods and services

26. Ibid., p. 185.   27. Ibid., pp. 185–6.

necessary to maintain and to reproduce the labourer. In so far as the capitalist pays the labourer wages high enough to permit the worker to continue to live and to work, he has paid the full value of labour and the exchange-relation defined in the wage contract is a relation of equivalence. The capitalist has paid the full and fair exchange-value of the commodity. But what he has, in fact, purchased is a certain number of hours of control and disposition over the worker's productive activity, over his ability to create, his capacity to labour. Here Marx introduces for the first time the shift in terminology which corresponds to his discovery of the 'essentially different category'. What the worker sells is not 'labour' but *labour-power* (*Arbeitskraft*); not a commodity like any other, but a commodity which is unique.[28] Labour alone has the capacity to create values where none existed before, or to create greater values than those which it requires to sustain itself. Labour alone, in short, is capable of creating *surplus value*. The capitalist purchases control over this creative power, and commands this power to engage in the production of commodities for exchange during a specified number of hours. The worker's surrender of control over his creative power is called by Marx exploitation.

This is not the occasion to review in detail Marx's theory of surplus value, of which the ideas here formulated are the cornerstone. Suffice it to say that Marx here begins not only to solve the problem of how exploitation can occur despite the fact that the wage-contract is an exchange of equivalents, but begins also the essential scientific task of quantification. Exploitation is for Marx a process verifiable in specific empirical variables which are at least in principle subject to precise measurement along the economic dimension. The variables which Marx would have us measure, however, are not those which are usually cited in critical reviews of his theory. Exploitation does not consist in the disproportion between the income of the working class and the income of the capitalist class; these variables measure only the disproportion between wages and profits. Since profits are only a fraction of surplus value as a whole, such an index would capture only a fracction of Marx's meaning. Nor is exploitation fully measured in the ratio of wages as a percentage of G N P; this index measures only the *rate* of exploitation in a given year. Perhaps more clearly than else-

28. Cf. Ibid., pp. 193–4 and R: 66. For 'control' and 'disposition' see pp. 193, 195, 201, 215, etc., or R: 66, 67, 73, 89, etc.

where, Marx states in the *Grundrisse* that the worker's impoverishment is to be measured in the power of the entire world which he constructs to capitalist specifications: 'He inevitably impoverishes himself ... because the creative power of his labour establishes itself in opposition to him, as the alien power of capital. ... Thus all the progress of civilization, or in other words every increase in the productive power of society, if you want, in the productive power of labour itself—such as results from science, invention, division and organization of labour, improved communications, creation of the world market, machinery, and so on—does not enrich the worker, but capital, and thus increases the power that dominates labour.'[29]

An index of exploitation and impoverishment which accurately captures the variables to which Marx was referring, therefore, would have to array on one side the net property holdings of the working class, and on the other side the value of the entire capital stock of all the factories, utilities, infrastructural investments, institutions, and military establishments which are under the control of the capitalist class and serve its policy aims. Not only the economic value, but also the political power and social influence of these established assets would have to be included in the equation. Only a statistic of this kind would be adequate to test whether or not Marx's prediction of increasing exploitation and increasing impoverishment had been validated by the course of capitalist development.

What is the fundamental contradiction?

The various steps by which Marx builds his fundamental insight that capitalist production involves a category radically different from mere commodity exchange into the fully fledged theory of capitalist accumulation which he later presents in *Capital* need not arrest us here. Exploitation proceeds 'behind the back of the exchange-process'; that is the basic insight which marks his penetration beyond the critique of bourgeois society as a market society. We may proceed now to examine to what extent the text of the *Grundrisse* justifies the sweeping claims made for Marx's new scientific achievements in his 1859 *Preface*. In particular we will be interested in knowing whether the *Grundrisse* provides further elucidation of the famous passage in the *Preface* about *revolution*: 'At a certain stage of their

29. Ibid., pp. 214, 215, and R: 88, 89.

development, the material forces of production in society come into conflict with the existing relations of production, or—what is only a legal expression of the same thing—with the property relations within which they had been at work before. From forms which developed the forces of production, these relations now turn into their fetters. Then comes the period of social revolution.'[30]

While there are echoes of this passage in some of the earlier works as well as on one occasion in *Capital*,[31] they remain on a level of generality so high as to be virtually useless. Above all, it is never made clear exactly what is meant to be included under the rubric of 'forces of production' or 'relations of production'. Are we to understand 'material forces of production' as meaning merely the technological apparatus, and 'relations of production' as the political-legal system? In other words, is the phrase 'material forces' only another way of saying 'infrastructure' and does 'relations' mean 'superstructure'? What precisely do these terms refer to?

The basic clue for the deciphering of what Marx had in mind with the phrase 'relations of production'—to begin with this half of the dichotomy—is already provided in the *Preface* itself. Marx writes that legal-political forms such as property relations are not these 'relations of production' in themselves, but are merely an *expression* of these relations. From this starting point, the text of the *Grundrisse* can be seen as an extensive and detailed commentary on the nature of these 'relations'. For what else is the chapter on money? Here Marx demonstrates, as we have seen, that money in bourgeois society is no mere natural object, but rather the objectified form of the basic *social relation* within which capitalist production takes places. Money is the social bond which links the otherwise isolated producers and consumers within capitalist society together, and which forms the starting and ending points of the process of accumulation. The social relation which lies at the basis of all capitalist legal and political relations, and of which the latter are mere expressions—as Marx shows in the chapter on money—is the exchange-relation. It is the social imperative that neither production nor consumption can take place without the mediation of

30. W13: 9 and *Selected Works* I, p. 363.

31. W4: 181 and *Poverty of Philosophy*, p. 174; *Manifesto*, W4: 467 and *Selected Works*, I, p. 39; *Capital* I, W23: 791 and *Capital*, I, London and New York, p. 763.

exchange-value; or, in other words, that the capitalist must not only extract surplus value but must also realize surplus value by converting the surplus product into money, and that the individual must not only have a need for consumer goods, but must also possess the money to purchase them. Far from being immutable natural laws, these twin imperatives are characterized by Marx as historically produced social relations specific to the capitalist form of production.

As for the other side of the dichotomy, it is easy to be misled by the word 'material' in the phrase 'material forces of production'. Indeed, the German original (*materielle Produktivkrafte*) could as well be translated as 'forces of material production', and it is clear in any case that the term 'material' for Marx did not refer merely to the physical attributes of mass, volume, and location. A machine is always a material thing, but whether it is utilized in a productive capacity, whether or not it becomes a force of production, depends on the social organization of the productive process, as Marx goes to great lengths to point out in the *Grundrisse*.[32] The forces of production are themselves a social and historical product, and the productive process is a social process for Marx. It is necessary to emphasize this point in order to make clear that the important role which Marx assigns to the development of the material production forces under capitalism does not make Marx a technological determinist. Quite the opposite is the case; it is not technology which compels the capitalist to accumulate, but the necessity to accumulate which compels him to develop the powers of technology. The basis of the process of accumulation, of the process through which the forces of production gain in power, is the extraction of surplus value from labour-power. The force of production is the force of exploitation.

It is apparent, then, that the dichotomy formulated by Marx in the *Preface* is identical to the dichotomy between the two distinct processes which Marx identifies as basic to capitalist production in the *Grundrisse* : on the one hand, production consists of an act of exchange, and on the other, it consists of an act which is the opposite of exchange. On the one hand, production is an ordinary exchange of equivalents, on the other, it is a forcible appropriation of the worker's world-creating power. It is a social system in which the worker, as seller, and the capitalist, as purchaser, are juridically equal and free contracting

32. *Grundrisse*, pp. 169, 216, 579, etc., and R: 89–90.

parties; and it is at the same time a social system of slavery and exploitation. At the beginning and at the end of the productive process lies the social imperative of exchange-values, yet from beginning to end the productive process must yield surplus values. The exchange of equivalents is the fundamental social relation of production, yet the extraction of non-equivalents is the fundamental force of production. This contradiction, inherent in the process of capitalist production, is the source of the conflicts which Marx expected to bring about the period of social revolution.

The road to revolution

The problem of precisely how this contradiction can be expected to lead to the breakdown of the capitalist system is one which has plagued students of Marx for at least half a century. The volumes of *Capital* provide no very clear answer. This deficiency is at the root of the 'breakdown controversy' which agitated German Social Democracy and which continues intermittently to flare even today. Veritable rivers of ink have been spent in an effort to fill up this gap in Marx's theoretical system. Yet this gap is present not because the problem was insoluble for Marx, not because he saw no answer, but because the conclusions he had reached in the *Grundrisse* lay buried and inaccessible to scholars until twenty years after the First World War. *Capital* is a work which proceeds slowly and carefully from pure forms of economic relationship step by step towards a closer approximation of economic-historic reality; nothing is prejudged and no new theories are introduced until the basis for them has been prepared. At that rate, it is easily conceivable that several more volumes of *Capital* would have been necessary before Marx could catch up with the point he had reached in the outline of his system in the *Grundrisse*. *Capital* is painfully unfinished, like a mystery novel which ends before the plot is unravelled. But the *Grundrisse* contains the author's plot-outline as a whole.

From the very beginning, the economics of the *Grundrisse* are more ambitious and more directly relevant to the problem of the capitalist breakdown than the economics of the extant portions of *Capital*. In the latter work, Marx relegates the relationship between persons and commodities (the utility relation) to a realm with which he is not then concerned, and he accepts the level of consumer needs which prevails in the economic system as a historical given which receives little further analysis.[33] In general, he takes consumption for granted, and concentrates his investigation on the how, instead of on the whether, of surplus realization. In the *Grundrisse*, however, he begins with the general assertion that the process of production, historically considered, creates not only the object of consumption but also the consumer need and the style of consumption.[34] He specifically criticizes Ricardo for consigning the problem of utility to the extra-economic sphere, and states that the relation between the consumer and the commodity, because this relation is a product of production, belongs squarely within the proper purview of political economy.[35] That he is aware not only of the qualitative but also of the quantitative aspects of the problem of consumption is apparent from excerpts such as this: 'Incidentally, ... although every capitalist demands that his workers should save, he means only *his own* workers, because they relate to him as workers; and by no means does this apply to the remainder of the workers, because these relate to him as consumers. In spite of all the pious talk of frugality he therefore searches for all possible ways of stimulating them to consume, by making his commodities more attractive, by filling their ears with babble about new needs (*neue Bedürfnisse ihnen anzuschwatzen*). It is precisely this side of the relationship between capital and labour which is an essential civilizing force, and on which the historic justification—but also the contemporary power—of capital is based.'[36]

These general remarks are then set aside with a reminder to himself that 'this relationship of production and consumption must be developed later'.[37] A hundred pages later on the problem is taken up again. After a critique of Ricardo's neglect of the problem of consumption, and Sismondi's utopian panaceas against overproduction, Marx formulates the inherent contradiction of capitalism as a 'contradiction between production and realization' of surplus value. 'To begin with, there is a limit to production, not to production in general, but to production founded on capital. . . . It suffices to show at this point that capi-

33. *Capital* I, W23: 49–50, Sect. 1, Ch. 1, p. 1.
34. *Grundrisse*, pp. 13–18 and R: 14–18.
35. Ibid., pp. 178–9 n., 226–7, 763.
36. Ibid., p. 198 and R: 71.
37. Ibid.

tal contains a *specific* barrier to production—which contradicts its general tendency to break all barriers to production—in order to expose the basis of *overproduction*, the fundamental contradiction of developed capitalism.' As is apparent from the lines which follow immediately, Marx does not mean by 'over-production' simply 'excess inventory'; rather, he means excess productive power more generally.

> These inherent limits necessarily coincide with the nature of capital, with its essential determinants. These necessary limits are:
>
> 1. *necessary labour* as limit to the exchange value of living labour-power, of the wages of the industrial population;
> 2. *surplus value* as limit to surplus labour-time; and, in relation to relative surplus labour-time, as limit to the development of the productive forces;
> 3. what is the same thing, the *transformation into money*, into exchange-value, as such, as a limit to production; or: exchange based on value, or value based on exchange, as limit to production. This is again
> 4. the same thing as *restriction of the production of use-values* by exchange-value; or: the fact that real wealth must take on a *specific* form distant from itself, absolutely not identical with it, in order to become an object of production at all.[38]

While a proper analysis of the implications of these rather cryptic theses would require a book, it is immediately apparent that these four 'limits' represent no more than different aspects of the contradiction between 'forces of production' and 'social relations of production'. The task of maintaining the enormous powers of surplus-value extraction within the limits set by the necessity of converting this surplus value into exchange value becomes increasingly difficult as the capitalist system moves into its developed stages. In practical terms, these four 'limits' could be formulated as four related, but mutually contradictory political-economic alternatives between which the capitalist system

38. Ibid., pp. 318–19. A five-element model of a closed capitalist system, from which Marx deduces the impossibility of expanded reproduction due to the impossibility of realization, appears on pp. 336–47. More on realization on pp. 438–42 (R: 174–6) and elsewhere.

must choose, but cannot afford to choose: 1. Wages must be raised to increase effective demand; 2. Less surplus value must be extracted; 3. Products must be distributed without regard to effective demand; or 4. Products that cannot be sold must not be produced at all. The first and second alternatives result in a reduction of profit; the third is capitalistically impossible (except as a political stopgap); and the fourth means depression.

Surplus labour

What is most remarkable and ought most to be emphasized about Marx's theory of capitalist breakdown as we see it at this point is its great latitude and flexibility. Cataclysmic crises rising to a revolutionary crescendo are only one possible variant of the breakdown process; and indeed, Marx lays little stress on this type of crisis in the *Grundrisse*. For every possible tendency towards breakdown, Marx names a number of delaying tendencies; this list includes the development of monopoly, the conquest of the world market, and, significantly, Marx mentions the payment by capitalists to workers of 'surplus wages'.[39] All things considered, Marx's breakdown theory in the *Grundrisse* provides important amplification of the statement in the *Preface* that 'no social order ever disappears before all the productive forces for which there is room in it have been developed'.[40] When one considers the requirements that must be met, in Marx's view, before the capitalist order is ripe for overthrow, one comes to wonder whether the failure of previous revolutionary movements in Europe and the United States is not imputable simply to prematurity.

The great historic role of capital is the creation of surplus labour, labour which is superfluous from the standpoint of mere use value, mere subsistence. Its historic role is fulfilled as soon as (on the one hand) the level of needs has been developed to the degree where surplus labour in addition to necessary subsistence has itself become a general need which manifests itself in individual needs, and (on the other hand) when the strict discipline of capital has schooled successive generations in industriousness, and this quality has become their general property, and (finally) when the development of the productive powers of labour, which capital, with its unlimited urge to accumulate and to realize, has constantly

39. Ibid., p. 341.   40. W13: 9 and *Selected Works*, I.

spurred on, have ripened to the point where the possession and maintenance of societal wealth require no more than a diminished amount of labour-time, where the labouring society relates to the process of its progressive reproduction and constantly greater reproduction in a scientific manner; where, that is, human labour which can be replaced by the labour of things has ceased.'[41]

Noteworthy in this long sentence, among many other things, is the statement that the capitalist order is not ripe for revolution until the working class—far from being reduced to the level of ragged, miserable brutes—has expanded its consumption *above* the level of mere physical subsistence and includes the enjoyment of the fruits of surplus labour as a general necessity. Instead of the image of the starving proletarian slowly dying from an eighteen-hour day in a mine or a sweatshop, Marx here presents the well-fed proletarian, scientifically competent, to whom an eight-hour day would presumably appear as a mere waste of time. In another passage, Marx goes further; he envisages a capitalist productive apparatus more completely automated than that of any presently existing society, and writes that nevertheless, despite the virtual absence from such a social order of a 'working class' as commonly defined, this economic organization must break down.

To the degree that large-scale industry develops, the creation of real wealth comes to depend less on labour-time and on the quantity of labour expended, and more on the power of the instruments which are set in motion during labour-time, and whose powerful effectiveness itself is not related to the labour-time immediately expended in their production, but depends rather on the general state of science and the progress of technology.... Large industry reveals that real wealth manifests itself rather in the monstrous disproportion between expended labour-time and its product, as well as in the qualitative disproportion between labour, reduced to a pure abstraction, and the power of the productive process which it supervises. Labour no longer appears as an integral element of the productive process; rather, man acts as supervisor and regulator of the productive process itself.... He stands at the side of the productive process, instead of being its chief actor. With this transformation, the cornerstone of

41. *Grundrisse*, p. 231 and R: 91.

production and wealth is neither the labour which man directly expends, nor the time he spends at work, but rather the appropriation of his own collective productive power, his understanding of nature and his mastery over nature, exercised by him as a social body—in short, it is the development of the social individual. The theft of other people's labour-time, on which contemporary wealth rests, appears as a miserable basis compared to this new one created by large-scale industry itself. As soon as labour in its direct form has ceased to be the great wellspring of wealth, labour-time ceases and must cease to be its measure, and therefore exchange-value the measure of use-value. . . . With that, the system of production based on exchange-value collapses. . . . Capital is its own contradiction-in-process, for its urge is to reduce labour-time to a minimum, while at the same time it maintains that labour-time is the only measure and source of wealth. Thus it reduces labour-time in its necessary form in order to augment it in its superfluous form; thus superfluous labour increasingly becomes a precondition—a question of life or death—for necessary labour. So on the one side it animates all the powers of science and nature, of social co-ordination and intercourse, in order to make the creation of wealth (relatively) independent of the labour-time expended on it. On the other side it wants to use labour-time as a measure for the gigantic social powers created in this way, and to restrain them within the limits necessary to maintain already-created values as values. Productive forces and social relations—both of which are different sides of the development of the social individual—appear to capital only as means, and only means to produce on its limited basis. In fact, however, these are the material conditions to blow this basis sky-high.[42]

This passage and similar ones in the *Grundrisse* demonstrate once again, if further proof were needed, that the applicability of the Marxian theory is not limited to nineteenth-century industrial conditions. It would be a paltry theory indeed which predicted the breakdown of the capitalist order only when that order consisted of child labour, sweatshops, famine, chronic malnutrition, pestilence, and all the other scourges of its primitive stages. No genius and little science are required to reveal the contradictions of such a condition. Marx, however, proceeds

42. Ibid., pp. 592–4 and R: 209–11.

by imagining the strongest possible case in favour of the capitalist system, by granting the system the full development of all the powers inherent in it—and then exposing the contradictions which must lead to its collapse.

THE UNKNOWN PIVOT

The gradual emergence of the *Grundrisse* out of obscurity into the consciousness of students and followers of Marx should have a most stimulating influence. This work explodes in many ways the mental set, the static framework of formulae and slogans to which much of Marxism has been reduced after a century of neglect, ninety years of social democracy, eighty years of 'dialectical materialism', and seventy years of revisionism. To put it more pithily, the *Grundrisse* blows the mind. A number of conclusions seem inescapable.

First, this work will make it impossible or at least hopelessly frustrating to dichotomize the work of Marx into 'young' and 'old', into 'philosophical' and 'economic' elements. Hegel-enthusiasts and partisans of Ricardo will find the work equally stimulating or, conversely, equally frustrating, for the *Grundrisse* is so to speak the pineal gland through which these two great antecedents of Marx engage in reciprocal osmosis.[43] It contains passages which formulate Ricardian ideas with Hegelian language and Hegelian ideas with Ricardian language; the intercourse between them is direct and fruitful. Although we have not here examined this point in detail, a reader of the *Grundrisse* will find a direct line of continuity going back to many of the ideas of the 1844 *Manuscripts*, and from the perspective of the *Grandrisse* it will not be clear whether the earlier manuscripts were indeed a work of philosophy at all, or whether they were not simply a fusion of economic and philosophical thoughtways for which there is no modern precedent. Likewise, from the perspective of the *Grundrisse*, the often apparently 'technical' obscurities of *Capital* will reveal their broader meaning. Between the mature Marx and the young Marx the *Grundrisse* is the missing link.

On the other hand, the fact that Marx makes a number of fresh discoveries and advances in the course of the *Grundrisse* must make students and followers of Marx more sensitive to the

43. The editors have provided a most thorough index of all overt and covert references to Hegel, as well as Marx's index to the works of Ricardo.

economic deficiencies of the earlier works. The *Grundrisse* contains the graphic record of Marx's discovery and systematization of the theory of surplus value, about which his theory of capitalist breakdown is constructed. If it was not already clear, a reading of this work makes it clear that the theory of surplus value was not a functional element of the economic model on which the *Manifesto* is based. Marx was aware, in 1848, of the *existence* of a surplus; but certainly he was not aware of the *importance* of this element. There is evidence of Marx's awareness of the Ricardian theory of the surplus in other early economic writings (the *Poverty of Philosophy* and *Wage-Labour and Capital*), but these works equally demonstrate that the surplus-value theory had *not* become a functional part of the economic model on which Marx based his predictions. Marx's early theory of wages and profits, for example, is clearly a function of a supply-demand model of the economic system; and it will be necessary to re-examine this early theorizing critically in the light of the later surplus-value model. In at least one important problem-area, the question of class polarization, it can be demonstrated that the prophecy of the *Manifesto* is explicitly contradicted by Marx on the basis of his theory of surplus value in a later work.[44] How many other such discrepancies exist, and how many of them are traceable to the differences between the early market-model and the later surplus-value model, is a question which ought to be examined not only for its own sake, but also to clear up the confusion which often results when it is asked what precisely Marx had to say on the question of increasing impoverishment, for example.

It follows that the most important Marxian political manifesto remains to be written. Apart from the brief *Critique of the Gotha Programme* (1875) there exists no programmatic *political* statement which is based squarely on the theory of surplus value, and which incorporates Marx's theory of capitalist breakdown as it appears in the *Grundrisse*. No grounds exist to reject the 1848 *Manifesto* as a whole; but there is every reason to submit all of its theses and views to critical re-examination in the light of Marx's own surplus-value theory. Many startling surprises might come to light, for example, if an edition of the *Manifesto* were published containing thorough and detailed

44. Cf. Martin Nicolaus, 'Hegelian Choreography and the Capitalist Dialectic: Proletariat and Middle Class in Marx', in *Studies on the Left*, VII: 1, Jan.-Feb., 1967, pp. 22–49.

annotations drawn from the later writings, point by point and line by line. Clearly the theory of surplus value is crucial to Marx's thought; one can even say that with its ramifications it *is* Marx's theory. Yet how many 'Marxist' political groupings and how many 'Marxist' critics of Marx make the surplus-value theory the starting point of their analysis? The only major contemporary work in which the surplus plays the central role is Baran and Sweezy's *Monopoly Capital.*[45] Despite the deficiencies of that work, it points the way in the proper Marxian direction and forms the indispensable foundation for the type of analysis which must be made if Marx's theory of capitalism is to reassert its political relevance.

Unfortunately from several points of view, *Monopoly Capital* ends with the conclusion (or, perhaps more accurately, begins with the assumption) that domestic revolution within the advanced capitalist countries is not presently foreseeable. This argument can and must be confronted with Marx's thesis in the *Grundrisse* that all of the obstacles to revolution, such as those which Baran and Sweezy cite, namely monopoly, conquest of the world market, advanced technology, and a working class more prosperous than in the past, are only the preconditions which make revolution possible. Similarly, it cannot be said that Marx's vision of the central contradiction of capitalism, as he states it in the *Grundrisse*, has ever been thoroughly explored and applied to an existing capitalist society; here *Monopoly Capital* falls short quite seriously. The results of such an analysis might also contain some surprising insights. In short, much work remains to be done.

That, we may conclude, is after all the most important conclusion to be drawn from the *Grundrisse*. Because this work underlines the deficiencies of the earlier economic writings and throws into sharp relief the fragmentary nature of *Capital*, it can serve as a powerful reminder that Marx was not a vendor of ready-made truths but a maker of tools. He himself did not complete the execution of the design. But the blueprints for his world-moving lever have at last been published. Now that Marx's unpolished masterwork has come to light, the construction of Marxism as a revolutionary social science which exposes even the most industrially advanced society at its roots has finally become a practical possibility.

45. Paul Baran and Paul Sweezy, *Monopoly Capital*, Monthly Review Press, New York, 1966.

15

Structure and Contradiction in *Capital**

MAURICE GODELIER

In this essay Maurice Godelier investigates the two different types of contradiction which Marx analysed in Capital. *One is the contradiction between capitalists and workers which arose and developed along with capitalism itself; since it originated with capitalism it cannot by itself lead to the revolutionary replacement of capitalist social relations by a higher form of social rationality (socialism). This latter transformation is prepared by another type of contradiction which capitalism only develops in its later phases: namely the contradiction between the increasingly social nature of the forces of production and the still private character of appropriation.*

Maurice Godelier is Professor of Economic Anthropology at the Collège de France, author of Rationality and Irrationality in Economics *(London 1972).*

Is it possible to analyse the relations between an event and a structure, or to explain the genesis and evolution of that structure, without being forced to abandon a structuralist viewpoint? These two questions are topical, and some have already hazarded an affirmative reply. A new situation is emerging, one of the aspects of which is the resumption of a dialogue between structuralism and Marxism. This is hardly surprising, as Marx himself, a century ago, described the whole of social life in terms of 'structures', advanced the hypothesis of the necessary existence of correspondences between infrastructures and superstructures characterizing different 'types' of society, and, lastly, claimed the ability to explain the 'evolution' of these types of society by the emergence and development of 'contradictions' between their structures.

* This essay first appeared in *Les Temps Modernes*, No. 246, November 1966. The translation is by Ben Brewster.

But the appearance of the word 'contradiction' might seem to cut short this resumed dialogue, for we all remember the dialectical 'miracles' of Hegel and many more or less well-known Marxists. But can the question be so simply answered; is Marx's dialectic the same as Hegel's? Marx's own statements on this point are equivocal: it sufficed to 'turn the dialectic right side up again' to make it 'scientifically useful', and to strip off all the mystifications with which Hegelian idealism had surrounded it.

I should like to reconsider this question by returning to the text of *Capital*. In fact, I think I can show that, in basic principles, Marx's dialectic has nothing to do with Hegel's, because they do not depend on the same notion of contradiction. Traditional exegeses of Marx then collapse, giving place to a Marx largely unknown even to Marxists, a Marx capable of providing unexpected and fruitful elements for the most up to date scientific reflection.

1. *From the visible functioning of the capitalist system to its hidden internal 'structure'*

What does Marx mean by an economic 'system'? A determined combination of specific modes of production, circulation, distribution, and consumption of material goods. In this combination, the mode of production of goods plays the dominant rôle. A mode of production is the combination of two structures, irreducible to one another: the productive forces and the relations of production. The notion of productive forces designates the set of factors of production, resources, tools, men, characterizing a determined society at a determined epoch which must be *combined* in a specific way to produce the material goods necessary to that society. The notion of relations of production designates the functions fulfilled by individuals and groups in the production process and in the control of the factors of production. For example, capitalist relations of production are relations between a class of individuals who have private possession of the productive forces and of capital, and a class of individuals without this property who must sell to the former the use of their labour power in exchange for a wage. Each class complements and presupposes the other.

For Marx, the scientific understanding of the capitalist system consists in the discovery of the internal structure hidden behind its visible functioning.

Thus, for Marx, as for Claude Lévi-Strauss,[1] 'structures' should not be confused with visible 'social relations' but constitute a *level of reality* invisible but present behind the visible social relations. The logic of the latter, and the laws of social practice more generally, depend on the functioning of these hidden structures and the discovery of these last should allow us to 'account for all the facts observed'.[2]

A very crude summary of Marx's thesis might go as follows: in the practice of the capitalist system everything *occurs as if* the wage were paid for the worker's labour, and as if the capital had of itself the property of automatic growth and of rendering a profit to its owner. In day to day practice there is no *direct* proof that capitalist profit is unpaid workers' labour, no *immediate* experience of the exploitation of the worker by the capitalist.

For Marx, profit is a fraction of the exchange value of commodities which remains in the hands of their owner after deducting prime costs. The exchange value of commodities presupposes a unit of measurement which makes them commensurable. This common unit cannot be the utility of the commodities since there is nothing in common at the level of use value between vegetables and a fountain pen. . . . The exchange value of commodities can only derive from what they have in common as products of labour. The substance of value is therefore the socially necessary labour for the production of these commodities. Profit is a fraction of the value[3] created by the use of workers' labour power which is not paid as wages. Profit is thus unpaid labour, free labour. But in practice, in the eyes of capitalists and workers, everything takes place as if the wages paid for all the labour provided by the worker (bonuses, piece rates, overtime rates, etc.). Wages thus give the workers' unpaid labour the appearances of paid labour : 'This phenomenal form, which makes *the actual relation invisible*, and,

1. Claude Lévi-Strauss, 'On Structure' in *Structural Anthropology*, Ch. XV, p. 279.

2. Ibid., p. 280. [This is a direct translation of the French text used by Godelier (*Anthropologie Structurale*, p. 306); Lévi-Strauss' (original) English version reads : 'make immediately intelligible all the observed facts'—*Translator's note*.]

3. This is a deliberate simplification, for profit may or may not correspond to the surplus value really produced in an enterprise.

indeed, *shows* the direct opposite of that relation, forms the basis of all the juridical notions of both labourer and capitalist, of all the mystifications of the capitalistic mode of production.'[4]

In fact, once wages appear as the price of labour, profit can no longer appear as unpaid labour. It necessarily appears as the product of capital. Each class seems to draw from production the revenue to which it has a right. There is no visible exploitation of one class by another. The economic categories: wages, profits, interest, etc., thus express the visible relations of day to day business and as such they have a *pragmatic utility*, but no scientific value. Once economic science bases itself on these categories it, in fact, does no more than '*interpret, systematize and defend* in doctrinaire fashion the conceptions of the agents of bourgeois production who are entrapped in bourgeois production relations. It should not astonish us, then, that vulgar economy feels particularly at home in the estranged outward appearances of economic relations ... and that these relations seem the more *self-evident* the more their internal relationships are concealed from it. . . .'[5]. The intelligibility and coherence introduced by this systematization of the current conceptions of members of the society can only result in mythology. 'To talk of the price of labour is as irrational as to talk of a yellow logarithm.' Myth here consists of a coherent theory of appearances, of what *seems* to happen in practice. The scientific conception of social reality does not 'arise by abstraction' from the spontaneous or reflected conceptions of individuals. On the contrary, it must destroy the obviousness of these conceptions in order to *bring out* the hidden internal logic of social life. Therefore, for Marx, the model constructed by science corresponds to a reality concealed beneath visible reality. But he goes even further; for him this concealment is not due to the inability of consciousness to 'perceive' this structure, but to the structure itself. If capital *is not* a thing, but a *social relationship*, i.e. a non-sensible reality, it must inevitably disappear when presented in the sensible forms of raw materials, tools, money, etc. It is not the subject who deceives himself, but *reality* which deceives *him*, and the appearances in which the structure of the capitalist production process conceals itself are the starting-point for individuals' conceptions. For Marx, a determined

4. *Capital*, I, p. 540 (Moscow, 1961). Emphases M.G. unless otherwise stated.

5. *Capital*, III, p. 797.

mode of *appearance* corresponds to each determined structure of the real, and this mode of appearance is the starting-point for a kind of *spontaneous* consciousness of the structure for which neither consciousness nor the individual are responsible. It follows that the scientific understanding of a stucture does not abolish the spontaneous consciousness of that structure. It modifies its rôle and its effects, but it does not suppress it.[6]

When Marx assumes that structure is not to be confused with visible relations and explains their hidden logic, he inaugurates the modern structuralist tradition. And he is fully in accord with this tradition when he proposes the priority of the study of structures over that of their genesis and evolution. Before getting on to this new theme, I should like to set down, without developing it, a rough comparison of Marx's scientific practice with Lévi-Strauss', by resuming the principal characteristics of the latter's celebrated analysis of the Murngin kinship system, to be found in *Les Structures Élémentaires de la Parenté*.[7]

This Australian kinship system was considered 'aberrant' by specialists, because it could never be exactly classified in a typology of the so-called 'classical' Australian systems. The latter are of three types, according as to whether the number of matrimonial classes is two, four or eight. It had been established that a moiety system prescribed marriage between cross cousins, but forbade it between parallel cousins. The four-section Kariera system was the same. Nothing was changed, therefore, in the order of prescriptions and prohibitions on passing from a two-class matrimonial system to a four-class matrimonial system. On the other hand, in the Aranda eight-subsection system, marriage between any first cousin, cross or parallel, was prohibited.

But the Murngin system differs both from the Kariera and from the Aranda systems. It contains eight subsections, just as the Aranda system does, but for all that, it authorizes marriage with the matrilateral cross cousin as the Kariera system does. But while the Kariera system authorizes marriage with both the cross cousins, the Murngin system forbids it with the patri-

6. In the same way for Spinoza knowledge of the second kind (mathematical knowledge) does not suppress that of the first kind (everyday experience).

7. Claude Lévi-Strauss, *Les Structures Élémentaires de la Parenté*, Paris, 1949, Ch. XIV, pp. 216–46. See also A. Weil's algebraic study, Ch. XIV, pp. 278–87.

lateral cross cousin, thus introducing a dichotomy between cross cousins. It also has other singular features: it demands seven lineages while four suffice for the Aranda system and two for the Kariera; its kinship terminology includes seventy-one terms, while that of the Aranda has forty-one and that of the Kariera twenty-one.

The dichotomy of cross cousins, preferential marriage with the matrilateral cross cousin and the other peculiarities of the system thus demand an explanation. Claude Lévi-Strauss has shown that this can be given if we assume the existence and action—beneath the explicit system of restricted exchange between eight subsections which is the appearance of the Murngin system—of an implicit four-section system of a quite different structure, of which the Murngin themselves are not conscious, and which the ethnologists specializing in kinship had not yet really identified and theorized: a structure which Lévi-Strauss calls 'the structure of generalized exchange'.

While in a system of restricted exchange, marriage always conforms to the same rule since if a man of A marries a woman of B, a man of B can marry a woman of A, in a system of generalized exchange, if a man of A marries a woman of B, a man of B will marry a woman of C, and a man of C a woman of A. A will then have taken a woman from B, but 'in exchange' grants a woman to C. Here reciprocity takes places between a certain number of partners by the interplay of relations oriented in a determined and irreversible direction: $A \rightarrow B \rightarrow C \rightarrow A$. It can be shown that in a system of generalized exchange with four sections the matrilateral cross cousin is always in the class immediately succeeding that of Ego, whence he can always take a wife, while the patrilateral cross cousin is always in the preceding class, which is forbidden. The structure of such a system thus provides the theoretical formula for Murngin marriage, and establishes the law of the dichotomy of cross cousins.

It is then easy to show that if matrilineal moieties are added to a four-section system of generalized exchange, each section is redoubled into two subsections, producing an eight-subsection system which has the *appearance* of a double system of restricted exchange of the Aranda type. At the same time, all the other peculiarities of the system, the number of lineages, the enormously extended terminology, appear as so many necessary consequences of the functioning of this implicit structure, as complementary aspects of its internal logic.

The immense importance of Lévi-Strauss' demonstration is easily seen. While seeking to account for a peculiar, aberrant,[8] case, not classifiable under the rubrics of the traditional ethnological typology, he discovered the existence[9] and explained the nature of a new family of structures, which was much more complex than those previously known, and, in particular, much more difficult to identify because the exchange cycle determined by it is not 'so immediately perceivable'. A new classification of kinship systems became necessary and possible, including within it the old typology of systems of restricted exchange whose peculiarity was now manifest. In the practical sphere a tool was now available to set out on a study of certain complex kinship systems in China, India, S.E. Asia, and Siberia, which had so far seemed outside the notion of exchange.

Lévi-Strauss' methodological principles and conclusions had no less importance in the epistemological sphere. Whether a structure is implicit,[10] as with the Murngin, or explicit, as with the Katchin, it is never directly visible and decipherable at the empirical level, but has to be discovered by theoretical labour in the production of hypotheses and models. Lévi-Strauss' structural analysis therefore rejects in principle Radcliffe-Brown's functionalist structuralism[11] and, in general, the whole

8. Compare the consequences of the experiment on 'black-body' radiation, a tiny 'detail' (cf. Bachelard) which upset the whole of the nineteenth-century physical perspective which grew out of Newton's work.

9. This is not precisely true. Lévi-Strauss gives Hodson the merit for the discovery of the correlation between the rule of matrilateral cross cousin marriage and the existence of a specific social structure. But Hodson thought that this structure could only be tripartite and patrilinear, while it can contain any number of sections and it is only necessary that it be 'harmonic'. (*Les Structures Élémentaires de la Parenté*, pp. 292–3; Hodson, *The Primitive Culture of India*, 1922.)

10. This case makes its discovery even more difficult as the appearance of the system suggests another structure, that of the Aranda system. But 'instead of the true symmetry of the Kariera and Aranda systems, we find a pseudo-symmetry which in reality arises from two super-imposed asymmetrical structures.' *Structures Élémentaires*, p. 242.

11. A. R. Radcliffe-Brown, *Structure and Function in Primitive Societies*, London, 1952.

of Anglo-Saxon empirical sociology, for which structure is part of empirical reality.[12]

Structure is part of reality for Lévi-Strauss as well, but not of empirical reality. A structure cannot therefore be opposed to the theoretical model built to represent it. The structure only exists in and through the human mind (*esprit*), and this is a rejection equally of the idealist and of the formalist structuralisms that lay claim to Lévi-Strauss.[13] The latter's position is put, more explicitly than anywhere in *Structural Anthropology*, in a reply to Maybury-Lewis who had accused him of discovering pseudo-structures contradicting the ethnographic data: 'Of course the final word should rest with experiment. However, the experiment suggested and guided by deductive reasoning will not be the same as the unsophisticated ones with which the whole process started. They will remain as alien as ever to the deeper analysis. The ultimate proof of the molecular structure of matter is provided by the electronic microscope, which enables us to see actual molecules. This achievement does not alter the fact that henceforth the molecule will not become any more visible to the naked eye. Similarly, it is hopeless to expect a structural analysis to change our way of perceiving concrete social relations. It will only explain them better.'[14]

A secondary consequence of the structural method is its critique of all psychologism and sociological teleology. From *Structures Élémentaires* on, Lévi-Strauss showed that Warner's psychological considerations gave an illusory answer to the problem of the existence of seven Murngin lineages.[15] Warner tried to explain this by the need to resolve the tensions which would be produced in the group between Ego and his mother's brother, i.e. the father of his matrilateral cross cousin, his future wife, without this multiplication of lineages.[16] We have

12. Claude Lévi-Strauss, 'On Manipulated Sociological Models' in *Bijdragen tot de taal-, land- en volkenkunde*, Deel 16, *Anthropologica*, 's-Gravenhage, 1960, p. 52.

13. Hence Lévi-Strauss' many critiques of the idealism and formalism which have, in fact, become the principle adversaries of scientific structuralism; cf. 'La Structure et la Forme', *Cahiers de l'ISEA*, and the preface to *Le Cru et le Cuit*.

14. 'On Manipulated Sociological Models', op. cit., p. 53.

15. *Structures Élémentaires*, p. 253.

16. Warner, 'Morphology and Function of the Australian Murngin Type of Kinship', *American Anthropologist*, Vols. 32–3, pp. 179–82.

seen that the answer owed nothing to psychology, but was to be found in the logic of the system of generalized exchange itself, while Warner did not even suspect the existence of the latter.

More basically, the analysis of the logic of a structure allows us to bring its possibilities and capacities for evolution into the open. Research into the origin and genesis of a structure is in some sense 'guided' by a knowledge of its mechanism. In the Murngin case, Lévi-Strauss assumes that they had borrowed from elsewhere the eight-subsection system which they were forced to make compatible with their original matrimonial system.[17] He then shows that such a system is 'unstable', determining its possible forms and modes of evolution. He demonstrates that this instability is characteristic of all systems of generalized exchange which belong in principle to the 'harmonic' régime, since their rules of filiation are the same as their rules of residence in the definition of the social status of an individual, while systems of restricted exchange are in principle 'dysharmonic and stable'.[18] He concludes from this that here is the basis for the unequal capacity of appearance and evolution of these two families of structure.[19] These capacities are thus objective properties of the structures, properties independent of individuals and remaining essentially unconscious to them. For example, if the Murngin system is the product of borrowing and adaptation it is thereby the product of a conscious and desired activity, but, in essentials, the Murngin remained unconscious of the logic and evolutionary capacity of their new system which were not at all dependent on their intentions. In this perspective social evolution ceases to be a series of accidents of no significance.[20]

This very brief analysis of a few fragments of the earliest work of Lévi-Strauss nevertheless suffices for a comparison

17. Cases of borrowings of all or part of a social institution in the range of kinship, myth, dance, etc., are common in Australia. Stanner was able to observe directly a case of borrowing a kinship institution by the Nangio-meri (*Structures Élémentaires*, p. 227).

18. For example, the Kariera system is matrilateral and patrilocal.

19. 'This characteristic (of harmonic régimes) explains why the realization of a system of classes is so rare wherever marriage is determined by a law of generalized exchange' (Ibid., p. 272).

20. Hence Lévi-Strauss' critique of nineteenth-century associationist evolutionism (Ibid., pp. 128 and 185).

between Marx and modern structuralism. It has allowed me to isolate in Lévi-Strauss' practice two principles of structural analysis: the first, that structure is part of reality, but not of visible relations, the second, that the study of the internal functioning of a structure must precede and illuminate the study of its genesis and evolution. I have already shown that the first principle can be found in Marx. I shall now go on to show that the architecture of *Capital* cannot be understood without the second.

2. *The priority of the study of structures over that of their genesis and evolution*

This priority is apparent from a simple glance at the architecture of *Capital*. The work does not start with the theory of capital, but by setting out the theory of value, i.e. by the definition of a group of categories necessary to the study of any system of commodity production, whether this is based on the labour of a free peasant, a slave, a serf, or a wage labourer, etc. This group of categories is developed from a definition of the exchange value of a commodity. Money is then introduced as a special commodity with the function of expressing and measuring the exchange value of other commodities. Coin is defined as a form of money. Coin ceases to function as a simple means of circulation of commodities and begins to function as capital when it brings in coin, when its use adds value to its initial value. The general definition of capital whatever its form—commercial, financial, or industrial—is that it is value that makes value and brings in surplus value.

By the end of the second section of Volume I of *Capital* Marx thus has at his disposal the theoretical instruments necessary to identify the specific structure of the capitalist economic system, the capital-labour relation, and to construct the theory of capital. Before this theory could be undertaken, a rigorous definition of the notion of commodity was essential, for within the capital-labour relation labour power appears as a commodity. This makes possible an analysis of the internal structure of the capitalist system, i.e. a study of the mechanism of the production of surplus value through the capital-labour relation. Volume I analyses at length the two forms of surplus value: absolute surplus value (obtained by lengthening the working day without increasing wages) and relative surplus value (obtained by decreasing the costs of employing the worker, by increasing the productivity of labour in the branches producing the means of subsistence of the workers and their families).

Only at the end of Volume I does the reader find Marx setting out the problem of the *genesis* of the capitalist production relationship via a discussion of what the classical economists called 'the problem of primitive accumulation'. Marx's procedure thus marks a break with any historicism or reliance on events. The genesis of a structure can only be studied under the 'guidance' of a pre-existing knowledge of that structure. To study the genesis of the specific structure of the capitalist system is to determine the particular historical circumstances of the emergence of individuals who are free in person, but deprived of the means of production and of money and forced to sell the use of their labour power to other individuals who possess the means of production and money but are forced to buy others' labour power to set these means of production in motion and breed their money. But Marx only sketches this genesis in a rapid perspective of some of the conditions, forms and stages of the appearance of capitalism in Europe, and this does not constitute a history of capitalism. Among these stages we might mention the disbanding of feudal retinues in England, the expropriation and partial expulsion of cultivators, the 'enclosures' movement, the transformation of merchants into merchant-manufacturers, colonial trade, the development of protectionism. All these appeared in the fifteenth, sixteenth, and seventeenth centuries here and there in Portugal, Spain, France, and England, and generally resulted in the emergence of a large number of producers without means of production and their use in a new structure of production.

The capitalist system *presupposes* the complete separation of the labourers from all property in the means by which they can realize their labour. As soon as capitalist production is once on its own legs, it not only *maintains* this separation, but *reproduces* it on a continually extending scale. The process, therefore, that clears the way for the capitalist system, can be none other than the process which takes away from the labourer the possession of his means of production; a process that transforms, on the one hand, the social means of subsistence and of production into capital, on the other, the immediate producers into wage labourers. The so-called primitive accumulation, therefore, is nothing else than the historical process of divorcing the producer from the means of production. It appears as primitive, because it forms the prehistoric stage of capital and of the mode of production corresponding with it. The economic structure of capitalistic society *has grown out of* the economic structure of feudal society. The dissolution of the latter sets from the *elements* of the former.[21]

Thus to analyse the historical genesis of a structure is to analyse the conditions of emergence of its internal elements and the way they come into relation with one another. In its constitution, economic history presupposes that these elements and this relation are already identified, so it presupposes economic theory. In Marx's text the genesis of one system is described simultaneously with the dissolution of another, and these two effects depend on the same process, the development of internal contradictions within the old system (which must also be theorized).

This general progress from the identification of the structure to the study of its genesis might seem to founder on an obstacle that Marx himself considered. For how can the hypothesis of the appearance of internal contradictions inside a system be reconciled with the thesis that the functioning of this system necessarily *reproduces* its conditions of functioning? For example, the capitalist system's functioning mechanism ceaselessly reproduces the capital-labour relation on which it is built. The mechanism of profit and wage always allows the capitalist class to accumulate new capital and to reproduce itself as the ruling class, while on the other hand it forces the working class to put its labour power up for sale again, and to reproduce itself as the ruled class.[22] The capital-labour relation appears as the *constant element* in the capitalist economic structure throughout all the latter's variations: the passage from the capitalism of free competition to private or state monopoly capitalism, the appearance of new productive forces, changes in the composition of the working class, in its forms of trade union and

21. *Capital*, I, pp. 714–15.
22. This is not weakened by the phenomenon of social mobility which allows certain workers to become capitalists, or which is produced by competition and the ruin of certain capitalists or category of enterprises.

political organization etc. The discovery and definition of this constant constitute the necessary point of departure for the scientific study of the system, of its genesis and evolution. The latter appears as the study of *variations compatible* with the reproduction of the constant element of the system structure. At this level the passage from political economy to economic history is once again set out. Synchronic and diachronic studies are possible (analyses of the various *states* of a structure corresponding to various *moments* in its evolution). But diachronic analysis of the variations which are compatible with the reproduction of a constant relation does not produce any structural incompatibles, any conditions of change.[23]

But can incompatible variations be produced *within* the functioning of a system if the very maintenance of the system proves that they are compatible with its reproduction? Before I analyse Marx's notion of contradiction in detail, I should like to develop further that of 'structural compatibility', for it plays a decisive double rôle which illuminates the whole method and plan of *Capital*. It allows Marx to account for the visible forms of the functioning of the capitalist system which he had initially rejected. It also allows him to explain the new rôle and new forms which the 'antediluvian' forms of capital[24]—commercial capital and finance capital—take on when they function in the framework of modern capitalism. I shall summarize these two points briefly so as to be able to deduce their methodological consequences. As we have seen, Marx first of all analysed the production mechanism of surplus value and showed that it consisted of production from unpaid labour. He then showed that the internal and necessary connection between surplus value and labour disappears once surplus value is put into relation with all the capital advanced by the capitalist rather than

23. This diachrony seems to be always recreated in the synchrony or at least to show the multiple modes of existence of the same structure, once given the local variations of its conditions of functioning. Cf. Marx: '... the same economic basis—the same from the standpoint of its main conditions—due to innumerable different empirical circumstances, natural environment, racial relations, external historical influences, etc. (is not prevented), from showing infinite variations and graduations in appearance, which can be ascertained only by analysis of the empirically given circumstances.' (*Capital*, III, p. 772).

24. *Capital*, III, p. 580.

with the wage paid to the worker, i.e. it disappears once surplus value appears as profits. The results of Volume II allow him, in Part 1 of Volume III, to analyse the complex conditions for the realization of a maximum profit by the capitalist entrepreneur. I can leave aside these problems—those of the relations between value and price, price and profit, normal profit and super profit, rate of profit in various branches, and at the level of the national economy, etc.—without loss for our purposes. What is essential is that we should remember Marx's conclusions. From his profit, which at the limit seems to have little relation to the real exploitation of his own workers, the capitalist must subtract a portion for the ground rent of the proprietor of the land on which his factory stands, another which goes as interest to a lender or to a bank, another which he owes to the State as taxes. The remainder constitutes the profit of his enterprise. By showing that the mechanism of the production of surplus value is the common origin of the visible forms of capitalist profit even though certain categories of capitalists seem to have no direct link with the production process, Marx made possible the analysis of the articulation of the internal structure of the system to the visible forms which he avoided on principle at the outset of his work.

Marx returns to these visible forms by defining at one and the same time their real function in the system and their internal compatibility with the essential structures that were given priority in his study. In modern terms, his progress would constitute a kind of ideal genesis of the various elements of a system on the basis of its laws of internal composition. Marx defined it himself in respect to money:

> Everyone knows, if he knows nothing else, that commodities have a value-form common to them all, and presenting a marked contrast with the varied bodily forms of their use-values. I mean their money-form. Here, however, a task is set us, the performance of which has never yet even been attempted by bourgeois economy, the task of tracing the *genesis* of this money-form, of developing the *expression* of value implied in the value-relation of commodities, from its simplest, almost imperceptible outline, to dazzling money-form. By doing this we shall, at the same time, *solve* the riddle presented by money.[25]

25. *Capital*, I, pp. 47–8.

But I must avoid a misunderstanding which might arise from what I have called the ideal genesis of economic categories. For if an object becomes a commodity once it is produced for exchange, this exchange could be by barter and thus not imply the existence of any money. The exchange of commodities necessitates the specialization of a commodity in the function of expressing and measuring the exchange value of other commodities only in determined concrete conditions (whether this commodity be cocoa, sea-shells, cattle, or gold does not alter its function). Other precise conditions are necessary if a precious metal is to be imposed as the general form of money. Marx is thus not working as a Hegelian by the 'deduction' of one category from another. He makes explicit the functions of one element within a structure, or of one structure within a system and explains the ranking of these functions. There is therefore no need to wait for the discovery of where and how the first money was invented to solve the 'riddle presented by money'. The object of economic theory is to render explicit these functions and their ranking in a given structure, and thus to articulate one to the others in a kind of logical genesis. But this genesis is not the real genesis and does not replace it. Once more economic theory, without being confused with economic history, provides it with the guide line for its analyses while developing thanks to its results. Here Marx totally rejects any historicism and any priority of the historical study of a system over its structural study, and anticipates by more than half a century the crises of linguistics and sociology which led de Saussure and Lowie to reject nineteenth-century evolutionism.

Rent *cannot* be understood without capital, but capital *can*, without rent. Capital is the all-dominating economic power of bourgeois society. It must form the starting point as well as the end and can be developed before land-ownership is. After each has been considered separately, their mutual relation must be analysed. It would thus be *impractical* and *wrong* to arrange the economic categories in the *order* in which they were the *determining* factors *in the course of history*. Their order of sequence is rather determined by the *relation* which they bear to one another in modern bourgeois society, and which is the exact *opposite* of what seems to be their natural order or the order of their historical development. *It is not a matter of* the *place* which economic *relations* occupy in the *historical succession* of different *forms of society*. Still less is it a matter of the order of their succession 'in the Idea' (Proudhon) (a nebulous conception of historical movement). It is a matter of their *articulation* within modern bourgeois society.[26]

This explains why the functioning of a structure must be compatible with the functioning of other structures, or must become so if they are to belong to the same system. It illuminates the status of the analysis of commercial and financial capital in *Capital*. Commodity production is not, in fact, exclusively characteristic of modern capitalism. To the extent that an important exchange of commodities existed in some societies with as different relations of production as the great states of the ancient East, Greek and Roman slave societies and the feudal societies of the Middle Ages, the functions of commerce and to a certain extent those of credit had also to exist. But in both cases the forms and importance of these commodity relations changed. Marx shows, for example, that the rates of usury in money trade and the immense gains from international commodity trade characteristic of many pre-capitalist societies were incompatible with the development of industrial capital, and that this last imposed the creation of new forms of credit and the establishment of much lower interest rates. This profoundly altered the proportion of the value of commodities returned to commercial or financial capital.

> The credit system develops as a reaction against usury. But this should not be misunderstood. . . . It *signifies* no more and no less than the *subordination* of interest-bearing capital to the *conditions and requirements* of the capitalist mode of production.[27]

Thus the appearance of new structures modifies the conditions of existence and rôle of older structures which are obliged to transform themselves. Our analysis closes with the emergence of the notion of a *limit* to the functional compatibility of different structures. We have once again arrived at the problem of the genesis of new structures and of Marx's notion of contradiction.

26. *A Contribution to the Critique of Political Economy*, trans. N. I. Stone, Chicago, 1904, pp. 303–4. [Corrected—*Translator's note*]

27. *Capital*, III, p. 586.

3. Two notions of contradiction in Capital

I shall start by listing the various contexts in which we find Marx talking of contradiction. First of all there is the contradiction between workers and capitalists. Then there are the economic 'crises' in which contradictions appear between production and consumption, between the conditions of production of value and surplus value and the conditions of their realization, and basically between production forces and relations of production. Finally there are the contradictions between capitalism and small peasant or artisan property, capitalism and socialism, etc. This simple list reveals differences of nature and importance among these contradictions, of which some are internal to the system, and other exist between the system and other systems. They must therefore be analysed theoretically.

The first contradiction presented is that between capital and labour, between the capitalist class and the working class. One owns the capital, the other is excluded from ownership of it. One's profit is the unpaid labour of the other. What characterizes this first contradiction? It is inside capitalist 'relations of production'. It is thus an 'internal contradiction of a structure'.

This contradiction is specific[28] to the capitalist mode of production. It characterizes it as such, distinguishing it from other, slave-based, feudal, etc., modes of production. As it is specific, it characterizes the system from the beginning, and the functioning of the system continually reproduces it. It is therefore original, in the sense that it is present from the beginning, and remains until the disappearance of the system. It develops with the development of the system, it is transformed by the evolution of capitalism from free competition to monopoly and by the evolution of the trade union and political organization of the working class. This contradiction is antagonistic: the function of one class is to exploit the other. It reveals itself in the class struggle. It is visible to and to some extent deciphered by the psychologist and sociologist, who distinguish individuals by their different functions and statuses, by the economist and the historian; finally, the philosopher may take it as his object when reflecting on justice, inequality, etc.

Is this basic antagonism, which would seem to occupy the forefront of the historical stage in fact the basic contradiction of capitalism? No. For Marx, the latter is the contradiction

28. *Capital*, III, p. 856.

between the development and the socialization of the productive forces and the private ownership of the means of production.

The contradiction, to put it in a very general way, consists in that the capitalist mode of production involves a tendency towards absolute development of the productive forces, regardless of the value and surplus-value it contains, and regardless of the social conditions under which capitalist production takes place; while, on the other hand, its aim is to preserve the value of the existing capital and promote its self-expansion to the highest limit (i.e. to promote an ever more rapid growth of this value).[29]

How is the contradiction visible? 'This collision appears partly in periodical crises.'[30]

In a crisis, the basic contradiction appears in the contradictions between production and consumption and between production and circulation of commodities. More profoundly, it appears in the tendency for the rate of profit to fall.

What are the characteristics of this contradiction?

It is not a contradiction within a structure, but *between two structures*. It is thus not directly a contradiction between individuals or groups, but between the structure of the productive forces—their ever greater socialisation—and the structure of the relations of production—the private ownership of the productive forces.

Now the paradox is that this contradiction, which is basic because it explains the evolution of capitalism and its inevitable disappearance, *is not original*. It appears at 'a certain stage' of evolution,[31] at a 'certain stage of maturity'[32] of the system. And this stage is the stage of large-scale industry, i.e. a certain state of development of the productive forces. Marx clarifies this in a letter to Kugelmann: 'He would have seen that I represent *large-scale industry* not only as the *mother* of the *antagonism*, but also as the *creator* of the material and spiritual *conditions* necessary for the *solution* of this antagonism.'[33]

In the beginning, on the contrary, far from contradicting the developing of the productive forces, capitalist relations of production pushed it ahead and gave it its impetuous progression

29. *Capital*, III, p. 244.   30. *Capital*, III, p. 258.
31. *Capital*, III, p. 237.   32. *Capital*, III, p. 861.
33. Letter to Kugelmann, 17th March, 1968.

from the organization of manufacture to the appearance of mechanization and heavy industry. Mechanized industry, completing the separation of agriculture and domestic rural industry (which is annihilated), 'for the first time, conquers for industrial capital the entire home-market' and gives it 'that extension and consistence which the capitalist mode of production requires', the latter having become 'combined and scientific'[34] with the progress of the division of labour. Before machinery, manufacturing production could not achieve this 'radical transformation'.

Thus, initially, far from there being a contradiction between capitalism and the development of the productive forces, there was a correspondence, a functional compatibility which was the basis for the dynamism of technical progress and the capitalist class. But this very structural correspondence between capitalism and the forces of production means a non-correspondence of these forces of production and feudal relations of production. And for Marx this non-correspondence is the foundation of the objective contradiction between feudal and capitalist relations, between the seigneurial class and the capitalist class. For as we have seen, if there are to be capitalists, there must also be labourers facing them, free in their person, forced to put their labour power up for sale. i.e. excluded from ownership of the means of production.[35]

> The immediate producer, the labourer, could only dispose of his own person after he had ceased to be attached to the soil and ceased to be the slave, serf or bondman of another. ... Hence, the historical movement which changes the producers into wage-workers, appears, on the one hand, as their emancipation from serfdom and from the fetters of the guilds. (The industrial capitalists') conquest of social power appears as the fruit of a victorious struggle both against feudal lordship and its revolting prerogatives, and against the guilds and the fetters they laid on the free development of production and the free exploitation of man by man.[36]

Thus the basic contradiction of the capitalist mode of production is *born* during the development of the mode of production, and *is not present* from the beginning of the system.

34. *Capital*, I, pp. 748–9.
35. *Capital*, I, p. 168.
36. *Capital*, I, p. 715.

This contradiction appears without anyone wishing to make it appear. This contradiction is therefore *unintentional*. It is a result of the action of all the agents of the system and of the development of the system itself, and is never the project of any consciousness, is never anyone's goal. Marx is therefore drawing attention to *aspects of reality which cannot be referred to any consciousness nor explained by consciousness*. It is the mode of production itself, the valuation of capital, which produces this result 'unconsciously'.[37]

But this basic, unintentional, non-original contradiction is not the opaque involuntary residue of intersubjective action. It is unintentional and without teleology; but transparent to *science* because it is 'significant'. It signifies the *limits* within which it is possible that capitalist relations of production, based on private property, may correspond to the development of the productive forces to which they have given birth.

These limits are 'immanent' to capitalist relations of production, and cannot be 'overcome',[38] since the valuation of capital depends on the exploitation of the great mass of producers; they are thus limits expressing *objective properties* of the capitalist mode of production (not of capitalists or workers as individuals or economic agents).

> The entire capitalist mode of production is only a relative one, whose barriers are not absolute. They are absolute only for this mode, i.e. *on its basis*.[39]

These limits are the limits within which the relations of production can remain constant, allowing for gigantic variations in the productive forces. These limits are thus objective properties of the system and these properties establish the necessity for its evolution and disappearance. They can act on the system itself and are the *causality* of the structure on itself. 'The *real barrier* of capitalist production is *capital itself*.'[40]

This causality acts everywhere, but it is impossible to localize its effect anywhere. It intervenes everywhere between one event and another to give each all its dimensions, whether conscious or not, i.e. the field of its effects, whether intentional or not. For Marx, the set of properties of the structure always

37. *Capital*, III, p. 254.
38. *Capital*, III, p. 254.
39. *Capital*, III, p. 252.
40. *Capital*, III, p. 245, Marx's emphasis.

comes between a cause and its effects, giving the action its objective dimensions.

Thus, while ceaselessly developing the productive forces, capital '*unconsciously* creates the *material* requirements of a higher mode of production',[41] and necessitates the transformation of capitalist conditions of large-scale production based on private property into 'general, common, social conditions'.[42] The development of capitalism makes possible and necessary the appearance of a socialist economic system, of a 'higher' mode of production. But what does 'higher' mean here, what is the criterion on which this value-judgment is based?

The criterion is the fact that the *structure* of socialist relations of production *corresponds* functionally with the conditions of rapid development of the new, gigantic, more and more socialized productive forces created by capitalism. The criterion thus expresses the possibilities, the objective properties, of a historically determined structure. This correspondence is totally *independent* of any *a priori* idea of happiness, of 'true' liberty, of the essence of man, etc. Marx demonstrates the necessity and superiority of a new mode of production, thus establishing a value-judgment *without starting with* an *a priori* criterion of rationality.[43] This value judgment is not a judgment of 'people', it does not demonstrate any progress in 'morality', any victory of 'ethical principles' in socialist society as against capitalist society. It is a judgment of the 'properties' of a structure, of the particular conditions of its appearance and functioning.

The necessity for the appearance of a new mode of production no longer derives from a teleology concealed in the mysteries of the essence of man as revealed to the philosopher alone, be he materialist or idealist, for it is no longer possible to read into the historically determined contradiction of capitalist relations of production with a determined level of the productive

41. *Capital*, III, p. 254.

42. *Capital*, III, p. 259.

43. Engels writes, in a letter to Paul Lefargue, 11th August, 1884: 'Marx rejected the "political, social and economic ideal" you attribute to him. A man of science has no ideals, he elaborates scientific results, and if he is also politically committed, he struggles for them to be put into practice. But if he has ideals, he cannot be a man of science, since he would then be biased from the start.' (*Correspondence Engels-Lafargue*, Éditions Sociales, Paris, p. 235.)

forces the philosophical drama of the revolt of the 'true essence' of man against the 'dehumanized existence' imposed on the workers by the bourgeoisie.

In *Capital*, the analysis of the contradictions of the capitalist system radically separates economic science from any ideology, and Marx has nothing more to do with the young Marx. For ideology consists precisely of transforming the 'merely historical transitory' necessity of the mode of production into a characteristic attributable to 'Nature'.[44] Marx's analysis rejects all the 'humanist' justifications which might be given for the superiority of socialism. This does not mean that he rejects the real problems that may be expressed in a humanist ideology if it is materialist. But to analyse these problems theoretically is to determine the new possibilities for social evolution specific to socialist structures.[45] By suppressing capitalist relations of exploitation and domination, the socialist society creates new conditions of social evolution just as the capitalist system did by destroying the earlier feudal society and its forms of slavery.

I have distinguished two types of contradiction in *Capital*, and shown that the basic contradiction illuminating the evolution of the system is the contradiction *between* its *structures*, and that this contradiction is born of the objective *limits* to the relations of production maintaining themselves constant while the productive forces vary in certain proportions. Now I can attempt a definition of the theory of contradiction which is implicit in Marx, and, which I think, radically opposes Marx's dialectic to that of Hegel.

4. *The radical opposition between Marx's dialectic and Hegel's dialectic*

The terms which still obscure Marx's and Engels' presentation of this problem are well known. On the one hand, Marx declares that his dialectical method is the 'direct opposite' of Hegel's, Engels that the dialectic was 'useless in its Hegelian form' and that only Marx's dialectic is 'rational'. But at the same time,

44. *Capital*, III, p. 237.
45. See Marx's whole discussion of the Gotha Programme and his savaging of its humanist declarations of 'equal rights', justice for labour, etc.

Marx adds that it suffices to put the Hegelian dialectic 'right side up again' to find its 'rational form', and to set it right side up again is to remove the 'mystifying side' introduced by Hegel's absolute idealism. The matter seems simple and reassuring. But in recent articles[46] Louis Althusser has torn off this veil of words and forced us to see the unlikely absurdity of this hypothetical 'inversion of Hegel'.

> It is inconceivable that the essence of the dialectic in Hegel's work should not be contaminated by Hegelian ideology . . . that the Hegelian ideology could cease to be Hegelian and become Marxist by a simple, miraculous 'extraction'.

For Althusser the specific difference of Marx's dialectic is to be found in the fact that the latter's contradictions are 'over-determined' in principle. This answer does not seem to me to grasp the essential point, although it provides valuable positive elements at another level. To take up the problem from another angle, Marx describes two kinds of contradiction. One of these, within the structure of the relations of production, appears before the other which is produced little by little between *the two structures* of the capitalist mode of production, the relations of production and the productive forces. The first contradiction appears and disappears with the mode of production. The second appears with the development of the system as an effect of the functioning of the first contradiction, but it is this second one which creates the material conditions for the disappearance of the system; it is the fundamental contradiction. The relation between the two contradictions thus shows that the *first* contradiction, within the relations of production, *does not contain within itself the set of conditions for its solution*. The material conditions of this solution can only exist outside it as the productive forces are a *reality completely distinct* from the relations of production and *irreducible* to them, a reality which has its own internal conditions of development and its own temporality.

The other conditions of solution of the contradiction in the relations of production are found at the level of the political, cultural superstructures, and these structures are equally irre-

---

46. 'Contradiction et Surdétermination' and 'Sur la Dialectique Matérialiste', re-edited in *Pour Marx*, Paris, 1965; 'Contradiction and Overdetermination', *New Left Review*, No. 41, Jan.-Feb., 1967.

ducible to the relations of production and have their own modalities of development. For Marx the solution to an internal contradiction of the structures of the relations of production is not created solely by the internal development of this contradiction. The greater part of the conditions of this solution is outside the contradiction, and irreducible to its content.

On the other hand, the possibility of resolving the second contradiction, between the structures of the economic system, is born of the internal development of the system (and, as we shall see, from the movement of all the structures of the society). The solution to this second contradiction is a change in the structure of the relations of production *to make them correspond* with that of the productive forces. This change implies the exclusion of private ownership of the means of production, thus suppressing *the very basis of the internal contradiction* in capitalist relations of production. But this suppression is only possible at a certain moment in the development of the mode of production, a moment in the development of the productive forces. The class contradictions within the relations of production may 'simmer' but no solution will emerge necessarily, unless there is development of the productive forces (on the contrary, there may be a cyclical reproduction of social conflict, stagnation, etc.).

Our analysis definitely excludes the possibility that Marx could have held a theory of the 'identity of opposites'. This hypothesis was, in fact, invented by Hegel to show that there is an *internal solution to the internal contradictions of a structure*. If such a solution is possible, each of the elements contradicted within the structure must at the same time be its own opposite. The thesis must be itself and its opposite the antithesis if the synthesis is already contained in their contradiction. Marx's work radically excludes this possibility, for neither the elements in contradiction within a structure, nor the structures in contradiction within a system *are reducible to one another*, identical to one another.

This shows that the identity of opposites, the basic structure of the Hegelian dialectic *is only necessary* to provide 'proof' of absolute idealism and *to establish Hegelianism* as the absolute knowledge of the absolute spirit, a totality which itself contradicts itself in the exteriority of nature and the interiority of the Logos, maintaining its identity through all its contradictions. The identity of opposites is, in fact, the magical operator which

Hegel had to provide himself to build the palace of ideas[47] which is absolute knowledge, and to give a rational appearance to the ideological sleight of hand which serves as the unprovable point of departure for absolute idealism. Thus Hegel's philosophical idealism determines the specific internal content of this notion of contradiction, and this structure, based on the principle of the identity of opposites, is the direct inverse of Marx's making the dialectic 'useless for science'.[48] In fact anything, i.e. nothing, can be proved with the hypothesis of the identity of opposites.

It is now easy to understand why Marx declared from the *Contribution* on: 'Hence, *it is the simplest matter* with a Hegelian to treat production and consumption *as identical* . . .'[49] and added: 'The result we arrive at *is not* that production, distribution, exchange, and consumption are identical, but that they are all members of one totality, differences within one unity.'[50]

And in *Anti-Dühring*, Engels defended Marx's dialectical method by showing that it could not be reduced to 'these dialectical . . . mazes . . . this mixed and misconceived idea (according to which) *it all amounts to the same thing in the end*,'[51]

47. In *The Concept of Dread*, Kierkegaard takes issue with Hegel and rationalism over this point, opening the way to existentialism.

48. When Lenin declares that the dialectic is 'the theory of the identity of opposites' or 'the study of the contradiction in the very essence of things', I suggest that he is proposing a false equivalence between these two definitions.

In the same way, Mao Tse Tung constantly confuses the unity of opposites with their identity: 'How . . . can we speak of identity or unity (of opposites)? The fact is that a contradictory aspect cannot exist all by itself. If there is not the opposite aspect, each aspect loses the conditions of its existence. . . . Without landlords, there would be no tenant-peasants; without tenant-peasants, there would also be no landlords. Without the bourgeoisie there would be no proletariat; without the proletariat there would also be no bourgeoisie. . . . All opposite elements are like this: Under certain conditions they are on the one hand opposed to each other and on the other hand interconnected, interpenetrated, interpermeated and interdependent; that is what we mean by identity.' (*On Contradiction*, Peking, 1960, p. 47; and in *Selected Works*, I.)

49. *A Contribution to the Critique of Political Economy*, p. 282.

50. Ibid., p. 291. [Corrected, *Translator's note*]

51. *Anti-Dühring*, p. 169.

where the negation of the negation serves 'as the midwife to deliver the future from the womb of the past', and consists of 'the childish pastime of ... alternately declaring that a rose is a rose and that it is not a rose'.[52]

Here Althusser's analyses are really relevant. The postulate of the identity of opposites guaranteed Hegel at any time an imaginary internal solution to the internal contradictions to be analysed, and this solution is usually a magical ideological operation within a 'simple' dialectic.

How then can we explain the impotence of Marx's commentators in the localization of the radical differences between Marx and Hegel? The answer is hardly complex. The *theoretical distinction* of the two kinds of contradiction (within and between structures), and the clarification of their reciprocal articulation were never explicitly stressed or developed by either Marx or Engels. This being so, the 'eyecatching' contradiction was that between capitalists and workers, and the second contradiction was confused with this one, i.e. with the structure's internal contradiction. Analysis thus slid over into the sphere

52. Ibid., p. 195. As Marx and Engels well knew, the dialectical method did not lead Hegel to confuse all opposites in their identity, nor to incoherence in his philosophical discourse. No doubt the identity of opposites is both *the principle and the object* of this discourse, and therefore, its *imaginary basis*, the speculative foundation of the theoretical validity of absolute idealism. But it is not the sole principle invoked by Hegel since the principle of the identity of opposites *a fortiori* establishes the principle of their unity. There can therefore be positive islands in the sea of Hegel's speculative discourse, induced from a reflection on the unity of opposites. For example, in the *Phenomenology of Mind*, the master-slave relation, within the speculative identity of master and slave (the master is the slave of his slave, the slave the master of his master), the relation of master and slave is constituted by two assymetrical relations, that of master to slave, and that of slave to master, which are not superimposed or confused. The master-slave relation is polarized by this fact, and evolves in a determined, irreversible direction.

Perhaps what Marx meant by the positive 'nucleus' (*Kern*) of Hegel's dialectic is the following group of properties: the unity of opposites, the asymmetry of the relations within this unity, a relation oriented in a certain direction and animated with an irreversible movement. Perhaps certain Hegelian analyses, of secondary importance, could be added to this group of properties: for example, the hypothesis of the transformation of quantity into quality.

This illuminates the two metaphors used by Marx to indicate the of Hegel's mystified and mystificatory dialectic, the fascinating dialectic of the identity of opposites, the internal solution, etc. And Marx's and Engels' equivocal formulations did not help to dispel this fascination, nor did the antiscientific habits of dogmatic Marxism:

> The capitalist mode of appropriation, the result of the capitalist mode of production, produces capitalist private property. This is the first negation of individual private property, as founded on the labour of the proprietor. But capitalist production begets, with the inexorability of a law of Nature, its own negation. It is the negation of the negation.'[53]

But what is for Marx no more than a metaphor, a way of expressing the movement of capital, becomes for Engels 'an extremely general—and for this reason extremely far-reaching and

---

relations of his dialectical method with that of Hegel: the metaphor of the 'nucleus' and that of the 'inversion'. For it was not sufficient to put the Hegelian dialectic back onto its feet to give it a completely 'rational' air, since it was first necessary to amputate the principle of the identity of opposites which was both its first methodological principle and the last basis of absolute idealism. Such nuclear fission shows that the nucleus itself was not preserved intact within Marx's dialectic as the metaphor pretends.

But it is difficult to imagine that Marx, the only nineteenth- or twentieth-century thinker to revolutionize both philosophy and a domain of scientific knowledge, could be *completely* mistaken about his relations to Hegel. Probably what Marx conceived as his theoretical debt to Hegel, as the positive heritage handed down to him, was this fragment of the nucleus: the concept of the unity of opposites and the group of attached properties. In that case it has to be stated—as Marx himself did—that as an *explicitly developed theory* of the unity of opposites, the dialectical method has as yet no scientific, i.e. no real existence. This is even more true if, as we shall see, the various kinds of contradiction should perhaps be linked to the concept of the 'limit', which means that there were already —as the very existence of *Capital* proves—as many *implicitly* dialectical analyses as there were scientific practices elucidating the limits of functioning in domains of 'objects' investigated by the sciences. But nothing ensures *a priori* that, once explicit, the methodological principles of each of these practices (whose operational norms work in the shadow of the scientific exploit) will take their places in one unique, unifying dialectic.

53. *Capital*, I, p. 763.

important—law of development of nature, history, and thought'.[54]

In fact, to the extent that the specific character of Marx's notion of contradiction remained unanalysed, the notion of the negation of the negation was the only general Hegelian concept which still *seemed rational* when the mystification of the identity of opposites had been got rid of.

As I understand it, Marx's analysis of the basic notion of contradiction between structures tallies with the most recent scientific practice.[55] The notion makes explicit certain objective properties of structures, the objective *limits* to their possibilities of reproduction, to their remaining *essentially constant*, given the variations of their internal and external conditions of func-

54. *Anti-Dühring*, p. 193; cf. p. 190, the fifteen-line sketch of the dialectical evolution of humanity from primitive communism to real communism via private property.

55. And within this practice, mathematics and cybernetics have a privileged place in the exploration of the notion of the 'limit'. This is one of the reasons their use is becoming more and more general in the social sciences. But the real effectivity of mathematics is circumscribed in principle within the limited set of problems which can already be formalized and for whose treatment mathematics has sufficient operational power.

For more complex problems of structural analysis—for example the analysis of the *modalities* of the *connection* of the structures of a system (whether social or not) so as to be able to explain why these modalities induce a *dominant function* within these connected structures—the scientific concept of structure is apparently still too narrow. Further, to use the concept of a limit is to determine the set of relations *allowed* between the structures of a system, the set of variations compatible with these structures. It is also to determine the set of incompatible variations which would provoke the elimination of one of the connected structures and change the system. If the first already seems to have been partially explored (for example, the mathematical concept of a *category* of sets takes as its object a set of things *and* the system of functions allowed between these things), we are still largely ignorant as far as the second is concerned.

As soon as mathematics is applied to a field of problems for which it is still too weak, there is a risk of creating illusory knowledge, scientific phantoms. There is also a risk that without knowing or wishing it, i.e. *with no ideological intent*, the invisible but real line which always separates scientific knowledge from ideology will have been crossed.

tioning, and, more *profoundly*, to their reproducing their relations, their *connection* with other structures. The appearance of a contradiction is, in fact, the appearance of a limit to the conditions of invariance of a structure. Beyond this limit a change in structure becomes necessary. In this perspective, the notion of contradiction I am putting forward would perhaps be of interest to cybernetics. This science explores the limit possibilities and internal regulation that allow any system, physiological, economic, or whatever, to maintain itself in spite of a determined range of variation of its internal and external conditions of functioning. This analysis brings together the sciences of nature and the sciences of man. To give a frivolous example, I could suggest that if a glaciation caused the disappearance of the dinosaur from the face of the earth, this species did not perish through the spontaneous development of its internal contradictions, but through a contradiction between its internal physiological structure and the structure of its external conditions of existence.

My theory of contradiction should therefore be able to restore to the dialectic its scientific character, and, for the same reasons, this scientific dialectic can only be materialist. For if the dialectical method no longer depends on the hypothesis of the 'identity of opposites' and if the contradictions born of the functioning of a structure express its 'limits' and are partially conditioned in appearance and resolution *outside* that structure, there is *no internal teleology* regulating the evolution of nature and history.

On this basis it should be possible to establish a new dialogue —centring on the hypothesis of the necessary correspondence of structures—between the sciences and Marxism and between structuralism and Marxism. I should like to close this essay with a confrontation of this hypothesis and another of Marx's theses which might seem to contradict it, or at least to reduce its importance by ideological sleight of hand: I mean the thesis of the determinant rôle played 'in the last instance'[56] by economic structures in the evolution of social life.

Everyone is familiar with the famous sentence from the *Preface to A Contribution to the Critique of Political Economy*:

56. Engels: letter to Joseph Bloch, 21st September, 1890: 'If somebody twists this into saying that the economic element is the *only* determining one, he transforms that proposition into a meaningless, abstract, senseless phrase.' (Marx-Engels, *Selected Works*, II, p. 488).

(The) relations of production correspond to a definite stage of development of (the) material powers of production. The set of these relations of production constitutes the economic structure of society—the real foundation, on which legal and political superstructures arise and to which definite forms of social consciousness correspond. . . . The mode of production of material life determines the general character of the social, political, and spiritual processes of life. . . . With the change of the economic base the entire immense superstructure is more or less rapidly transformed.[57]

The peculiar causality that Marx grants to the economic in the interplay of the set of all the reciprocal causalities of infrastructure and superstructures has generally been misinterpreted. We have seen that even within the infrastructure Marx distinguishes between relations of production and productive forces, and never confuses these two structures. This irreducibility of structures cannot be confined to the economy, and we must start from the fact that each social structure has for Marx its own content and mode of functioning and evolution. This irreducibility immediately excludes two kinds of interpretation of the determinant causality of the economy.

On the one hand, non-economic structures cannot 'emerge' from economic relations; the causality of the economic cannot be the genesis of the superstructure from within the infrastructure. On the other hand, non-economic structures are not simple 'phenomena' accompanying economic activity with only a passive reaction on social life while the economic relations are the sole active causality with more or less 'automatic'[58] effect. In either case, it is hard to see by what bizarre alchemy the economy becomes, say, kinship, or for what mysterious reason it should be (badly) hidden behind kinship. We must therefore look elsewhere for an answer, and study the notion of 'correspondence' of structures more closely.

For example, let us examine the process of production in our capitalist society. The relations of production between capitalists and workers and the latter's obligation to work for the former seem largely independent of the religious, political, or even familial ties which they may have among themselves.

57. *A Contribution to the Critique of Political Economy*, pp. 11–12; Marx-Engels, *Selected Works*, I, p. 363. [Corrected, *Translator's note*]
58. Engels: Letter to Starkenberg, 25th January, 1894.

Each social structure seems broadly 'autonomous', and the economist tends to treat non-economic structures as 'exogenous variables', and to look for a rationality that is economic 'in itself'. The correspondence of structures therefore seems mainly 'external'. In an archaic society, this is not the situation. The Marxist economist, for example, easily distinguishes between the productive forces of these societies (hunting, fishing, agriculture, etc.), but he cannot distinguish their relations of production 'in isolation'. Or at best, he can distinguish them in the functioning of the kinship relations themselves. The latter determine the rights of individuals to the land and its products, their obligations to work for others, to receive or to give. They also determine the authority of certain individuals over others in political and religious matters. In such a society, kinship relations dominate social life. How, within Marx's perspective, can we understand both the *dominant* rôle of kinship and the *determinant* rôle of the economy in the last instance?

This is impossible if economy and kinship are treated as base and superstructure. In an archaic society kinship relations *function* as relations of production, just as they function as political relations. To use Marx's vocabulary, kinship relations are here *both* infrastructure and superstructure[59] and it would be a fair guess that the complexity of kinship relations in archaic societies relates to the multiple functions they take on in such societies.[60] It could also be suggested that the dominant rôle

59. In *The Origin of the Family, Private Property and the State* (Marx-Engels, *Selected Works*, II, p. 170, Preface to the First Edition), Engels, by declaring that 'the determining factor in history is, in the last resort, the production and reproduction of immediate life', implies that kinship plays a determinant rôle *alongside* the economy, whereas in these societies it is really an element of the economic infrastructure.

60. This plurifunctionality of kinship has led Beattie and other anthropologists to claim that kinship has no content of its own, but is a container or symbolic form in which the content of social life is expressed (economic, political, religious relations and so on), i.e. that kinship is merely language, a means of expression. While not quarrelling with the notion that kinship functions as a language symbolizing social life, Schneider objects that kinship also has its own content which can be brought out by *substracting* from its functioning the economic, political, and religious *aspects*. The set of relations of consanguinity and alliance which serve as the means of expression of social life and serve as the *terms* of the symbolic

and complex structure of kinship relations in archaic societies are related to the general structure of the productive forces and their low level of development, which impose the co-operation of individuals and therefore group life for subsistence and reproduction.[61]

In this abstract example, the economy-kinship correspondence no longer appears as an external relation, but as internal correspondence, without for all that confusing economic relations between kinsfolk with their political or sexual relations, etc. Thus, to the extent that kinship in this kind of society really functions as relations of production, the determinant rôle of the

---

language of kinship will then appear. Here kinship is both a particular content of social life and serves as the mode of appearance and expressions of all other contents.

But when he sets out to rediscover a content for kinship in this way, Schneider hardly evades the biologism for which he condemns Gellner. Everyone knows that the set of biological relations of consanguinity and alliance is not kinship, as kinship is always a particular 'group' of these relations within which descent and alliance are socially regulated. Because these relations are selected and 'retained', real kinship is not a biological fact, but a *social* one.

Schneider and Beattie have in common the error of looking for the content of this kind of kinship *outside* the economic, the political and the religious, since kinship is neither an external form nor a residual content but functions *directly* and internally as economic and political relations and so on, and therefore functions as a mode of expression of social life and as a symbolic form of that life.

The scientific problem thus becomes the determination of why this is so in many types of society, and, in the methodological sphere, the conclusion would seem to be that the conceptual couples : form-basis, container-content are not the right ones for an account of the functioning of social structures.

Gellner, 'Ideal Language and Kinship Structure', *Philosophy of Science*, vol. XXIV, 1957; Needham, 'Descent Systems and Ideal Language', Ibid., vol. XXVII, 1960; Gellner, 'The Concept of Kinship', Ibid., vol. XXVII, 1960; Barnes, 'Physical and Social Kinship', Ibid., vol. XXVIII, 1961; Gellner, 'Nature and Society in Social Anthropology', Ibid., vol. XXX, 1963; Schneider, 'The Nature of Kinship', Ibid., vol. XXXI, 1964.

61. On this see Claude Lévi-Strauss, 'The situation is quite different in groups for which the satisfaction of economic needs rests entirely on conjugal society and the sexual division of labour. Not only are man and woman differently specialised technically, and

economy does not contradict the dominant rôle of kinship, but is expressed through it.[62]

This perspective makes it possible to predict one of the contributions Marx will make in the future to the scientific study of social structures and their multiple evolution, a contribution profoundly different from those his exegesists attribute to him, or deny him. For what are, in fact, irreducible are the functions and evolution of structures, so their differentiation should be explained by the transformation and evolution of their functions. It would be possible, for example, to guess that the appearance of new conditions of production in archaic societies will modify their demography, demand new forms of authority, and bring with them new relations of production. It is a fair guess that beyond a certain limit the old kinship relations will no longer be able to fulfill these new functions. The latter will develop outside kinship and will bring forth distinct political and religious social structures which will in their turn function as relations of production. It is not the kinship relations that are transformed into political relations, but the political function of the old kinship relations which develops on the basis of new problems. The kinship relations will shift into a new rôle with a different social importance, and the political and religious relations, charged with new functions (both infra- and superstructural), will come to occupy the liberated central place.

To explain the determinant rôle of the economy is at the same time to explain the *dominant* rôle of non-economic structures in a given type of society, and societies distinct in time

---

therefore depend on one another for the construction of the things necessary for daily tasks, but they devote themselves to the production of different kinds of food. A complete, and above all a regular diet thus depends on that veritable 'production co-operative', the household.... Particularly in primitive societies, where the harshness of the geographical environment and the rudimentary state of technique make hunting and gardening, collecting and gathering equally hazardous, existence is almost impossible for an individual left to himself.' (*Structures Élémentaires*, p. 48.)

62. Marx wrote of the 'rank and influence' of social structures in a society characterized by a determined production: 'It is the universal light with which all the other colours are tinged and are modified through its peculiarity. It is a special ether which determines the specific gravity of everything that appears in it.' (*A Contribution to the Critique of Political Economy*, Introduction, p. 302.)

and place belong to the same 'type' if their *structure as a whole* is comparable, i.e. if the *relation* between their social structures determined by the *functions* and the *importance* of each of them is comparable. This perspective makes it possible to reconcile the usual oppositions: structure-event (anthropology-history) and structure-individual (sociology-psychology) in a new way.

An event—whether from outside or inside—always acts on the whole structure by acting on one of its elements. The set of known and unknown properties of one or several structures always intervenes between a cause and its effects. This structural causality gives an event all its consciousness and unconscious dimensions and explains its intentional and unintentional effects. It is therefore incorrect to abandon the structuralist viewpoint or to *leave structure aside to account for events*. When, by their acts, men create the conditions for the appearance of new structures, in fact, they open up the way to new fields of objective possibility of which they are largely ignorant, which they discover through events and whose limits they submit to necessarily when the conditions of functioning of these structures vary, and when these no longer fulfil the same function and are transformed. The intentional behavioural rationality of the members of a society is always inscribed within the basic unintentional rationality of the hierarchical structure of the social relations characterizing that society. Instead of starting from the individuals and their hierarchies of preference to explain the rôle and relation of the structures of a society, it is necessary rather to explain this rôle and this relation in all their aspects, known or unknown by the society, and look in this hierarchy of structures for the basis of the hierarchy of 'values', i.e. the social norms of prescribed behaviour. This hierarchy of 'values' could then illuminate the hierarchy of needs of individuals playing a given rôle with a given status in the society.

This would make it impossible to challenge history with anthropology[63] or anthropology with history, to set psychology and sociology or sociology and history in sterile opposition. The possibility of human 'sciences' would definitely depend on the possibility of discovering the laws of the functioning, evolution and internal reciprocal correspondence of social structures.

63. Cf. Roland Barthes, 'Les Sciences Humaines et l'Oeuvre de Lévi-Strauss', *Annales*, Nov.–Dec., 1964, p. 1086.

And one day these human sciences could give the lie to Aristotle by becoming sciences of the 'individual' as well. The possibility of human 'sciences' depends on a generalization of a method of structural analysis which has become capable of explaining the conditions of variation and evolution of structures and their functions. This generalization is today very unevenly developed, depending on whether the study is economics, kinship, politics, or religion. Perhaps Marx's work, purged of equivocation, could help accelerate this development.

16 Marxism: Science or Revolution?

LUCIO COLLETTI

Marxism is frequently discussed as if it were only a better method for studying social relations. In this essay Lucio Colletti is concerned to stress that the scientific vocation of Marxism is not to be separated from its integral relation to the socialist revolution.

Lucio Colletti is Professor of Philosophy at the College of Rome and the author of From Rousseau to Lenin: Studies in Ideology and Society (*London, 1972*) *and* Marxism and Hegel.

Marxism as science or Marxism as revolution? There was and there still is this alternative. To resolve it is not so easy as is often thought. I shall begin with the first horn of the dilemma —Marxism as a science. The broad outlines of the argument might be presented as follows. Marxism is a theory of the *laws* of development of human society. In *Capital*, Marx has studied and analysed the laws governing the development of capitalist production, he has taken this 'mechanism' to pieces and described it. As a scientific doctrine, Marxism essentially consists of the discovery of objective causal relationships. It discovers and analyses the laws which make the system work, describes the contradictions which undermine it from within and signal its destiny. But, insofar as it is a work of science and not ideology, *Capital* will not allow this analysis to be tainted with 'value judgments' or subjective choices: instead it makes only 'judgments of fact', objective judgments, affirmations which in the last analysis are universally valid. Scientific propositions are in the indicative. They do not advance 'choices' or finalities. It is impossible to deduce imperatives from the objective and impartial statements of science. This is the well-known argument developed by Hilferding in the preface to his *Finance Capital* (the argument of more or less all the orthodox Marxism of the Second International). 'Marxism is only a theory of the laws of development of society.' 'These laws which obtain their general formulation in the Marxist view of history, are applied by Marxist economics to the epoch of commodity production.' 'Marxism, which is a scientifically logical and objective doctrine, is not bound to value judgments.' The task of Marxism as a science is to 'describe causal relationships'. Though they are always being confused, 'socialism' and 'Marxism' are *not* the same thing. Socialism is an end, a goal, an objective of political will and action. Marxism on the other hand, being a science, is objective and impartial knowledge. One can accept the science without desiring the end. 'To recognize the validity of Marxism,' says Hilferding, 'does not at all mean to make value judgments, much less to point out a line of practical action. It is one thing to recognize a necessity, and quite another to put oneself at the service of that necessity.'

This view clearly allows no room for a link between *science* and *class consciousness*, between science and ideology, let alone for the 'partisanship' of science. Socio-economic development is seen as a process unfolding before the observer and the scientist like the movement of the stars. 'Economic laws' are objective laws, external to classes and independent of our wills just like the laws of nature. The 'law of value' is like the law of the fall of heavy bodies. More or less present in this conception is always a 'theory of breakdown'. The laws of the capitalist mode of production inescapably lead the system to its end. The extinction of capitalism is inevitable. It is made fatal and almost automatic by the explanation of its own laws. Nuances and slight variations apart, this was more or less the view which prevailed in the Third International too. While it existed, and above all with Stalin, all that was added was the criterion of 'partisanship' (an element anyway already latent in Lenin). But apart from the blind and sectarian way in which it was advanced, this criterion was only juxtaposed to that of naturalistic objectivism.[1] Juxtaposed, never mediated with it; i.e., united with it only by paste and string.

This 'physicalist' position, in infinitely more cultivated and refined forms, is still the dominant one among the best Marxist economists. The case of Oskar Lange is typical, and still more

1. See, for example, Stalin, *Economic Problems of Socialism in the Soviet Union.*

so is that of Maurice Dobb (who in general is a very serious scholar). Dobb sees the law of value as a law which allows us to reconstruct, unify, order and explain all the major mechanisms and movements of the system.

> Only with the work of Adam Smith, and its more rigorous systematization by Ricardo, did Political Economy create that unifying quantitative principle which enabled it to make postulates in terms of the general equilibrium of the economic system—to make deterministic statements about the general relationships which held between the major elements of the system. In Political Economy this unifying principle, or system of general statements cast in quantitative form, consisted of a theory of value.[2]

This passage stresses above all the ultimate social neutrality of the law of value. The law makes it possible to relate together the most important quantitative factors of the system, to establish certain quantifiable relationships between them—just as the law of universal gravitation does in its own field (Dobb's very example). But what does not come out here is the particular, 'fetishistic' or 'alienated' nature of the quantitative factors related together by the law. For Marx, commodities and capital have not always existed, and what is more, their existence must come to an end. Apart from the relationships *within* the system, Marx analyses and criticizes the *system* itself. He discusses why the product of labour takes the form of a 'commodity'; why human labour is represented by the 'value' of 'things'; he discusses why (that is, under what conditions) capital exists and reproduces itself. Dobb, on the other hand, argues a little like Smith and Ricardo, who see the commodity as the 'natural' and inevitable form of the products of labour and the *market* as an institution which must always exist, and present the law of value as a law of permanent quantities or factors (often, in fact, confusing it with the problem of the 'measurement' of values).

There is no reason to dwell on this point here. Suffice it simply to note that for Marx too the law of value is an objective law, a law operating independently of consciousness and even 'behind the backs' of men : except that for him a quite peculiar kind of objectivity is involved. It is, so to speak, a false objec-

2. Maurice Dobb, *Studies in the Development of Capitalism* Routledge, 1946.

tivity and one which must be abolished. The laws of the market
—Marx writes—are a 'natural necessity' for men. The movements of the market are as unpredictable as earthquakes, but
this is not because the market is a 'natural' phenomenon. What
has taken the objective form here of *things* and interactions
between things, is really nothing but the social relationships of
men to each other. 'These formulae,' Marx writes, 'bear it
stamped upon them in unmistakable letters that they belong
to a state of society in which the process of production has the
mastery over man, instead of being controlled by him.' A
little earlier he had pointed out : 'The life-process of society,
which is based on the process of material production, does not
strip off its mystical veil until it is treated as production by
freely associated men, and is consciously regulated by them in
accordance with a settled plan.' And this can obviously come
about only through revolution.

In the Ricardian interpretation, then, the law of value tends
to be naturalized and appear as a socially natural law. The laws
of nature have no class character. And by the same token, the
production of commodities and the existence of a market have
no class character. Hence the constant familiar speeches. The
'market' and 'profit' are not seen as the inevitable survivals of
bourgeois institutions in the first phase of socialist society, which
is *par excellence* a *transitional* society, but as 'rational criteria
or measurements of economic activity', as something positive
which must always exist. There is a 'socialist' market and there
is 'socialist' profit. The revolution is not made to abolish profit, that is, to abolish exploitation. The revolution is made only
for the pleasure of marching, well-drilled and cheering, past a
speakers' platform.

Another basic distortion, closely related to the first, is the
misinterpretation of the nature and meaning of Marx's work.
For Marx, political economy is born with the extension and generalisation of commodity production. It is born with capitalism
and dies with it (that is, with the progressive extinction of its
surviving elements in the transitional society); which explains
why all Marx's major works have the title or sub-title of the
critique of political economy. For many Marxists today, however, the contrary is true : there must always be political economy,[3] just as there will always be law, the State, and those

3. See the *Manual of Political Economy*, U S S R Academy of
Sciences.

who tell the masses what the masses themselves ought to think and believe.

I must interrupt the argument developed so far in order to look at the problem in another way and from a different angle. Open the first of Marx's really important writings, the *Critique of Hegel's 'Philosophy of Right'*. It has a remarkable structure. Not only does the work begin with a critique of the Hegelian *philosophy* of the State, and imperceptibly turn into a critique of the *State*: but in both cases—that is, both on the question of the way Hegel sees the State, and on the question of the State itself—the critique is developed by the use of a single model. Not only is Hegel's *representation* of the reality of the State upside down and 'standing on its head' but, Marx says, so is the actual *reality* generated by the State. 'This uncritical spirit, this mysticism,' he writes, 'is the enigma of the modern constitution ... as well as the mystery of Hegelian philosophy.'

This point of view is undeniably abstract, but it is the abstraction of the political State as Hegel himself develops it. It is atomistic too, but it is the atomism of society itself. The point of view cannot be concrete when the object of the point of view is abstract. In general, an author criticizes another by showing him that things are not as he has described them. He criticizes him in the name of reality and on the basis of reality. But here the procedure seems to be different: the death sentence pronounced on the old philosophy at the same time applies to its *object* too. Marx does not only want to see the end of the Hegelian *philosophy* of the State: he wants to see the actual 'dissolution' of the State. This again is because he understands that not only is the philosophical representation of reality false, metaphysical, and 'standing on its head'—but so is reality itself, that is to say, the particular type of social régime which takes the form of the modern representative State or parliamentary Government.

There is an analogous situation in *Capital*. Here too Marx does not restrict himself to criticizing the 'logical mysticism' of the economists, their 'trinity formula': Land, Capital, Labour. Their 'fetishism' is explained by the fetishism of reality itself, that is of the capitalist mode of production. This is quite evident in a whole series of expressions. *Capital* contains such phrases as: 'the mystical character of commodities', or 'the whole mystery of commodities, all the magic and necromancy that surrounds the products of labour as long as they take the form of commodities'; or, finally, that the 'mystical veil' is not an invention of the bourgeois interpreters of the 'life-process of society which is based on the process of material production', but actually belongs to this process, which therefore *appears* to political economy as what it really *is*.

In fact, reality itself is upside down. It is therefore not just a question of criticizing the way in which economists and philosophers have *depicted* reality. It is necessary to overturn *reality* itself—to straighten it up and put it 'back on its feet'. 'Until now the philosophers have only interpreted the world: the point however is to change it.' In the foregoing I have looked at Marxism as a science; now I come to Marxism as revolution.

I urge the reader not to get too excited, but to keep his eyes open and use his head. In the argument I have just outlined there is a somewhat dubious and even dangerous point. An author criticizes another by appealing to *reality*, showing him that things are not as he had described and depicted them. This is the only correct kind of procedure. But Marx—with Hegel as with the economists—*seems* to be unable to do this: unable to, because the reference criterion—reality—is already itself a counterfeit standard. If this was really all, Marx would only be a prophet (which is not much), and we would be revisionists. On what basis do we say that the reality of capitalism is upside down? According to Bernstein, on the basis of the *moral ideal*. The idea of 'justice', Kant's ethics, tell me that the world should be corrected and reformed. Value and surplus value are mere words. Socialism is the product of good wishes. Change the minds of men! Abandon scientific socialism for utopian socialism. Reality is not important. 'Facts' are of no account. Reality is denied to make room for the realization of the ideal. Reason is Revolution. The contemporary Bernstein seems to lie to the left—in the petit bourgeois anarchism of Marcuse and of all those who have taken him seriously.

I must stop here a moment to put some order into the argument. Reality is certainly upside down—otherwise revolution would not be necessary. On the other hand, Marxism also needs to be a science: if not there would be no *scientific* socialism, only messianic aspirations, or religious hopes. In short, if Marx is a scientist, he has to measure his ideas and those of others against the facts, to test hypotheses experimentally against reality. In simpler and more familiar terms, this means that when Marx criticizes Hegel, the economists and all the reality of capitalism, he still has to do it in the name of reality and *on the basis of reality*. The criterion of his critique, in short, cannot be the *ideal* (which is still the ideal of just anyone). It must be a criterion drawn from and rooted in reality. If I may summarize this briefly, I would say that there are *two realities* in capitalism : the reality expressed by Marx, and the reality expressed by the authors he criticizes. I shall now try to demonstrate this as simply and quickly as possible, by examining the relationship between capital and wage labour.

I shall begin by seeing how this relationship looks from the point of view of the capitalist. The capitalist invests his money in the purchase of spindles, cotton, and labour. He finds these things on the market, that is, as commodities. He buys them as anyone might buy a whip, a horse and a carriage. After making these purchases (suppose he buys at no more than their actual value), the capitalist then puts the worker to work at the spindles to transform the cotton into thread. At this point, Marx says, 'the labour process is a process between things that the capitalist has purchased, things that have become his property. The product of this process belongs, therefore, to him, just as much as does the wine which is the product of a process of fermentation completed in his cellar.'

The capitalist's eye, accustomed to synthesis and the overall view, does not deign to distinguish between the various things he has bought. From his point of view, wage labour is a *part* of capital, in the same way as machinery and raw materials : it is the 'variable' part of capital, the 'wages fund', as distinct from the part invested in the purchase of means of production. The fact that, besides reproducing his own value, that is the wage, the wage labourer produces surplus value, is a happy circumstance which raises no theoretical problem for the capitalist. To him, this fertility of labour appears directly as the *productivity of his own capital* : the capital of which labour is itself a part, being one of the purchases. This is, as we know, the thesis of all non-Marxist economists, what Marx calls the fetishism of political economy. It is not only labour which produces value, but capital too. Wages pay for the productivity of the former, profits pay for the latter. Land produces the harvest;

capital or machinery produce profits; labour produces wages. To each his own. Then let harmony be established once and for all, and let the factors of production collaborate.

You will say that this is the 'bosses' ' point of view. But the important thing to understand is that more than a subjective point of view is involved: it is a point of view which corresponds in a certain sense to the actual course of things. The working class reproduces its own means of subsistence, and at the same time produces surplus value (that is, profit, rent, and interest); with its labour it provides the revenues of all the basic classes of society. And—*as long as it is kept down*—the working class is in fact only a cog in the mechanism of capitalism. Capital is produced by labour: labour is the cause, capital the effect: the one the origin, the other the outcome. And yet not only in the accounting of the enterprise, but in the real mechanism, the working class appears only as 'variable capital' and as the wages fund. The 'whole' has become the 'part', and the part the whole. Such is the reality 'on its head' already mentioned: the reality which Marx not only rejects as a criterion and yardstick, but which he wants to overthrow and invert.

Think of the American working class. It is only a cog of capital, a part of the capitalist mechanism. More strictly speaking, it is not even a 'class' (it does not have *consciousness* of being a class): it is an agglormeration of 'categories': car workers chemical workers, textile workers, etc. When it reacts and goes on strike, its relationship to the whole of the social 'mechanism' is like that of a bilious irritated organ to the human body: it demands no more than a pill to make it feel better. This class (though every working class has passed through this stage, and in a certain sense remains in it until it takes power), this class is, really, a *part* of capital: although (to distinguish it from the imperialist exploitation of workers in other countries) it is also true that the thing of which it is *part* (capital), is in its turn a *part* of the value produced by the working class.

The point of view adopted by Marx is in fact the expression precisely of this other reality. Capital, of which wage labour is only the variable component, is in reality part of this its part (which is therefore the 'totality'): it is the product of 'living labour'. Without then repeating Bernstein's moralism or Marcuse's 'utopias', Marx overthrows the arguments of the economists and points to the overthrow of capitalism itself, pivoting on an aspect of *reality*. Marxism is therefore science. It is an analytical reconstruction of the way in which the mechanism of capitalist production works.

On the other hand, as well as being a science, Marxism is revolutionary ideology. It is the analysis of reality from the viewpoint of the working class. This in its turn means that the working class cannot constitute itself as a *class* without taking possession of the scientific analysis of *Capital*. Without this, it disintegrates into a myriad of 'categories'. The working class (dreamers awake!) is not a given factor, it is not a product of nature. It is a destination point: the production of *historical action*, that is, not only of material conditions but also of *political* consciousness. In short, the class becomes a class when, going beyond economistic spontaneism, it develops the consciousness of being the antagonist of the whole system: the consciousness of being the protagonist of a revolution which emancipates not only the workers but the whole of society. This consciousness, through which the class constitutes itself in political organization and takes its place at the head of its allies, cannot be derived from anywhere but *Capital*. It is in this sense, I think, that Lenin said that the construction of the party also requires something 'from without'.

Further Reading

As a number of contributions to this volume have specialist bibliographies appended to them I will only indicate here some of the major works in English in the field of Marxism and avant garde bourgeois social theory.

Some advanced posts of academic social theory are to be found in the following: in sociology Alvin Gouldner's *The Coming Crisis in Western Sociology* (U S A, 1970); in economics Piero Sraffa's *The Production of Commodities by Means of Commodities* (U K, 1960) and the associated work of the Cambridge School (discussed in this volume by Edward Nell, Ch. 4); in historiography E. H. Carr's *What is History?* (U K, 1962) and the writings of the group of French historians associated with *Annales* (Paris); in political science *The Political Theory of Possessive Individualism* by C. B. Macpherson (U K, 1962); in anthropology the work of Claude Lévi-Strauss and, in Britain, E. R. Leach. Developments in linguistics and psychoanalysis challenge many of the assumptions and methodologies now prevalent in academic social theory; as just two instances of the influence such developments can exert see *Elements of Semiology* by Roland Barthes (U K, 1967) and *Madness and Civilisation* by Michel Foucault (U S A, 1966). Of direct relevance to theories of society are developments in the philosophy of science such as Paul Feyerabend, *Against Method* (U K, 1972) and Gaston Bachelard, *La Formation de l'Esprit Scientifique* (France, 1952).

In a somewhat different category from the above—which are explicitly concerned with theory—come those substantive investigations with implicit methodological significance. These would include Barrington Moore's *Social Origins of Dictatorship and Democracy* (U S A, 1966); Oscar Lewis, *The Children of Sanchez* (U K, 1968); Edward Thompson, *The Making of the English Working Class* (U K, 1964); Peter Brown, *The World of Late Antiquity* (U.K, 1971); Robert L. Heilbroner, *The Making of Economic Society* (U S A, 1962); Eric Wolf, *Peasant Wars of the Twentieth Century* (U S A, 1968); Ronald Fraser (ed), *Work: Twenty Personal Accounts* (U K, 1966); P. Bachrach and M. S. Baratz, *Power and Poverty* (U S A, 1970); Arno J. Mayer, *Politics and Diplomacy of Peacemaking* (U S A, 1967); Eugene Genovese, *The Political Economy of Slavery* (U.S A, 1966); a useful corrective to the academic re-interpretation of American history will be found in Robert Hummel (ed), *Marxist Essays in American History* (U S A, 1968). See also Gabriel and Joyce Kolko, *The Limits of Power* (U S A, 1972). Although much contemporary social theory draws on Marx, there can be no substitute for studying the original texts themselves.

The more important shorter texts will be found in Karl Marx and Frederick Engels, *Selected Works* (in one volume, U K, 1968), notably *The Communist Manifesto; The Eighteenth Brumaire; Value, Price and Profit; The Civil War in France* and the *Critique of the Gotha Programme*. Much attention has been lavished on Marx's early writings—this should at least be complemented by a study of those of his writings which mark a break with his early perspectives, especially *The Germany Ideology* and *The Poverty of Philosophy*. Our view of the achievement of the mature Marx will certainly not be complete until we can set the forthcoming English translation of the *Grundrisse* beside *Capital* and the *Theories of Surplus Value*. Engels' contribution should not be neglected: see, for example, *The German Revolutions* (U S A, 1965).

The best introduction to Marx's ideas is probably *Karl Marx* by Karl Korsch (U S A, 1968); D. Ryazanov's edition of the *Communist Manifesto* (U K, 1928) furnishes an extensive guide to Marx's later work; there is a useful biography of Marx by the same author published jointly with this edition (see also the *Life of Karl Marx*, by Werner Blumenberg, U K, 1971).

The best account of Marx's economics is to be found in the work of Ernest Mandel; notably the brief *Introduction to Marxist Economic Theory* (U S A, 1968), *The Formation of Marx's Economic Thought* (U S A, 1972) and the two volume *Marxist Economic Theory* (U S A, 1968) which is an extensive restatement of theory drawing on a wide range of economic, anthropological and historical research.

The nature of Marx's new science of the social formation has led to the creation of a number of rival schools. The interpretation which dominated the early part of the century may be studied most conveniently in G. V. Plekhanov, *Fundamental Problems of Marxism* (U K, 1969) and N. Bukharin, *Historical Materialism* (U S A, 1968). Georg Lukacs *History and Class Consciousness* (U K, 1970) rejected a positivist interpretation of Marxism and sought to insist on the importance of Hegel in the formation of Marx's thought. *Marxism and Philosophy* by Karl Korsch (U K, 1970) adopts a similar perspective but with less reliance on the German historicist and sociological writing that influenced Lukacs. Subsequently a whole current of German Marxism has employed a parallel emphasis to that of the early Lukacs and Korsch: see, for example, Herbert Marcuse, *Reason and Revolution* (U S A, 1940), Theodore Adorno, *Prisms* (U K, 1968); Walter Benjamin, *Illuminations* (U S A, 1969); and Alfred Schmidt, *The Concept of Nature in Marx* (U K, 1971). The writings of Lucien Goldmann have sought to develop the insights of the early Lukacs both in studies of particular thinkers (*The Hidden God*, U K, 1964 and *Immanuel Kant*, U K, 1972) and in discussions of methodology (*Philosophy and the Human Sciences*, U K, 1968). The importance of the Hegelian element in Marxism is also stressed by Henri Lefebvre, *Dialectical Materialism* (U K, 1968).

In France two attempts have been made to derive a general Marxist theory of society: Jean-Paul Sartre's *Critique of Dialectical Reason* (of which only the introduction, *Search for a Method*, U K, 1965, is available in English), and, from a very different perspective, Louis Althusser and Etienne Balibar, *Reading Capital* (U K, 1970). Althusser's work seeks to establish the scientificity of Marx's thought and to distinguish it from all varieties of humanism and historicism (see *For Marx*, U K, 1969 and *Lenin and Philosophy*, U K, 1971). In Italy the writings of Lucio Colletti have also insisted on the scientific nature of Marx's undertaking but rejected the idea that Marx wished to provide theoretical schema for understanding society in general rather than capitalist society and its contradictions in particular (see *From Rousseau to Lenin*, U K, 1972).

Recent notable contributions to Marxist economics include: Paul M. Sweezy, *The Theory of Capitalist Development* (U S A, 1943 and 1968); Paul Sweezy and Paul Baran, *Monopoly Capital*

(U S A, 1964); Maurice Godelier, *Rationality and Irrationality in Economics* (U K, 1972); A. Emmanuel, *Unequal Exchange* (U K, 1972); Ernest Mandel, *The Economics of Late Capitalism* (U K, 1973).

In the field of political theory and analysis *The State in Capitalist Society* by Ralph Miliband (U K, 1969), *Fascism and Dictatorship* and *Political Power and Social Class* by Nicos Poulantzas (U K, 1973) are undoubtedly the most significant recent contributions. The writings of the founder of the Italian Communist Party, Antonio Gramsci, furnish many crucial concepts for Marxist political analysis: see his *Prison Writings* (U K, 1972). In the writing of history Marxism exercises a very pervasive influence but the work of two writers should be singled out for substantive and methodological reasons: that of Issac Deutscher (notably *Stalin*, U K, 1964, and the Trotsky trilogy) and that of E. J. Hobsbawm (notably *Industry and Empire*, *Labouring Men* and the *Age of Revolution*). Marxist concepts are to be found in much anthropological writing (see the survey in Maurice Godelier's preface to *Sur les Sociétés Précapitalistes*, Paris, 1970) though there are not many systematic presentations of a Marxist anthropology; but see E. Terray, *Marxism and Primitive Societies* (U S A, 1972), and also the last section of Maurice Godelier, *Rationality and Irrationality in Economics* (U K, 1972).

In the development of Marxism there has always been a close relationship between political struggle and intellectual production. Marx believed that scientific analysis was a necessary foundation for a correct political practice; that is why he wrote *Capital*. In the twentieth century the most vital contributions to Marxist theory have invariably had this goal of clarifying the field of political practice. Lenin's *Development of Capitalism in Russia* (actually published in 1899) and *Imperialism* had this aim; Mao's *Report of an Investigation of the Peasant Movement in Hunan* sought to establish the basis for a particular political strategy through a study of the class struggle in the Chinese countryside; Trotsky's *Permanent Revolution* analysed the class dynamic of revolution in backward capitalist states in order to determine the type of class alliance appropriate to the revolutionary movement. In other cases the relation between theory and politics is even closer; namely when analysis concerns the consequences and lessons of a particular political experience. Thus Marx's theory of the revolutionary State was a direct investigation of the experience of the Paris Commune;

Lenin's *State and Revolution* similarly depended on the experience of the Soviets and Trotsky's *Revolution Betrayed* on the experience of the Soviet Union after the installation of the Stalinist bureaucracy. Equally important is Trotsky's remarkable study of the nature of capitalist democracy to be found in *The Struggle Against Fascism in Germany* with an introduction by Ernest Mandel (U S A, 1972). A good introduction to Lenin's thought will be found in *Lenin* by Georg Lukacs (U K, 1970) and to that of Trotsky in Denise Avenas, *La Pensée Politique de Trotsky* (Paris, 1970): see also *The Age of the Permanent Revolution* by Leon Trotsky (edited and with an introduction by Isaac Deutscher, U S A, 1966).

Fontana Modern Masters

General Editor: Frank Kermode

This series provides authoritative and critical introductions to the most influential and seminal minds of our time. Books already published include:

'This series is just what is needed by the so-called "general reader" in search of a guide to intellectual currents that clash so confusingly in a confused world.'

The Times Literary Supplement

Hitler: The Führer and the People

J. P. Stern

His life, his times, his policies, his strategies, his influence have often been analysed. But rarely is the most elementary question of all raised – how could it happen?

How could a predominantly sober, hard-working, and well-educated population have been persuaded to follow Hitler to the awful abyss of destruction? What was the source of his immense popularity? What was the image projected in his speeches, his writings, and his conversation?

Hitler: The Führer and the People is a compelling attempt to reconstruct the nature of Hitler's political ideology, its roots, logic, and function.

'Who really wants or needs another book on Hitler? The short answer is, when the book is as good and original and brief as Professor Stern's, that we all do.'
Donald G. MacRae, *New Statesman*

'Stern's book is, on all counts, a significant achievement.'
Geoffrey Barraclough, *New York Review of Books*

'. . . an excellent book, all the more so because it concerns itself, via Hitler, with the more general problems of the relationship between society and the individual leader, between ideas and action, between myth and reality.'
Douglas Johnson, *New Society*

'His short book is one of the most remarkable studies of Hitler and Nazism to have appeared.'   Christopher Sykes, *Observer*